D1588517

PARENTS OF POOR CHILDREN
IN ENGLAND, 1580–1800

PARENTS OF POOR CHILDREN IN ENGLAND, 1580–1800

•

PATRICIA CRAWFORD

OXFORD
UNIVERSITY PRESS

OXFORD
UNIVERSITY PRESS

Great Clarendon Street, Oxford OX2 6DP

Oxford University Press is a department of the University of Oxford.
It furthers the University's objective of excellence in research, scholarship,
and education by publishing worldwide in

Oxford New York

Auckland Cape Town Dar es Salaam Hong Kong Karachi
Kuala Lumpur Madrid Melbourne Mexico City Nairobi
New Delhi Shanghai Taipei Toronto

With offices in

Argentina Austria Brazil Chile Czech Republic France Greece
Guatemala Hungary Italy Japan Poland Portugal Singapore
South Korea Switzerland Thailand Turkey Ukraine Vietnam

Oxford is a registered trade mark of Oxford University Press
in the UK and in certain other countries

Published in the United States
by Oxford University Press Inc., New York

British Library Cataloguing in Publication Data

Data available

Library of Congress Cataloging in Publication Data

Data available

Typeset by SPI Publisher Services, Pondicherry, India
Printed in Great Britain
on acid-free paper by
MPG Books Group,
Bodmin and King's Lynn

ISBN 978-0-19-920480-9

1 3 5 7 9 10 8 6 4 2

PREFACE

Parents of Poor Children in England 1580–1800 is Patricia (Trish) Crawford's final work. The completed manuscript was sent off to Oxford University Press on 9 March 2009, but sadly Trish did not live to see her book in print. She died peacefully at home after a long and courageous battle with cancer on Tuesday, 28 April 2009.

The seeds of a project about parenting in early modern England had been germinating in Trish's mind, so she says, at least as far back as 1998. Originally, Trish intended that the project would encompass the experiences of parents from across the social spectrum. Upon the recurrence of cancer in 2006, however, she decided this would be too large to be manageable, and the project was revised into its present form. It remains, nevertheless, a work of considerable scope and readers will no doubt be struck by the sheer volume of material that Trish has examined and the breadth of ground she has covered. That the manuscript was completed barely six weeks before her death, when she was already struggling with the final stages of the disease, is also testament to her determination to see the book finished. When Trish realised that she was to be denied that satisfaction, I was asked to take responsibility for seeing the book through the publication process.

Naturally, I agreed. I have had the privilege of working with Trish at the University of Western Australia since 2003, when she became a supervisor of my doctoral thesis. We got on so well, that the arrangement continued and Trish saw me through to completion. Ever keen to support young scholars, she gave me casual work as a research assistant, which consisted initially of checking out books from the library and printing journal articles.

I was already assisting Trish with research and copy-editing on various small projects, when she engaged me to help with the completion of her book. My duties were probably fairly typical of what is expected of young research assistants: proofreading the manuscript, checking references for footnotes, formatting files, organising the permissions for illustrations, and generally dealing with the tedious technical and administrative bits and pieces that Trish no longer had the energy to wrestle with. I hope, too, that I was able to give her some measure of support and encouragement, especially as treatments sapped her energies. I sometimes found myself in the role of supervisor, drawing on some of the very same sensible advice Trish had given to each of her postgrads in those anxious months before submission. In the event, however, Trish's determination saw the manuscript completed before she became too sick to work. All that has been left for me to do, really, are the technicalities: copy-editing, checking, proofing, and indexing. The words, the ideas, the observations are all the author's.

Trish was not a typical academic. There was almost nothing of the 'grand dame' about her—she did have a sense of her entitlement to respect, but never demanded it—colleagues regarded her with a quiet veneration. She always took an interest in the work of younger scholars. Many of the students she supervised later counted Trish amongst their friends and relied upon her for advice and mentoring. As her acknowledgements show, many people generously shared their ideas and sources, or read and commented on chapters. Scholarship for Trish was collaborative and egalitarian and, as was frequently remarked upon in the days following her death, she had a remarkable talent for friendship. She didn't see the need to draw strong distinctions between her work and private life.

Trish will be fondly remembered, and terribly missed, by many, for many different reasons. Of course, she will be remembered for her energy and drive, her intellectual generosity and passions, and her feminism to name but a few. Especially, however, she will be remembered—with the publication of *Parents of Poor Children*—for the compassion and sensitivity she showed for her subjects: the ordinary men, women, and children of early modern England. It has been my great privilege to ensure its completion.

Lesley O'Brien
July 2009

ACKNOWLEDGEMENTS

It is with more than usual gratitude that I acknowledge the help of many friends and scholars. I began research for a book about parents in 1998 on an ARC grant, but most of it has been written since I was diagnosed with breast cancer in 2001, which recurred in 2006. In this situation, on the other side of the world from so many archives, scholars and friends have been wonderfully generous in checking manuscripts for me, discussing points by email, and reading and commenting on drafts.

Several scholars have taken the trouble to read and comment on chapters, and I am deeply grateful for their observations (even if I have not always taken their advice). I thank Judith Bennett, Amanda Capern, Ruth Wallis Herndon, Steve Hindle, Alysa Levene, Jane Long, Philippa Maddern, Sara Mendelson, Tom Nutt, Jeska Rees, and Judith Richards. Laura Gowing, Phyllis Mack, and Lyndal Roper have read the entire manuscript, and that more than once, and I thank them deeply not just for their knowledge and insights, but for their friendship, humour, and support.

It will be obvious to the readers of this book that my work owes much to both Sara Mendelson and Laura Gowing with whom I have worked and shared ideas and sources over many years: Sara has responded to many requests, and Laura's ideas about precarious parenting have been significant for chapter 1. For their generous sharing of references and ideas, I thank especially Jeremy Boulton, Timothy Hitchcock, and Margaret Hunt.

I have enjoyed many conversations over the years with other scholars in addition to those named above. Audiences at seminars and conferences at the University of Western Australia, and in Australia and New Zealand have offered valuable comments. In particular I would like to thank, in Australia, Alan Atkinson, Susan Broomhall, Sybil Jack, David Lemmings, Philippa Maddern, Katharine Massam, Joanne McEwan, Wilfrid Prest, Richard Read, Kate Riley, Pam Sharpe, Stephanie Tarbin, Jacqueline van Gent, Claire Walker, and Charles Zika; in England, the late Gerald Aylmer, Amy Erickson, Frances Harris, Joanna Innes, Anne Laurence, John Morrill,

Margaret Pelling, Mary Prior, Alexandra Shepard, Paul Slack, Naomi Tadmor, Joan Thirsk, Sir Keith Thomas, and Tim Wales; in the United States, Cynthia Herrup and Keith Wrightson; in Canada, the late Sylvia Bowerbank and Mary O'Connor.

Research assistance has been provided by Sue Hart, Alicia Marchant, and Jeska Rees. In preparing the manuscript for print, I have benefited greatly from the excellent research skills of Lesley O'Brien, whose assistance has ranged from comments on the text to an eagle editorial eye.

I thank the Australian Research Council for funding, and the University of Western Australia for financial support. Many librarians, especially at the Reid Library at UWA, have assisted in helping me to locate material, and have answered my queries.

Christopher Wheeler, Matthew Cotton, and editorial staff at OUP have been most kind and helped me to complete the manuscript. Steve Hindle's assessment of the manuscript for OUP was extremely helpful, as was his willingness to continue discussing specific points.

The categories between scholarship and friendship blur, but there are some more personal thank yous. I thank the medical professionals who have kept me alive, especially Henrietta Bryan, Arlene Chan, and Diana Hastrich. Family and friends have supported me in different ways through the ordeal of cancer treatments, and I thank them all: Robin and Iain Adamson, Ursula Aylmer, Vic Burrows, Jill and Iain Cameron, Joan Eveline, the late Fay Gale, Mary and Ken Green, Pat Grimshaw, Helen and Bill Henderson, Kandy-Jane and Graeme Henderson, Gail Jones, Nada Murphy, Sandra and John Penrose, Cedar Prest, Rosemary and Christopher Wake, Stasia Zika. Above all, I thank my family, Rupert, Mandy, Xavier, and Michael, and my husband, Ian.

Perth, Easter 2009

CONTENTS

LIST OF FIGURES

ABBREVIATIONS

BL   British Library, London
Bodl   Bodleian Library, Oxford
CUL   Cambridge University Library
fo.   folio number of manuscript
GL   Guildhall Library, Manuscripts Section, London
HWJ   *History Workshop Journal*
JBS   *Journal of British Studies*
JP   justice of the peace
LMA   London Metropolitan Archives
MS   manuscript
OBP   *The Proceedings of the Old Bailey, 1674–1913*, consulted on http://
              www.oldbaileyonline.org before 30 November 2008. [Note that I have
              extended the recommended citation, including the crime for which the
              person was tried, and the verdict. The date of a case is in the reference
              number. Thus t17620114-11 signals a date of 14 January 1762.]
Rec. Soc.   Record Society
RO   Record Office
sig.   signature, referring to a gathering of pages in a printed book
SPCK   Society for Promoting Christian Knowledge
TRHS   *Transactions of the Royal Historical Society*

NOTE CONCERNING DATES AND SPELLING

Until Britain adopted the Gregorian calendar in 1752, the year was taken to begin on 25 March, and was 11 days different from dates on the Continent. Here the year is taken to begin on 1 January throughout.

Spelling of original sources has been retained with some silent emendation of contractions.

INTRODUCTION

Early one cold December morning in 1596, Mary Monsloe gave birth to a son.[1] She was unmarried, probably a servant in the household of Thomas Welch and his wife Sara in St Botolph Aldgate in London. By 7am, within an hour of the birth, the midwife, Mrs Jane Greene, and another woman, carried Mary's baby into Whitechapel where Mrs Greene delivered the baby to a waiting and allegedly unknown nurse. When Mary later asked Mrs Greene where her son was: 'Marry,' said the midwife, 'hee is well & kepte Bravelye wth his vellet Capp & fether.' He was in Kent, she said, and stood to inherit lands.

The story seems to turn on the desire of a gentlewoman to produce a male heir. Mrs Steede, 'a prettie woman,' was married to an old man in Kent, and was presumably childless, or at least without a son and heir, for she had sought out Mrs Green, the London midwife, to help her to 'buy' a newborn baby boy. Mrs Greene made enquiries: she 'did labour & perswade wth three other severale woomen at severall tymes that some one of them woulde let her have ye childe she wente wth.' Mrs Steede in turn visited pregnant Mary Monsloe two or three times at the Welches, and often prompted Mary 'to be of good cheare & that she woulde ease her of her childe,' while the midwife assured Mary that her son 'shoulde be broughte up like a gent[leman]'. In order that Mary's 'bastard' should be accepted as the Steedes' heir, Mrs Steede faked a pregnancy, preparing childbed linen, then 'lay Inne therewithall'. She also threatened to return the child should Mary ever reveal the secret. Nevertheless, childbirth was notoriously difficult to hide, and by the time the child was born, several women in St Botolph's parish knew the outline of the baby substitution plot.

Like so many incomplete stories, this one leaves us with puzzles. When the depositions were taken, the whereabouts of Mary's child remained unclear. Although one witness claimed that the gentlewoman took the boy to Kent, Mary's mistress, Sara Welch, implied that Mary was wet-nursing a baby: if Mary could not explain the where-abouts of her child, 'this Sara in her conscience thinketh yt the childe ye said Mary keepeth is her owne childe'. Was this a version of the

Moses story, where a woman higher up the social scale had 'adopted' a child and employed its own 'true' mother as a nurse, though in this case knowingly? If Mary was working as a wet-nurse to an unrelated child, then where was her baby? Was the story really about a suppositious heir being imposed on a credulous husband? Or was it about newborn child murder? Presumably it was neighbourhood talk and suspicions about the whereabouts of Mary's baby that prompted the formal enquiries.

The fragmentary evidence from which the story of Mary Monsloe's maternity has been constructed survives among the papers of St Botolph's parish, and probably belongs to a series of depositions taken on 28 December 1596 for the quarter sessions. Mary's story raises issues about parenthood which were important in early modern England. As a single mother, Mary either did not wish or was not able to keep her son; a married woman, Mrs Steede, wanted a child so desperately that she engaged in a series of complex and ostensibly secret negotiations so that she could pretend that Mary's baby was her own. Unmentioned in this evidence was the man who begot the child, the 'father'.

The story of Mary Monsloe and her illegitimate son raises questions about the parents of poor children with which this book is concerned. We know that in early modern England, many fathers and mothers of legitimate children saw their offspring as their family, their posterity, and their immortality. In many instances, parenthood was actively desired, and the absence of an heir, or even of a daughter, a source of grief to couples. But not everyone viewed parenthood in the same way. Motherhood and fatherhood in Mary's story were tenuous and uncertain.

Everyone today has a script about mothers and fathers in their heads, just as they did in early modern England. Whether parents are present or absent, good or bad, individual childhood experiences shape ideas about what it means to be a mother or a father. Beliefs shift, change shape, and blur over lifetimes; women think about their own mothers, their ideas alter if they become mothers, and as they watch their contemporaries cope with mothering; men reflect upon the meanings of fatherhood in their lives. Governments also have views about mothers and fathers. And most significantly for our understanding of the past, historians have their own memories and stories, the emotional content of which is significant. We may recognize universal elements in parental experiences across times and cultures, such as pleasure in children's behaviour, or sorrow if they should die. But we need to balance this with a recognition that parenting takes place in a particular historical context. Historically variable are attitudes to breastfeeding, to the disciplining of children, to the relative value of sons and daughters, to what rights and duties men and women have as fathers and mothers, and to what involvement the state has in their lives. The story of Mary Monsloe's single motherhood was shaped by the complex historical situation in Elizabethan England. Culture not sociobiology underpins this study.

Given present emotional and policy investments in parents, how can a historian approach a subject of such general significance? Most historians have seen families as relatively unchanging, belonging to the private world; they studied public events and national histories. A few late twentieth-century studies of 'the early modern English family' set agendas for discussion: did 'the family' change between 1500 and 1800 from an extended family to a nuclear family in which parents were more loving to their children, or was there a story of continuity of family forms? Did parents treat their children cruelly or lovingly?[2] Like early modern authors who wrote of the universal concern about 'breeding children'[3] and 'the common fortune of parents',[4] these historians assumed that there were common elements of parenting experiences across gender and class. Lawrence Stone wrote his history from the top down; he measured poor parents against the wealthy and found them inadequate.[5] But we cannot read the history of poor mothers and fathers as a pathetic attempt at the ideals and practices of the élite. Ideals did not simply trickle down from the upper social levels: the parenting of the poor must be considered in its own terms. Scarce resources and limited space may have created a different emotional climate between poor fathers, mothers, and children from that in wealthy families. In wealthy families, parents were more remote from their offspring, since servants were involved in childcare, and property and inheritance influenced family relations.

The labouring poor, whose economic circumstances were adverse, could embark on heterosexual activity before they could see their way to marriage. Parenthood was especially unwelcome to poor women and men who were not married to each other. If couples did marry, they might be unable to set up a household together. Others might cohabit illicitly. Poor fathers and mothers could find that another child overstretched their inadequate resources, causing further poverty. The assumption that there was a nuclear family of parents and children, as idealized by the Protestant reformers, is questionable: fragments of families seemed more usual among the poor. Poor parents were less able to protect their children from misfortune. Poverty meant poor accommodation and diet which in turn affected health and mortality. Because of late marriages, migrations, desertions, and deaths, many fathers and mothers did not live to see their children grown up. The disruption of poor families meant that alternative arrangements had to be made for the care of children. Remarriages, or informal relationships which passed as marriages, complicated children's experiences of parents. The children of deserted, widowed, or single mothers were more at risk of accidents and further misfortunes because mothers' work, always paid less than that of men, had to be combined with childcare.

My argument is that material circumstances mattered, and we need to discuss how the parents of poor children, single as well as married, brought up their children. Poverty rather than legitimacy may have affected what mothers and fathers did when they found themselves in difficulties providing basic maintenance and care. Economic circumstances could determine whether a family stayed together, and whether fathers and mothers could retain influence over their offspring's upbringing and lives.

Because material circumstances mattered, there can be no one history of *the* family.[6] Demographic historians of the family did not think too closely about the effects of poverty on how parents could rear their children, and some assumed that high infant and child mortality indicated a lack of maternal care. Historians thought that parents in early modern England seemed emotionally detached, unlike parents in the later twentieth century in the west, whose emotional investment in children was generally high. Even though historians argued that at the upper levels of society there was plenty of evidence about deep emotional bonds between parents and children, such evidence seemed lacking for the parents of the poor. But the absence of evidence does not allow us to argue for a lack of feeling.

The time frame chosen, from roughly 1580 to 1800, deliberately spans more than two centuries after the European Reformation. It begins in the late Elizabethan period when Protestant changes were taking effect, and English imperial expansion had begun, continuing through the eighteenth century when Britain industrialized and became a major imperial power.[7] During the sixteenth century, gender relations underwent a sea change: brothels were closed in the mid-sixteenth century, clerical marriage was permitted by the Elizabethan religious settlement, and an ideal of a godly family was promoted. Poor Laws, culminating in the statute of 1601, were enacted, and these shaped the administration of welfare until 1834. Protestant ideals of parents' duties inspired the men who made and administered the Poor Laws. The state involved itself in the family lives of the poor at a particular moment in the history of family forms.

This longer time frame across the early modern period has several advantages, although there is no metahistory of the poor across the early modern period. Historians have yet to agree on what changed for the poor; 1660 has been something of a watershed in the historiography as welfare historians accepted the views of earlier political historians that the Civil Wars and interregnum marked a major change in English politics and society. Only recently have social historians begun to examine the earlier Elizabethan period when Poor Law policies were being formed, and the seventeenth-century history of their operation.[8] Thus an advantage of a longer time span which departs from existing chronologies is that it poses new questions, and gives a new perspective on historical change.[9] Historians' periodizations—Tudor, Stuart, Hanoverian—are rarely determined by the lives of ordinary women and men. We do not know enough about mothers and fathers to decide when glacial changes occurred for the poor. Sometimes it appears that there was little alteration in their lives between 1580 and 1800: born to labour, they lived their lives in a cycle of poverty, which their children in turn inherited. Yet over the period, we see changes in the meaning of poverty, in attitudes to it, and a widening gap between the poor and their social and economic superiors.

CONTEXTS: SOCIAL STRUCTURE, FAMILY SIZE, AND THE POOR

This book, then, focuses on the parenting of poor children in particular historical circumstances. I shall begin with some brief comments about social structure and terminology. Over the early modern period, society became less one of hierarchies and more one of class. This meant that those of gentry status and above retained a certain social distinction, while wealthy merchants, manufacturers, and industrialists—the 'middling sort'—became increasingly important in eighteenth-century England and involved in public affairs. Men and women in diverse conditions of poverty were consolidated into a class of people, 'the poor', or 'the labouring poor'. From the late Tudor period, the poor became a more visible proportion of the population on the streets of London and other cities, but their circumstances varied between urban and rural, and over their life stages.

This study adopts a very broad tripartite division in society based on material wealth and social status: élite, middling, and poor. The term 'élite' is used here as a convenient shorthand to refer to those with wealth and social status. While this is not always satisfactory, it can be justified. As Lawrence and Jeanne Stone have argued, the élite was a comparatively closed social group.[10] Their wealth and status set them apart from the middling sort, and far distant from the poor. Although the mores of the landed gentry and wealthy urban men differed, the term 'élite' avoids the need for cumbersome references to 'the peers and gentry and wealthier people'. This group was the smallest of the three. The 'middling sort' here refers broadly to those whose material circumstances varied but were sufficient to allow them to live in some comfort. The 'middling sort' were a broad group, including professionals as well as manufacturers and craftsmen, small farmers, and men and women who earned a living in range of occupations. The middling sort reached down to the parish level of those who paid poor rates.[11]

There are a number of difficulties in defining who the poor were. First, they were a fluctuating proportion of the population who lacked material resources and depended on their labour. Secondly, a distinction should be made between those in absolute and relative poverty. Parents in absolute poverty were not even able to supply their food needs, while those in relative poverty lacked basic resources relative to others in their society. Contemporaries judged differently what these basic needs were.[12] Thirdly, contemporaries distinguished between those poor who were deemed worthy of relief, and those who were believed to be poor through their own moral failings, and therefore to be set to work, and denied welfare. 'The poor' were always a larger proportion of the population than those in receipt of formal assistance who were always a small proportion of those in need.

Contemporary estimates of the proportion of the population who were poor varied: from the late sixteenth to the early seventeenth century, urban poverty was judged to be from 5 per cent to 25 per cent, depending on the criteria used. Those in receipt of relief were a minority. The most detailed census, that of Norwich in 1570, confirms that while 5 per cent of the population was receiving relief, another 20 per cent would have had a claim to aid in difficult economic circumstances. Beyond those who received some parish or charitable relief were those who worked hard, yet found difficulty in meeting their needs for food. Agricultural labourers, cottagers, and paupers have been estimated to amount to 47 per cent at the end of the seventeenth century.[13]

Thus the term 'poor' as used here broadly encompasses those who laboured for meagre wages as well as those who received poor relief at different stages of their life-cycle. Some historians have estimated that in eighteenth-century London, about 50 per cent of the population needed parish relief at some point.[14] In difficult years, around 20 per cent of the population could not have afforded bread, even if they made no other expenditure at all; in a very hard year, 45 per cent would be in destitution.[15] Individuals moved in and out of destitution. Orphaned children of labouring parents were in need of relief until they were capable of supporting themselves. Women were usually far more vulnerable to poverty than men. Fear of poverty was widespread, as adverse circumstances such as desertion or widowhood could plunge even middling individuals into indigence.

Population growth and changes in the English economy altered the situation of the poor over the period 1580 to 1800. The population grew until the mid-seventeenth century, followed by half a century of decline, with growth resuming in the mid-eighteenth century.[16] Changes in agriculture meant that poor parents lost access to land and became more dependent on wages.[17] Developments in industries, manufactures, commerce, and trade led to the growth of cities, and many people migrated from the countryside to the towns in search of work. Economic opportunities opened up in some industrial areas for unskilled and low-paid workers. Thus the context in which parents raised their children was very different in 1800, and as people had generally become more prosperous, the gap between the poor and others had widened. Poor parents struggled to rear their children in a society where others were enjoying greater affluence.

A basic question with which historians of poverty have grappled is whether it was a product of life-cycle difficulties or inherited. Following Rowntree's account of poverty in a late nineteenth-century urban context, historians have recognized that one life-cycle event occurred after marriage when parents had a growing family of young children. A mother's responsibilities for childcare prevented her from being employed, and the children were too young to contribute or to leave home, so that the whole family were dependent on the meagre wages of the father. Thus when a father was in his early thirties, his family was likely to need some support.[18] Richard Smith, in modelling this life-cycle, has pointed out how mortality and other chance factors could vary this pattern. If a child died, then there was less pressure on resources, but if it was the father (on whose earnings the family depended) who died, then the remaining fragmented family needed relief.[19]

Other historians have argued that those born to poor parents were likely to inherit their poverty and welfare dependence. In one study of a Hampshire village, Stapleton found that for many, their need for assistance dated to the birth of a first child, and was largely a consequence of inadequate wages for agricultural labourers. This situates the onset of poverty close to marriage, an earlier stage of the life-cycle than that associated with an increased number of children. Over the generations, more families inherited poverty and were likely to experience indigence and formal relief as a permanent condition.[20] I would argue that both inherited poverty and life-cycle poverty played a significant role. Many who might be termed the labouring poor had been born to parents with limited resources. They were vulnerable to both life-cycle poverty and general crises, such as poor harvests, and disruptions of trade, as well as personal misfortunes such as sickness and death. Most of those whom we might term 'the labouring poor' were likely to be reduced to destitution and need assistance in bad years or at some stage of their lives: as orphans, in sickness, in widowhood, or in old age when they could no longer work. Disease and debt could reduce parents to indigence. Such difficulties, combined with inherited poverty, could create acute distress. Poor children were thus both those who inherited their parents' poverty and those plunged into poverty by their parents' misfortunes or deaths before the children were able to provide for themselves.

Yet although 'the poor' were frequently lumped together, they were not an undifferentiated mass: they were 'a jumble of social groups and individuals'.[21] There were differences between men and women, and many subcategories, including rural and urban, arable and pastoral, north and south, and people of different ages. Some had settlements (formal entitlements to relief), while others were unsettled. The labouring poor included agricultural labourers, charwomen, hawkers, artisans, sailors, soldiers, and servants. Formal poor relief and charities selectively focused on particular groups. By 1700, however, after a century of parish-administered relief, contemporaries were beginning to think of the poor as a class of people different from others. There were social distinctions between those who paid rates to relieve the poor, those who received relief, and the group in between who might need parish relief in hard years. Furthermore, some contemporaries distinguished between the labouring poor and the miserable, others between the 'good' or 'worthy' poor and the idle and improvident.[22]

The category of 'the poor' thus had multiple meanings. It could even serve rhetorical purposes, being invoked by plebeians who were not destitute themselves, to establish a moral claim against 'the rich' in their disputes.[23] Certainly, in many of the surviving records which relate to poor relief, the poor themselves were anxious to emphasize their poverty as a means to exact greater assistance. Social relations between those who were poor and their superiors were always more complex than the rhetoric surrounding 'the problem of the poor'.

Of course the boundaries between the élite, middling, and poor are hard to delineate, and many individuals lived their lives on the margins. Boundaries are not my central concern. Rather, the purpose of this broad categorization is to contrast the material circumstances in which family life was lived. Unlike many demographic historians, I do not consider that a particular form of the nuclear family was typical of all social levels in early modern England.[24] The publicly circulated discourse of wealthy literate men about parents and children masks the vastly different economic resources of parents. The dynamics of wealthy titled families, their stories, and their beliefs were all largely irrelevant to the families of poor women and men whose major preoccupations may have been how to feed, clothe, and house their children, and prevent the fragmentation of their families.

While it has been widely thought that English parents in the past wanted large families to enjoy extra labour and assistance with agriculture and domestic industries, poverty and gender affected parents' attitudes to numerous births. In poorer families, merely subsisting was difficult, so that far from being an economic asset, any young children were a liability. Individual families as well as society were on a knife edge between too few and too many children.[25] At all social levels, fathers and mothers divided their scant resources between their children. But what could they do about 'family planning'? Reliable contraceptive knowledge was lacking. So far as people knew, any act of heterosexual penetration carried the risk of pregnancy and more children.[26] Family size was determined by God.

However, the number of children a woman bore was to a large extent affected by her age at marriage. In the sixteenth and seventeenth centuries, the majority of women married at around 26 years of age, men around 28 years of age, with both women and men marrying at younger ages in the eighteenth century.[27] Ordinary women married later than did the daughters of the peers and gentry, and historians have suggested that this pattern of 'prudential' marriage was a means of family limitation. Certainly people knew that marriage meant children, so when birth intervals were around two years, a later marriage for women meant fewer births.[28] Furthermore, the labouring poor may have delayed marriage for other reasons: they needed to save the economic resources to establish and support a household. Women's attitudes to marriage were affected by their capacity to earn as single women. As their wages dropped from two-thirds of the male wage in the late seventeenth century to one-third in the early nineteenth, marriage became more necessary.[29] Pregnancy also made women seek marriage. Marriage decisions for both women and men were complex.

While demographic historians have given us a great deal of information about the size and structure of families in past times, their reliance on family reconstitution has major weaknesses so far as the family life of the poor is concerned. First, the parish registers of baptisms, marriages, and burials, on which so many of their calculations were based, focused on settled family groups. Those families whose data could be reconstituted lived in one parish long enough to have all their vital events (births, marriages, and deaths) recorded. Since parishes did not want pauper families to settle because they would then be entitled to parish relief, records of the births of their children and the deaths of poor parents were frequently scattered in different parish registers and have probably slipped through the cracks of demographic research. The picture of family life which emerges from reconstitution studies may be unrepresentative for the poor.[30]

Secondly, the lives of those who migrated in search of work were likely to be more unstable than those who remained in one parish. Since the poor were least likely to be able to afford marriage to legitimize a pregnancy, and most likely to engage in repartnering without the attention of the church, their patterns of family life are frequently invisible in the records and so unlikely to be part of demographers' data. Poor couples could pass as married for several years; illegitimate children were not always baptized, so escaped the parish registers. Women were harder to trace over time because they

changed their names on marriage, so inevitably demographic historians have prioritized men's lives over women's.[31] The methodology of
family reconstitution replicates the significance of male lines of descent, making female lines marginal. The families of mothers of
illegitimate children are those least likely to be traced.

A third group of criticisms relates to the assumptions inherent in
demographic research. Miranda Chaytor showed that not all people
in a household over 14 years of age and with different surnames could
be viewed as life-cycle servants; many had kin relationships to the
household.[32] Bridget Hill questioned what marriage meant in the
eighteenth century, when many couples simply cohabited without a
marriage in church.[33] Finally, numbers can be misleading, for, as
Margaret Spufford has observed, once historians have viable statis-
tics, they tend 'to lose all sense of individual people'.[34]

THE POOR LAWS AND HISTORIOGRAPHY

Because the Poor Laws feature so largely in the lives of poor mothers
and fathers, a brief account of these is necessary at the outset.[35]
Attempts to address issues of social welfare had a long history, as
from the later middle ages, the state had attempted by statute, pro-
clamations, and regulations, to relieve the deserving and set others to
work.[36] Statutes were passed in the reign of Henry VIII to punish
vagrants, to relieve the 'impotent' poor, and to put poor children to
work. In Elizabethan times, further legislation established a welfare
system which lasted, though with some adjustments, until 1834.
Alongside the provisions for secular welfare, individual Christians
continued charitable activity.

The main principle animating the legislators and administrators of
the Poor Laws was that the true poor—widows, orphans, and the
worthy who had suffered misfortunes—should be relieved, while the
rest should be set to work. By a statute of 1563 (5 Eliz. I c. 3), each
parish was to collect rates for the relief of the poor, while by another
of 1576 (18 Eliz. I c. 3) the idle poor were to be forced to work. Acts
were consolidated in 1597 (39 Eliz. I c. 3), and re-enacted in 1601
(43 Eliz. I c. 2).

No strangers could claim relief from a parish, and by acts of 1572
(14 Eliz. I c. 5) and 1598 (39 Eliz. I c. 40) vagrants were to be
punished. The issue of who belonged to the parish, and was therefore entitled to relief, was clarified by Acts of 1662 (13 & 14 Car. II

c. 12) and 1692 (3 Will. & Mary c. 11). Individuals could acquire a 'settlement' in a parish by birth, by working in the parish for a year, or by property. Parishes judged that any wandering poor people did not belong and so they remained outside the relief system.[37]

While legislators judged that idle adults were frequently work-shy, they believed that children over about 7 years of age were trainable. From 1547, statutes directed that poor children were to be set to work. In 1598, an Act for the Relief of the Poor (39 Eliz. I c. 30) required the appointment of an overseer for every parish, and by a consolidating act of 1601, 43 Eliz. I c. 2, churchwardens and overseers were ordered to bind out poor children as apprentices if they judged that their parents were not able to maintain them. Over the next two centuries, although the Poor Laws were modified, a constant principle was to train the children of the poor to be useful workers.

This study of poor parents draws extensively upon a rich historiography which has two main strands: the first focuses on the making of the laws and their administration, the second on experiences of poverty. Histories of the laws began in the eighteenth century.[38] Subsequent historians depicted the history of the Poor Laws in terms of the development of welfare. In the early twentieth century, Sidney and Beatrice Webb wrote their monumental history of the old Poor Laws,[39] and others worked on specific aspects and time periods. E. M. Leonard wrote of the Poor Laws in the early seventeenth century before the Civil Wars, and Dorothy Marshall of the poor in the eighteenth century.[40] Subsequently Ivy Pinchbeck and Margaret Hewitt traced welfare policies towards children.[41] Historians have been divided between those who judged that the system established was a reasonable form of welfare, and those who condemned its harsh provisions, not least its effects on the family life of the poor. Some have also distinguished between a more compassionate approach to poor children, which emphasized education and training before the later seventeenth century, with the harsher regime of work discipline later.[42]

In the twentieth century, socialist histories of the administration of the Poor Laws have given way to more nuanced studies such as those of Paul Slack and Joanna Innes.[43] Margaret Pelling has analysed the relationships between local authorities and the poor, and shown how authorities attempted to care for the health of the poor.[44] Steve Hindle's important study of parish relief from the mid-sixteenth to the mid-eighteenth century analyses the relationship between the Poor Law authorities and the recipients, revealing the micro-politics of the parish.[45] Likewise, studies of the development of philanthropy and of specific charitable institutions, such as Christ's Hospital, charity schools, and the Foundling Hospitals have enabled us to see the widespread concern of English men and women with poor relief.[46] Social historians have focused on the experience of poverty. Detailed analyses of Poor Law records, including settlement examinations which often contain mini-biographies (though from the point of view of those determining settlement entitlements), have yielded stories of pauper lives. Historians including Keith Wrightson, David Levine, Tim Wales, and Jeremy Boulton have depicted poor people in specific local contexts, revealing much about the varied patterns of relief, while Tim Hitchcock, Peter King, Pam Sharpe, and others have chronicled the experiences of poverty from the perspective of the poor themselves. Although there have been significant advances, Keith Snell's 1985 comment, that there is 'still a long way to go for the family history of the poor', remains valid.[47]

PATRIARCHY AND THE ENGLISH FAMILY

Early modern discourse reiterated certain basic ideas about fathers and mothers. Both God and nature had planted in parents a love for their children; it was one of the strongest principles 'which the wise Author of Nature has implanted in the human Breast', wrote Jonas Hanway in 1762. Humans, like animals, had to nurture their young: 'The very Tyger teaches us what is due to our own Children.'[48] The corollary was that those who did not care about their children were unnatural.

The metaphor for the parent–child bond was 'blood': those related by blood were the only ones 'on whom nature has laid an obligation'.[49] Gender was fundamental to family experience; fathers' and mothers' roles differed, and gender relations were established and negotiated as men and women reared their children. Feelings were gendered. Women's bodies, softer and more delicate than men's, were generally thought to produce feelings correspondingly tender.[50] Man's stronger body ideally demonstrated emotional control; fathers aspired to a stern and 'manly' demeanour. No matter what happened in practice, everyone agreed that a father's duty was to maintain his family, and exercise authority as head of the household.[51] A father

Figure 1 'The Society betwixt Parents, and Children' (1672). In the ideal family, 'The Father maintaineth his Children by taking Pains' while the mother nurtured them. In the family scene pictured here, the father sits apart, while the mother sits with her six children. She suckles one, while an older girl assists with feeding a toddler.

was deemed responsible for overseeing the education and marriages of his children, while a mother nurtured her children and cared for her household, subject to her husband's authority.[52] Women did the work of motherhood which was first a bodily experience, and later physical work. Being a mother was a crucial component of many women's emotional lives, with profound personal meaning as well as implications for their position in families and in society.

The patriarchal family, church, and state were all fundamentally connected in early modern thinking. Metaphors about the family as a microcosm of church and state were commonly used. The family, said Thomas Cobbett, a minister at Lynn in 1656, was 'the original' of state and church; it is 'the Mother Hive, out of which both those swarms of State and Church, issued forth'.[53] The church's ultimate authority rested on Scripture, and sixteenth- and early seventeenth-century translators of the Bible into English normalized the text in the light of their own cultural and religious ideals. Thus Scripture in turn supported, as a God-given model, a family in which a patriarchal father exercised authority.[54] Society had an interest in how fathers and mothers reared their children. The religious education of children, explained an eighteenth-century divine, was of great moment 'to the Publick at large'.[55] Such language which separated 'family' and 'the Publick' allowed fathers to be rulers at home while being subjects abroad. Although being a father was an intensely individual experience, men constantly spoke of the connections between the private world of the family and the public worlds of the parish and the state.

The religious changes of the sixteenth century modified rather than altered moral values, but it can be argued that paternal power was enhanced: fathers were kings and priests in their household, and the Protestant clergy—now married, and no longer living either in communities of other men or with concubines—were themselves active promoters of a patriarchal ideal. Some clergymen equated their own wills with those of God, and regarded disobedience to an earthly father as a despising of God.[56] Early modern fathers exercised the legal power to discipline their dependents, and were the legal representatives of their children until they reached adulthood.

'Patriarchy', a key concept deployed in this book, has been variously understood. Many historians have been wary of the term, particularly challenging the feminist argument that patriarchy was oppressive.[57] Patriarchy remains a slippery concept with multiple meanings, but any discussion and clarification is worthwhile because it was a fundamental term for seventeenth-century political theory as well as for individuals and families. Here I have followed Sylvia Walby's definition of the term as 'a system of social structures and practices in which men dominate, oppress, and exploit women'. In less abstract terms, Walby argues that sets of practices in economic and social life underpin the patriarchal social structure.[58] Patriarchy here has two related meanings. It was a system of paternal authority and inheritance in families—in theory, fathers ruled, and primogeniture obtained—and was a wider system in society whereby men were advantaged in relation to women.[59] At all levels of society, fathers believed that they possessed authority relative to wives, children, and servants in their own households and were responsible for the care of those subject to them.

However, more recent scholarship has drawn attention to the ways in which patriarchy, the rule of fathers, could also be used by some men to subordinate others.[60] While all men had some interest in patriarchy, sharing in what Shepard has termed 'the patriarchal dividend', it was as fathers in families and heads of household that men could subordinate their sons as well as their daughters, and any other males in their households. Exercising public authority as fathers of the poor, 'civic fathers' reduced poor men to the status of children. A patriarch in both families and the state was defined as the 'chiefe father'.[61]

The book adopts a critical perspective on the patriarchal assumptions about fatherly power which justified the intrusion of the state into the family life of the poor. Gender affected family relationships, and men whose sense of self depended on the successful exercise of authority in both their families and outside them were constantly vulnerable to challenge; no man could ever feel himself secure. Being a father in a family affected men's attitudes to public patriarchal policies; however poor a father was, he shared an interest in upholding paternal authority. There was a dialectical relationship between the attitudes and values of the men who framed and administered the Poor Laws and the mothers and fathers of poor children.

Although patriarchy has been central to understandings of early modern politics, how it related to men's roles as fathers has been less considered. Indeed, John Gillis argued that scholars have not taken fatherhood as seriously as motherhood: 'Fathers occupy a very modest place in our symbolic universe—always at the threshold of family life, never at its centre.'[62] Studies of masculinity have concentrated on sexualities, but devoted comparatively little attention to the centrality of heterosexuality in shaping families and in socializing boys and girls into appropriate gender roles.[63] In 1990, Laqueur was 'annoyed that we lack a history of fatherhood': 'Fatherhood . . . has been regarded as a backwater of the dominant history of public power.'[64] Sara Ruddick questions fathers' absence from the work of nurturing children, and argues that we need to 'attend to fathering as a kind of work'.[65] Although there have been studies of men as fathers, to date British historians have been more interested in questions about how men's honour was bound up with their exercise of authority over wives and children than in exploring what men actually did as fathers.[66] They argue that men were threatened not so much by women as by other men with authority who had power to harm them.[67] Of course these divisions between men within patriarchy were significant. For poor fathers patriarchy was Janus-faced: on the one hand, those who could not maintain their wives and children were humiliatingly subject to the authority of the magistrates and overseers; on the other, within their immediate family, their fatherhood was the source of their authority.

Families were central to patriarchy, but although historians are aware of their changing nature, over the last three decades they have been strangely resistant to feminist reconceptualization of 'families'.[68] Terms such as 'the Protestant family' or 'the English family' are inadequate to encompass the diversity of family and household forms. Is a single mother and her child 'a family'? Those who have followed early modern patriarchs in viewing 'the family', rather than the individual, as the basic social unit inevitably find that mothers of children born 'outside' the family do not fit into their histories, but rather into histories of prostitution and bastardy. Likewise, terms such as 'family economy' and 'household economy' obscure the different interests of individuals—mothers, fathers, sons, daughters, servants, apprentices, and other dependents—within the family. In early modern England, there was no such thing as 'the family' or 'the household': there was only a diversity of family types, constantly changing as individuals were born and died. Families were complex and dynamic social institutions.

Two key structural factors affected all families in early modern England, namely, class and gender. Most studies of family dynamics have focused on the middling and élite levels of society where marriage strategies, property relations, and lineage were closely interrelated. But what did patriarchy mean for fathers and mothers of poor children whose family life was less affected by inheritance strategies and primogeniture?[69] Maybe some poor fathers did see their sons as heirs, and their daughters' marriages as enlarging kinship networks, but their thinking about the future had a different context from that of their social superiors. Lack of literacy among the poor means we have great difficulty in documenting ongoing family ties.

Historians have depended on qualitative evidence from the pens of the literate who were largely male and of middling and upper social status to discuss family relationships. Lawrence Stone posited a transition in characteristic family types from 'the Open Lineage Family' to 'the Closed Domesticated Nuclear Family', and argued that parents became more loving over the early modern period.[70] Ralph Houlbrooke emphasized continuities in family life and affection rather than cruelty.[71] Studies of individual gentry families, such as the Verneys, and the Newdigates, have enhanced our knowledge of parent–child relations among the élite.[72] Middling families of the eighteenth century have been studied by Margaret Hunt, using family archives, and Richard Grassby, focusing on business papers.[73] While qualitative evidence about ordinary mothers and fathers is undoubtedly limited, it is important to be aware that the family forms and patterns of behaviour among the 'top levels' are not necessarily found among the families of the poor.[74]

In the developing historiography of 'the family', parents of the poor have fared ill. Lawrence Stone's compelling and influential narrative of change in the early modern English family, in which an open lineage extended system changed to a nuclear family based on companionate marriage and affection for children, was unsympathetic to the poor. His token account of parent–child relations caricatured his generally critical assessment of early modern parents who were 'improvident in begetting children...improvident and careless in disposing of them once they had arrived: easy come, easy go'. Stone cited uncritically the hostile observations of the social superiors of the labouring poor, such as those of the midwife Elizabeth Cellier, who wrote of the great number of children 'overlaid and wilfully murdered by their wicked and cruel mothers'. Like Cellier, Stone ascribed bad motives: if children could work, parents treated them 'as slave labour', deliberately keeping them out of school and so illiterate.[75] In the subsequent abridgement of his book, Stone acknowledged that his critics were correct in pointing to the weakness of his evidence about 'the lower classes'. His response was to concentrate explicitly on families in 'the top levels of society', which again had the unfortunate effect of leaving poor parents without a history.[76] The work of social historians has to some extent modified general understandings of the early modern family, and Houlbroke in particular was aware of how poverty affected the basic functions of parents.[77]

The dearth of first-person writing by poor mothers has allowed the assumption that high infant and child mortality was the result of a lack of maternal affection and failures of nurturance to remain unchallenged.[78] Although surviving documents do not allow us to answer earlier questions about parental emotions, for instance whether mothers and fathers loved their children, I argue that we can read accounts of mothers' and fathers' behaviour as evidence of care and of commitment to their children. We cannot always interpret parental actions: did those who sought to reclaim their children from institutional care do so because they had regarded this as a temporary expedient? Or did they see their children instrumentally in terms of their economic value, and intend that such offspring should contribute to their own upkeep or to the family budget? We should leave open the possibility that as older children required less direct care, parents could manage to have them living at home. (As we will see, parents frequently applied for places in institutions for one child as a means of allowing them to focus resources on others.)

As for the history of childhood, in the 1970s, Lloyd de Mause and his collaborators asserted that all parents in the past were cruel, and the history of childhood a nightmare.[79] Linda Pollock, on the other hand, argued from a study of diaries, autobiographies, and newspapers that parents loved their children and did their best for them; little changed over the period 1500 to 1900.[80] Historians are beginning to discuss the lives of children who were poor but children's voices remain elusive. Thus, while recognizing that parenting is always a two-way process, I have concentrated on the experiences of parents rather than children.

Initially, feminist historians, of whom I count myself one, were drawn to the history of women's bodies, and histories of motherhood focused largely on the archetypal experiences of pregnancy, birth, and the nurture of infants.[81] We have not always been keen to situate women's lives in a family context because it can obscure other aspects of their lives, such as work. In our study of early modern women, Sara Mendelson and I sought to consider women as individuals rather than as wives and mothers, since the majority of females in early modern England at any one time—girls, single women and widows included—were not married.[82] However, 'the family' remains in western societies in tension with 'the individual', both concepts retaining profound political significance. Just how significant is debatable. Alan Bray, in his work on male friendship, challenged both past and present assumptions about the centrality of the parent–child relationship, compared with the role of friendship in the life of the individual.[83] Even so, the family was vitally important as a social institution which created and reproduced gender relations.[84]

Feminist scholars have another problem with traditional studies of 'the family', for inevitably they focus attention on men as fathers and heads of the household; reasserting the centrality of men to history has never been part of the feminist project. Nevertheless, it is my hope that by taking a critical view of men as fathers we may better understand the gender division of labour and how men gained and kept power over women. Fathers were not expected to teach sons to nurture, but rather to inculcate the values of manly independence; the physical care of children was women's work, ideally taught by mothers to daughters. Essential for men was the exercise of authority in their families, and even the poorest fathers shared in this 'patriarchal dividend' as Connell has termed it.[85] In the public world, studies of masculinity have shown that being able to assert authority over other men was a crucial ordering principle between men.[86] Civic authorities had power over other men as well as women; and here, as we shall see, the poorest fathers were diminished.

Gender affected the roles of mothers and fathers. Taking the view that motherhood was work emphasizes what women did—how they fed, clothed, sheltered, and attempted to socialize, discipline, and train their individual children—rather than what they felt.[87] Again, in the absence of first-person statements, evidence about mothers' work tells us something about poor women's attachment to their daughters and sons.

Family behaviour was not static over time, though it seems as if continuities in attitudes and values were predominant. We tend to think that the teaching of gender roles to each individual was reinforced by powerful psychological mechanisms. As social psychologists have shown, behaviours can be taught, but some are so deeply embedded within the individual that they are accessible neither to reason nor to change. While I do not want to proceed via psychoanalytic theory, I use some of its concepts. Establishing a gender identity involves the child, as psychologists and psychoanalysts have argued, in negotiating with their primary nurturer, the mother. Girls and boys were viewed as different even before they were born. Psychoanalysis has endeavoured to explain how parents socialize their children, so that before they reach adolescence girls' and boys' gendered identities are deep in their unconscious. Freudian theories are useful in explaining the role of sexual difference in creating an unconscious as well as a conscious emotional attachment to the gender norms of a particular society.[88]

Parents had a crucial role in the transmission of cultural values; gender, class and nation were made part of each individual woman and man in their earliest years. When an infant was born, much of its class and gender position was already determined by its family of origin. How do practices of parenting shape individual children, turning them into men and women, rich and poor, English, British, and 'other'? All of these concepts—gender, class and nation—were relational. Thus to be a man meant not being a woman; to be a gentleman meant not to be ignoble; to be English meant not to be a savage, an 'other'. Men emerged with a sense of entitlement which separated them from boys and from women. Cultural representations became part of individuals' subjective identities.[89]

Across the period 1500 to 1800, England changed profoundly, becoming a class society and a nation, Great Britain, forged from England, Wales, Ireland, and Scotland, with an empire.[90] As men served in the armies and navies of Britain's empire, so ideas about other peoples filtered into the lives of the poor. Empire introduced black people to English society. Children's ideas about being British and imperialists as well as about gender and class were created by myriad quotidian interactions which defined individuals in relation to others. Of course, children's interactions were not just with parents.

Nevertheless, it was fathers and mothers, or those who acted as such, who had a crucial role in shaping their social identities.

TERMINOLOGY: WHO WERE PARENTS?

Beneath the common designation of 'parents' and 'children' was a range of relationships. Families were not straightforward, but muddled, as in the case of Mary Monsloe and her baby with which this introduction began. As in modern families, parents were defined on the basis of blood and marriage. 'Mother' and 'father' were not synonymous. Mothers were genetic and gestational, fathers genetic only. Both women and men were expected to be social parents, but men were not expected to be fathers to their illegitimate children, although single mothers who refused to nurture their offspring were deemed unnatural. In addition to mothers and fathers who had a 'blood' connection, remarriages created stepparents. As an anonymous catechist explained in 1616, parents included stepfathers and stepmothers.[91] (Those whom we term stepparents were referred to as 'mother-in-law', and 'father-in-law'; usually in-laws were simply termed mother and father.) Informal adoptions created surrogate parents, as relatives or strangers took in orphans. Thus 'parents' included foster parents: 'All of these which are not in the right line, although they be not properly and immediately parents; yet is their dutie all one, in respect of Christian education.'[92] While contemporaries deemed the responsibilities of 'natural' parents as limitless—there were 'no bounds of their office'—others such as guardians served only until children married or could shift for themselves.[93] However, as we shall see, in practice fathers and mothers made subtle distinctions between children who were 'their own', their stepchildren, orphaned relatives, illegitimates, and foundlings.

In contemporary discourse, masters and mistresses of servants and apprentices were said to be *in loco parentis* rather than in an economic relationship. In 1630, Robert Cleaver explained that the householder was called 'Pater Familias, that is, a father of a familie, because he should have a fatherly care over his servants as if they were his children'.[94] Masters might interfere in the marriages of contracted servants or bound apprentices.[95] Nevertheless, employers and masters were fundamentally different from parents. Employers never considered themselves bound to love and care for their servants and apprentices until death, nor were employees their heirs. Though fathers and mothers invested much of their own emotional life in their children, employers did not. Their regime was designed to produce disciplined bodies. Many households had two tables with different food for parents and children, and for apprentices and servants. The latter fared worse, and there were complaints of hunger. Indeed, withholding of food could be a form of bodily discipline (designed to lower the 'high blood' of adolescents). Similarly, the clothing and general accommodation of apprentices was inferior to that provided for children. Familial language extended to some work relationships, and obscured their economic base. A senior freeman in a workshop might see himself as father: in 1683, Joseph Moxon wrote that every printing house is a chapter, and the oldest freeman 'is the Father of the Chappel'.[96]

Commentators on the fifth commandment—Honour thy father and thy mother—used the concept of fatherhood to define relations between superiors and inferiors.[97] From Tudor times 'parents' included civic and religious authorities.[98] A 1581 catechism explained that the fathers and mothers to be honoured included 'the fathers of our Countrie'.[99] The name 'parent', according to the anonymous author of a 1616 treatise, was 'a name which equivocally is given to the Magistrate, who is called, Pater patriae, the Father of the country'.[100] The 'fathers of our country', or 'civic fathers', as I shall term them, were increasingly significant in the lives of poor children in the early modern period (as Chapter 5 shows). Clergy were spiritual fathers: the pastor was father of the flock, God the father of all Christian believers, and 'the Church is named Mother of us all'.[101] Teachers, too, were fathers and mothers: 'Look upon thy Teachers as thy second Parents', urged Samuel Brewster in 1703.[102]

I have used the term 'civic fathers' as a convenient shorthand to refer to a broad social group of men who exercised public fatherhood on behalf of the state or charitable institutions. Justices of the peace and governors of charities were the most obvious civic fathers, but I have included even churchwardens and overseers of the poor in parishes. While overseers served for only a year, and might themselves end their lives on parish poor relief, nevertheless when they were in office they shared in the exercise of public fatherly power that the state vested in those administering welfare policies. This 'state' was different from the nation states of the nineteenth and twentieth centuries; its development was shaped by social interests.[103]

'Children' refers both to those who were physically young, and also to those who all their lives remained in a relationship to their fathers or mothers. These relationships were individual to each child, and changed over lifetimes. The period of childhood, an abstract notion about the years of girls' and boys' dependency, varied according to social levels; in early modern times, parents of the élite and middling sort protected their children for longer than the poor were able to. But there is a further meaning of the term 'children'; 'children' came to include all of the poor, 'Gods familie', for whose welfare the magistrates, the civic fathers, were responsible.[104] When authority figures were fathers, by implication all subordinated were children, perhaps even unruly children. Finally, in early modern usage the terms 'family' and 'friends' could designate both wider kin and immediate family, parents and children.[105]

The language of parental relationships permeated early modern society. Christian religious beliefs were articulated in family terms, as were political relationships, which made abstract concepts seem comprehensible. A catechist explained in 1617 that all superiors were called 'by the name of mother and father...because they are sweet and pleasant names' signifying affection of superiors to inferiors, and also persuading inferiors to perform their duty cheerfully.[106] God's honour was more involved with his children 'than any parents can be in the behaviour of his owne children', urged the minister John White in 1647.[107]

SOURCES

This study depends on multiple primary sources. Qualitative evidence across lifetimes or minute and detailed observations of parent–child interactions are rare even for the highest social levels in early modern England. What we have for poor parents is even more incomplete, and usually from the pens of others. Many historians as well as early modern observers have confessed how hard it is to get within poor families.[108] Yet there is no dearth of material about the lives of poor mothers and fathers; the administration of the Poor Laws and the proceedings of courts left massive records.[109] Such evidence, created for administrative purposes, historians have read against the grain to deduce something about the lives of the poor themselves. As one instance, Linebaugh and Rediker expanded a brief paragraph written by an elder of the Bristol Church of Christ about a seventeenth-century woman servant, 'a Blackymore maide named Francis'. By showing what it meant to be a servant, and a black woman in Bristol in the 1670s, they allow us to understand something of the social context in which Francis was both a radical presence and an accepted member of the church.[110] Incomplete evidence in surviving court records may need to be expanded, and we may need to speculate about the meaning of stories.[111] Unless historians attempt the challenge of interpretation, the voices of the poor are silenced.

Literary scholars have accused historians of taking insufficient account of genre, of the shape and form of sources, yet characteristically much historical research involves a careful understanding of both the value and limitations of each source, and the deployment of a wide range of records, each of which offers a distinctive perspective. So far as the poor were concerned, most surviving records share the view from above; the voices of the poor are mediated by their social superiors. The main groups of sources are described briefly below.

The administration of poor relief and charities created a vast body of records. Parish records enable us to see the interactions of poor parents with the civic fathers, although because parish practices varied, and the survival of continuous series of records is uneven, it is always difficult to generalize about how the law operated. 'Bastardy depositions', those formulaic documents required under the Poor Laws in order to filiate (that is, establish a father of) an illegitimate child, may reveal something of women's and men's attitudes to becoming parents. Other administrative records may include details of apprenticeships and employment, allowing us to observe the transition of poor children from parental care to the semi-independence of adolescence. The increasing use of printed forms from the later seventeenth century meant that information was more likely to be standardized and individual stories to remain unrecorded.[112]

Chiefly though, the poor sought to gain relief, and petitioned both parish and charitable authorities for assistance. With knowledge of the purposes for which these petitions and narratives were written—not necessarily by the poor themselves—we can interpret them to give detail about parents' attitudes to their children, about their economic circumstances, and even something of their hopes.[113] Over the period, poor petitioners struggled in their applications to adapt their stories to the values of the authorities. They drew upon multiple discourses in their culture—legal, medical, and moral—to offer acceptable presentations of themselves. Sometimes, as Garthine Walker reminds us, the voices are the speakers' own; 'sometimes they are the voices of the culture' against which individuals struggle. There is potentially something personal in each story.[114]

Fragmentary documents can be suggestive, cautioning us about how we attempt to write the lives of 'others'.

A rich, much studied collection is the petitions for the admission of infants to the Foundling Hospital in the second half of the eighteenth century.[115] Women did not always write these petitions themselves, so the terms in which the petitions were expressed may well echo contemporary views of ideal motherhood. Nevertheless, the petitions contain information about single motherhood, such as how they tried to look after their infants, and how they managed their economic resources. Some petitions included statements about maternal feelings.

Ordinary men and women inhabited a world steeped in commonplaces about parenting. Those who made and administered the laws relating to poor relief were familiar with the genre of fathers' advice which had a long history; circulated initially in manuscript, it proved popular with the advent of print. Many early modern advice texts echoed those from medieval times in didactic tone and topics addressed.[116] Sermons publicized the norms of good parenting. William Gouge's influential treatise, *On Domesticall Duties*, was first preached at Blackfriars, and reached a wider audience in print.[117] Such domestic advice manuals mediated what was already known about parenthood and articulated ideas about something new. Élite discourses about fathers and mothers informed the policies of the civic fathers towards the poor. While many poor parents, especially mothers, were illiterate, they could attend sermons where they were made familiar with the main commonplaces about parental duties.

Imaginative literature such as drama and fiction engaged in various ways with parental relationships and their meaning: mothers and stepmothers were differentiated, and parents were shown to respond differently to favoured children, or to sons and to daughters.[118] Didactic literature was published for children, sometimes in the guise of moral tales.[119] Such literature reached poor fathers and mothers only indirectly. However, oral traditions of story telling were widespread, and fairy stories about parents, particularly stepparents, exercised a powerful hold on imaginations.[120] Popular sayings and ballads popularized the dangers of not disciplining children: 'cocking Dads make sawsie lads', warned Thomas Tusser.[121] An early seventeenth-century ballad told of the consequences of a mother's indulgence:

> And, when her husband fell full sicke,
> and went to make his will,

> 'O husband, remember your sonne', she said,
> although he hath beene ill.

Subsequently the wicked son attempted to blacken his widowed mother's name, was imprisoned for his evil conduct, and hanged himself.[122]

Parent–child relationships feature in many tales, but historians, as Lyndal Roper has pointed out, have difficulties with documents 'which we do not believe to be factual'. Discussing confessions of witchcraft, Roper argued that these were not products of realism, but 'vivid, organized products of the mind'.[123] Such an approach helps us interpret surviving evidence. Stories could echo written texts, of which the Bible was the most influential, for although both Old and New Testaments were based in cultures very different from that of early modern England, popular narratives told of prodigal sons, of paternal favouritism, and of how to distinguish true mothers from false. Since the meanings of such stories were never absolutely fixed, they could be reshaped in the reading and in the telling, and individuals could impose their own version of the past.[124]

In oral traditions, mothers' tales featured prominently, although men were more likely to be the scribes; Alice Beare told Anthony à Wood's father 'many stories of the family' which Anthony subsequently recorded.[125] Benjamin Shaw, a mechanic (a skilled manual labourer) from Lancashire, was one of the very few ordinary writers who attempted to set down something of his knowledge of his family partly for himself, and partly for his children, recording 'what I remember to have heard, by word of mouth, or seen'.[126] Here we would be less concerned for 'truth' (which I would argue is none other than individual perceptions in family stories) than for plausibility, arguments, rhetoric, and stereotypes.

Stories could resonate at many social levels and appear in more than one guise. Mary Monsloe's 1596 story of single motherhood and child substitution, with which this discussion opened, was echoed in 1677 in an Old Bailey case. A midwife, either determined to satisfy her husband 'who was very Impatient to have a child' or to preserve her credibility as a midwife, pretended to have a child. She faked a pregnancy by wearing a small pillow, and sought a baby, alive or dead. She bribed two women searchers to bring her the dead child of a very poor woman who would thus save the cost of a burial. The court concluded that the case showed 'a strange extravagant humour' but was not murder.[127] Again in 1688, after the birth of a Prince of Wales, the whole nation canvassed tales about suppositious births and the substitution of a male child via a warming-pan.[128] Individual episodes of such stories recurred because of the importance of male heirs in some families, and because fears of deceitful and desperate women had a hold in popular imagination.[129]

Church courts, criminal courts, and quarter sessions all offer other tales. Framed by the particular proceedings of a court, the participants—defendants and witnesses—all recount versions of events. What we hear, of course, are the words of the scribes, not the voices of the past.[130] Although court narratives were contested, incidental detail may prove telling; brief biographical statements may survive in court proceedings, which offer tiny glimpses of individual lives and relationships. Especially rewarding is the published collection of stories told in the London court of the Old Bailey from 1674, now beguilingly accessible on a magnificent new website. The *Proceedings* must, like all other sources, be placed in historical context.[131] The procedure and reportage of the Old Bailey trials changed over the period. Witness statements became first-person accounts in the 1710s, and the length of the reports increased in the 1730s and 1780s, reducing in the 1790s;[132] not until the 1730s was defence counsel allowed.[133] Yet if we bear in mind the limitations of reportage, the *Proceedings* can offer a window into plebeian mentalities. Whereas once those on trial may have been viewed as a criminal class, historians now see that they, together with witnesses, were all were 'part of an eighteenth-century working class'.[134] Other court proceedings offer glimpses of the rural population, though there is no other single such valuable source; the quality and survival of county records varies enormously. Closest to the events described are depositions to a justice or to coroners' courts.[135] While court stories may not be true, they can be analysed as fictions which probed motives and constructed meanings in ways that were believable by contemporaries, however extraordinary they may seem to later readers.[136] Because the fragments may seem opaque to the modern reader, I have speculated a little about possible narrative meanings, although the meaning of silences and absences remains elusive.

The illustrations selected here offer another source about poor parents. Visual images were produced by print-makers, engravers, and artists whose purposes included the desire to make money. Some woodcuts, engravings, and paintings offer a further view from above, depicting the poor as objects of fear, and as subjects for reform. By contrast, pictures of public performances and public institutions, and portraits of wealthy philanthropists, promoted an idealized version of charity and philanthropy.

In selecting examples from a wide range of sources across a long time span, my aim is to undermine the notion that there is a single history of parents. So much of our imagined view of early modern family life is derived from the compelling testimonies left to us from the pens of the social élite, and their views of the poor especially in the eighteenth century were generally unsympathetic. By focusing on the qualitatively different evidence about the lives of poor mothers and fathers I invite the reader to reassess how social level, or class (to use the term simply as a shorthand) affected relationships between parents and children. Over the early modern period, poor fathers and mothers struggled to provide their children with the basic necessities, while many others in their society were growing richer in wealth and consumer goods. Parents' individual stories—the anecdotes—have both common elements and differences across the period 1580 to 1800 as they adapted to social and economic changes.

Thus there are two basic arguments in this book. First, class and gender mattered. Poor mothers and fathers were different from parents of the gentry and aristocracy because their poverty placed them in a different material world. We can learn about the poor as mothers and fathers from a discussion of what they did for their offspring, how they brought their children up. The second argument addresses the connection between fatherhood in a family and public fatherhood in the state. The Poor Laws which gave power to civic authorities over poor fathers and mothers perpetuated a particular form of domestic patriarchy, formulated in the later sixteenth century, that gave all adult men who headed households an investment in upholding paternal authority.

The book is structured around different perspectives on being a mother or a father of a poor child. The first two chapters focus on the most extreme cases of the difference gender makes, by discussing the contrasting experiences of mothers and fathers of an illegitimate child. Pregnancy, giving birth, and responding to the needs of the newborn child involved mothers in all the demands of motherhood, albeit in the doubly adverse circumstances of being unmarried and being poor. Paternity, by contrast, was always uncertain, and never more so than in the case of children begotten of illicit sexuality. Men's experiences of fathering illegitimate children resembled those of the fathers of legitimate families only in limited ways. The second chapter reveals the diversity of men's responses to illicit paternity, and their general unwillingness to undertake even the basic duty of maintenance.

The next two chapters focus on what mothers and fathers actually did in order to bring up their children. While Chapter 3 discusses the ways in which material circumstances shaped how parents could nurture and educate their offspring, Chapter 4 focuses on the lamentable straits to which they were reduced when poverty increased. Sometimes the mere fact of more children to be cared for made parents desperate, and the pressure of poverty fractured family groups. At other times, sickness and mortality reduced the family to destitution. For parents who both inherited poverty and experienced life-cycle crises, keeping children alive and bringing them up was never easy.

The formulation and implementation of Poor Laws from the late Elizabethan period brought public fatherhood into poor families. Chapter 5 examines the rhetoric and practices of these civic fathers, who, in exercising their paternal authority and granting or withholding relief, reduced all the poor including adults to the state of childhood. Furthermore, the authority of these public fathers was applied not only to the poor in England, but to the indigenous inhabitants of Britain's empire.

A concluding chapter draws some of these themes together, reflecting upon the experiences of mothers and fathers who were poor in contrast to those of higher social status. Despite the bleak picture which poverty always presents, it argues that many poor parents derived social status and personal satisfaction from their struggles to do their best for their offspring.

MOTHERS OF 'THE BASTARD CHILD'

In 1773, Anne Newman petitioned for the admission of her baby to the London Foundling Hospital: 'though her child is illegitimate and obnoxious to the Laws yet the natural Affection of a Mother is still the same'.[1]

Anne Newman was right: her child was 'obnoxious to the Laws' of the country, which deemed a 'bastard' to be the child 'of no man'. Further, according to the bastardy legislation and the Poor Laws, those who called themselves 'fathers of the poor' directed the fate of such 'bastard' children. Yet parents of illegitimate children were often termed 'natural parents', and if 'the natural Affection of a Mother' was still the same, why was Anne Newman petitioning for someone else to care for her child? Illegitimate parenthood challenged the ideals of a properly ordered society, raising questions about the meanings of motherhood and fatherhood in early modern times.

Single women who bore illegitimate children were undoubtedly a minority of mothers, even of the poor. But their fate matters, because the fear of bearing an illegitimate child structured the behaviour of young women on the cusp of marriage. Low levels of extramarital conceptions were achieved only by society exerting immense social pressure on young women and men. Women had to balance their fears of pregnancy with their desires for sexual pleasure and for marriage.

Contemporaries censured single mothers as 'bastardbearers', and told tales of their ignorance and indifference. Sir Nicholas LeStrange recounted a story about his grandmother Stubbe, who had asked the young woman she employed to produce a testimonial: 'O Mistresse sayes she, I have one of those above in my Boxe; and up she runs, and for her Testimoniall, brings down a very faire and formall warrant, signifying that she had lately had a Bastard, and was to be passed from Constable to Constable.'[2]

Early modern terminology about single mothers and their children sounds censorious: mothers were 'lewd', 'bastard-bearers', 'strumpets', or 'unnatural' whores, and their children 'bastards'.[3] To call a person a 'bastard' was derogatory: in 1652, Southampton authorities investigated someone who had said that Christ 'was a Bastard'.[4] The term was also actionable at law, because it could deprive a person of an inheritance.[5] Most historians have generally adopted the contemporary language of bastardy (which did have a legal meaning). Peter Laslett referred to a 'bastardy prone sub-society',[6] and introduced the term 'repeaters' for women who bore more than one illegitimate child.[7] Historians' use of the contemporary terminology of 'bastard-bearers' erases the maternity of single women, and makes them marginal to the history of 'the family', a unit headed by a husband and father. When 'bastardy' is related to inheritance, property, and exclusion, then the experiences of unmarried mothers are occluded.[8] However, alternative language is difficult to find. The term 'illegitimate' is itself problematic, because it refers to the sexual relationship of the adults, not to the child. As a character in Henry Fielding's novel *Tom Jones* (1749) observed: 'the words "dishonourable birth" are nonsense...unless the word "dishonourable" be applied to the parents; for the children can derive no real dishonour from an act of which they are entirely innocent'.[9] The term 'natural' for the child can be ambiguous. Rather than follow the contemporary language of 'whores' and 'bastard-bearers', I have chosen to use terms which emphasize maternity. I will generally seek non-censorious language wherever possible, referring to children as illegitimate, and problematize other terms such as 'father' with scare quotes.[10]

The apparently small number of illegitimate compared with legitimate children can make single motherhood seem relatively unimportant.[11] Certainly, the illegitimacy ratios (understood as the proportion of illegitimate baptisms to all baptisms)[12] that demographers have calculated are comparatively low, fluctuating from 2.8 per cent of all baptisms 1580–84, to 5.05 per cent 1795–9. There were variations within five-year periods: the proportion was 3 per cent around 1600, but in the later 1630s it fell to below 2 per cent. The mid-seventeenth century marked a low point, and in the later eighteenth century the ratio had doubled to between 4 and 5 per cent.[13] Illegitimacy ratios varied across regions. In the period from roughly 1580 to 1650, demographers estimate that London had a lower ratio than the rest of England,[14] despite single young women being a higher proportion of the population.[15]

All these figures underestimate the number of illegitimate births. We do not know how many babies died between birth and baptism;

illegitimates, typically born in more difficult circumstances, were more likely to die. Not all illegitimates were baptized and registered in the Anglican Church. Some parish clergy recorded legitimacy status. A Hertfordshire clergyman entered the baptisms of base children, one begotten by 'her master', another in Gloucestershire of 'supposed daughter of', and 'Sarah the reputed daughter of William Pope (shearman) & Sarah Clark *als* Hobbs his supposed wife'.[16] Others refused to set down any mark distinguishing bastards, saying 'that when the Childe is Christned yt ys noe bastard'.[17] Illegitimacy has to be inferred in many instances because recording practices were flexible.[18] Although historians have wondered whether poor people cared about legitimacy, and whether there was a 'bastardy prone sub-society',[19] shame gave single mothers good reasons for not presenting their illegitimate offspring for baptism. By the early nineteenth century, about 40 per cent of illegitimate children were not recorded.[20]

Numbers give a spurious sense of certainty about the changing proportions of illegitimate children. In practice, the legality of marriages was often uncertain, especially at the lower levels of society.[21] While studies about changing illegitimacy ratios contribute to our understanding of the context of unmarried motherhood, many questions about single mothers are not answerable by counting.[22] We do not know how many single women bore more than one child. Figures do not tell us whether single women who were genetic and gestational mothers undertook social motherhood.

The mothers and 'fathers' discussed here and in the next chapter were parents whose illegitimate children were *liable* to be a charge to the parish ratepayers; excluded are those wealthier mothers and fathers who escaped the Poor Law authorities. As Dalton explained in his 1618 manual, *The Countrey Justice*, parents who could keep their 'bastard' child were exempt from 18 Eliz. I c. 3; the problem the legislation addressed was not bastardy *per se* but pauper bastardy.[23] This and the next chapter draw on the records of the Poor Law and of charitable institutions, and on wide reading of different kinds of archives across England.

How did women react to pregnancies and births outside marriage, and what happened to them and their children? This chapter first discusses the legislative context in which women bore their illegitimate children, then their pregnancies, childbirths, and initial responses to their infants. Secondly, it examines how single mothers managed to both work and bring up their children, and what support they could draw on. The parish was important, but not all poor single mothers were assisted by parish welfare. In two Bedfordshire parishes, c.1760–1814, only 44 per cent of unmarried mothers whose babies were baptized received parish relief. In Chelmsford 1814–34, the proportion was even less: 37 per cent.[24] Finally, the chapter assesses evidence about single mothers and older children to suggest how these families of mothers and children survived and to discuss whether this can be read as evidence of care and affection.

THE CONTEXT

Over the early modern period, the social context for single motherhood changed. In the late Elizabethan and early Stuart periods, single mothers were censured and liable to be punished for illicit sexuality, but parishes might help them to marry by coercing men. Failing marriage, parishes would provide some small maintenance, which they attempted to recover from the 'fathers'. By 1800, society was no more accepting of women's single motherhood, but the Poor Law authorities concentrated on forcing fathers to pay maintenance for their 'bastards'. Whereas in the earlier period society condemned the *joint* wickedness of men and women who sinned 'against their owne bodies',[25] by the end of the eighteenth century, women were more likely to be regarded as victims of male seduction.

Because the canon law of marriage and the poor relief laws determined so much of the context in which single women experienced maternity, some brief account of the legislation and how it affected pregnant single women is necessary. (How the legislation affected 'fathers' is discussed further in Chapter 2.) This helps us understand why single mothers might see the parish as the last option, and try to manage on their own.

Late Tudor legislation created a different context for ordinary women giving birth outside marriage. In the fifteenth century, the church courts prosecuted for fornication or adultery leading to the birth of an illegitimate child. Mothers could apply for maintenance orders against the 'fathers', and the courts attempted to filiate base-born children, and to determine the level and duration of paternal support, with the sanction of excommunication for non-compliance.[26] Although by canon law such children might be legitimated by the subsequent marriage of their parents, common law categorized them as 'bastards'.[27] However, common law did accept as legitimate children who were *conceived* before their parents' marriages.

After the Reformation, as McIntosh points out, 'older social values were being appropriated and modified, not discarded'.[28] The sixteenth-century Protestant church continued the Catholic tradition of viewing extra-marital sexual activity as a sin, and any resultant children as illegitimate, but the state, rather than the church, became responsible for overseeing the relief of 'bastards'. From 1576, by the statute 18 Eliz. I c. 3 and the subsequent Poor Law of 1598, 39 Eliz. I, secular not canon law enforced the duties of both fathers and mothers to provide for their illegitimate child. Whereas church court proceedings for maintenance were expensive and initiated by individuals, new laws made parishes responsible for illegitimate children, and gave parishes a vested interest in finding men who could pay to maintain their offspring, just as did fathers in legitimate families. The church courts continued to issue support orders, but the practice fell into desuetude, and was non-existent by the mid-eighteenth century.[29] From 1576, by the law 18 Eliz. I c. 3, secular authorities were responsible for finding a 'father' and ordering him to pay maintenance, on threat of punishment and imprisonment. Two justices took depositions to meet the legal requirement of affiliating (determining the father of) the child, so that they could make an order for the father to pay maintenance. Many single women were examined before the child was actually born; others were questioned when they were in labour; after 1733, they were not examined for at least a month after giving birth.[30] If the father could not be found, or defaulted, then illegitimate children were to be maintained at the expense of the parish rate-payers. By the Poor Laws of 1597–1601, the parish was given residual responsibility for maintaining and overseeing the upbringing of illegitimate children, so there was an increasing parochial determination to collect maintenance from 'fathers'.[31]

Legislation was designed to deter extra-marital births; mothers and the alleged fathers were liable to physical punishment. Mothers were most likely to be punished in the period before 1640. By the statute 7 & 8 Jac. I c. 4, they could be whipped and/or sent to a house of correction for a year.[32] Whipping was to be deferred until woman had recovered from lying-in 'or the childe [may] miscarry'.[33] In Wiltshire in the 1620s, Ingram found that the justices usually ordered 'bastard bearers' to the house of correction for a year.[34] How commonly such harsh punishments were inflicted is unclear. Quarter session records for the seventeenth century suggest considerable local variations. In Jacobean Somerset, the justices did not order whippings of all unmarried mothers; perhaps some additional moral outrage prompted the decision in particular cases. Thus in 1621, they ordered that Susan Wallys 'for her notorious offences to be severely whipped to put her in mind how she doth offend in the like hereafter'.[35] In Cheshire, mothers were not usually whipped unless an initial order was disobeyed.[36] Westminster civic authorities ordered both private and public whippings at the cart's tail in the early seventeenth century.[37] However, in three local studies before 1660, King estimated that 80 per cent of parents—unfortunately he did not separate mothers and fathers—were punished.[38] Public shame and censure were probably greatest before 1660 when concern over the multiplication of the numbers of the poor combined with the sterner sexual morality associated with Puritanism. Yet even after the 1650 Act to suppress incest, adultery, and fornication, administrators did not distinguish bastardy from fornication, and attempts to tidy up the law failed.[39] A study of the administration of the law in Devon suggests that magistrates were no harsher in the 1650s than at other times.[40] At the end of the eighteenth century, corporal punishment for bastardy was rare.[41] By 1800, while a single mother was still shamed as a 'fallen' woman, emphasis had shifted onto the issue of economic support for both herself and her child.

In the early modern period, the relationship of formal marriage to sexual intercourse was never so clear-cut as the clergy and legislators wished. Illegitimacy and legitimacy were not simple alternatives: many women bore their first child to a man they subsequently married. Promises to marry could be treated as binding and lead to sexual intercourse, but the couple might not marry, sometimes because economic difficulties intervened.[42] Marriage involved not just the couple, but also parents and kin who would be expected to help the couple establish an independent household; without assistance it was difficult for a couple to marry, and births could occur before the process was completed.[43] Thus the law's definition of a 'bastard' was not necessarily that which ordinary people generally entertained. One effect of the growing hostility to bastardy from the later sixteenth century was to strengthen the importance of church marriage.[44]

Attitudes to premarital fornication as well as to illegitimate births may have fluctuated with economic conditions. Difficult times in some areas in the early seventeenth century led to harsher attitudes to the sexuality and marriages of the poor.[45] There was a national peak in the illegitimacy rate just after 1600.[46] This could reflect the higher incidence of births outside marriage, but it could reflect greater community anxiety about supporting illegitimate children in times of economic adversity, and so a greater desire to register illegitimacy and affiliate any children.

This legal and social context affected single mothers in many ways. First, they were likely to have civic authorities intrude into their lives. Parishes were not always keen to see the parents of an illegitimate child marry,[47] because then they would be liable to support a growing family of paupers. Female-headed households were thought disorderly,[48] so justices and parishes discouraged single mothers and their children from living alone with a parish pension. In the late sixteenth and seventeenth centuries, parishes preferred to board the illegitimate child out. In theory the authorities would enforce the right of those under 7 years to be nurtured by their mothers, but they could imprison and punish the mother in a house of correction with or without her child for up to a year. Because a single mother's sexual behaviour was the subject of local gossip, she would find it difficult to obtain work, especially as a live-in servant, and her family would be shamed as well. By the 1662 law of settlement, 'bastards' were to be relieved in the parish where their mothers gave birth. Thus the child's legal settlement (entitlement to be relieved) could be different from the mother's own place of settlement, and in such cases mother and infant could be separated. Even if she kept her child, when she or he reached the age of 7 years, it was likely the overseers would order the child to be apprenticed. This was no apprenticeship to learn a trade: briefly, a small premium (of around £1 in eighteenth-century Devon) would be paid so that a master could have service in housewifery or husbandry from the young child. Formal indentures for pauper apprentices were infrequently recorded compared with a classic apprenticeship.[49] A mother would have no control over what happened to her child.

Secondly, since the parish ratepayers would become liable for the maintenance of her child, a single mother would be pressed to name the father. Until the eighteenth century, this affected the assistance she received when giving birth. Midwives licensed by the bishops were sworn to withhold their services when the woman was *in extremis* until she named the true father; it was assumed that no woman would want to die with a lie on her lips.[50] The ecclesiastical courts heard complaints against unlicensed midwives who did not insist that the mother name the father. Thus in 1727, Jane King of Moor was cited for unlicensed midwifery: she 'does not Cause the Naugty [sic] Women to filiate their Children'.[51] But single mothers were often unwilling to confess, because men disliked having their names in public contention, and sometimes threatened to deny maintenance if their lovers named them.

Thirdly, there were punishments associated with illicit maternity. After a single mother recovered from giving birth, she might be whipped, and/or ordered to a house of correction for a year, with or without her child. She was subject to legislation if her newborn child died. In fifteenth-century England, those involved in the suspicious deaths of any newborn children were indicted in the church courts, where a guilty verdict would lead to penance, but after 1624, by the statute 'to Prevent the Murthering of Bastard Children', if an unmarried woman concealed the birth of her child and it was found dead, then she was presumed guilty of murdering it, and subject to the death penalty.[52] Unlike a married mother, an unmarried one was always suspected of criminal intentions.[53] Before the Restoration, many deeply religious parishes were convinced that if they did not see justice done on the perpetrators of infanticide, they would share in 'the guilt whereof we are anxious not to contract'.[54]

Single mothers' need for maintenance involved the parish. Although the Poor Laws applied nationally, they were administered in different ways all over England. Justices exercised considerable discretion, so there were great regional, temporal, and inter-regional variations, although administration was more routine in the eighteenth century.[55] The laws were shaped by local needs, where civic authorities had their own concerns about illegitimacy and poverty. Élite and middling men knew that illegitimacy endangered orderly inheritance in their own families, so they viewed 'bastard-bearers' harshly, applying a double standard of sexual morality. While authorities wanted 'fathers' to bear the costs of their children, they knew that paternity was uncertain and suspected that mothers lied, and so they gave other men the benefit of the doubt. By the time of the reform of the Poor Law in 1834, some élite men were convinced that nine out of ten single mothers in towns falsely swore the paternity of their children.[56]

Over the period, parishes became more hostile to women giving birth in their parish, and there was less scope for individual relief. The Poor Laws made it harder for a woman's family to help her. In the eighteenth century, mothers were less likely to receive parish support to care for their infants, as parishes preferred to place children in the institutional care of the workhouse while mothers earned a living outside. The laws made the procedures for making the 'fathers' pay maintenance more routine, but mothers were subject to community pressure to name as 'father' a man who could afford maintenance; naming a poor man added to his economic burdens and delayed his prospects of marriage as well as reducing his capacity to pay Poor Law rates to the parish.

Thus Poor Law legislation, framed initially as concepts of marriage and family were being redefined after the Protestant Reformation, created a different context in which an unmarried woman experienced pregnancy and maternity. Over the next two centuries, changing ideas about motherhood in general were bound to affect single mothers in particular. Although single mothers differed from those who were married, they were still mothers, and, as a legal treatise of 1699 explained, like all mothers they owed a natural duty of nurture to their children.[57] Sentimental views of maternity increased during the eighteenth century, and influential writers and thinkers struggled to establish new ideas of virtuous motherhood.[58] Romanticism coloured maternity, and breastfeeding was seen as a crucial marker of womanliness.[59] Trumbach argues that by the mid-eighteenth century, 'a new gender role' for most women 'stressed their maternal feelings' in contrast to those of women who became prostitutes.[60] But by 1800, even attitudes towards prostitution had softened, which in turn affected how single mothers were viewed.[61] They were regarded with some pity as 'fallen women', rather than as lewd whores, who were potentially reformable so that they could re-enter the labour market, but as single women divested of their offspring, not as single mothers.

Attitudes to childhood and children also became more sentimental over the early modern period. In the seventeenth century, parents were influenced by doctrines of the child's original sin, but in the eighteenth century, childhood was seen more as a stage of innocence that needed adult protection. Emphasis on the spiritual health of the child gave way to greater concern with the development and education of the individual. How the child was represented had implications for state policies. If childhood was supposed to be happy, then contemporaries noticed that the children of the poor were exploited.[62]

Such changing ideas affected levels of tolerance for single mothers raising their own children. The context in which unmarried women mothered was generally negative. Beliefs in heredity were powerful, and it was still thought that women who engaged in illicit sexuality transmitted their 'bad blood' to their offspring, especially their daughters: 'bastards by chance are good, by nature bad'.[63] 'The good wife would not seek her daughter in the oven if she had not been there before.'[64] In 1690, Henry Prescott, the deputy registrar of the court of the Chester diocese, saw not single mothers but 'a slovenly crowd' of 'whores...[who] carry and show in their arms their wailing and wretched children'.[65] Lawmakers judged that single mothers, 'bastard-bearers', defrauded 'the Releefe of the impotent and aged true poore'.[66] Negative attitudes towards the children themselves were casually expressed throughout the early modern period. Congenital idleness would infect 'bastards' unless they were trained to work.[67] When the London Foundling Hospital was seeking inspectors for the nurses of the infants in 1758, all the gentlemen in Southwark refused, 'saying they would not be troubled about Bastards'.[68] Such contemptuous views restricted charitable relief, and contributed to the hostile social context in which single women attempted to mother their children.

WHO WERE SINGLE MOTHERS?

Irrespective of marital status, all women who gave birth were mothers; their maternity was an embodied experience. Their responses to the immediate needs of their newborn infants—feeding, cleaning, clothing, and nurture—were individual, complex products of their own historical and personal circumstances. The term 'mother' generally covers three aspects of maternity: the conceiving and bringing forth of the child (the generative and gestational roles) and the social role.[69] Social motherhood thus refers to the work of nurturing and raising a child, as distinct from giving birth to it.[70]

Most of the single mothers to whom the Poor Laws applied were from labouring, mechanic or farming backgrounds. Many worked as household servants. During the 1620s mothers were servants in 61 per cent of Essex quarter sessions cases, compared with 24 per cent in Lancashire.[71] In the 1650s, servant women made at least 19 out of 49 bastardy depositions in Essex, and in at least 11 cases the alleged fathers were the servants' masters.[72] Over the seventeenth century, as the illegitimacy rate declined, Levine and Wrightson concluded that illegitimate births became 'more and more the province of the poor and the obscure'.[73] In eighteenth-century London, where the illegitimacy ratio was higher, in trials for infanticide at the Old Bailey 1730–74, over half (35 of 61) of the single mothers were servants.[74] Many of those in London had come from the countryside. Servants were liable to dismissal for illicit pregnancy. Indeed, by the late seventeenth century, pregnancy could be an accepted cause for dismissal: a

Nottinghamshire employer successfully claimed that the woman 'hath disabled herself by being with child from doeing him yt service wch he might jusley [sic] expect from her'.[75] In 1771, Grace Scott lost her place 'of a common servant' because of her pregnancy.[76]

While the majority of mothers of illegitimate children were single women, some were wives or widows. The child of a long-deserted wife was deemed a bastard,[77] though legally her child was legitimate unless proven otherwise. Thus in 1786, although the mother of 14-year-old Thomas Denty was a soldier's wife, her son was deemed a 'bastard' because her lawful husband 'had been absent several years in Germany or elsewhere in foreign parts'.[78] Children whose parents 'passed' as married, or who had married bigamously, could also come under the bastardy legislation if poverty drove their parents to seek relief, and the unorthodox marital status of their parents was exposed.[79]

Single mothers shared some experiences with the mothers of legitimate children. The illegitimacy ratio and the proportion of firstborn children conceived premaritally were strikingly similar. Wrigley calculated that in the late sixteenth and seventeenth centuries, roughly 15 per cent of all rural brides were pregnant at marriage, 35 per cent in the later eighteenth century. For a proportion of women, courtship and premarital sex had ended happily, even though the married couple were liable to troublesome proceedings in the church courts for premarital fornication.[80] Young women who became single mothers probably became sexually active at around the same ages as those who bore legitimate children. Both single and married women gave birth to their first child at around 26 years. In eighteenth-century London, John Black found that single mothers were of similar mean age to plebeian women at first marriage.[81] Furthermore, between 1561 and 1640, within ten years of giving birth, 42 per cent of single mothers in western and north-western regions of England later married, either the fathers of their children, or other men.[82] Single mothers were likely to marry subsequently, although at a later date this pattern may have altered. Steven King found that in the early nineteenth century, unmarried mothers were drawn from a distinct socio-economic group, and that multiple illegitimate births were relatively common in a section of rural communities suggesting a degree of tolerance of unmarried maternity.[83]

Among ordinary people, there was some confusion over what constituted a valid marriage: in the fifteenth and sixteenth centuries, a promise of marriage followed by sexual intercourse was accepted as a valid though irregular marriage.[84] Courtship followed by sexual intercourse should have been followed by some public ceremony, and there are hints that neighbours held a more accepting attitude towards consequent illegitimate births. But there is little sign overall that single mothers belonged to a tolerant sub-society. They had not deliberately avoided marriage. Rather, many consented to their lovers' sexual demands in the hope that marriage would take them out of service and into a secure and socially desirable life. Women no more chose to be single mothers than men chose to undertake the responsibilities of fatherhood when they engaged in illicit heterosexual activity.

PREGNANCY, ABORTION, PARTURITION, INFANTICIDE, AND 'ABANDONMENT'

When a single woman found herself pregnant, she may have been uncertain what to do. An illicit pregnancy was usually her first, so she was ignorant and inexperienced. She might interpret her bodily symptoms as a menstrual disorder, or a disease, and seek cures; she might talk to her suspicious women neighbours of colic, wind, or the absence of menstruation. Unlike deserted wives or widows, pregnant single women lacked access to the female culture around pregnancy and childbirth. Confiding in another woman was dangerous.[85] Choices facing her were stark. Unless she could marry, or conceal her pregnancy and giving birth, she risked unemployment, punishment, and familial as well as public censure.

Responses and experiences differed. Shame led some to try to abort themselves. Before 1803, this was not a crime if the child had not yet quickened. No records would be made if women were successful; that pregnancy would not make them mothers. They might seek abortifacients under the guise of remedies for menstrual disorders.[86] We know that some pregnant women, like Deborah Brackely in 1651, rejected their lovers' suggestions of abortion as immoral.[87] Shame also led some to suicide.[88]

If her lover refused to help, with either marriage or maintenance, a pregnant single woman was on her own, facing dismissal from her employment and marginalization in her local community. She was unwelcome in the parish where she worked, as her pregnancy reflected 'evil rule' in a household rather than godly order, and in her own parish, her child would be viewed as a liability, a burden on the parish rates. If she migrated from shame and lack of support, either during pregnancy or after the birth of her baby, she was even more desolate, distant from previous networks of support, lacking the 'belonging' which would give her an entitlement to parish assistance, and likely to be punished as a vagrant.[89] Pregnancies made women objects of suspicion to householders in any parish, so they would be 'moved on'. In 1596, one poor London parish threatened that anyone who took in a pregnant woman whose child was liable to be chargeable, would be forced to pay for its keep themselves.[90] The church courts had prosecuted householders who allowed their premises to be used for immoral purposes; by the end of the sixteenth century, they prosecuted those who harboured pregnant women and assisted them in escaping punishment.[91] Once women were wandering from place to place, they were likely to be punished as vagrants.[92]

An early seventeenth-century story illustrates what hostile parishes could do. Women of the parish of Ryarsh in Kent dragged Joan Jacquett, a single women, over the parish borders when she was actually in labour, so that she would give birth in the adjacent parish, which would then be liable for the illegitimate child. Joan gave birth 'in a little straw, under a tree, in the common highway'.[93] Similar stories were told elsewhere.[94] Poor Law authorities would insist that illegitimate babies be settled in the place where they were born, even if the mother's own settlement was elsewhere.[95]

Pregnant single women, outside female networks of support for childbirth, had trouble making arrangements for lying in.[96] There were thought to be places where single women could give birth without too many questions asked, but the poorest women may have lacked access to them.[97] Thus the midwife and any other women who attended the labour of poor women insisted upon the disclosure of the father's name, and justices used such confessions made *in extremis* to affiliate the child and determine maintenance payments. Quarter session records contain examinations of mothers and witnesses, which could be complex. Essex justices, in one case of 1589 involving a married master, questioned ten witnesses, even before the man appeared in court.[98] In a Gloucester case of 1720, Hannah Lyly bore twins with Mary Tindale assisting as midwife. After the first child was born, Hannah named one man, but the midwife, knowing that there was a second child, demanded an additional name, threatening to abandon Hannah:

the sd informant tould her she was on the brinke of Eternity and if she did not confesse the whole truth she would goe away and leave her upon which she tould the informant that Joseph Milman of Kingswood aforesaid had to Doing with her or knowledge of her body to[o] to yt purpose . . . [99]

The midwife's insistence on a second man's name hints at a popular view that twins had different fathers (which would not be raised in the case of a married woman's twins). Mothers' sworn statements had a crucial role in the justices' orders, though men, as we will see in the next chapter, frequently challenged them.

Single mothers' babies were more likely to die than legitimate children. Parish records may underestimate mortality rates as well as illegitimacy rates; illegitimate babies may not have survived long enough to be baptized.[100] Adair concluded from a study of twenty-five rural parishes in the period 1550–1750 that foundlings frequently escaped registration.[101] Single mothers' pregnancies may have involved migration, and subsequently their nutritional levels and inexperience may have made their infants less viable.

After giving birth, a single woman was confronted with difficult decisions. If she breast-fed her child, her shame and dishonour became public knowledge, and her bad reputation might prevent her finding another place in service. But how was she to live, support herself, and her child?

Some new mothers seem to have made no plans, though if they had concealed their pregnancies and given birth secretly, and the babies were stillborn or died, they could be convicted of infanticide. Several excellent studies have examined the cases of infanticide and newborn child murder in the early modern period.[102] These show that women had concealed their pregnancies, given birth in secret, then left their babies somewhere, or even killed them. Such single women may simply have extended their psychological state of denial to include ignoring the child's existence. In a modern study of neonatal infanticide, Julie Wheelwright argues that many mothers were in what she terms 'a dissociated state', so traumatized as to erase the whole painful experience of giving birth from their memories.[103] There was a medical context in the early modern period which acknowledged the physical and emotional stresses involved with pregnancy and labour.[104] In 1696, one single mother pleaded 'that when she was delivered, she cried out, and that she was in a great Trance'.[105] In 1737, a parish overseer investigating a suspected infanticide—the baby's body was later found concealed in a chimney with its throat cut—felt pity at the sight of the mother: 'the poor Creature, the Prisoner, was sitting upright in her Bed, with a Book in her Hand, and the Tears ran plentifully down her Face.'[106]

It is difficult to interpret the stories of infanticidal mothers, because historians have to take account of the legal, religious, and cultural narratives that they were addressing.[107] Some mothers seem to have found it impossible to tell their stories.[108] In 1731, Martha Busby resumed her work after secretly giving birth, but was haunted by her experience. She was picking strawberries when she asked the woman working beside her, 'If she did not hear a Child cry? saying, she had continually the Noise of a New-born Child in her Ears'. Her baby's body was later found in a house of office (a privy) wrapped in an old blanket. In prison, Martha told a witness that she did not escape because 'she knew herself to be Guilty, and had no Power'. The jury was not persuaded she had killed the child, so acquitted her.[109] Seventeenth-century pamphlet literature emphasized maternal savagery, but a minority of reports after 1670 alluded to economic circumstances: Sarah Dent's lover had died, so 'not knowing how to maintain it [her child]', she had killed it.[110]

If a baby's body were found, midwives and other women searched women's bodies for evidence of secret births. In 1694, Mary Maye of Stines initially denied that a dead baby was hers, but confessed when a search revealed a plaster 'upon her Breasts to dry up the Milk'.[111] In 1696, a woman identified only as M— S— denied giving birth, but after her mistress and some women found 'Milk in her Breast', she was indicted of infanticide.[112]

Sympathetic witnesses at infanticide trials spoke of young women's inexperience. In 1790, in an Old Bailey infanticide case, a midwife testified that Martha Miller went to the water-closet, and 'from ignorance of her state, she went there to relieve herself'. The midwife's testimony, that the child might have been stillborn, from Martha's 'ignorance of rendering it proper assistance', convinced the jury who found Martha not guilty.[113] Earlier, in a similar case in 1745, a servant 'pleaded ignorance because she never had had a child; for people who have been in labour knew more than those who have not'.[114]

Juries might be merciful to a mother who had simply allowed her child to die, but if there were signs of violence, then there was little scope for acquitting her, and she faced the death penalty.[115] In Southampton in 1649, Mary Gash's illegitimate child was found in a house of office with marks around its neck. Mary confessed that she had given birth alone, and thrown the child into the privy: 'she sayth that she did it in hope to keep it private and herselfe from further shame, and to keepe the greife & shame of it from her friends.'[116] There was a high rate of execution for those convicted. In Essex between 1620 and 1680, over 40 per cent of accused mothers were hanged,[117] a higher rate of execution than those indicted for witchcraft. (In Essex between 1560 and 1700, there were 299 persons indicted for witchcraft of whom 82, around 27 per cent, were executed.[118]) However, attitudes softened over the seventeenth century. Whereas in Sussex before 1640, 53 per cent of women accused of infanticide were convicted, and of those 88 per cent hung, Amussen found that by the end of the seventeenth century in Norfolk, most women were acquitted.[119] By the early eighteenth century, there were low levels of conviction and execution for infanticide. Women found that the courts frequently accepted various standard defences, such as that they had prepared for the birth and confided in friends.[120]

Not all unmarried mothers accused of infanticide were young and inexperienced. Sarah Wilmshurst claimed she already had ten children, but when she gave birth in 1743, she had not seen her husband for two years.[121] Mrs Wilmshurst had denied her pregnancy: 'and People have laughed at her for denying it'. At market, the butchers said 'she should have Things cheaper than another because she was with Child, and she always said it was Fat'. She gave birth at Mrs Kendry's house, cared for her daughter for a month, then left the baby to be nursed there, paying 3s. a week until, she claimed, her lover refused to contribute. Neither her father nor her family, apart from her mother, knew she had had the baby. After the 3-month-old child's body was found in the house of office, she was tried, convicted, and sentenced to death for murder. Mrs Wilmshurst denied any thoughts 'of making away with the Child, for all the World knew me to be a tender Mother'. Five women and one man called as witnesses supported her claims to being 'a very indulgent Mother', 'a tender Mother to all her Children'. Perhaps in her case the shame of an illegitimate child and the economics of surviving without a husband's or a lover's support explained why she could not mother her illegitimate daughter.

As Laura Gowing has argued, 'women's experiences of secret pregnancies, labours, and alleged infanticides were shaped by some profound tensions about the reproductive body and about maternity.'[122] Parishes and neighbours, she argues, never accepted denials of

pregnancies and secret births, and sought to create a maternal relationship. In Bradford, Yorkshire, when a dead child was found in
Mary Butler's bed-straw, the searcher confronted her, saying 'Mary
this is your child'. Mary confessed, but claimed the child was stillborn, and she had not hurt it.[123] Communities wanted women who
gave birth to be social mothers.

Unwilling birth-mothers might refuse the 'natural' duty of nurture.
In 1609, the Somerset quarter sessions found that the mother of a
'bastard' had refused to breastfeed, she 'having unmotherly and most
unnaturally stopped and dried upp her brestes'.[124] Other mothers
placed their infants with a nurse, then disappeared. In 1768, Elizabeth
Tapscott reported to the Foundling Hospital that she had met with a
miserable object, a 6-week-old baby girl, 'a Natural [i.e. illegitimate]
child', whose parents 'had both run away and left it to a beggar to
take care of it'.[125] Some women simply refused to be social mothers,
and fled. In the 1650s, the Norwich quarter sessions ordered the
overseers to pay a grandmother 18d. weekly for a child, because the
mother had run away.[126] But mothers may have initially cared for
their babies. In 1741, the billet sealed at the Foundling Hospital for a
2-month-old boy noted that his mother Dorothy Smith had deserted
him, he was not christened, and his father was not to be found.[127]
Similarly, in 1770, Mary Clifton left her baby at the Hospital after
struggling for five months. She had pawned 'all her things to support
her Child' before she disappeared, 'is gone no body knows where and
has left the Child with a poor woman where she lodged'.[128]

'Abandonment', or 'dropping' a child, can be read as a denial of
maternity, and most historians have followed contemporaries and
viewed 'abandoning' mothers negatively. Wrightson considered that
those who gave their babies to vagrant or otherwise unsuitable nurses
were virtually infanticidal.[129] Hitchcock saw 'abandoning' mothers
as going on to lead new lives.[130] However, from a study of German
cases around the same date, Rowlands argued that such women were
experiencing shame, anger, and resentment which made mothering
impossible.[131] Historians have observed that there was a preference
for leaving girls rather than boys in most of Europe, but Fildes's study
of foundlings in London from the 1560s to the 1790s showed that the
only fifty-year period in which the percentage of girls exceeded that of
boys was the second half of the seventeenth century, and then not by
much.[132] Similarly, Levene argues from an analysis of petitions to the
Foundling Hospital 1741–99 that the sex ratio of children admitted
was almost exactly the same as the sex ratio at birth, namely 104

males to every 100 females.[133] This pattern suggests that the economics of single motherhood rather than a particular preference explains mothers' pattern of relinquishment.

Leaving a child in a public place was a known way of providing alternative parents: foundlings, whose legitimacy was unknown, could be informally adopted. Thus some mothers left their babies in the porch of a parish church, at a wealthy man's door, or the precincts of the London charitable institutions, showing, as Gowing argues, 'a gesture of faith in charity'.[134] Parents might even help their daughters to find alternative parents for their babies. In 1615, Robert Hartwell was indicted in Middlesex because his wife had conveyed their 'daughter's bastard' and laid it at someone's (perhaps the putative father's) door.[135]

The advertisement placed by St Dionis Backchurch in 1766 offering a two-guinea reward to anyone finding the parents of a 3-month-old baby girl, indicates that there had been careful deliberation on the part of whoever left the child. The girl, 'with two teeth' (which suggests that she was older than 3 months), was 'laid upon a small Bed of Wood Shavings' at 8pm near the passageway under the charity school: the bed would keep the baby safe until she was found, and 8pm was perhaps late enough for secrecy but not so late in the evening that she would lie out all night. The child's clothing, worn and makeshift, indicated poverty: she 'had on an Old Cap with a ragged Crown, an old Ragged Shirt, and an old Red & White Line Gown, a Man's old-torn Flannen [flannel] Waistcoat, and a Bit of an old Blanket bound with White'.[136]

Mothers may have sought alternative care for their infants as a temporary arrangement. Some eighteenth-century London parish records show that in many instances mothers were reunited with their children (whose legitimacy status was unstated), although it is unclear whether this was because the parishioners found the mother, or whether she had a change of heart.[137] On 1 December 1767, St Sepulchre's workhouse recorded the admission of eight children into their workhouse, six of whom were under 6 years. Two mothers absconded the same day and took their children away. Three others continued to be nursed by mothers.[138] The overseers of St Paul's Covent Garden recorded in 1774 'a dropt Child taken away by the mother', and in 1789, 'a Casual Child' returned to her mother the day after she was 'dropt'.[139]

In early modern culture, nurturing infants was a mother's duty, so single mothers who failed to care for their infants were condemned as unmaternal and unwomanly. Little account was taken of their material circumstances. Discussion of maternal failings has diverted attention from both the 'fathers' whose lack of support created an impossible situation, and from the bastardy laws designed to deter illegitimate births by punishing mothers.

MARRIAGE OR FINANCIAL ASSISTANCE

How her lover responded to her disclosure of pregnancy determined much of a woman's subsequent history and that of her child. Marriage meant an honourable status for herself and a father for her child, even though she might be shamed as a pregnant bride, and the new family might be unwelcome in a parish. From Tudor times, some parish ratepayers objected to pauper marriages, fearing increases in the number of poor.[140] Couples might circumvent this opposition by marrying clandestinely in an adjacent parish.[141]

In the seventeenth century, illegitimate maternity may have been 'an unfortunate outcome of the sexual anticipation of marriage'.[142] Many single mothers insisted that they had consented to sexual intercourse only after promises of marriage.[143] But during the eighteenth century, the rate of illegitimate births increased, which has led historians to suggest that courtship practices changed. Marriage was less likely because sexual intercourse would be followed by marriage only if the couple were able to afford it. This left many women pregnant and unmarried.[144] Women's petitions to the London Foundling Hospital suggest that they had continued to see premarital sexual intercourse as leading to marriage, and many told of men's promises broken, either deliberately or by mischance. Anne Sugg had held out against the seductions of her lover, Henry Willis, until early 1799, when the banns for their marriage were read at St Andrew Holborn. Subsequently, Willis absconded and could not be found. Witnesses who had known Anne from infancy gave her a good character and spoke of how Willis 'used many arts to seduce her'.[145] Mary Lake claimed that she had married a fellow servant on 24 January 1771, but it subsequently transpired that he had a wife already 'with whom he is gone off', leaving Mary pregnant, stripped of her savings and even of a great part of her clothes.[146] Some petitioners presented themselves as gullible victims of deceitful lovers: one was 'unhappily drawn aside by a Villain'.[147] Such a tale of frustrated marriage plans may have been what civic authorities wanted to hear.

It is difficult to judge whether there was a new willingness of men to seduce and abandon by the later eighteenth century. Certainly the social context of courtship altered as a result of labour migration. Supervision of young women and men's courtships was weaker. John Black's analysis of the social characteristics of 'putative fathers' of illegitimate children in London, from a sample of over 2,000 bastardy depositions, suggests a pattern of courtships that failed under economic stress. But not all illicit births were the products of failed courtships. In the parish of St Clement Danes in the 1770s, a proportion of young professional men who had no intention of marrying their lower-status lovers fathered illegitimate children.[148] Trumbach suggests that at least a quarter of the single mothers making bastardy depositions in the West End named gentlemen whom they could never have hoped to marry.[149] We should also remember that throughout the period many unmarried women bore children to men who were married already. In Terling, over the period 1570–1699, 31 per cent of illegitimate births were the product of such 'sexual delinquency'.[150]

Mothers' stories were complex. The main sources we have for their experiences are bastardy depositions, petitions to the London Foundling Hospital, and settlement examinations. While we know that mothers themselves gave bastardy depositions, these were statements about the child's paternity, not revelations of women's expectations of their lovers. Their petitions to the London Foundling Hospital frequently told something more of the circumstances in which they became mothers, but these petitions too had a formula, a particular kind of story, and women did not write the majority themselves.[151] Settlement examinations were taken by the parish if a family required assistance: children were entitled to a settlement in their father's parish, or, if they were illegitimate, where were they born.[152]

Women's narrative strategies about any sexual encounters were limited. In the seventeenth century, as Garthine Walker has shown in her important discussion of rape, women stressed submission and consent to sexuality, but since these were the expected female responses, this made it difficult for women to speak of rape or sexual desire.[153] Medical theories also influenced whether women were seen as active or passive in sexual encounters. Whereas in the Elizabethan period women's agency in illicit sexual encounters was generally accepted, by the eighteenth century theories of conception had altered, so mothers could plausibly present themselves as sexually passive.[154] Petitioners to the Foundling Hospital spoke of pregnancies as happening without their active involvement: Mary Brown

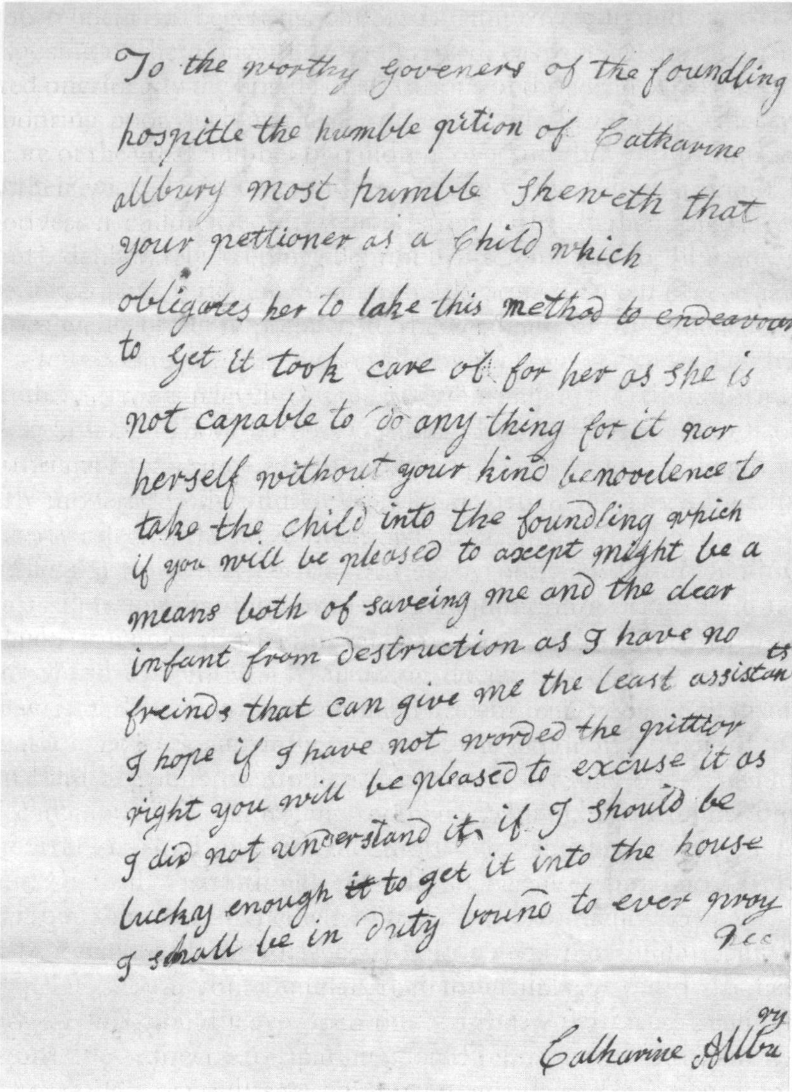

To the worthy goveners of the foundling
hospitle the humble pition of Catharine
allbury most humble sheweth that
your pettioner as a Child which
obligates her to take this method to endeavour
to get it took care of for her as she is
not capable to do any thing for it nor
herself without your kind benovelence to
take the child into the foundling which
if you will be pleased to accept might be a
means both of saveing me and the dear
infant from destruction as I have no
freinds that can give me the least assistants
I hope if I have not worded the pittion
right you will be pleased to excuse it as
I did not understand it if I should be
lucky enough it to get it into the house
I shall be in duty bound to ever pray
&c

Catharine Allbury

Figure 2 Petition of Catharine Allbury to the Governors of the London
Foundling Hospital (1782). From 1742 (apart from the period 1756–60),
admission of children to places in the London Foundling Hospital was by
petition. Individuals, usually mothers, submitted a petition explaining their
circumstances. Frequently, an administrator from the hospital checked with
landlords or neighbours to confirm the petitioner's veracity. Most of the
petitions were written by others on the mother's behalf, but Catharine Allbury has written this one herself.

'Unfortunately become the mother of an Infant'.[155] In curiously detached formulaic language, women referred to the child's conception as the consequence of a momentary lapse from virtue: Mary Taylor was 'in an unguarded moment deluded',[156] and 'in one unguarded Minute, she [Ann James] was ruined'.[157]

By baptizing their babies with the father's name, single mothers asserted a claim to *de facto* marriage, and perhaps strengthened their entitlement to maintenance. Thus in 1687, Martha Garrett charged John Cooper 'for the naturall & lawfull father of the said Child' whom she called Arabella Cooper.[158] In 1749, Rachel Peters gave birth to an illegitimate daughter, naming her Sarah Stanley, for the father, Samuel Stanley, who had lived in Peters' mother's house. Similarly, on 30 July 1750, Margaret Ludgate (whose own surname suggests she may have been a parish foundling) told the parish of St Botolph Aldgate that she had been prevailed on by John Younger, and had her daughter baptized Margaret Younger.[159] By the second half of the eighteenth century, illegitimate babies in Colyton were more commonly baptized with the father's surname.[160] It is unclear whether these naming practices refer to men's willingness to acknowledge paternity, planning to marry the mothers in the future, or mothers' determination to secure a father for their infants and remove the slur of bastardy.

Neighbours were often unsure of mothers' marital status: 'Is she married?' the court asked one witness. 'Not that ever I heard of' was the reply.[161] Single women who bore three or four children to the same man may have regarded their *de facto* relationships as marriages. Their stories emerged only when poverty forced mothers to ask for parish assistance. When in 1779 Ann Winter, a druggist's servant, appealed to the parish of St Clement Danes, it transpired that she had borne three children to her master.[162] In London, Trumbach found several bastardy declarations from women living in long-term, irregular unions in the second half of the eighteenth century; Evans suggests that at that date in the East End there was a culture of cohabitation.[163] Similarly, Sharpe found that in Colyton the pattern of women having more than one illegitimate child was more obvious in the same period; from 1740 to 1839, nearly a quarter of the mothers of illegitimate children bore more than one child, not always with the same father.[164] Multiple fathers may reflect a series of failed relationships.

Single mothers expected financial assistance from their lovers, but many applying to the London Foundling Hospital in the later eighteenth century had been disappointed. Sarah Brown declared that the father was snatched from her (she does not say how, but presumably by death) so she was deprived of the aid 'which he was bound to give to his natural child'.[165] Another petitioner asserted that she was 'deserted by him who should have supported me in my great distress' and had been forced to eat nothing but vegetables.[166] Mary Seymour complained in 1776 that her lover had left her destitute, 'without defraying even the Expenses of Child-Birth'.[167] Even though their lovers had failed to honour promises of marriage, single mothers refused to accept sole responsibility for their babies and held men morally obliged to assist financially.

By marrying, even if not to the 'father' of her child, a woman could integrate her illegitimate child into a family. The passage of time and the birth of further children obscured the legitimacy status of the 'bastards'. A settlement examination in St Botolph Aldgate in 1789 uncovered one such illegitimate child. Hannah Gotschin (also spelt Getehin), married for seventeen years, admitted that she had never married the sailor father of her three adult children with whom she had lived for eleven years. Hannah had applied for help for her 26-year-old son, Alexander Lewis/Frazer, who had been apprenticed as a mariner by a parish officer, but whose master had sailed away two weeks later, then died, leaving Alexander 'now a Lunatic and incapable of supporting himself'.[168] But for the death of his master, Alexander's status as a 'bastard' would not have been revealed.

Since illegitimate children could be an obstacle to a woman's marriage, her relatives may have taken in her illegitimate children.[169] Some mothers may have sought institutional assistance. A pauper examination in 1746 revealed that Katherine Stark had asked Catherine Cole to 'drop' her 2-year-old son, Edward Hardy, in Nightingale Lane, so that the parish of St Botolph Aldgate would provide for him. Cole refused, but later saw the little boy standing at the door of St Botolph's workhouse 'crying for its Nurse'. His mother Katherine had since married a sailor, but the witness thought that Edward was still in the workhouse.[170] Perhaps after two years, Katherine Stark may have been unable to manage any longer without either employment or marriage, and her new husband may have been unwilling to accept her illegitimate son. Economic circumstances may have forced mothers to make very difficult decisions.

WORK AND CHILDCARE

For a single mother on her own, economics were crucial. Whatever support a lover or her parish provided in the way of weekly maintenance, she needed both to work, and to arrange for childcare. Her options were slightly different depending on her location. In the towns and cities, she might more easily find work as a live-in servant, but then she needed to look for a nurse; in the country, she might turn to her family for childcare assistance while she worked, and in industrial districts she might work at home.[171] The opening of the Foundling Hospitals in the mid-eighteenth century offered another option.

Throughout the period, family assistance was invaluable but family responses varied. Some parents rejected their daughters, reducing them to poverty speedily. In 1775, a clergyman's daughter, Elizabeth Everett, petitioned the London Foundling Hospital for the admission of her child: 'she was bred a Gentlewoman, her friends will not look upon her'.[172] But social status was no key to parental attitudes: in 1768, Elizabeth Bloxham was 'turned out of doors by her parents, being very poor and indigent'.[173] Mary Pell was 'willing as far as in her Power lay to Maintain her child, Endeavouring that it should not be Burdensome to any Person', but pleaded for family assistance.[174]

Shame deterred some single mothers from seeking help either from their parents, kin, or their parish. Elizabeth Baxter, the daughter of 'a Reputable Tradesman', dared not apply to the parish; she was 'unwilling to disgrace my family as knows nothing of the matter, by Swearing the Child'.[175] Mary Smith, the daughter of 'People of Credit and Character', quitted her business as a milliner: 'For was her situation made known to Her Family they would forever desert her to Infamy and Ruin'. She begged the Hospital to take her child to 'preserve her Parents from Shame! and her from Misery!'.[176] Jane Forder, 'born of good Parents tho poor', was blackmailed by her lover. Jane had concealed her pregnancy from her parents, but he threatened to expose her if she troubled him.[177] Although women's pleas to shield their parents from disgrace seem routine, they were none the less real, affecting how single women managed.

In the earlier period, supportive parents could themselves be cited before the church courts if they sheltered their daughters and helped them to evade punishment.[178] Typically, parishes prohibited parents from taking in their pregnant unmarried daughters as boarders.[179] From the 1580s, London parishes attempted to restrict householders taking in inmates.[180] In 1642 in Warwickshire, one parish dispatched a pregnant single woman, who had returned to her father, back to the parish of her employer.[181] In 1661, Warwickshire quarter sessions heard that Joan Corbison was reportedly living with her mother, while awaiting her delivery.[182] Parishes were especially concerned to prohibit those who received parish assistance from taking in their children 'eyther married or marriageable', lest the parish be liable for any illegitimate children.[183]

Despite the Poor Laws, many single mothers had help from their parents and kin. In 1631, when the parish of Callocke presented Thomas Loriman and his daughter Anne Loriman who had borne a 'bastard child', Loriman defied the parish, asserting 'that he was bound by nature to receave her being his dauther'.[184] Parents sheltered their daughters during pregnancy and giving birth, and may even have helped conceal newborn infant deaths. If parents subsequently provided childcare, they may have passed their grandchild as one of their own, as we know they did in the nineteenth and twentieth centuries; evidence would be hard to find as such family secrets brought disgrace. The poet John Clare (1793–1864) wrote that after his own father learnt of his illegitimacy, he went away from his mother and his village.[185]

The autobiographical writing of Benjamin Shaw, a mechanic from northern England, hints at this practice of taking in illegitimate grandchildren. Shaw's aunt Mariann Noddle, who mostly lived in service, returned home pregnant. Her son was baptized in 1783: 'the child lived & she left it at home with her mother & went into Service again.' Subsequently, Mariann married, but 'it was said she was with child again'.[186] Shaw also recounted the complicated history of his own illegitimate grandchildren, born in the early nineteenth century. Unlike Benjamin, who married his lover, Betty, after she found she was pregnant, these young people remained single. In 1815, William Shaw, their second son, had two children born within a month 'fathered' on him: 'he Paid a while & Some time after was put in to the House of Correction for debt, for his child' until he finally married one of the mothers. Soon after, the second mother died '& the child was Brought up by her Parents'.[187] The Shaws' eldest daughter Bella (b. 1799) bore an illegitimate child in 1819: 'She continued to live with her Parents, who brought up the child, untill She was married' in 1822.[188] Hannah, the next daughter, was illicitly pregnant when she was only 17 years old; Benjamin and his wife then 'had Bella Child to keep, & all the trouble attending it, & now likely to have another. Parents trouble is not done when they have reared their Children.'[189] Greater sexual freedom could mean greater trouble and constraints for young people and their parents. Benjamin and Betty saw their son imprisoned for debt, and clearly felt an obligation to assist their daughters' children and grandchildren, irrespective of their legitimacy status.

Detailed stories offer glimpses of emotional bonds between poor parents and their adult children. In 1772, Elizabeth Brooks was a 30-year-old single mother. She had been a servant since she was 14 years old, but left her place to nurse her blind mother, the wife of a Sussex day-labourer. There Thomas Bowman courted her for two years, until 'in an unhappy hour' she yielded. Bowman had promised to marry her when he had saved enough to hire a house, but after she proved pregnant, he refused both marriage and support. Elizabeth had spent all her savings on her mother, but she dared not apply to the parish, lest her shame become known, 'which will hasten ye Death of her poor Mother, and by ye Loss of Character render her unable to get again into an honest service'.[190] In another case in 1773, the grand-mother Mary Williamson petitioned the Foundling Hospital on be-half of the baby of her seduced daughter, who had been reduced to insanity by grief. Mrs Williamson had paid 5 guineas for her daughter to be confined for a month but could do no more, having 'done more then lies in my power to pay... without Reducing myself to the lowest Degree'.[191]

Poverty always limited the support maternal kin could offer. Thus in October 1654 in Somerset, a mother petitioned that she was unable to care for the 'bastard' of her widowed daughter, Rose Gillingham, who had fled; the justices ordered the parish to take the child.[192] A single mother in Colchester appealed for some parish aid so she could 'labour for myself and my child', as her own mother could do no more than give her a bed and some small furnishings.[193] In the later eighteenth century, many single mothers explained to the London Foundling Hospital that their parents were utterly incapable of assist-ing because of their own poverty. Typical was Elizabeth Harris, who alleged in 1773 that she was 'of a poor reduse & destrest Familey'.[194] Sarah Page in 1770 alleged that she had no support 'but an old Mother wich is sixty years old and hath nothing to Depend on but her Hard Labour'. Sarah's mother had sold some of 'her Households' to help, but now neither mother nor daughter had a morsel of bread.[195]

Usually we know of kin assistance only when it failed.[196] Even when maternal kin joined together across generations, their resources were limited.[197] Nevertheless, maternal kin offered other kinds of support. In 1652, a Norfolk father obtained an order from the ses-sions that the yeoman who had seduced his daughter, then refused to marry her or to contribute maintenance, should pay 2s. weekly.[198] Grandmothers could help with childcare. Some enjoyed the babies, even if they were illegitimate. In the 1630s in Oxfordshire, the widow Hulet said 'I do love to dandle a child in my old age.'[199] Illegitimate children may have lived with kin for some years, and indeed have been useful as they grew older. The Norwich Census of 1570 recorded how an 11-year-old lad, 'a bastard of hir daughters', lived with his 80-year-old widowed grandmother, Eme Stowe, who was lame in her arm; both were idle and begged.[200] Some siblings took in orphaned illegitimates. In 1773, after Hannah Smith died, her widowed sister, Sarah Evans, kept her illegitimate niece for six months, although Mrs Evans had four children of her own.[201] Other siblings proved harsh. In 1781, Anne Sowerby petitioned the Hospital because her brother, whose housekeeper she was, 'turned her out of Doors as soon as he was informed of her situation'.[202]

Towns and cities allowed greater anonymity, and some pregnant single women found some support from landladies or neighbours. But

Figure 3 'Buy any Wax or Wafers' (1711). The marital status of this poor hawker whom Laroon depicted selling letter writing supplies is unclear. A single woman in so visible a state of pregnancy would not usually be employed as a servant. Hawking on the streets would provide some livelihood.

Buy any Wax or Wafers.
Cire d'Espagne, et oublies.
Ostie e cera spagna.

Mauron delin:

P Tempest ex:
Cum Privilegio

as new mothers were usually out of service or unemployed, they quickly used up their scant resources on giving birth and lying-in. Comments left with babies at the Foundling Hospital in the 1740s attest to maternal deprivation written on the infants' bodies: 'almost starved & would not take food';[203] 'seemed stupified with Opium'.[204] Eleanor Richardson said that she was too weak to breastfeed her baby herself, but unable to pay for a wet-nurse.[205] The Hospital usually noted whether the babies were wet or dry nursed, but it is not always clear whether by their mothers or a nurse. A mother who spoke of 'the Calamity of Sore Breasts' was probably struggling to breastfeed her child.[206] Single mothers may have been less likely than others to breastfeed their own infants because they could not combine it with employment. Sarah Aviary had successfully concealed 'her Condition' from her employers; if the Hospital would take her child, her former employers would receive her again, and thus she would avoid 'the disgrace attendant on Misfortunes like hers'.[207]

A single mother's wages and work opportunities were less than those of a man, yet she had to combine the responsibilities of both mother and father. In London, the economics of single motherhood were increasingly desperate by the end of the seventeenth century. Mothers could rarely earn enough to support both themselves and their children.[208] All ordinary mothers without men to earn for the family were in difficulties. Society failed to provide an ideology and an economic structure that would allow working women to support their children.[209]

One option, if secrecy about her unmarried status was unnecessary, was for the mother to work for reasonable wages as a wet-nurse. Single mothers would probably work privately rather than be employed by the parish or the Foundling Hospitals. (The nineteenth-century novel, *Esther Waters*, which focused on the options of an unmarried mother, dramatized her situation as wet-nurse in the house of more prosperous parents.)[210] In 1747, one single mother, Elizabeth Fletcher, was suspected of infanticide when an infant's body was found because she had milk in her breasts. Her Old Bailey trial revealed that Elizabeth's 2-year-old child was in the workhouse while she worked as a wet-nurse.[211] In 1768, Mary Hendrie, a seduced servant from Edinburgh, put her own child out 'to Nurse' while she was employed in London as 'a good Nurse for a child' for six months. When the nursling was weaned, Mary resumed the care of her own child.[212]

The key equation was between the costs of childcare and a woman's wages as a servant. The nursing of an infant was always more expensive than the care of an older child and usually beyond a mother's wages. In the later seventeenth century, church court depositions suggest that wet-nurses' pay was around 3s. weekly and more, amounting to annual rates of £7. 16s. to £9. 15s.[213] Rates varied. In 1773, an unnamed mother was unable to meet the nurse's pay of 3s. 6d. weekly.[214] There was no discernible pay difference between wet and dry nurses employed by the London Foundling Hospital; pay was usually around 2s. 6d. weekly (amounting to £6. 10s. per annum).[215] In 1780, the London parish of St Faith under St Paul paid nurses 3s. per week (£7. 8s. per annum) for children of an unspecified age.[216]

The wages of a servant 'are nothing near sufficient to defray the expenses of a Child', declared Sarah Middleton in 1768.[217] She was right, for though servant's wages varied, few women earned enough to pay for childcare. In Chelsea in 1766, one servant who bore an illegitimate child declared that her wages were £4 per annum, plus board and lodging; another earned 6 guineas, plus board and lodging.[218] In London in the mid-eighteenth century, mean wages for women servants aged 22 to 26 years (the ages at which many fell pregnant) ranged between £3. 5s. 10d. to £4. 7s. 9d. and included board and lodging.[219] Women servants' wages in Lincolnshire from 1768 to 1785 were considerably less, £2. 15s.[220] The gender gap for servants in husbandry was greater than between London servants.[221] A servant's wages did not allow a single mother to pay for the nursing of her child and to keep herself, unless she had help from her lover or family. As Mary Bassett said, 'being only a Servant is utterly unable to Cloath herself and support her child by her Wages'.[222]

In 1768, Mary Jewitt, whose lover had died before their marriage, spelt out the economics of single motherhood: by going into service 'for small wages of £6' per annum, she would be unable to pay 4s. per week for childcare, amounting to £10. 8s. per annum.[223] Elizabeth Sarah Mills was in service in 1799, while her offspring was at nurse for 1 guinea per month (amounting to £12. 12s. per annum). Since her wages were £5 per annum, she was £7. 12s. short, and lacking assets, having 'made away with all her Clothes except those in daily wear'.[224] Single mothers thus had little choice and limited control over the nurses they employed, unlike parishes and institutions who could demand satisfactory performance of childcare duties.

Paid nurses had a bad press throughout the early modern period. Some nurses confessed to taking money privately then abandoning the baby elsewhere.[225] Other care was so suspect as to be a form of infanticide. In 1658 in London, Abigail Hill worked as a parish nurse, and when the children died, she borrowed her neighbours' children for the quarterly parish inspection.[226] In 1684, Mary Compton was accused at the Middlesex quarter sessions of murdering several babies. Subsequently, in 1714 the House of Commons reported that children were 'inhumanly suffered to die by the Barbarity of Nurses, especially Parish Nurses'.[227] In the language of the late nineteenth century, these nurses were murderous 'baby farmers'. Whereas parishes could in theory dismiss unsatisfactory nurses, single mothers may not have been able to afford better care. Even so, they may have found nurses more easily in towns and cities than in rural areas.

Inability to pay for childcare could force a single mother to give up work. In 1799, Margaret Beaumont, from Wensley in the north, told how she had been persuaded to come to London 'for the purpose of Secrecy', 'to preserve my Character from being injured by my unpardonable conduct'. The man she termed her 'seducer' paid for her lying-in and a nurse, but when he stopped payment, Margaret faced unemployment because she could no longer afford childcare: 'I am under the necessity of taking my Child back from the nurse & give warning for leaving my situation.'[228]

Self-employed mothers had more chance of combining childcare with gainful work, but much of their labour was poorly paid. Needleworkers in the mid-eighteenth century could earn no more than 5s. to 6s. per week, and although a rate of upwards of £13 per annum was better than service, a woman had to buy lodging and food for herself and her child.[229] In 1788, Charlotte Davies, who earned her living by her needle, explained that she was incapable of maintaining her child as well as herself: 'the profit of her work—supposing she could always get employed wch is not the Case being barely sufficient for her own Support' was too small.[230] Furthermore, self-employed mothers were at risk of economic fluctuations as well as personal misfortunes such as ill health. A mantua-maker kept her child for six months, but by April 1776, 'work being Slack', she could no longer provide both for herself and her child.[231] Such women may have looked for casual work, or even turned to illegal activity such as prostitution or petty theft.[232]

THE LONDON FOUNDLING HOSPITAL

Institutions caring for foundlings had existed in European cities for some time, but in England, earlier proposals had not developed.[233] From 1741, when the London Foundling Hospital opened to receive 'abandoned' or 'foundling' children, single mothers had a further option for the care of their illegitimate children.

Initially, mothers left their babies with identifying tokens and the Hospital documented their admission with specific billets.[234] During a four-year period known as the General Reception, 1756–60, the Hospital accepted all infants presented up to 1 year old. The London Hospital attracted national attention and many babies came from long distances. The Hospital also established several local branches. However, when Parliamentary funding ceased, operations contracted, and from 1761 the governors admitted only a limited number of London children with no fixed parish.[235] Mothers applied for places by petition, and if their stories were found on checking to be truthful, the petitioners were admitted to a public ballot. The number of infants accepted depended on Hospital funds. Initially, infants were to be aged no more than 8 months old, but after 1772 the age of reception was lowered to 6 months.[236] Mothers had to time their applications according to the Hospital's fluctuating admission policies as well as their own economic circumstances; for much of the time, if they delayed making a decision until their babies were 6 months old, they would have no chance at all. Nearly half the mothers (44 per cent) in the period 1768–72 waited until their babies were over 2 months old, and 22 per cent until over 4 months.[237] Their petitions provide details about their material circumstances. Mothers had pawned or sold any assets, and drawn on their own savings, their families, their friends, their neighbours, landladies, and former employers, before they turned to the charity.

Whereas Adrian Wilson claimed that the thousands of mothers who took or sent their children to the Foundling Hospital 'have left us almost no trace of their feelings',[238] I would agree with Outhwaite, Evans, and others, that the petitions *do* reveal much about maternal emotions.[239] While we know that most of the petitions were written by scribes or others, not by mothers themselves, the information was supplied by mothers or someone on their behalf,[240] and can be read as mothers' responses to desperate circumstances. It is unfortunate that

Figure 4 *An Exact Representation of the Form and Manner in Which Exposed and Deserted Young Children are admitted into the Foundling Hospital* (detail) (1749). If a mother's petition was found to be truthful, she was admitted and seated in the ornate Court Room of the Foundling Hospital. Only if she drew a white ball in the ballot was her child admitted immediately. It was unlikely a mother would ever see her infant again since the majority of children died. Observing the ballot was a source of interest for wealthy Londoners.

we lack comparable evidence for the seventeenth and early eighteenth centuries.

Although the Hospital claimed that it saved children from wicked and abandoning parents, mothers ignored this negative rhetoric, and claimed to be good mothers who sacrificed themselves for their children's welfare. Mary Graves declared herself incapable of 'Discharging my duty to my child to prevent it from perishing with Hungar'.[241] Some mothers judged that the Hospital's quality of care was better than that offered by the parish, as did Jane Bowring in 1781: 'she & her friends thinks they [the children] are better taken care of both in Manners & Morals.'[242] Jane Forder concluded that the Hospital was preferable to the parish workhouse.[243] Most single mothers did not relinquish their babies lightly. In 1741, observers noted the grief of both those who left their children and of those whose children could not be admitted: 'a more moving Scene can't well be imagined.'[244] Mothers left tokens, clothing, and notes about the names and perhaps the baptismal status of their infants, to ensure that children could be identified so that they might reclaim them.[245]

Some intended that the Hospital would be a temporary expedient, as did Anne Ramsden, a lady's maid who hoped 'by her Industry in a few Years to ennable her Selfe to take the Care of her Child on her Selfe'.[246] Initially the Hospital's policies were a major deterrent to

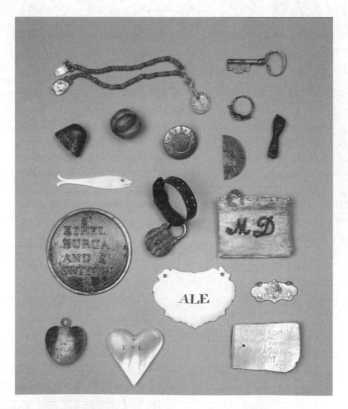

Figure 5 Tokens given by mothers to their children on leaving them at the London Foundling Hospital (18th cent.) Mothers attached tokens to their babies, hoping that these would enable them to identify their children when they came to reclaim them. A sample of these tokens pictured here poignantly shows small items of little value, including a button, a pendant, a key, and a thimble.

reunions, because those reclaiming the child were required to discharge the expense of care, and to leave a bond for £80. This requirement was waived in 1764.[247] In the same year, seven years after placing her child in the hospital, Mary Barnes asked for her child's return. Her new husband was 'not the father: But he is willing to support it, he bears a good Character.' Her child, however, like about two-thirds of those admitted, was dead.[248] Actual numbers of mothers applying to reclaim children were small. Only 1.2 per cent of Levene's sample of 1,650 children the Hospital admitted in 1756–60 were actually reclaimed.[249]

Maternal families could be supportive, but others tried to force their daughters to put their babies in the Foundling Hospital. Sarah Williams, seduced by a gentleman's servant in the country, journeyed to London in search of her lover, giving birth at her sister's house. In 1776, Sarah's landlady explained that the family had petitioned the Hospital on Sarah's behalf: they 'pressed her [Sarah] earnestly to part with her child . . . wch she was always very much against but supposed they had persuaded her to it now'. However, Sarah failed to appear with her baby on the appointed day, so we may deduce that she intended to keep her child.[250] In 1762, Jane Marriott begged the Foundling Hospital to refuse admission to her baby. Her father would not allow her to marry, and wanted his grandson to go to charity, which neither Jane nor the child's father wished: 'its true I agreed to its going' her petition stated, but she changed her mind. She wanted her father to maintain the child because he was 'a man of great property and can very well take care of it'.[251]

The question of single mothers' agency is vexed: while they were not oppressed victims lacking all power, their choices were between a number of undesirable options. Looming over single mothers was the parish.

THE PARISH

The parish was not usually a single mother's first choice of support. While it provided a basic safety net to women who had Poor Law settlements, the terms on which assistance was delivered were such that many single mothers may have preferred to manage without the public involvement.

No parish wanted the burden of supporting 'bastards', so single mothers were liable to hostile questioning over the paternity of the child. Between 1576 and 1733, when bastardy depositions were frequently taken *before* the birth of the child, a woman had an incentive to name a single man, rather than a married one, in the hope that the parish would pressure him to marry her. Once the child was born, a marriage was less likely, so the parish may have encouraged her to name a man who could afford maintenance. In other words, mothers may have experienced a slight pressure towards naming a single man of equal social status before the child's birth, and a man of higher status after.

Mothers and children could be victims of inter-parish disputes. Before 1662, there were no clear guidelines for establishing which parish was legally liable for the child's relief. The dismal story of Katherine Talbot shows what could happen. In 1656, Talbot was examined before the Northern Assizes for the child she had borne eighteen months earlier. Her attempts to obtain relief from the quarter sessions, the constable of the Forest of Bowland, and the overseers of Slaidburn had failed, and she was advised to leave the baby where it was born. Slaidburn parish relieved the child for nine months until an overseer and constable made Katherine Talbot take her child, promising to help her maintain it, which she did 'and said she would gladly live with it'. Daily she craved relief, 'a house or place for her to sit in and she would work for her child and her own maintenance'. The threat of starvation drove her to beg until in the end she 'sat down with her child and it died in her arms'. Katherine left her child where it died, and subsequently got a living by spinning 'here and there as she could get work'.[252]

Parishes moved babies to and fro. In the early seventeenth century, a midwife who delivered an illegitimate child at Hatfield persuaded a poor woman at Stansted to wet-nurse it. Since the wet-nurse had acted without her husband's authorization, she later returned the child to Hatfield, but the next day, some women from Hatfield brought the child back to Stansted, tricked the nurse into suckling the hungry baby, then ran away. The nurse accompanied by the Stansted constable then tried to return the child to the midwife, but her husband's servants returned it to Stansted where parishioners in turn tricked a woman who was not settled there into keeping it.[253] These journeys, amounting to roughly 60 miles over several days, cannot have improved the newborn infant's chances of survival. The whereabouts of the single mother was not mentioned; she may have died, or fled. The 1662 legislation made the parish of the child's birth liable.

If the justices ordered the mother to the House of Correction without her child, then they sent her infant to a nurse. The cost was to be covered by the alleged father and mother, or the parish rates. Nurses were usually poor women in need of work and supervised by the parish.[254] A single mother had limited control over her child's future in such circumstances, but in practice some insisted on their rights to intervene in their children's interests. In 1656, the widowed mother of an illegitimate child, Mary Mortlocke of Weathersfield, petitioned the overseers because they had put her child out to nurse 'unto a poore woman who for want of fitt allowance doth almost starve the said Child'. The Essex justices ordered the parish to pay Mary the same amount, 18d. weekly, to care for her child.[255] Over a century later, on 24 May 1780 Mary Neale complained to the vestry of St Faith under St Paul that her 'bastard child' at nurse at Isleworth 'was not taken proper care off [sic] for which reason she had taken it away and begged that she might have the usual Parish allowance for the maintenance thereof'. The vestry awarded her 3s. per week.[256] This child was more fortunate than one who died in 1624 in an Aldgate parish in poor conditions: 'hee that loveth his dogg would not put it in such a place to be brought upp.'[257]

From the late seventeenth century, there was public concern about the abuses of parish nurses, and the very high mortality rates—up to 75 per cent—of children in their care.[258] The stereotypic image of the parish nurse was of a child murderer, and contemporaries blamed single mothers for not caring for their babies themselves. In 1731, Defoe wrote of those 'merciless Mothers' who could not murder their offspring themselves who got it done 'by dropping their Children, and leaving them to be starved by Parish-Nurses'.[259] Nurses who drank gin and administered opiates to sedate their charges all aroused contemporary ire. Jonas Hanway argued that it was always 'less expensive to the parish, to *let a child die*, than to keep it alive'; parishes never wanted to pay a mother 2s. 6d. a week for the support of her child, because she would ensure that it would live, whereas if the parish employed a nurse, the child would probably die.[260] While Hanway's cynicism probably overstated the case against the parishes, there was a grain of truth: keeping 'bastard' children alive was a burden on the ratepayers. There were certainly instances of parishes attempting to place even legitimate children into the Foundling Hospital when it seemed likely they would be a burden on the rates.[261] Public concern about nurses was such that parishes exercised more supervision in the later eighteenth century. In 1767, an Act offered an incentive payment: nurses who kept children alive should be paid 2s. 6d. extra.[262] Studies of the nurses employed by the Foundling Hospital show that the inspectors supervised and tried to prevent abuses.[263] The governors paid a premium of 10s. if the nurse kept the child alive for a year.[264]

However, not all parishes employed nurses, since it was generally held that a bastard child, whether of a vagrant or a settled mother, had an entitlement to maternal nurture, even going with her into a Bridewell or a house of correction.[265] The length of time which the parish allowed to single mothers to care for their children varied. In Essex in 1653, the justices resolved that a female bastard was to stay with her mother since she was under 7 years of age, 'and therefore cannot be removed from her mother'.[266] Other mothers may have kept their children with them for around ten years. A justices' manual of 1683 stated that the mother should nourish the child, and the father was to pay 20s. immediately, and every Friday pay 16d. until the child was 10 years of age.[267] Justices were torn between ideas about the 'natural' rights of children to nurture and their desire to deter illegitimacy. In the seventeenth century, justices sometimes ordered fathers to pay maintenance until the child was around 12 years of age (thereby leaving the children with mothers or nurses), but by the eighteenth century, it was agreed that 7 years were sufficient 'for Nurture', and parish officers 'usually and very properly' left the very young child with its mother since to separate it was 'unnatural and cruel'.[268]

Mothers who named 'fathers' had to contend with the hostility of men's families and friends in local communities. Maintenance orders were affected by the justices' judgments of the woman's sexual morality.[269] Awards against mothers, who usually earned smaller wages than men, were less than those against 'fathers' because it was assumed that the mother provided nurture by breastfeeding her child. If she refused, parishes might employ a nurse and make the mother contribute. Likewise, if she were better able to pay than the father, maintenance payments were adjusted accordingly. In 1602, the Norfolk justices ordered that a couple be whipped together for a bastard child, then pay 16d. weekly between them, he 4d. but she 12d., 'in consideracion of her better abilitie'.[270]

Maintenance payments could involve public shame. In the early seventeenth century, in Somerset, for example, both parents were ordered to pay maintenance at the communion table every Sunday and to publicly 'confesse their faulte and offence'.[271] Since the parish had already known of the single mother's giving birth to a 'bastard', she may have experienced less shame than her lover, who had tried to conceal his paternity. However, in the eighteenth century, Blackstone observed that 'the very maintenance of the child' was 'a degree of punishment' for the single mother.[272] Because the issue was a moral one, not surprisingly justices' decisions varied.

When the medieval church courts ordered a father to pay maintenance for his illegitimate child, enforcement depended on a suit of the mother, which involved her in travel and expense. From the late sixteenth century, mothers who had obtained an affiliation order were able to count on her parish paying a small basic weekly sum to care for the child, even if the 'father' defaulted. If the parish failed to pay, a mother could appeal to the justices. Dorothy Marshall argued that parish accounts showing money received and paid for the children rarely balanced.[273] Although parishes disapproved of single mothers, paradoxically they gave considerable relief to them and their children; at this stage of their lives poor single women received maximum assistance.[274] With the help of a parish pension, mothers may have suckled their babies for a year and a half; in some instances, they may have continued until the child was two or three.[275] If the payments from the putative father ordered by the justices did not reach the mother or child, mothers could appeal. In a Cambridgeshire case, Anne Brand of Chesterton complained that she was receiving no money for her illegitimate child; it transpired that the overseers had kept the 'father's' lump sum payment.[276]

A parish might insist that the woman's own parents or even other kin support her and her child (even though they did not like families taking in their pregnant kin): a Sussex husbandman in the eighteenth century gave a bond for £14 for his pregnant sister by which he agreed to maintain the child until it was 21 years of age.[277]

By the eighteenth century, unmarried mothers could find that justices took on the role of protectors against the men who seduced and abandoned them.[278] The price of having civic fathers enlisted on the side of single mothers in negotiations with putative fathers was that mothers increasingly presented themselves in more passive roles: they had been deceived by lying men who had promised marriage. Deference to the authorities and reliance upon the civic fathers reinforced a gender order in which women were dependent.

Poor Law records are unclear about what happened after mother and child were released from the House of Correction. Given early modern patriarchal ideology, it is unlikely that the little family would be allowed to exist in a separate household. Manchester had regulations 'that no single woman unmaryed shalbe at her owne hande to kepe house or chambr . . . but she shall reforme thym selves'.[279] Other towns and cities had similar policies.[280] How single mothers managed seems another area of women's makeshift economy: some casual work here and there, and perhaps some charitable gifts of food and cast-off clothing from neighbours, or 'supported only thro' small Donations, and Benefactions of a few charitable Persons'.[281] Those who successfully evaded the parish overseers may have enjoyed more freedom to decide what was best for themselves and their children. But if they could not cope, then their children came 'on the parish': Ann Clark had a 2-year-old whom she kept 'as long as she could'. When she was taken to prison, she left her child at her lodgings, and so to the parish.[282]

Many parishes stopped employing nurses around the end of the seventeenth century and insisted that it was a cheaper and more efficient system to put children in the workhouse in the care of paid nurses or inmates. Mothers disliked putting their children into the workhouse: as one said, if she sent her child there, 'that would ma[ke] her unhappy conduct publick', ruin her reputation, and prevent her working.[283] In 1780, Elizabeth Eaton tried to get her baby admitted to the Foundling Hospital, explaining that the parish had refused to care for her child unless she too entered the workhouse.[284] In early eighteenth-century Westminster, Boulton calculated that when paupers used the parish or the workhouse for childcare, half the children under 6 years were subsequently returned to their parents.[285] Contemporaries thought that the infant mortality rate in workhouses was high. Hanway estimated the mortality rate of children under 4 years, legitimate as well as illegitimate, at around 46 per cent, but for sample years in the Chelsea workhouse, Hitchcock calculated it was only around 23 per cent.[286] However, for St Margaret's Westminster workhouse, Hitchcock calculated that of 106 children under 20 months admitted, 83 died.[287] Mortality rates were similarly high in the London Foundling Hospital.[288] In an institution, infants may have received less individual care than with a parish nurse.

Sometimes a workhouse took in the child, while the mother was employed and lived outside. Judith Defour's 2-year-old daughter was in the workhouse when she took the girl out and sold her new clothes to purchase gin. (Defour was subsequently convicted of murder for leaving the child naked in a ditch with strangle marks around her neck.)[289] When the parish placed illegitimate children in the work-house, links with their mothers were attenuated. Those who gave depositions to workhouses about older children reported either that the mothers were dead, or that they knew little about them.[290] The children lacked friends who might help them. As Fanny Hall explained when she applied to the Foundling Hospital to take her child in 1799, 'i have been deprived of parents ever since i have been five years old an have not a friend to apply to'. Fanny Hall had worked as a servant since she was 14 years of age, but did not say how she had lived in the intervening period, between the ages of 5 and 14.[291]

By the later eighteenth century, when parishes usually received a lump sum from an alleged father, they had a financial interest in doing as little as possible for the 'bastard child'. There were even stories of parishes kidnapping chargeable bastards and attempting to place them in the Foundling Hospital, by which they would be discharged from any further responsibility.[292]

Some evidence suggests that single mothers kept their children with them as long as they could. Agnes Banes kept her illegitimate son James for eight years 'at her own charge', before leaving the child in 1602 with her aged mother and stepfather. After nine months, they were forced to turn to the parish.[293] In the London parish of Chelsea near the end of the eighteenth century, over a third of the illegitimate children whose mothers applied for relief were not newborn but up to 10 years old, suggesting that only when they were desperate would mothers surrender their illegitimate children to the parish.[294]

One story pieced together from over twenty years of entries in the records of the Warwickshire parish of Salford shows the complexity of a single woman's maternity. In 1625, the widowed Margaret Doughty applied for relief. Born around 1573, she had six children, two were lame, and the youngest, who was probably illegitimate, was under 5 years of age, too young to beg. By 1633, Margaret had a house and garden rent free, and had only her 13-year-old illegitimate child with her. Although the overseers resented her clamour, they still allowed her 6d. weekly while the child was with her, to be reduced to 4d. after the child left. Finally, in 1649, when Margaret was aged 76 years and in extreme poverty, she was granted a weekly pension which was increased in 1652.[295] Perhaps in practice some parishes helped single mothers to keep their children for several years.

MATERNAL FEELINGS

Most of the evidence about single motherhood is in institutional and administrative records where the physical work of motherhood, such as feeding, washing, nursing, and supervising left no traces. Even harder to perceive is the evidence of maternal affection conveyed by bodily gestures, such as hugging, rocking, and kissing.

Nevertheless, single mothers left some traces of their feelings in their petitions to the London Foundling Hospital. Some expressed hostility and resentment, referring to their child as 'that Incumbrance', or 'this Burthen'.[296] Mary Brown confessed that 'she was almost Tempted by the Devil to destroy it'.[297] Others referred to maternity as an interruption in their lives: 'when rid of that Incumbrance',[298] she could resume her employment. More commonly, women deployed the stereotypic rhetoric of maternity, referring to 'the anxious solicitude of a Mother'.[299]

Leaving a child to the care of others, as in the biblical tale of rival mothers, involved maternal sacrifice. Laura Gowing recounts a 1599 story of a London widow who gave birth to a child of questionable legitimacy. Accompanied by the midwife, she carried the baby to another parish and left it on a stall in Cornhill, but then had a change of heart and wanted to return for her child: 'thou fool [said the midwife] it will be kept better then thou art able to keep it.'[300] Similarly, many mothers may have believed that the Foundling Hospital ensured a better future for their children. As Elizabeth Sugars explained, she was not able to do that justice to her offspring as she wished, 'being oblig'd to go to hard labour every day'.[301]

A few mothers who left their children in the London Foundling Hospital later changed their minds. Jane Marriott (mentioned earlier) who initially consented to her father's desire to put the child in the Hospital, subsequently petitioned for its return: 'not that I have a doubt of its being taken proper care of but the thoughts of never seeing it any more distrest me beyond Expression'. In a further plea, she added 'if I lose my child I dont know what will be come of me'.[302] Another mother seized her child from his nurse in Surrey, declaring 'that the Child was hers, and now she had found it, she would carry it away with her, for that she had been out of her senses ever since ye child was taken from her.'[303] Her reported language was of distraught, determined, and unapologetic maternity.

Single mothers could impress their neighbours as good mothers. When in 1743, 27-year-old Elizabeth Shudrick of Harefield, who lived with her widowed mother, was indicted for killing her newborn infant, a witness testified in her favour by referring to her maternal affection: Elizabeth had 'a Child of five Years old last Valentine's-Day, and *no Woman could ever be fonder of a Child than she is of that* (emphasis mine)'.[304]

Perhaps the most eloquent testimony of all about single women as mothers is that many kept their children with them for several years. Their maternity was outside the records unless they fell foul of the law. Grace Martyn was found wandering and begging in Salisbury in 1598, with four children. When she was sent to her place of birth in Cornwall, three of the children accompanied her, but her son who was over the age of 14 years was sent to his place of birth, in Somerset.[305] In 1636, two women punished in Kent for vagrancy had 11 children with them and no husband.[306] The children's legitimacy status was not mentioned. So disorderly a group was far from a conventional nuclear family, but it is telling that the women were responsible for so many children. Nor were they atypical; many single mothers tried to protect their children for as long as possible. Parish authorities did not go looking for responsibilities, so if a mother and her child were managing without assistance, they would not interfere. In 1756, a Wiltshire settlement examination discovered that 33-year-old Elizabeth Pope, who travelled the country carrying wooden bowls and dishes to sell, had kept company for years with Thomas Hilliar, a scribbler (petty writer), by whom she had two children, a daughter aged 13 and a son of 10 years.[307] Records for Mitcham, Surrey, for the late eighteenth century reveal that in the 1790s one single mother, Ann Miles, had four illegitimate children with her aged between 10 and 3 years, all born in different places, and another single mother had a 13-year-old.[308]

Later in life, illegitimate children spoke of how their mothers tried to provide them with the crucial inheritance for poor people, a parish settlement. Although Burn stated that the mother of a 'bastard' could give no settlement, because the 'bastard' was not a part of her family,[309] mothers tried to integrate their illegitimate children into the welfare system. Thus in 1750, St Botolph's recorded of Sarah Barber, a single woman, that 'she has been oftentimes informed by her Mother & other persons that she this Depon[ent] was born a Bastard . . . in the parish of St Dunstan Stepney', which gave her a claim on

Figure 6 'Three beggars met together' (17th cent.). The vagrant group pictured here shows the blurred outline of 'the family' among the poorest people. While the relationships between the mother, her three children, and the two men are unclear, the mother has kept the children with her. We lack pictures of poor single mothers, although there were portraits of aristocratic mothers and their illegitimate children.

St Dunstan's.[310] Single women's settlements were highly contested, and pregnancy complicated the situation.[311] Pamela Sharpe argues that a single woman, a *femme sole*, could acquire settlement rights,[312] but I have found no evidence that poor single mothers did in fact transmit them to their illegitimate children. More likely was that the parish where the child was born remained liable.

Single mothers were preoccupied with material circumstances. Bringing up children was demanding work, and they had no husbands to help maintain their children. Inevitably, their motherhood was precarious, for if they were unable to provide for their children, they risked being separated from them. Mothers had to teach their offspring how to survive. They shared many difficulties with poor mothers of legitimate children, juggling work and childcare, but did so in a context in which they and their children were stigmatized. Many historians, like the Poor Law authorities, have judged single mothers harshly, but 'the state', as well as the men who begot the children, created the specific legal and economic context that made mothering difficult. Nevertheless, many single mothers made pragmatic solutions to the births of their illegitimate children, asserting their maternal status and contrasting their honesty with that of men who had broken their promises.[313] Single mothers' refusal to be degraded was important to their and their children's survival; survival involved self-esteem as well as material things.[314] Finally, single mothers did not necessarily remain outside the boundaries of the reputable household. Many married, albeit at older ages than other women at first marriage, and thereby their illegitimate children blended into complex families, so common amongst the poor.[315]

2

'FATHERS' OF ILLEGITIMATE CHILDREN

Men's attitudes to their illegitimate sons and daughters differed from those to their legal offspring. Legally, a 'bastard child' had no father and was *filius nullius*. Indeed, a man might never know that he had begotten an illegitimate child.

In the later sixteenth century, there were some changes in expectations of the fathers of families. The Protestant reformers of the sixteenth century denied any special virtues in celibacy, and priests were to be married men, model fathers of families. The godly man, head of his family, was responsible for the good behaviour of his wife, children, and servants. As a father, he was to oversee his wife's nurture of their young children, and when they reached 7 years of age, to undertake their education. A father was to train his sons so that they could maintain themselves in employment, and to see his daughters suitably married.[1]

Society's expectations of 'fathers' of illegitimate children were limited and contradictory. 'Bastards' were not included 'under the words *family* or *children*', explained Richard Burn in his influential treatise about the Poor Laws in 1755. A bastard, as a child of no man, was theoretically incapable of inheriting.[2] A man who admitted paternity had no legal rights to custody even when his child was under 7 years of age.[3] Formally, the illegitimate child, lacking a legal relationship to a father, was outside the family, although there were some cases at the highest social levels where a title did pass to a bastard. A blood connection was recognized between father and illegitimate child, even though the blood transmitted was 'base', and the same incest taboos operated as between a man and his legitimate offspring.[4] Some 'natural' paternal feeling was expected. Legal commentators continued to reiterate the view of medieval canon law: the begetters of illegitimate children were legally obligated by 'ties of nature'.[5] Thus a 1679 pamphlet censured Robert Foulkes, a minister convicted of the murder of his bastard child: 'to destroy an innocent

Babe, had cruelty enough in it; but to offer violence to the fruit of ones own body, was such a monstrous piece of barbarity, as admits not of a parallel.'[6] As the social critic Jonas Hanway observed later in the eighteenth century, fathers should be made to discharge their legal obligations to maintain their illegitimate children, even if they did not marry the mothers as they should.[7] In the forceful words of Defoe, directed to both fathers and mothers, 'My Child, is my Child, let it be begot in Sin or Wedlock, and all the Duties of a Parent are incumbent on me so long as it lives'. Nevertheless, Defoe considered that no father ever intended to set his bastard 'on a Footing' with his legitimate children.[8]

Contemporary terminology reflects men's ambiguous relationship to paternity outside marriage: they were simply 'alleged', 'reputed', or 'putative' fathers. Since fathers belonged to the legal and social worlds of marriage and family, I will refer to those who begot illegitimate children as 'fathers' to draw attention to their problematic status.[9] All women who gave birth were mothers, and contemporaries expected that they would 'naturally' undertake the duties of nurture involved in social motherhood, even if their offspring were illegitimate. But many fewer men who were genetic fathers of 'bastards' were prepared to be social fathers.

So far as the 'fathers' of children subject to the bastardy and poor laws were concerned, not many accepted any duties beyond the bare minimum: maintenance. In many instances even this duty was enforced by the civic authorities. That 'fathers' and not the parish bore the cost of illegitimate children became a constant principle of the administrators of the bastardy laws and the Poor Laws.[10]

Propertied men's concerns about illegitimacy were different from those of men whose illegitimate children were liable to require parish relief. Élite and middling men had inheritance concerns—legitimate heirs might be challenged by 'bastards'—and they had moral concerns about the turpitude of 'bastards'. Wealthier fathers who managed their affairs so that their illicit paternity never came into public discussion by civic authorities are outside the scope of this chapter. Yet over the early modern period, even gentlemen could find it increasingly difficult to evade the notice of the parish overseers. Experience showed parishes that private arrangements could easily come unstuck, and that illegitimate children would then become a parish liability. Because parishes were concerned to minimize the cost of maintaining pauper 'bastards', they were determined to make 'fathers' responsible. Thus poorer men may have been less concerned about illegitimacy *per se*, but for them, illegitimate children were an economic burden and could affect their marriage plans; potential parish involvement meant they could not easily disregard the off-spring of their illicit sexuality.

Marriage and children affected labouring men and women differently. For an adult woman, whose earning power was so much less than that of a man of similar status, marriage or remarriage was necessary for assistance in supporting her children. However, for a man, the primary earner, marriage meant responsibility and a growing financial burden as more and more children were born. Thomas Chubb (b. 1679), who lived single, judged it 'greatly improper to introduce a family into the world, without a prospect of maintaining them'.[11] In the late Tudor period, marriage decisions even among the labouring poor required some support from the couple's 'friends', namely their parents and kin. In financial terms, kin support may have declined over the early modern period.[12] Another constraint upon poor people marrying in rural society was the availability of housing, as many landowners and parishes refused accommodation, and the law upheld them.[13]

Around 1600, ordinary labouring men married in their late twenties; their wives were usually in their mid-twenties, and became mothers within a year. By 1800, men's age at first marriage dropped from 28 years to 26.4; women's, from 26 to 24.9 years.[14] Society's expectation that fathers would be the head of a household, maintaining their wives and children, and exercising authority over those within their households, coloured the experiences and responses of men to their lovers' illicit pregnancies. Being a married father and head of a household enhanced a man's status; the corollary was that if his family life turned out badly it reflected adversely upon him. Fatherhood could subject him to humiliations.

As we have seen in Chapter 1, from 1576, if men could not or would not marry their pregnant lovers and the children were liable to be poor, then secular law as well as canon law was involved. The bastardy laws and the Poor Laws gave the state a role in forcing 'fathers' to pay maintenance for their illegitimate offspring.[15] Over the early modern period, the laws were strengthened to increase the parish's power over alleged fathers. Men charged with paternity were liable to penalties for failure to appear before the justices of the peace, or to comply with maintenance orders. Determining the father of any child was no easy process. The common law simply presumed that all children born to a marriage were of the husband's begetting, unless circumstances made this impossible, and this legal fiction resolved many paternity issues. But since the illegitimate child lacked a legal father, determining the father, affiliation, came to rest on the mother or her midwife swearing his name to the justices; it depended on a judgment whether the women's words were believed. Men could, and did, challenge women's words and their reputations, as we shall see.

Paternity outside marriage thus focuses attention on fatherhood, men's concepts of honour, what it meant to be a man, and a head of a household. Inevitably, illicit paternity aroused complex responses. This chapter discusses men's responses to illicit fatherhood. Individual reactions depended on many factors. The laws shaped the general context but, as Hanway observed in 1759, everyone determined responsibilities differently.[16] Marriage was one option, but some 'fathers' were married already. Men's feelings for their lovers affected their attitudes to pregnancies. Most hoped that paternity allegations would never become public and that they could resolve the issues involved in any illicit birth without outside interference. Taking or evading responsibility for mothers and children—being a father or refusing to be a father—affected men's lives deeply. In the following discussion, I have selected examples which illustrate particular aspects of the general pattern of men's responses to illicit paternity.

FATHERS, HONOUR, AND PATRIARCHY

Socially, the men who begot illegitimate children liable to be a burden on the parish were a more varied group than were the mothers. 'Fathers' were both single and married. Whereas most single mothers were young women in their later teens or twenties, and most worked as servants, the age range of fathers was greater, their marital status varied, and their economic resources were generally greater than those of their lovers. (Even if the men and women were both servants in a household, there was always a gender differential in pay; men were paid more.)

The social status of 'fathers' changed over the early modern period, in response to religious, social, and economic changes. Clerical marriage meant priests were no longer commonly named as fathers as they had been before 1500.[17] The households of Protestant ministers were expected to be exemplars of the godly family: in 1697 one clergyman declared that the ability of a minister as a spiritual father in the house of God 'would best be measured by the condition of his own Family at Home'.[18] It was scandalous if ministers erred.

To the humiliation of being publicly subjected to civic authorities was added the threat of further legal proceedings and even imprisonment should they refuse to obey, and all on the words of the women who swore their paternity. 'Fathers' were often angry, feeling dishonoured in any subjection that involved women. Perhaps their loss of autonomy to women returned them to the dependence of infancy, a vulnerability which may help explain the fury and venom some showed towards their former lovers. Hannah Bradley's lover, a London attorney's clerk who lodged with Hannah's mistress, swore that 'if one single half penny would save her and the child that he would not give it her, and pushed her out of his office'.[19]

Before the Civil Wars, poorer men might be subjected to public shame and humiliating physical punishment as well as affiliation and maintenance orders. In the parish of St Swithins by Londonstone, a married man who had fathered a 'bastard' was ordered by the Court of High Commission to stand in a white sheet while the minister preached and later published a sermon of 'warning to whore-mongers'.[20] Men of higher social status were usually able to buy their way out of public humiliation. Thus in 1629, an ecclesiastical court in Oxfordshire heard Thomas Lovel plead that the penalty of doing penance as a putative father would 'be a disparagement unto him', so the court permitted him to pay £3 and to be discharged.[21]

Thus more than expense was involved in 'bastardy' proceedings: a 'bastard' had the potential to shame a man. Much of the discussion of the 'fathers' of illegitimate children has to date involved questions of male honour. Bernard Capp has argued that from the Elizabethan period a woman's naming of a man as the father might expose him to unpleasant consequences, including physical punishment, shame, penance, and financial responsibilities. Sexual reputation was so important to men that it gave women a 'lever' against them.[22] While men might boast about their sexual prowess, as did William Hodge in 1786 at a public house the morning after allegedly raping his servant, it was another matter to attend the quarter sessions to justify themselves publicly.[23] Married men were especially vulnerable to the dishonour of bastardy orders against them.[24]

Since men considered that fatherhood was their own private business, their honour was sullied if the justices believed the mother's words against their denials. 'Sexual prowess was one dimension of the meaning of manhood', Griffiths has argued, claiming that sexuality 'helped define masculinity itself'.[25] Masculinity could be undermined by women's allegations of illicit paternity for, as Alexandra Shepard has argued, men subject to the authority of others were judged as failing the patriarchal manly ideal of independence and autonomy.[26] The higher their social status, the more men resented appearing publicly before the justices, and being subjected to orders in matters related to their most intimate sexual lives. The 'most precious thing that a man hath in this world is a good name', preached Richard Cooke in 1629. Cooke rebuked men who were humiliated by subjection to the magistrates, thinking themselves superior: 'these beastly creatures thinke they can either over-looke or over-top authoritie, by being greater or better...then the Magistrate'.[27] Throughout the period, there are stories of men reacting angrily to the 'bastardy' orders against them. In the early seventeenth century, Somerset magistrates heard that John Hunt was furious when a tithingman delivered a justice's warrant: 'hast thou brought a warrant for mee you rogue? take it and wipe thy arse with it, I care not a turd for thee nor the warrant, nor for him that sent it.'[28] Similar examples of men scorning the civic authorities continued in the eighteenth century. In April 1728, St Sepulchre's sent for John Smithers about a 'bastard child': 'he bid defiance to the power of the Committee.'[29] The repercussions of a bastardy order could even affect a man's credibility as a witness in another law case, and provoke conflicts between men in local administration and higher courts.[30]

Illicit births thus affected a range of patriarchal relationships and take us to the heart of gender and power in family and household relations. As we have seen, heads of household would be called to account if they entertained pregnant single women under their roofs, or allowed a woman to give birth and leave without reporting her for punishment.[31] While responsibility for reporting was not new, the Protestant reformers' delineation of the key role of husbands and fathers in that fundamental unit of social order, the godly household, meant that men who failed to maintain good order were more publicly visible as failing.[32] In 1616 in Nottinghamshire, a father was indicted because he dismissed a maidservant 'made pregnant by his son' instead of accepting responsibility for the mother and child.[33] Even gossip and rumour could prompt investigation. William Aldworth and his wife testified in an Oxford church court case in 1617 on behalf of the good name of their maidservant, allegedly the mother of a bastard child. Aldworth declared 'that he thinkes it concerneth him and his wyfe to maintaine and preserve the good name of the said Joane soe far forth and noe otherwise then an honest and weldisposed master and mistres for a carefull and honest servant'.[34]

Masters 'as heads of household' could demand sexual relations of their women servants, who would find it difficult both morally and physically to deny them. The layout of many houses meant that servants slept in the same space as their masters, sometimes on truckle beds. Prosecutions of heads of household for illicit sexual relations under their roofs may have been more common in the early seventeenth century than later, possibly because in the earlier period authorities were more concerned with the moral disorder than with the economics of maintenance payments. In the eighteenth century, household heads who could afford secret maintenance were less likely to come to the attention of authorities.

DENIALS

When men were accused of fathering a bastard, a common response was denial. Very few voluntarily accepted even the minimal duty of maintenance. Instead, they sought to evade responsibility and expense; their own social and economic standing and honour were more important than the claims of any children. Men voiced their denials in terms of contemporary cultural stereotypes: paternity was uncertain because women who were sexually active outside marriage were whores; their words were untrustworthy. Unlike single mothers, however, in a pre-DNA age, men's bodies bore no incontestable witness against them.

Men who begged their lovers to abort the foetus tacitly admitted responsibility. Women told the courts of men that their lovers tried to persuade them that they had no need to fear 'a great belly' 'for that there was severall things that would destroy it'. A Buckinghamshire case in 1711 told of Elizabeth Goldsworth whose lover James Neale complained that she should have told him of her pregnancy earlier: 'he blamed her for not discovering it to him before and saying that had he known it sooner it might have been prevented for she might have took something by which he meant that she ought to have destroyed 'em in her womb.'[35] Such allegations were plausible, if not always true.[36] Eighteenth-century northern assizes records include instances of men forcing their pregnant lovers to take abortifacients from which they subsequently died.[37]

Flight was an easy form of denial, an option more open to single than to married men. Single men fled because they were either unwilling or unable to marry or pay maintenance, as numerous early modern bastardy depositions attest. A common tale told by mothers petitioning the Foundling Hospital later in the eighteenth century was that their lovers had simply vanished. In 1771, Mary Sims explained that her seducer was 'incapable of providing for himself & Family, and by this unhappy incident obliged to disappear, thro fear of the consequences'.[38] The father of Mary Marsh's child was her fellow servant 'who has Eloped lest he should be compelled to pay for the Nursing of his Child'.[39] By the eighteenth century, Britain's wars and overseas empire created increased economic opportunities for men outside their parishes. In 1781, Jane Bowring explained that the father was John Barnard, 'and to avoid Marrying her or keeping the Child is run away she believes gone to Sea'.[40] Trumbach calculated that of the 780 petitions for single women who offered children to the Foundling Hospital in 1768–9, the whereabouts or occupations of the alleged fathers was mentioned in over half, and over a third of those men had gone abroad, to sea, to America, been impressed, or were soldiers.[41] Those forcibly enlisted had little choice. As single mother, Mary Marr, explained in 1779, the young man with whom she was intimate had used his utmost endeavours to support her, but he was impressed and 'gone to America'; their child was now 4 months old.[42] In 1781, Elizabeth Mitchell's lover was aboard a man-of-war ship; John Barnard 'has Rune of[f] to See'.[43] Britain's overseas empire presented men with other opportunities. Mary Redman's lover was an attorney who went to the West Indies in December 1799.[44] Whether a man volunteered or was impressed, the burden of providing for the child still remained with the mother.

While there is considerable evidence of maternal kin helping their daughters with their pregnancies and their infants, men's kin were generally hostile to their sons' lovers and 'bastards'. A bastardy allegation could upset parents' marriage plans for their sons. There are plenty of instances across the early modern period of men's fathers and mothers helping their sons evade the unwanted responsibilities of marriage and fatherhood.[45] In 1588, an Essex father, William Grimes, conveyed his son away.[46] In 1667, when a constable attempted to arrest a Cheshire man for fathering a bastard, he was set upon by a group of women, including the widowed mother of the accused.[47] In 1769, Mary Brown, in her petition to the Foundling Hospital, claimed that her lover had wanted to marry her, but his parents had sent him to the East Indies.[48] In 1772, an angry father threatened the parish constable in Surrey who tried to serve a warrant on his son for 'getting a bastard child': 'if ever he came to his house after his son he would do for him'.[49]

'Fathers' in some cases assisted in secret births and subsequent infanticides. In 1681, when Susanna Watkin was in labour, a witness heard her call for a midwife, but her master, the child's father, refused, 'for he had a mind to conceal it in this world and in the next let him and her shift it'.[50] 'Fathers' were, however, less likely than mothers to be involved directly in the deaths of newborn children. Malcolmson found that only about two dozen of his 350 infanticide cases involved men, nearly always the fathers.[51] In 1767, John White stayed with his lover Ann Usher while she gave birth in a field, carried the baby away, and refused to tell what had become of it. Two years later, when she threatened to speak of his taking her child, he offered £50 for her silence, threatening that if she spoke, 'he would stab her'.[52] Similarly, 'fathers' featured little in women's accounts of infanticides, unless the births involved incest between a man and his daughter or stepdaughter. In a 1683 case before the Old Bailey, Elenor Adams was sentenced to death for infanticide, while her stepfather 'by evidence of his extraordinary kindness to his Daughter more than to his Wife' was suspected of paternity but not of involvement in the infant's death.[53] Significantly, legal and popular representations of newborn child murder usually focused on the actions of unmarried mothers rather than fathers, erasing the evidence of men's violence.[54]

Nevertheless, indirectly men's hostility to being fathers adversely affected the lives of their illegitimate offspring. By refusing financial assistance, they made a woman's pregnancy and lying-in more difficult; poverty affected her ability to nurture her infant. Other 'fathers' went further and gave their babies to vagrant nurses, which Wrightson has suggested was a form of infanticide.[55] In 1696, John Dee negotiated with a woman who demanded £5 to take the child for ever, but only £1 to abandon it in another parish; Dee chose the cheaper option.[56] A late seventeenth-century case of fraud before the Old Bailey told of three women who, 'under the species of Nurses', had taken money from both the 'natural Parents' and then secured parish pensions for nursing the same children. One father had given them £5 for his base-born twins.[57] In 1773, Ann Smith petitioned the London Foundling Hospital for the admission of a baby. She pretended to be the mother, but when the Hospital's officer checked, Ann admitted that she had been persuaded to impersonate the mother by 'a Man in the Country'. Presumably he was the 'father', who no longer wanted to pay 12s. per month to nurse the child. (The governors rejected the petition.)[58]

The Bloudy Mother,

1544

OR

The moſt inhumane murthers, committed
by *Iane Hatterſley* vpon diuers Infants, the iſſue of her
owne bodie: & the priuate burying of them in an Orchard
with her Araignment and execution.

As alſo, The moſt loathſome and lamentable end of *Adam
Adamſon* her Maſter, the vnlawfull begetter of thoſe vnfortunate
Babes, being eaten and conſumed aliue with Wormes and Lice.

At Eaſt *Grinſted* in *Suſſex* neere London, in Iuly laſt. 1609.

Figure 7 *The Bloudy Mother* (1609). The text on the pamphlet's title pages focuses attention on the woman servant, Jane Hattersley, who kills her child, thus playing down the complicity of Jane's master, Adam Adamson, in the conception and death of the infant. The visual image, however, depicts both the servant and her master, who was presumably the child's 'father', burying the body of one child with the bones of other infants scattered nearby. Jane Hattersley was executed, while 'the unlawfull begetter of those unfortunate Babes' was 'eaten and consumed alive with Wormes and Lice'.

Historians have suggested that the establishment of foundling hospitals throughout Europe allowed parents to ease their guilt for abandoning their children.[59] Some determined men kidnapped their children and put them in the Foundling Hospital. In the mid-eighteenth century, one Oxley had passed as married to Sarah Bathe for five years, and their illegitimate son was baptized Timothy and 'took the Sir name of the father Oxley'. Taking advantage of Sarah's temporary absence, Oxley took their son to the Foundling Hospital. Timothy, whose return his mother sought, was 11 months old and wearing 'a stript bed gown of cotton blue & white, red shoes & stockings a coral necklace with a silver penny'. Sarah, supported by her own father, alleged that this was the second child the 'father' had disposed of: Oxley had 'by the same clandestine means' taken away an earlier-born son named Thomas Oxley.[60] Clearly Oxley was happy to have Sarah as his supposed wife, but refused to be a social father to any of their children.

The archives of the London Foundling Hospital reveal other stories of men whose actions fell short of deliberate murder, but indicate a callous disregard of their children's welfare. In 1759, Elizabeth Simpson from the North Riding, in Yorkshire, enquired of the Foundling Hospital about the whereabouts of her son whom her lover, a gentleman, Henry Kilvington, said he had arranged to place there. The narrative suggests Kilvington's considerable determination to be rid of the child against Elizabeth's wishes. Elizabeth had given birth and lay in at a house for seven weeks, taking care of her son. Then, with Henry's consent, she gave the baby to Dorothy Denis to feed, while she went to York on horseback with Kilvington's brother William, where she stayed with her aunt 'until she had lost her milk'. When Elizabeth returned to Renton, 'Expecting to see her Child', Henry Kilvington said he'd sent the child to another nurse. Suspiciously, she had questioned him minutely about their son's welfare, asking 'if her Child slept all the Way when he carried it to the wet nurse near Beddale'. Kilvington said that the baby had slept, because he got something from the doctor to make him. Subsequently Elizabeth was told that Jane Denis, presumably related to the nurse Dorothy Denis, had taken her baby to the Hospital, but 'cannot believe it', and suspected that Kilvington and the nurse had done the child some mischief. Kilvington admitted to Elizabeth that he had sedated their son, presumably with an opiate, for the journey from Yorkshire to the London Foundling Hospital, a journey of perhaps a week.[61]

Elizabeth Simpson's story hints at careful planning by her gentleman lover to conceal his paternity. Kilvington had the financial resources to support Elizabeth while she gave birth and suckled her child, then to pay for a wet-nurse while her milk dried up. He was assisted by his kin, and could call upon other women to help him. Elizabeth's anxieties about her son's welfare and her attempts to find him demonstrate her attachment. She was supported by her own kin in her search for her baby. Kilvington's concern seems to have been to rid himself of any responsibility for his son, while keeping the matter private.

In the same year, 1759, Elizabeth Smith told the Foundling Hospital governors a similar story of the kidnapping of her 22-week-old child by his father, John Winter. Winter (like Henry Kilvington) was abetted by his brother. John seized the child from his mother's arms at 10pm and 'sent it away by his brother Harry Winter the same Night'.[62] Whether Elizabeth Smith was able to recover her son is unknown. Other stories of kidnapping were less detailed. In 1759, Elizabeth Brunsel of St James Clerkenwell petitioned the Hospital for the return of her bastard daughter named Elizabeth Banks, 'Sir-name of the Father', who she said had been seized by two men and a woman, and put in the Hospital, though she 'was both able and willing to support it'.[63] Again in 1759, a supervisor of the Hospital's nurse-children in Berkshire reported that an alleged father had seized a 6-week-old baby from his cradle in his grandmother's house; the grandmother was powerless against the gang of men. The mother complained to the justices that she feared that her son had been murdered or placed as a foundling, and was reportedly 'inconsolable for the loss of her child'.[64] Here a single mother was caring for her child with the support of her family. We can only speculate about the father's attitudes. Perhaps the child's very existence caused him shame.

A few fathers featured in cases of 'spiriting away' children, sending them aboard ships to the new world. Even though these children were older, and had presumably lived in the households of their legal fathers, these men had stayed emotionally detached, believing that the children were the products of adulterine bastardy and therefore spurious heirs.[65] While some men sought to disappear, or to make their illegitimate offspring vanish, others concentrated on private negotiations with their lovers so that the matter would not become public.

ACKNOWLEDGEMENT: TACIT ADMISSION AND PRIVATE ARRANGEMENTS

Wealthier men who did not want their paternity publicly known could pay private maintenance. In many cases they were married, so that any public discussion of their illicit sexuality reflected not just on their reputations but also on their wives at home. Cases in the seventeenth-century church courts suggest that some 'fathers', whether married or single, privately assisted their lovers and babies, thereby acknowledging some responsibility for their children but avoiding the intervention of the parish officers. Indeed, 'fathers' might make considerable contributions in recognition of their responsibilities, *provided* they were not legally obligated.[66] Quarter sessions records show that men were sensitive to the dishonour of being named. In Oxfordshire in 1712, William Young admitted 'that he did not matter keeping the Child, but only the disgrace'.[67]

Lovers offered various kinds of financial inducements so that their paternity remained secret. They attempted to bribe women to swear the child to someone else, thereby calling into question another man's honour and perjuring women. In 1629, the Banbury church court heard some local gossip: William Watton said 'Roland Bull begot his maid with child and hired another to father it, and so might your master do for ought I know.'[68] In 1762, the parish of St Leonard Shoreditch heard that Elizabeth Woodfin was pregnant to Thomas Yate, a victualler, who offered her 6 guineas to name another man, or to marry any young man she liked. Woodfin declined to take a false oath, but offered to accept the 6 guineas and trouble Yate no further. Yate refused to pay unless Elizabeth committed perjury, threatening that he would prosecute her, put her in the pillory, 'or transport her'.[69]

Some men agreed to acknowledge their paternity if the child proved to be a boy, as did one early seventeenth-century Somerset man, adding 'but if it was a maid she should lack a father for it'.[70] In 1650, a Southampton widow, Margaret White, told the justices that her lover, James Lock, had desired her to conceal the matter 'and he would send her to London and if her child were a boy he the sayd Lock would make him a tobacco cutter'.[71]

In fraught negotiations over maintenance, 'fathers' risked public exposure. After an elaborate charade to present his pregnant lover, 'Payne's daughter', as his wife in 1714, Roger Quartermaine of

Chalgrove reneged on his promise to give his lover a bond for maintenance payments. The landlady Mary Lawrence heard Payne say that she would be carried to Chalgrove '& the said Quartermaine should keep her & the Child'.[72] By threatening to make Quartermaine's sin public knowledge in his own parish, Payne sought to shame him into paying maintenance. While the emphasis in recent historiography has been to view single mothers' accusations critically, it is important to remember that we can rarely determine the truth of the allegations; innocent men and lying women are as unsubtle stereotypes as any others.[73]

A wealthier man could bribe another man to marry his pregnant lover and be a father to the child. A Tudor minister offered another man cows, money, and a house, to no avail.[74] In the 1590s, another minister Robert Dey married off his pregnant servant, Elizabeth Purkey, using his brother-in-law to negotiate a dowry. When he failed to pay part of the dowry, Elizabeth came to evening service and left her baby on the chancel steps.[75] In 1635, Elizabeth Haddon confessed that at the time of her marriage to Higgins, she was pregnant by Robert Toms, whose two brothers had negotiated a payment of £4. 10s. with Haddon's brother to be paid to her husband.[76] In this case, a 'father's' kin assisted him in negotiations, but something had gone wrong, so the story went to court.

From the lengthy proceedings of the church court in Devon in 1679, we can reconstruct a complex case in which one 'father' went to elaborate lengths to provide secretly for his 'bastard'. The court prosecuted Roger Chanon, 'a strong water man' of Exeter, for his involvement in the birth of an illegitimate child. Chanon was not poor, and may have been married already.[77] His attempts to organize private maintenance involved a wide circle of people who suspected his paternity. Before the mother—some thought one Grace Bomer—lay in, Chanon commissioned a certain Gendell, a tiler, to hire a wetnurse. Gendell made enquiries and contacted Elizabeth Northcote from the nearby parish of Farringdon. Mrs Northcote agreed to collect the baby in Exeter in a fortnight's time and nurse it at an agreed monthly fee. When the baby was born earlier than anticipated, Mrs Northcote was summoned to Exeter to the house of one Richard Gantony, a fell-monger (a dealer in animal hides), where she collected an infant about 2 days old, and a box of clothes. Chanon paid her 6s. in advance for two weeks' nursing, and both she and her husband suspected that Chanon was the baby's father. Two or three days later, the Farringdon parish officers, fearing that their parish might become liable for the 'bastard', ordered Mrs Northcote to return it. The nurse, who was illiterate, had a letter written to Chanon and Gantony, but although the two men offered a bond to discharge the parish from maintenance of the child, the Farringdon parish officers refused it.

The quest for a wet-nurse continued. This time the fell-monger Gantony rode off looking for another nurse. In the parish of Crediton, to the north-west of Exeter, he was recommended to Jane South-combe, who agreed to nurse the child for 12s. per month. Gantony took the wet-nurse behind him on his horse to Exeter, where the next day various women became involved. Gantony's wife took the nurse to Hevitree, an intermediate point where, at John Watkyns' house, the men resumed negotiations. Chanon met with the new nurse's husband, Nathaniel Southcombe. The first nurse and her husband transferred the baby. Chanon paid Mrs Southcombe 12s. in advance for the first month's nursing, and gave the whole party a dinner, after which the Southcombes returned with the baby to Crediton. But Chanon's troubles were not over, for in Crediton, the parish officers wasted no time and were soon questioning Nathaniel Southcombe for 'entertaining the child'. Nathaniel Southcombe, the nurse's husband, went to Exeter, told Gantony about the matter, and soon after Gant-ony and Chanon travelled to Crediton, where the parish accepted the two men's bond for the child's maintenance. Three weeks later, the baby died, and one of Chanon, Gantony, or Gendell reimbursed the Southcombes for the funeral.

While there are unresolved puzzles about this case, what is striking is the complexity of the 'father's' subterfuges in attempting to arrange the secret maintenance of his illegitimate child. Clearly a number of people knew about the child (who was unnamed throughout). While Roger Chanon was generally thought to be the father, the name of the mother was less evident; the Southcombes had heard that Goody Cooper's daughter had given birth, not Grace Bomer. The marital status of neither Chanon nor the two suspected mothers was revealed. The relationships between Chanon and all the men helping him— Gendell the tiler, Gantony the fell-monger, and John Watkyns, the innkeeper at Hevitree—are also unclear; the men shared neither names nor occupations. Chanon and the child's mother may have drawn on friendship or kinship connections.

The length of time that 'fathers' actually paid informal mainten-ance is difficult to determine, because we know of their failings only when mothers were forced to seek the assistance of the parish or a charity. Many maternal petitions to the Foundling Hospital referred to their disappointments: lovers had promised financial support, but defaulted.[78] In Westminster in the early eighteenth century, authorities heard that a married woman nursed an 18-month-old 'bastard' for five months and had been paid at the rate of 2s. weekly 'by the father's brother' until he defaulted.[79] Many fathers of illegitimates faced almost insurmountable difficulties in continuing maintenance payments, as they simply could not afford them. If they were married, then few earned enough to support two families. If single, they worked in the households of others, and maintenance payments postponed their own chances of marrying.

Incidental evidence indicates that some wealthier fathers maintained their 'bastards' for some time. Another seventeenth-century story from Devon tells of one Vernery who kept his illegitimate son in his own household; again, gossip led to a case in the church courts. Around 1679, Margery Osbourne appealed to the Devon church court to clear herself of the allegation that six or seven years ago, before her marriage, she had borne a bastard son in the moor at Vernery's house. Bartholomew Valance said that his brother John had seen the boy at Vernery's house.[80] Alehouse keeper Elizabeth Honywell, the 57-year-old wife of a blacksmith, heard Valance say that 'twas a pretty Curl'd Locked boy'; John Valance had said that the boy 'went without hose or shooe', presumably implying a lack of due paternal care.[81] We do not know how common such informal arrangements were.

If married men were forced to take some responsibility for their illegitimate children, the attitudes of wives were crucial. Wives might be angry with their husbands (and the single mothers), but nevertheless stand by their men. In 1591 in Essex, a mistress attempted to bribe her pregnant servant to blame the child's paternity on someone other than her husband. When the servant refused, the wife sent her to London to lie-in and found her another service there.[82] In 1608, Thomas Creede told Suzan More that he had no intention of fathering her child, and boasted of his wife's support: 'I will shift it off well enough and my wife will help to clear me of this matter and to shift it off as she hath shifted me of such matters as this is before now.'[83] Such stories were echoed in the popular ballads of the seventeenth century. A married man turned to his wife when the parish ordered him to pay maintenance:

> The Parish him inforced
> To see the Infant nursed,

Figure 8 *Rocke the Babie Joane* (17th cent.). A married man who had a maintenance order against him for his 'bastard' begged his wife to take the baby, to suckle it and rock it, thereby saving them the expense of paying a nurse.

> He being but lightly pursed,
> desir'd to save that charge:

He beseeched his wife to suckle the child herself, so that they would not have to pay maintenance:

> Suckle the Baby,
> Huggle the Baby,
> Rocke the Babie Joane.

Initially, Joan refused:

> I scorne to suckle the Baby,
> Unless it were mine owne.

Finally, while Joan acknowledged 'we be but poore yet', she agreed to 'rocke thy Baby, As well as 'twere my owne'.[84] A less happy outcome seemed likely in a Warwickshire case of 1657, when Anne Aldridge agreed to take in her husband's illegitimate child, and to 'breed it up with her own children rather than her husband should lie in prison, she being confident of her husband's honesty notwithstanding the harlot's affirmation'.[85]

Although much of men's illicit fatherhood is hidden in private negotiations and secret agreements, clearly some men did accept a measure of responsibility for their illicit offspring.

MARRIAGE OR COHABITATION

Although many single mothers claimed that their illicit sexual activity was linked to the promise of marriage, only some single fathers proceeded to marry. In the sixteenth and early seventeenth centuries, the couple might be subject to censure in the church courts for premarital fornication.[86] Nevertheless, judging by bridal pregnancy figures—from 1550 to the later eighteenth century, between 16 and 35 per cent of all first births were within eight months of marriage—many men did honour their promises, so their children were born legitimate.[87] They may have defied their parents or parish authorities with a clandestine marriage.[88] They may have married reluctantly, as did Benjamin Shaw, a mechanic, who tells us that in 1793 after Betty, with whom he had spent a night, told him she was pregnant he hesitated for months. Finally he married her, even while confessing that he 'wished that she might die . . . for we were so poor, & such a dark prospect before us'.[89]

Adverse economic conditions affected ordinary men's ability to marry. Because labouring men could not usually afford to marry and support a family until their mid- to late twenties, they were required to exercise sexual restraint in a society which acknowledged strong heterosexual desires. Furthermore, after the Restoration, there was a culture, mainly around the court, which celebrated sexual excess and promiscuity. The conflicting pressures on labouring men's courtship were reflected in popular ballads, in which men assured their partners that the Lord would help them.

> Jenny is poor, and I am poor.
> Yet we will wed, so say no more;
> And should the Bairns you mention come,
> (It's few that marry but what have some,)
> No doubt but Heav'n will stand our friend,
> And bread, as well as children, send.[90]

In practice, many men knew that their earnings were insufficient to maintain a family. However, if their lovers' pregnancies were related to long-term courtship and marriage plans, as we might judge from the number of pregnant brides, many marriages did follow.

In the 1650s in Essex, fathers from the lowest social levels were under-represented in bastardy proceedings: they were largely husbandmen and yeomen, artisans or tradesmen.[91] In eighteenth-century London, 'fathers' were usually men of higher-skilled occupations than mothers. John Black's studies of putative fathers in three London parishes in the eighteenth century found no sub-group of 'bastardy prone' men; instead, the men reflected the general adult male occupations.[92] Comparatively few masters of households were accused in the period 1740–1810; more typical fathers were younger professional men in lodgings, although in the Chelsea bastardy examinations 10 per cent of fathers were of the middling sort.[93] None were in a position to marry and set up households of their own.

'Fathers' appealed to a variety of circumstances to explain why they could not marry. Apprentices' indentures forbade young men from marrying until the age of 24.[94] Men were impressed into the army or navy. Others deliberately refused to marry their pregnant lovers, regarding it as a point of honour to marry a chaste woman. During the seventeenth century, men of varied social status from the courtier, Thomas Thynne, to James Godman, a village constable, denied marriage to the women they had impregnated. The constable contemptuously vowed 'he would not marry a whore'.[95]

Some men wanted nothing to do with family life. So terrified were they at what Benjamin Shaw termed the 'dark prospect' of family responsibilities, they disappeared. Economically, they were not ready to set up a family and household. A classic case was that of a blacksmith, the lover of Susan Draper, who came before the Exeter justices in 1652 as a 'bastard-bearer'. His response to her pregnancy was 'O Susan, what shall I doe? Trading is soe bad I cannot live heere.' He fled.[96] Taking on the responsibilities of a family were daunting prospects for labouring men, which perhaps explains why their average age at marriage was comparatively late at around 28 years. In London, from the 1740s, real wages declined.[97] Work was frequently intermittent, and it was widely known, as we shall see in Chapters 3 and 4, that an increasing family of children could easily lead to deeper poverty.

In some areas, men lived in long-term relationships for years, passing as married, and their *de facto* wives bore several children. Men who passed as married were more likely to live in urban rather than in rural England; villagers were suspicious of strangers whose marital status was uncertain.[98] However, Wrightson and Levine found a number of *de facto* couples in the coal-working area of Whickham in the early seventeenth century,[99] which raises the question of whether some local cultures condoned cohabitation, forming a 'bastardy prone sub-society' as Laslett termed it.[100] A study of early nineteenth-century Lancashire suggests that only a small minority of women bore multiple illegitimate children, of whom less than a third bore all their children by the same father.[101] We have no means of knowing how many men fathered illegitimate children with more than one woman. For the period 1740–1830, Black argues, men were named as fathers of children by more than one woman in only 22 of 2,000 possible cases found in three London parishes.[102] More usually, the legitimacy status of children would be revealed if the parish investigated the claims of *de facto* couples for assistance. In a settlement case in 1768, the parish of St Botolph Aldgate examined Elizabeth Hyman as a pauper. She had lived with Samuel Johnson and borne three daughters, Mary aged around 13 years, Elizabeth 12, both baptized under the name of Johnson ('although in truth they were never married'), and Sarah, born in St Botolph's, aged 6 years.[103] The two elder girls were liable to be sent away from their mother to the parishes where they were born.

Sometimes parishes deliberately instigated prosecutions for bigamy so that they would not be liable for any children. In 1787, St Clement

Danes forced Thomas Wardropper to marry, locking him up until he consented. In December 1791, Wardropper married Alice Doyle, while his first wife was still alive, as Alice knew: 'she was so infatuated with him, that she would have him in any event', and a month of so later, Alice took in his child 'that he had by his wife'. Subsequently, Alice cohabited with Wardropper for five years or so before she, having moved on to one Mr Douglas, prosecuted Wardropper for bigamy.[104] In 1797, another story involved Hampstead parish officers forcing Ambrose Rowe to marry. He was later charged with bigamy, but the case was confused, because there was some question about the legitimacy of his first marriage. Rowe 'frequently heard' that Kitty was not a widow, but had another husband living, and he was acquitted.[105] In many such complex cases, it is clear that neighbourhoods accepted couples as married, even though they might hear otherwise. Any children who were legally bastardized, however, could be separated from their parents and sent to their place of birth.

This was a society in which divorce allowing remarriage was impossible for ordinary men.[106] Unhappily married men, men who had migrated, or men whose wives had left them, had motives for bigamous marriages and may have had emotional attachment to their 'wives' and children. Their children, classified as 'bastards', could be sent to the place of their birth, or if they were older, given a settlement different from their fathers'. In 1789 when Hannah Puffey applied for relief for herself and four of her children (the elder two were, in the formulaic language of her settlement examination 'Emancipated from her'), she confessed that all six of her offspring were 'Illegitimate and Bastards' because she had married bigamously.[107] This bigamy (it is unclear whether the couple 'married' knowingly, or not) meant that two daughters, aged 12 and 11 years, were sent to St Bride's, where they had been born, and two younger children, Maria and William, aged 6 and 5 years respectively, were allowed to stay in St Botolph's.[108] Similarly, in 1773, John, aged 11 years, was removed to Bristol where he was born, away from his mother's care because her parish of settlement was in Devon; his father's bigamous marriage made him a 'bastard'.[109] Similarly, the children of married women born after a long absence of their husbands would be sent to their place of birth as 'bastards'. Even the historian Taylor, who takes a favourable view of the Poor Laws' attempts to keep families together, nevertheless judged that women and children who were the victims of bigamy were treated in a barbarous fashion.[110]

While good moral order would have required civic authorities to try to force couples to wed, in practice parish attitudes to marriages varied depending on the consequences for the ratepayers. One parish might promote a marriage which removed a pregnant single woman to a husband in another parish. Thus in 1793, one mother was forced to marry the man to whom she had sworn the child, while he 'was kept three days in the cage at Fulham'; after their marriage, he fled the same day without having further carnal knowledge of her.[111] There were cases where overseers and justices forced the man to marry. On 17 May 1744, the Wiltshire justice William Hunt recorded that when Grace Lane 'was with child with her seventh bastard', the alleged father was taken up by warrant, 'and obliged to marry her'.[112] In 1746, the complaint of the overseers of West Lavington against Jonathan Bartlet who had fathered a bastard child prompted an immediate marriage.[113] Parson James Woodforde married several reluctant men in Castle Cary; one in 1769 'came handbolted to Church for fear of running away'. In 1787, 'The Man was a long time before he could be prevailed on to marry her when in the church Yard; and at the Altar behaved very unbecoming.'[114]

However, many parish authorities, increasingly preoccupied with the costs of poor relief, discouraged pauper marriages.[115] They sought to prevent responsibility for 'a brood of legitimate children', who would burden their rates and defraud the 'true poor'. An Essex labourer, Robert Johnson, fathered a 'bastard' but subsequently ran off to London, averring that 'he would have married her [the mother] if the inhabitants would have suffered him'.[116] Parishes might even refuse a married couple the right to cohabit, lest their offspring should prove chargeable. A locally born man might be refused permission to bring his wife into the parish, his neighbours fearing 'he would breed up a charge amongst them'. Such harsh attitudes intensified with the passage of the settlement laws in 1662, and most of the evidence for hostility to pauper marriages originates from that date.[117] While authorities had no legal right to prevent marriages, in practice they could informally withhold housing, or settlement rights.[118]

Occasionally, men were prepared to marry, but the women refused. In a seventeenth-century Cheshire case, a man claimed that he was worth only £5 a year, while the mother of his child not only declined marriage, but refused to contribute anything from her wages as a wet-nurse, so their child was like 'to starve'.[119]

Men lost considerable independence when they fathered children on women who were not their wives, as the law deemed them responsible for maintenance even if they did not or could not marry the mothers.

AFFILIATION, PUNISHMENT, AND MAINTENANCE

So far, we have been considering the various responses of single and married men to their lovers' pregnancies and childbirths. Looming over all were the bastardy laws and Poor Laws which meant that civic authorities could intervene in what men judged to be their own business.[120] The justices and the parish authorities could punish men's sins, and attempt to ensure that they, the 'fathers', paid for their children's maintenance, not the parish ratepayers.

The implications of the public affiliation of a child differed for married and single men. Apart from the public dishonour, an affiliation and maintenance order on a married man placed him in difficulties with his wife, which in some cases he was able to negotiate successfully. In 1714 a Sussex husbandman, who refused to disclose the father of the male child born in his house, was bound with his wife to the parish to maintain the child for ten years on a bond for £50.[121] (It was likely that the husbandman himself was the father.) A single man might feel less dishonour, but he might come under pressure to marry and undertake the responsibilities of a family.

Justices affiliated a child on the basis of a deposition the mother made before or after the child was born, and by the evidence of midwives. It was a complex process.[122] Putative fathers were shadowy figures in these bastardy depositions. Records were usually brief, involved not with attitudes to fatherhood, but with the requirements of the law. Adair found that naming of fathers was more common in the north-west regions in the pre-Civil War period than in the east, where three-quarters of depositions named the mother only.[123] The need to find 'fathers' to pay maintenance intensified when economic conditions worsened. Nevertheless, the justices, recognizing that paternity rested on the words of women, accepted the legal dictum that accused men were 'putative' or 'alleged' fathers only, and usually gave men a sympathetic hearing.[124] In a complex paternity case in Essex in 1601—more than sixteen witnesses were examined at different times—Thomas Carter of White Colne denied any involvement. His lover, Mary Graunte, told a different story, namely that when she informed Carter that she was pregnant, he promised her maintenance provided she concealed him, but if she betrayed him, she would get nothing, and he would grow to dislike her. Carter boasted that he refused to be bridled by any justices, he 'beinge a man bothe of wealth and stomacke'.[125]

A major difficulty for the justices was whether to believe the mother rather than the alleged father. If a man persisted in his claim of innocence, the courts were usually willing to heed him. In October 1700, when James Wellington utterly denied fathering a bastard, the Salop sessions agreed that one of his own nominated midwives should attend the delivery and examine the mother upon oath in the extremity of her labour.[126] Alleged fathers complained that women had used unlicensed midwives, and so had not truly sworn. In a seventeenth-century Staffordshire case, Franch Allen, the alleged father of Elizabeth Edge's second illegitimate child as well as her first, complained that no proper interrogation of the mother had occurred.[127]

Some historians have viewed the father's plight sympathetically, as did the justices: Marchant wrote of the 'commendable reluctance' of justices to order corporal punishment of the reputed fathers on the word of the mother alone.[128] Capp argues that because women could threaten to name men publicly to force them to marry, they might even blackmail 'innocent' men.[129] The Commissioners who set out to reform the Old Poor Laws in 1834 were convinced that women lied, so that under the new law, the mother's oath was automatically doubted, and the onus of proof of paternity shifted to her.[130]

Certainly, there was evidence of false paternity allegations.[131] In 1621, the Dorchester justice Sir Francis Ashley examined the case of Thomasin Valence, who charged a husbandman with being the 'father' of her illegitimate child. Witnesses heard her admit 'that she was fayne to charge Thomas Squib to be the father of her child for that the trew father thereof was to[o] great of bloud to mary her or to be approached for the father'.[132] Ashley recorded another case in which a mother confessed that her false allegation had been prompted by the advice of a widowed midwife, her fellow prisoner in gaol.[133] In 1657, a couple was charged with 'a foule conspiracy' to persuade a woman to charge a woollen draper with being the father of her bastard daughter.[134] Dorothy Marshall cited evidence of single women extorting money from 'perfectly innocent' men in the eighteenth century.[135] However, historians who focus on questions of men's honour divert attention from the practical issue of maintenance: a child was to be provided for.

Physical punishment and public shaming of men for bastardy were more common in the earlier period, and in some areas rather than others.[136] In July 1617, Somerset justices ordered both father and mother to be publicly whipped until their bodies were bloody. Two fiddles were to play, to make known the couple's particular lewdness: they had begotten the base child on the Sabbath day when coming from dancing.[137] Prior to 1640, Marchant found that Lancashire justices would whip both father and mother, while those in Somerset less often subjected men to physical punishment.[138] In practice, Wrightson concluded that Lancashire justices reserved their greatest severity for repeat offenders: one man had fathered seven 'bastards'.[139] In Nottinghamshire in 1623, the father of a 'bastard born and dead' was still ordered to the stocks for two hours.[140] (If the child died, fathers were not liable for maintenance payments.) The 1720 edition of Giles Jacob's manual for justices noted that a father was rarely given corporal punishment, 'unless he is very poor, and not of Ability to indemnify the Parish'.[141] Like single mothers who had limited financial resources, poor men would suffer bodily punishment while wealthier men would escape with fines.

Justices exercised considerable discretion in dealing with alleged fathers. Initially in the seventeenth century, their orders were varied. 'Fathers' were either to take the child and maintain, keep, and provide for it, or pay maintenance.[142] Over the seventeenth century, orders were gradually standardized; increasingly, justices ordered fathers to pay weekly maintenance, and perhaps a sum of money to apprentice the child, or pay a lump sum, all of which was to be administered by the parish officers. Since there was no national scale of maintenance payments, local justices decided the amount to be paid weekly and for how long, as well as the size of a bond, whether it was to be used for the apprenticeship of the child, and whether the 'father' was to reimburse the parish for the mother's lying-in costs and associated expenses. In practice, justices used a combination of orders and punishments. In 1624, a Nottinghamshire yeoman, Henry Wheatley, was ordered to take his child into his keeping, or to pay a nurse 2d. per diem to care for it, and to be set in the stocks.[143] If an affiliated father fled, the justices might authorize the overseers to seize and sell his goods to defray the expenses of maintaining his illegitimate child.[144] By the eighteenth century, there was a more strongly gendered division of parenting labour: 'fathers' paid maintenance while mothers provided nurture. Mothers were rarely ordered to contribute economically unless they did not care for the child.[145]

Walter King, in his study chiefly of Lancashire in the early seventeenth century, concluded that justices were more interested in obtaining maintenance than in punishing, resorting to imprisonment usually only when 'fathers' refused to pay.[146] In the eighteenth century, putative fathers were commonly in trouble for failing to comply with maintenance orders. By the 1733 act, 6 Geo. II c. 31, justices could commit the reputed father to gaol unless he indemnified the parish or entered a recognizance to appear.[147] Men's extra-marital sexual conduct was increasingly bringing them into jeopardy. In contrast with the earlier pattern, by the eighteenth century, imprisonment was more likely to be used against 'fathers' than mothers.[148]

A maintenance order was unwelcome to any man. As Susan Amussen has pointed out, 'Men did everything in their power to avoid paternity accusations'.[149] In 1769, a Kentish parson was frightened by his lover (whom he referred to bitterly as 'Jezabel') for three or four months when she sought his advice about what to do about her pregnancy.[150] James Lackington, an eighteenth-century autobiographer, wrote with bravado of himself as lucky, for although Betty Tucker swore before the justices that he was the father, the baby was stillborn, 'so that I was never troubled for expenses'.[151] In local communities, men who fathered bastards suffered some social ostracism because their sexual activities imposed on their neighbours the burden of supporting their bastards.[152]

Thus parishes and mothers had a strong common interest in finding a man who could afford to pay maintenance for the 'bastard'. Parishes sometimes tried to persuade a mother to name men who could pay, as a 1589 case before the Essex quarter sessions demonstrates. A young servant, Alse Mathewe, admitted a sexual relationship with a 16-year-old fellow servant when she was working for Robert Gosvold of Pentlow, a yeoman. Initially, Alse had named her master as the father, but when questioned by the parish constable and another man, she confessed that Davie was the father, 'a very poor young man and as destitute of friends as herself'. The two parishioners privately urged her 'not to charge such a beggarly fellow with the child but rather such a one as [could keep her] and the child'. They threatened her with a whipping if she did not lie and name her master, encouraging her perjury by citing the case of another 'poor wench' who had perjured herself by falsely charging a neighbour as instructed; the neighbour, rather than 'have his credit be brought in question', paid up very willingly.[153]

The amount of maintenance payments fathers were ordered to pay varied across the parishes of England in the early modern period,

Figure 9 *Woman Swearing a Child to a Grave Citizen* (18th cent.). Here William Hogarth has presented the 'father' as a married man, whose wife berates him for his infidelity. The single woman who is swearing the child's paternity is supported by two men who may have been parish officials keen to transfer the burden of maintaining the illegitimate child to a man capable of paying.

especially in the period before the Civil Wars. The early seventeenth-century Somerset justices clearly varied their orders according to circumstances. In April 1621, they ordered a husbandman to pay 6d. weekly, and the money was to be reserved so his 'bastard' could be apprenticed. (The mother was to be whipped and to keep the child without any allowance.)[154] Other fathers were bound to pay various sums, such as 8d. weekly, or 14d. weekly.[155] Even in the eighteenth century, despite the legal decisions on appeal to King's Bench, magistrates continued to use their discretion,[156] although by 1800, standard weekly maintenance orders were usually 1s. 6d. to 2s.[157] Payments should be put in context. Men received higher wages than women, so could more easily earn a sum such as 1s.; it was a smaller proportion of a male's wage than of a female's, and a mother, of course, had to arrange childcare in addition to earning an income.

Justices varied the length of time for which 'fathers' were to pay. In 1619, George Rodbert was ordered to pay 10d. weekly for his base daughter, Mary, until she was 12 years old, and to give a bond with sureties for £20.[158] In a Norfolk case in the late Elizabethan period, a father was ordered to pay 16d. weekly until the child was 12 years of age.[159] In the earlier period, parishes often tried to extract 10 to 14 years of support from the alleged fathers;[160] later, support was for shorter periods. In 1687, a Portsmouth father's weekly payments were 'untill the age of eight'.[161] By the eighteenth century, the judges of King's Bench (to whom Poor Law appeals were made) thought that fathers should maintain children until 9 years of age, before which they could not be expected to provide for themselves.[162] In practice, as Pam Sharpe's study of parish apprentices in Colyton has shown, the most common age for apprenticing out children was after they were 8 years old.[163] Even so, the maintenance of a child until he or she was 8 years old was a heavy burden for a labouring man, making his own prospects of marriage more remote. Of course, maintenance could be demanded only so long as the child was chargeable.[164] If the child were apprenticed out, or died, the father would be acquitted from further payments.[165]

Men were also liable for lying-in costs, which could be considerable. For example, in Oxford in 1687, the expenses for the lying-in and sickness of Elizabeth Smith, a single woman, amounted to £9. 3s. 6d, a large sum for a labouring man to pay.[166] Again, costs varied. In 1732, the Hackney petty sessions ordered a payment of 38s. to Mary Kirby for nursing and maintaining Elizabeth George for four weeks' lying-in and for the care of her and her daughter.[167] In 1800, a Yorkshire father was ordered to pay 4s. towards lying-in costs and 2s. 6d. weekly so long as the child was chargeable.[168]

Paternal payments could be adjusted, at the behest of both parishes and fathers. In Warwickshire in 1661, the inhabitants of Allesley complained that since the mother of the child had run away making the parish liable for all the costs, 12d. weekly was too small a sum from the affiliated father; the justices ordered that a greater weekly allowance be considered.[169] In 1655, the Norfolk sessions considered the case of Leah Baker's illegitimate child. Leah had maintained it for seven years, but since she had fled, the justices ordered the reputed father to pay 40s., then 6s. 8d. maintenance weekly until the child was 10 years old, and afterwards £20 towards an apprenticeship. The sums involved suggest a more prosperous father, but he refused to pay, and so he was gaoled.[170] In 1647, Clement Caswell petitioned for maintenance relief, claiming that he had paid 2s. weekly until three years previously, had suffered losses, and besides, he added, Agnes Bull had subsequently borne another base child and never been punished.[171] Payments were also adjusted according to the child's age. In 1650, the Norfolk quarter sessions ordered Joseph Chapman to pay 2s. weekly to the overseers at first, then 1s. 6d. until the child was 10 years old, then 1s. until it was apprenticed. (The mother was sent to the House of Correction for a year, so presumably the father's payment was to cover the cost of the foster mother.)[172]

Although 1s. per week (£2. 12s. per annum) over seven years amounted to £18. 4s., no inconsiderable sum, it fell short of what was probably the cost of bringing up a young child. An Oxfordshire testamentary dispute in 1617 turned partly on the cost of raising an illegitimate child. Richard Parratt had died nine years earlier, leaving a bequest of £5 for his illegitimate 4-year-old daughter Mary. The parish refused to take her, because the sum was too small to cover their costs. John Bridge was offered the child for £5 but refused 'because she was too young and the money so litle'; at 3 or 4 years of age, Mary 'was not able to earne or helpe to gett her living'. Two men estimated that the cost of a young child was more like £5 *per annum*. William Parratt (whose relationship to the deceased was not specified) took Mary Parratt into his household, where she was given meat, clothes, and other necessities for about nine years. Perhaps William was the girl's uncle; a witness thought Mary had cost William money of his own.[173] Maintenance was only a *contribution* towards the child's upkeep.

In general, maintenance money was to be paid to the parish authorities, the vestry, or overseers.[174] Some early orders involved a weekly shaming penance, as 'fathers' were to pay their weekly maintenance to the parish officers in church on Sundays. In January 1653, the Essex justices ordered one reputed father either to take the child himself, or make a weekly payment of 1s. 6d. every Sunday in the parish church.[175] As we saw in Chapter 1, Somerset justices ordered both parents to pay weekly at the communion table and publicly 'confesse their faulte and offence'.[176]

Men could be bound over for non-compliance with maintenance orders, and an Act of 1662 allowed overseers to seize the goods of 'the Putative Fathers and lewd Mothers' for the 'bastard' child's maintenance.[177] Legislation of 1733 attempted to make fathers bear the administrative costs of securing maintenance orders.[178] 'Fathers' were required to give bonds to parishes for their payments. All

Hallows Lombard Street required a bond of Mr Deane to save the parish from the charge of Humphery Allhallowes, a young child of around 20 weeks; £10. 5s. per annum was to be paid to Mary Salter, the wife of Edward Salter who had taken charge of the boy.[179] By the eighteenth century, the payment of either a fixed sum or a substantial bond was common. Thus in 1738, one reputed father, a yeoman, gave a bond by which he agreed to maintain, educate, clothe, and bring up his daughter until she could provide for herself.[180] Indeed, payment for alleged paternity seems almost routine. Many 'fathers' made a single payment—often of around £5—to discharge themselves of all responsibility. In London parishes in the 1740s, comparatively few men bothered to appeal: most simply paid up.[181]

But after orders were made, did 'fathers' actually pay? Parishes varied in the effectiveness of their collections. From case studies of parishes in Essex and Yorkshire in the second half of the eighteenth century, Thomas Nutt found a high rate of collection of maintenance, the 'bastardy recovery rate'; between half and two-thirds of the costs were recovered, but the amounts varied regionally. In Sowerby in the West Riding in over 90 per cent of 649 affiliation cases between 1779 and 1834, putative fathers were paying something. But some 'fathers' were simply too poor; they were no different from any other men who found maintenance of children impossible. Nutt concluded that fathers were most likely to comply with orders if employment conditions were good and the maintenance payments relatively small.[182] However, Burn judged that men's ongoing responsibility for maintenance 'as long as it [the child] is or may be chargeable' was a constant grievance.[183]

'Fathers' who refused to obey the justices' orders faced further penalties for non-compliance. In 1611, William Price, a carpenter, was committed to Gatehouse prison until he provided sureties. (He was charged by Alice Hull with begetting her child, and was said to have begotten children on another couple of women earlier.)[184] Men's motives for non-payment were not recorded: typical was the Middlesex sessions order of 1615 which simply recorded that a reputed father who refused to pay 9d. per week maintenance was to be bound over.[185] Justices negotiated men's payments by a combination of threats, orders, and punishments, with varying degrees of success. In another case in 1615, a man who had 'secretly compounded' with a couple for the nursing of his child had been paying 6s. 8d. per month, but after he defaulted, the Middlesex justices ordered that he find sureties, and pay the arrears, or be put in Newgate.[186] If an absconding father was of some substance, justices might seek payment from his estate. In 1665 in Warwickshire, the justices ordered that an annuity of 40s. belonging to an alleged father be paid to the parish for the child's maintenance.[187] Justices issued warrants against defaulters: in 1744, justice William Hunt issued a warrant against James Damor for a bastard child;[188] another against James Nalmer in 1746 on the complaint of the parish officers of Market Lavington that he refused to pay 1s. per week for the maintenance of his 'male bastard child'.[189] Examples abound throughout the early modern period.

In the absence of paternal payments, some parishes attempted to extract support from men's kin, despite the legal fiction that the child was fatherless and therefore lacked a family. Whereas the justices had resolved that a reputed grandfather was not liable for the relief of his illegitimate grandchild, because a bastard was *filius nullius*, in Charles II's reign the chief justice in King's Bench resolved on appeal that it was reasonable that a grandfather contribute to maintenance if he could.[190] In 1773, Margaret Williams applied to the Foundling Hospital as the paternal grandmother of an illegitimate child aged 3 months. Her son was an apprentice, 'and has the Misfortune to have A Child Laid to his Charge Witch I have Supported from its Birth'; 'the Mother of the Child is Gone Away'.[191]

In the seventeenth century, some parishes required men to take direct responsibility for raising their children. Thus in Nottingham in 1604, Mary Arnold was ordered to keep her bastard son until he was 6 months old, then the reputed father was to receive him, 'and bring him up at his own expense'. (Mary was to be whipped three times.)[192] In the Shropshire parish of Shifnal, the justices ordered the overseers to deliver a bastard child aged around 10 years to the father.[193] It is unclear in this instance (as in many other cases) whether these 'fathers' were married men with households. How such children were treated we do not know. The gossip about the 6-year-old Vernery boy in Devon—he 'went without hose or shooe'—suggests that he was not well cared for. In a Norwich case in 1600, authorities wrote to an alleged father 'to keep his bastard at the town of Cringleford and not suffer him to run roguing about'.[194] At the end of the seventeenth century, the Lancashire justices rarely placed illegitimate children with their fathers.[195] They may have feared ill-usage, hearing stories of fathers disposing of unwanted children. By the early nineteenth century, Nutt found that the Essex Bench would not allow 'fathers' to take their children until they were 7 years old. In one instance in 1828, a mother refused her consent to the father having their 9-year-old; 'indignant at the brutal attempt to deprive her of her child only 9 years of age', she agreed to maintain it herself.[196] In many of these cases, the sex of the child is unclear; it may be that boys were more commonly sent to 'fathers'. Certainly, by the early nineteenth century, contemporaries would have judged that any boy or girl over 7 years of age was capable of contributing to its own keep.

People's attitudes to escaping fathers were coloured by family loyalties and economic considerations. The fathers and mothers of the pregnant woman were resentful while the parents of 'fathers' might be pleased to see them escape. Ratepayers had an interest in affiliated fathers paying maintenance, although ties of friendship or kinship might cut across this concern as they did in a Dorset case of 1623. A tithingman of Yetminster was entrusted with a reputed father, Edmond Chub, but had allowed him to escape, 'and refused to raise the hue and cry after him on the grounds that he was not a felon'.[197] 'Fathers' strongly objected to being pursued by their neighbours for the consequences of their sexual conduct and to being treated like felons for their defaults.

SURROGATE FATHERS

What of men who became stepfathers to base-born children? Evidence is limited. Men who married pregnant women may not have been the fathers, though they were legally deemed so, as were husbands whose wives committed adultery. Communities gossiped about suspected illegitimacy. Anne Travis claimed that her neighbour's son was the bastard of William Carricke for 'he was as like him as yf he had beene spatt out of his mouth'.[198] Furthermore, we know that many women with illegitimate children subsequently married, but not always the children's fathers. Some of the mothers' petitions to the London Foundling Hospital for the return of children stated that they had married, and that their new husbands were prepared to accept the child: in 1764, one mother petitioned for her 7-year-old, who 'was born previous to their marriage, Mr Barnes is not the father: But he is willing to support it, he bears a good Character'.[199] Not all husbands were willing. In Essex in January 1655, when his new wife's illegitimate child was brought to Robert Lawrence, he 'avoyded himselfe', thereby preventing the delivery of the child who was then left to the determinations of the parish overseers of Bocking.[200] A mother with children, whether illegitimate or not, was a potential burden on her new husband's parish, so no parish authorities tried to force stepfathers to accept the children.

Illegitimate children lacking fathers were more likely than legitimate children to be 'abandoned' for others to care for. Child abandonments, as Laura Gowing has argued, were collective events, and many people were usually involved.[201] Public authorities who undertook any parenting roles towards apparently abandoned children saw themselves in the guise of foster fathers. As the preacher of a charity sermon explained in 1708, God had made charitable men to take the place 'of Foster-Fathers to these exposed Innocents; to take them up when they were in danger of perishing' and rescue them from ignorance.[202] Mothers appealing to the governors of the Foundling Hospital might beg their 'Fatherly Care'.[203] Parishes frequently baptized foundlings with the surname of the parish: Ann Alban, for example, was named in 1643 after the London parish of St Alban Wood Street,[204] and St Christopher Le Stocks likewise gave girls and boys their surname from the parish name of Christopher.[205] As we shall see in Chapter 5, 'civic fathers' exercised increasing influence over illegitimate and poor children in the early modern period.

Individual men might become recognized as the social fathers of foundlings by various informal processes. (The only formal adoption process at this date involved the adoption of kin as heirs.) Men took in children whose status—'bastard' or legitimate—was unknown.[206] A man who was 'noe Relation' might care for a child, as did one Londoner for a lad, saying 'what he doth is purely for God'.[207] In 1650, after an explosion in the city killed an estimated sixty-seven people, a child in a cradle was blown onto the church roof. No kin could be found, so a charitable neighbour took the child in and named her Mary Aylmer.[208] Around 1709, a justice of the peace rescued a girl whose uncle had attempted to murder her. He kept her himself and 'loves it *as if it were his own*: for he has no Children himself'.[209] Even a woman might be permitted to adopt. In 1564, the Governors of Christ's Hospital placed the 7-year-old Elisabeth Trotter, a skinner's daughter, with Elizabeth Skollaker 'which child she hath taken as her own'.[210] The tradition of childless men taking in a child and caring for it 'as if it were his own' was kept alive in ballads and stories. Thus, in an early eighteenth-century story, a man who found an infant starving to death in a tree took it home to his wife:

> '(Quoth he) This Child from fatal Doom
> I happily did save it,
> Therefore I'll keep it as my own,
> Since I have none beside it:
> Tho' such a thing is seldom known,
> I will support and guide it.'[211]

Informal adoptions might receive some formal sanction. In 1630, a poor woman in Nottinghamshire took a child initially for a quarterly payment of 16d., then later discharged the town for a payment of 2s. 6d.[212] The parish of All Hallows Lombard Street took bonds from couples who were prepared to take responsibility for children. In 1699, John Barnard undertook to indemnify his parish for £10 if the child Mary, who was 'nursed and brought up by them the said John and Mary his wife for the said parish since the time of leaving it there' should be any burden to the parish.[213]

Wet-nurses and their husbands often wanted to keep the children, although parishes might object, fearing liability. Ann Stoaks wrote to the Shrewsbury committee of the Foundling Hospital in 1767, asking if she and her husband could take back the child Bernard Harris, whom they had cared for since he was a month old: they missed him. Her husband, she stated, earned 11s. a week as a paper-maker, and would teach Bernard the same trade.[214] Bernard was lucky: his foster-parents were attached to him and the parish apparently accepted the arrangement. But generally, illegitimate children lacked opportunities to form close emotional bonds with any father figures. Sometimes it is quite unclear who had looked after children. In 1784, Devon authorities examined a 12-year-old girl, termed 'a single woman . . . a vagrant . . . [who] saith she has neither father nor mother, nor knows where she was born'.[215]

Some stories, like that of Mary Monsloe with which this book began, tell of secret adoptions: the single mother relinquished her child, and the boy was transformed into a son and heir, as though he were part of an unexceptional nuclear family. But of course there was an explosive secret at the heart of this family's life known to the adopting mother but not the adopting father. While we cannot, of course, know what secrets other apparently 'normal' nuclear families kept hidden, it is as well to remember the possibilities.

THE 'NATURAL' FEELINGS OF FATHERS

Fatherly love was a principle of natural law, according to Blackstone, so strong that a father who beat his son's assailant to death was guilty of only manslaughter: such was the indulgence the law showed 'to the frailty of human nature, and the workings of paternal affection'.[216] Yet as we have seen, 'the workings of paternal affection' were different if the children were illegitimate. No one really expected men to love their illicit offspring. In his legal treatise of 1805, Michael Nolan wrote critically of such a 'father' who rid himself of his child: he 'may sell him, or make away with him, as too often happens'.[217]

Single fatherhood was a contradiction in terms, and virtually impossible in early modern England. A single father did not exist according to common law and had no social role: a father was a married man, head of a household. The Poor Laws gave men no authority over their illegitimate children. Their sole responsibility for children likely to be chargeable was for maintenance, which caricatured a father's role. Records relating to affiliation and maintenance payments are difficult to read for evidence about affection; as Thomas Nutt has argued, if a man failed to comply with an affiliation order, this does not mean that he rejected the burdens of fatherhood altogether.[218] Economics may have dictated his response.

Indirect seventeenth-century evidence indicates that some men were interested in their lovers' pregnancies. In 1682, a Yorkshire servant, mother of twins, blamed her mistress for their deaths at birth; she claimed that her lover 'did not wish her to make away her bairn when he got it but said he would keep it'.[219] Mary Witby, who abandoned her baby at Newport in 1615, said that her master, who was the father, would be glad of 'a man child' because he had none of his own. Since a maintenance order was later cancelled, we know no more of the case.[220] Fragments reveal fatherly attachment. A 1675 case which came before the Old Bailey saw two men sentenced to death. One, named only by his initials, L. O., had a great love in his life; instead of working, he took 'evil Courses' for 'the Maintenance of the Mother and the Child . . . his idleness not permitting him to take any better'. Under sentence of death, he reportedly 'desires his Friends to see her and bid her be careful of the Infant'.[221]

Those who begot children outside wedlock left little first-person testimony. Bastardy depositions focused on the relationship and sexual history of the couple only to determine responsibility for maintenance.[222] Nothing invited men to reflect upon their paternal duties or feelings. Perhaps those who could afford to make their own arrangements for their offspring fitted Augustine's observation: while no men desired bastards, they were usually fond of them after they were born.[223] In a similar vein, Richard Burn suggested that those fathers who acknowledged their children in some way were more likely to have had affection for them.[224]

Some men had little kindness for their illegitimate offspring. In Cumberland, from 1740 George Gibson gave maintenance money to Ann Moan but two years later, he asked Ann for their daughter, saying that his mother would care for her. Ann refused, they quarrelled, and Gibson admitted hitting her. When mother and child drowned in a dike gutter, Gibson was found guilty of their murder.[225] Ann may have suspected that Gibson had murderous intentions; he may have sought to be relieved of the cost of maintenance, so his attitude may have been only indirectly infanticidal. Or he may have loved the child and wanted her with his own family; we do not know.

Predictably, only married men or fathers who passed as married, either in long-term *de facto* or bigamous relationships, are mentioned in connection with older illegitimate children. Very occasionally, records of 'bastards' surface in their father's households, especially if men were higher in the social scale. In rural communities, fathers no doubt remained the subject of gossip, as did John Vernery and his curly haired boy, but at least the children may have had some connection with their fathers. The west and north-west regions seemed more accepting of illegitimacy than the south and the east.[226]

We know from wills that some wealthier fathers left bequests to their illegitimate children who may have been poor. In Hawkshead, Lancashire, a gentleman, William Braithwaite, remembered three illegitimate children in his will together with three legitimate children; perhaps they lived in his household.[227] In a study of wills in north-east Lancashire, John Swain found that 17 per cent of his sample mentioned bastards. However, these were not the wills of the poorest men; many testators had at least £40 in personal estate.[228] Swain argued that there were high levels of illegitimacy judging both from the baptism records—1 in 8 in the period 1600–40—and from the amount of attention devoted to illegitimacy in the quarter session records—57 per cent of the sessions' business in the period 1626–42 was bastardy. These findings offer further evidence that estimates of bastardy rates may be too low.[229] Although there is no indication that all these records related to poor men who fathered illegitimate children, they do show that some men felt responsibility and even affection for their illegitimate offspring. The presence (or absence) of legitimate sons in a family may have affected a father's attitude, and a boy's relationships with his *de facto* stepmother and his legitimate half-siblings.

Moral attitudes towards illegitimate children fluctuated over the early modern period. The bastardy laws and the Poor Laws increasingly affected attitudes towards men's paternal responsibilities for their children who were both illegitimate and poor. In higher social circles, a more indulgent code operated; illicit sexuality and fathering a 'bastard' child could be a matter of pride, attesting to male virility, the subject even of boasts and jokes.[230] However, before 1660, many parishes were influenced by the more zealous morality of those termed Puritans. Under the Commonwealth, they attempted to impose a stricter code of sexual morality.[231] Even so, there was a double standard: Stuart legislators who fulminated against the dishonour to God from 'lewd Mothers' referred only to 'Putative Fathers'.[232] In most churches, including Nonconformist ones, there was pressure on men to marry their pregnant lovers. By the eighteenth century, people knew that 'bastards' cost ratepayers money; fathering a bastard may have attracted some contempt. But fathers and mothers of illegitimate children were on a see-saw, mother up for censure at one date, then father. If women were more heavily censured in the earlier period, by 1800 'fathers' were likely to be viewed as dishonourable since notions of weak womanhood cast men in the role of villains, responsible for seductions. As Hunter explained in 1784, 'the mother is weak, credulous, and deluded', so her seducer left her to 'compleat *ruin* for *life*'.[233] Attitudes to sexual morality were always strongly affected by class and by notions of the complementarity of gender roles.

Having a father meant comparatively little to illegitimate children unless their parents cohabited and 'passed' as married. Since society accepted such families as legitimate, men were able to perform the role of fathers, maintaining, nurturing, training, and loving their sons and daughters. Such fathers brought up their children much as did other poor men.

CONCLUSIONS

Over the period 1580–1800, men whose illicit sexuality resulted in the births of children liable to be a burden on the parish rates found themselves in a disagreeable situation. An increasing proportion of brides who were pregnant suggests that many men did honour their promises and marry after sexual relations during courtship resulted in pregnancies. But men who were married already, or could not afford to marry, or refused to do so, found themselves in trouble. Before the Civil Wars, depending on the area in which they lived, they faced the threat of corporal punishment as well as demands for maintenance. Private arrangements with the mother might keep the matter hushed up, but if 'fathers' defaulted on paying maintenance, they were increasingly likely to find the justices and their former lovers in league against them. By the eighteenth century, their attempts to evade responsibility subjected them to penalties for disobeying orders. Whereas earlier magistrates were prepared to take a sympathetic view of their denials of paternity, later authorities were less concerned with men's innocence or guilt than in finding a man who could pay maintenance, and so absolve the parish ratepayers. By the later eighteenth century, authorities were more determined to make 'fathers' pay maintenance than to punish mothers. When the Poor Laws were reformed in 1834, the situation was reversed. The Commissioners were convinced that women lied about paternity, so the onus of proof was placed on mothers, allowing men to evade responsibility.

The overwhelming impression from the evidence discussed here is of the complexity of individual circumstances. Under the labels of 'fathers' and 'bastards' lie human stories of varying degrees of unhappiness. There seems little in the records about fathers' relationships with their illegitimate children. Most illegitimate children grew up knowing only mothers and their kin, and even then, the parish removed many children to other households once they turned 7 years. Children's own impoverished lives were made worse by the absence of a father's wages in their household; they usually lived in small households which were more likely to break up. Their experience of paternal authority came from the parish overseers and the more distant justices. Social attitudes towards illegitimacy were negative; children were of 'base blood', and were made to feel their inferiority. They grew up in a world where they observed men rejecting and deserting their illegitimate offspring.

3

BRINGING UP A CHILD

the care & labour common to rearing a family

Benjamin Shaw[1]

Many early modern parents complained of poverty. Even the wealthiest could find themselves short of cash to set up their younger sons or to provide portions for daughters. An improvident heir could go through the savings of generations, and speedily reduce a family to 'ruine and destruction'.[2] A peer's widow might write of 'how little a Pittance I haue made Shift to liue uppon' so as to help her children.[3] Such poverty was relative rather than absolute. More troubling even to middling status mothers and fathers was the prospect of struggling to provide food, clothing, shelter, and training for their sons and daughters. Parents were haunted by fears that businesses might fail, and families be plunged into poverty by an adverse turn of fortune's wheel, or the judgment of God.[4] As a great example 'of fortune's mutability', Gervase Holles recounted a story of Francis Holles, son of a close kinsman of the first earl of Clare, orphaned as a little boy, 'forced to beg his bread in the streetes amongst other poor children'.[5] A 'black sheep' of the Ferrar family, Richard Ferrar, wrote from London in 1636 begging help from his family at Little Gidding, without which he would have to turn to the parish. Nicholas Ferrar allowed his brother three shillings a week for himself, his wife, and two children.[6]

Such tales circulated among the more prosperous, warning men of the dangers of economic life, and of moral failings such as drink, gambling, and debt, and cautioning women against illicit sexuality and extravagance. But what of those who were born into labouring families and had limited means when they married and became parents? The daughters and sons of at least a third of the population lived on the margins of poverty all their lives. Becoming parents themselves, they faced a lifelong struggle to provide basic needs; they knew that the birth of each child spread their few resources more thinly. Children also restricted mothers' ability to undertake paid employment. Poor parents were vulnerable to any bad harvest, or downturn in trade, as well as to personal misfortunes such as sickness or death. Experiences of poor families varied temporally and spatially, between urban and rural, and between regions. The poor in the countryside experienced hard times when harvests failed, as in the 1590s, 1620s and 1630s, and 1690s,[7] or when the trade in woollen cloth was interrupted and spinners and weavers were not needed. Over the early modern period, changes in farming reduced the number of young people who worked as live-in servants, and enclosures in the eighteenth century affected the economy of those who depended on common rights. Meanwhile, London grew exponentially, and the poor crowded into poorly built housing, where disease and malnutrition took a toll.

Poor families lacked resources and therefore were the most vulnerable to failures of health, and to mortality. Economic misfortunes as well as deaths led to re-partnering, remarriages, and complex family structures. Poor children were more likely to have stepparents, as a result of either remarriages or cohabitation. Children who lived in such households had varying fortunes, depending on whether it was their father or mother who had remarried or informally cohabited. There is no single story about poor parents; not all poor families were alike. Many were more like fragments of disparate families, in which some children were legitimate and others not, and there were stepchildren who, as a result of serial remarriages, were biologically unrelated to either parent.

This chapter focuses on how poor mothers and fathers raised their children, and on what they understood their parental duties to be. It discusses how material circumstances affected their capacity to be good mothers and fathers, and attempts to examine what they and their neighbours considered to be a 'good' parent. Much of this account applies to the parenting of illegitimate children as well. In neighbourhoods, the legal status of children was often unclear. By the early eighteenth century, all single parents and their children were a charge on the parish, accounting, in the case of two London parishes, for upwards of 30 per cent of their total expenditure.[8]

Children here are those up until around what I term their 'social adolescence', when they left home for the semi-independence of service or pauper apprenticeships. Historians have found that the children of the poor left home earlier than most, at any age between 7 or 8 years and their late teens. We cannot always assume that there was a 'home' which these young people left; 'family economies' of the poor may have disintegrated by the time children reached adolescence. The next chapter looks more closely at parents' strategies in severe poverty.

Although we lack the letters, diaries, and autobiographies which reveal details about élite and middling mothers' and fathers' relationships with their offspring, records created by the administration of the Poor Laws and of charitable relief can be used to give some account of the experiences of poor parents and their children. Of course there are limitations to an understanding based on Poor Law records, not least because much of the experience of poor parents falls outside the net of parish relief. The Poor Laws were of limited relevance to all who lacked a 'settlement', the crucial entitlement to parish relief. Such parents had to use initiatives including migration and fragmenting their families in order to survive. Increasingly, the Poor Laws rigidified distinctions between good and bad poor. Fathers and mothers who could not maintain their children without assistance were liable to be censured as morally bad. In addition, as the élite and middling sort became more preoccupied with childhood as a state of innocence deserving protection, judgements of poor parents who apparently failed were more severe.[9]

Many historians have accepted those contemporary judgements uncritically and viewed poor parents, especially mothers, as deficient. Even a recent account of child murder argues that court cases 'reflect the scant value placed on the lives of infants in Georgian England. For some women in impoverished circumstances, children were seen as expendable.'[10] Counter to such views, this chapter offers evidence about the substantial time, effort, and sacrifice involved in raising children, arguing that poverty, rather than lack of commitment, characterized parenting at the lowest levels of society.

FAMILY FORMATION

During the early modern period, the age at marriage dropped. Whereas around 1600, most men married for the first time around 28 years, and women under 26 years, by the second half of the eighteenth century, men married at just under 26, and women around 24.[11] Many women were pregnant at marriage; roughly one-fifth in the seventeenth century, and two-fifths in the eighteenth.[12] Indeed, in the eighteenth century, the margin between married and single parents blurred, as premarital pregnancy rates rose. By 1800, half the first babies born were conceived out of wedlock, although in nearly 40 per cent of instances, the parents married before the child was born.[13]

Thus, pretty soon after marriage, the labouring poor had a family of young children. After the first birth, children were born at intervals of roughly every two years. Infant and child mortality rates were high; in the first fifty years of the eighteenth century, children under 10 years were more vulnerable than in any other fifty-year period between 1550 and 1800.[14] Within this broad general pattern of family formation, there were marked regional and individual variations. All over England, at different times, the relationship between wages and prices affected poor families. As Eden observed in his late eighteenth-century survey, in every district, there was 'a variety of complicated circumstances'.[15] A common feature, however, was that a few years after marriage, poverty was deepest because there were a number of young, dependent children who required a mother's care which prevented her from working.

Deaths fragmented poor families, although maternal mortality in childbirth improved after the mid-seventeenth century: of women who died in the age group 24–34 years, maternal mortality accounted for one in five deaths. Whereas maternal mortality rose from 1600 to a peak in the years 1650–74 of 17.0 per 1,000 live births, thereafter it fell, to nearly half—9.0 per 1,000—in the last quarter of the eighteenth century.[16] Many women suffered ill-health as a consequence of pregnancy and complications of childbirth. Many fathers died before their children reached an age when they might work for their own support. In Elizabethan Rye, nearly 60 per cent of fathers who died left children under 14 years of age.[17] Improvements in adult mortality in the first half of the eighteenth century lessened a child's risk of being orphaned. Improved mortality also raised the ages at which widowhood occurred, thus reducing the percentage of marriages in which one parent was widowed. Many parents were stepparents, affecting family dynamics, although children in the eighteenth century were less likely to have a stepparent than earlier.[18]

Although family size might ultimately be comparatively small—four or five children—each new birth tested maternal strength and stretched parental resources.[19] John Clare (1793–1864), the eldest of four children, two of whom died in infancy, judged that his parents 'had the good fate to have but a small family'.[20] The unusually detailed autobiography of Benjamin Shaw, a mechanic in the north of England, offers a case study of a poor family over four generations in the eighteenth and early nineteenth centuries. Childless couples, Benjamin reflected, 'led a life of Liberty without much care',[21] while he, his parents, and grandparents, struggled with unemployment, cold, and the cost of children: 'my father began to feel the effects of a growing family.'[22] Benjamin's aunt was lucky, as she and her husband had only one daughter, and so enjoyed marriage 'without much of the care & labour common to rearing a family'.[23]

Additional births could increase marital tensions. In 1735, a witness at a murder trial at the Old Bailey heard Charles Conyer, the husband of her neighbour Isabel who had just given birth, demanding 'how she [Isabel] thought he could maintain her and her four Children'. The relationships in this case are not clear: there was talk of 'his' 6-year-old son, and Isabel may have been a second wife. Nevertheless, Conyer was clearly angry and upset at the prospect of providing for yet another child.[24]

While poor fathers were expected to provide for families, their wages were usually inadequate, and so, in addition to nurturing children, mothers were required to undertake paid employment. The work of mothers thus had two aspects, but medieval and early modern historians have, for the most part, declined to incorporate maternity into their analyses of women's working lives. Alice Clark's projected study of 'the joys and responsibilities of motherhood', which she considered inseparable from women's productive lives, was never written.[25] Marjorie McIntosh begins her wonderful study of working women's lives across the medieval/early modern divide with a discussion of motherhood, but she deliberately excluded it from her analysis.[26] Thus the work of motherhood again escapes historical analysis, and is left in a timeless ethnographic present. However, if we separate social motherhood from the genetic and gestational aspects of maternity, we can move away from biological essentialism and understand more about motherhood in its specific historical context. In early modern England, the paid employment mothers undertook was an essential part of their maternal work. They needed money to supplement the inadequate or possibly nonexistent wages of their husbands or partners. Most poor mothers undertook the care of their own children, unless they were so destitute that they were forced to 'abandon' them for others to care for.

The material base for most ordinary fathers and mothers was so limited that the meaning of 'family' differed from that understood by the wealthy. Since the labouring poor generally married comparatively late and mortality rates were high, many never lived to be grandparents. Indeed, for Rye, around the early seventeenth century from,

Mayhew calculated that the mean length of marriage was only around 13 years, with marriages lasting around 15 years among the wealthier couples, but only about 10 years among the poor. Thus many poor fathers and mothers would never see their children reach 10 years of age.[27]

MATERIAL NEEDS: FOOD, CLOTHING, HOUSING, AND HEALTH

'...Poor Labouring People that have many Children, and make a hard shift to sustain them by their Industry'.[28]

Fathers and mothers knew that children required food, clothing, and housing. Boys' and girls' needs varied according to age. Evidence from different time periods and regions reveals something of the range of parental practices and experiences. However, while the struggles of poor parents to provide for their children were constant, they took place in a society in which material goods were making life more comfortable and pleasant for those who could afford to consume them. Although the range of household goods owned by the labouring poor increased in the eighteenth century, so too did their disadvantages relative to their social superiors.[29]

The pregnancies of poor mothers were less a time of indulgence than for women at higher levels of society. All mothers were thought to feed their unborn children with their blood, and they shared many beliefs about their pregnancy, such as about the harmful effects of maternal imagination on the foetus.[30] Midwives frequently had a clientele across social levels, though as we have seen many single mothers gave birth without attendants. The elaborate ceremonies associated with childbirth were absent from the births of poor labouring women and single mothers, but even among the labouring poor there were celebrations at christenings.[31]

Motherhood was corporeal, bodily work, and for much of their married lives, poor women were pregnant, lactating, and child-rearing. Mothers suckled their infants with their milk, which many understood to be simply blood turned white.[32] Breastfeeding was a touchstone of maternal goodness (though not for those aristocrats or gentlewomen wealthy enough to employ wet-nurses), so in the seventeenth century, mothers who refused to breastfeed their babies were censured. Poor mothers had little choice: they could rarely earn enough to pay a wet-nurse. Whereas aristocrats and gentlewomen were generally esteemed for the number of children, especially sons, whom they bore, the birth of an extra child to a poor mother was not always a matter for rejoicing.

Even breastfeeding may have been difficult for malnourished mothers; in 1740, some infants admitted to the Foundling Hospital were starved, almost too weak to suck, and others seemed 'Stupifyed with some Opiate'.[33] Nevertheless, the family reconstitution studies of the Cambridge Group for the History of Population and Social Structure indicate that women normally breast-fed their children for eighteen months or more, and suggest that poorer women may have suckled their children for longer, as breast-milk was a cheaper alternative to purchased food.[34] If a mother was employed, or could not breastfeed her infant, then the cost of a wet-nurse was higher than the cost for the care for older children. Contemporary physicians were aware that many poor women worked as wet-nurses, with sad consequences for their own infants.[35] Wet-nurses were especially liable for condemnation if their charges died.[36]

A female lore about child-rearing drew upon natural remedies and popular beliefs.[37] Breast-feeding women required good food: they should 'feed on good nourishment', explained Jane Sharp in 1671. While 'good wholesome meats and drinks' would increase milk, a woman could diminish her milk by slender diet.[38] 'Mothers who do not eat enough of solid food', advised William Buchan in 1769, could not provide 'proper nourishment to an infant'.[39] In a case of spousal murder before the Old Bailey in 1722, the marital dispute had erupted because Hannah Brinsden, a breast-feeding mother, wanted better food. She was sitting on the bed 'suckling her Child', and asked her husband for supper. Matthias said that supper was 'Bread and Cheese, can't you eat that as well as the Children?', but Hannah insisted that she wanted meat, although Matthias said he had 'no money' to buy any. He killed her with the bread knife.[40]

Providing meals was usually mothers' work, and a weaned infant competed for scarce food resources; we do not know whether mothers breast-fed sons longer than daughters. Mothers needed cash to purchase food especially in towns and cities. Diet varied in summer and winter as well as between town and country. Archer estimates that in Elizabethan London, a minimal daily requirement for food was around 1¼d. in the 1580s, rising to 2d. in the 1590s. In 1587, York authorities thought that 'a pore creator' could not live under 1½d. per day.[41] Alice Clark estimated that during the

Figure 10 *A child being taught to walk* (*c.*1635–7). In this charming chalk drawing, Rembrandt van Rijn pictured two women supporting a child while it learns to walk. The child wears a protective 'roller' on its head in case of falls.

seventeenth century, food for a child cost between 1s. to 1s. 6d. per week, depending on their ages.[42] Boulton calculated that London costs doubled in the seventeenth century.[43] In the 1690s, Gregory King estimated that expenditure in the whole kingdom was 16s. 5d. per head per week, while by the 1730s, an observer thought that the diet of a poor family cost 22s. 7.5d. per week per head, compared with 50s. 5od. for a middling family.[44] Bread featured largely in the diets of the poor in the south, supplemented in the north in the eighteenth century by milk, oatmeal, and potatoes.[45] The pleas of social reformers give a glimpse of how poor families fed: in 1650, Samuel Hartlib wrote of poor women who begged 'with little Children in their armes and hands, for bread, and broth, and beere . . . the chiefest things that children feed upon'. In the countryside, the very poor ate bread and pottage with roots in winter, and bread with herbs (salad) but not butter or cheese, in summer.[46]

The diet poor mothers provided may have been less monotonous than some institutional records suggest. Even at the Foundling Hospital children ate a variety of seasonal fruits and vegetables; indeed, McClure considered that foundlings had a better diet than those who lived with their parents.[47] Joan Thirsk's recent study demonstrates the extraordinary variety of diet in the rural areas, where food would have been fresher and more flavoursome. Some contemporaries thought that the diet of the poor was healthful, although they judged that those in London made poor food choices, preferring bread and butter and cheese to nourishing soups. While Gregory King thought that half the population never ate meat, Thirsk points out that all the wild birds of the sky were regarded as sources of meat. A skilful boy with a sling could contribute to his family's diet. Mothers transformed somewhat uninspiring ingredients into economical and tasty meals.[48]

In the debate over the standard of living in the eighteenth century, historians have used anthropometric data to determine children's nutritional status.[49] Studies of the heights of soldiers and of poor boys who entered the Marine Society in the 1770s revealed that adolescent boys were generally of small stature.[50] In 1744, the Navy Board required that children working in the dockyards should be 5 feet high, and if not, aged 16 years.[51] So far, no measures for female adolescent nutrition have been found. We know that within a family, mothers distributed food unequally, weighing the needs of husbands and fathers against those of individual children, and favouring one child over another. In the eighteenth century, an 'unfortunate husbandman', Charles Varley, complained in his autobiography that his stepmother sent him out into the fields hungry, while she and her children were 'snug and warm at breakfast', and she thrashed him for his thefts of food from the pantry.[52]

In the later eighteenth century, Armstrong, a London physician, criticized the diet ordinary mothers provided: 'many mothers here, amongst the lower sort of people, give fresh meat to their children while they are suckled, and fish'. Furthermore, he continued, they fed their weaned children the same diet as their own, namely beef, mutton, pork, bacon and the like, 'cramming' them with fat.[53] But others thought that the diets of the children of the poor were generally spare; in 1800 tea without milk or sugar was said to be inadequately nutritious to allow children in charity schools to work.[54] Tea, with sugar, unknown in the earlier period, was 'to be met with in most cottages in the southern parts of England' and was thought 'deleterious'.[55]

Miscellaneous evidence suggests that hunger was a common experience in poor families. One Essex father confessed that he had stolen and eaten a sheep in the winter of 1623–4, 'haveinge a wife and seaven smale children'.[56] In the country, some food could be grown, but frequently better food had to be sold for cash to pay rents. In the hard years around 1690, the Nonconformist minister Richard Baxter observed that servants fared better than poor tenants, who 'are glad of a piece of hanged bacon once a week'. Tenants could not afford to eat any eggs, apples, or pears that could be sold; they fed themselves and their children 'with skimd cheese and skimd milke and whey curds'.[57] Older children required more food.

Details about the limited food of poor Londoners surfaces in criminal trials. At a murder trial before the Old Bailey in the late eighteenth century, William Patmore, a staymaker at Mile End, was accused of starving his wife to death. The court asked many questions about the food Patmore provided for his wife, in comparison with how the rest of his family fared. Witnesses spoke of the quantity and quality of the food: of potatoes (only one, and that often rotten), of a thin piece of bread and butter, and of the distribution of a single red herring. Little preparation would be required for such a diet, most of which would have been purchased or scavenged. Although those downstairs fared better than the starving woman in the garret—their food included some meat—several witnesses spoke of Patmore's poverty.[58]

Seeing their children starve caused some parents intolerable anguish, even driving some to murder. In 1749, a mother killed her 3-year-old son because she could not feed him; in 1756, a schoolmaster father claimed that the crying of his 5-year-old son for bread drove him to murder; he realized 'that he would not long have bread to give it'.[59] Rabin argues that in murder cases defendants framed pleas based on 'popular perceptions of mental distress', suggesting that contemporaries found such parental pleas credible.[60]

Domestic advisers agreed that the care of young children 'especially lieth upon the mother'.[61] Keeping infants clean and dry was mothers' work.[62] Newborn children, who cried if they were not kept clean, required more intense work, although the practices of poor mothers are usually documented only when physicians wanted to censure them. Thus in 1797, Underwood urged that infants should be kept clean and dry, rejecting the 'vulgar notion, familiar to common people, that a frequent change of linen has a tendency to weaken new-born children; an absurditie'.[63] More to the point may have been

Figure 11 The Sense of Smell: A father's unpleasant duties (1631). This Dutch painting should not be taken as a reflection of social reality, but it raises questions about fathers' roles in the physical care of children. Whether a poor Englishman's masculinity would have allowed him to undertake the cleaning of a child is questionable. Domestic and medical advisers all judged that the physical care of an infant was women's work which they were expected to know instinctively. Thus in his advice book of 1651, Nicholas Culpeper offered no instructions about toilet training a child.

a comment about the difficulty of washing and drying babies' messy equivalents of nappies.

Clothing children was expensive, usually increasing with the age of the child. Historians consider that poor men would have been hard pressed to feed children, let alone buy new clothing.[64] Parishes in Elizabethan London allowed sums from 8s. to 20s. per annum to clothe a child.[65] An estimate of 5s. to clothe a child in Terling seems low, especially as Boulton suggests that there was inflation in the retail cost of clothing during the seventeenth century.[66] A young child's clothing would cost less than that of an older boy or girl. One London parish in the later eighteenth century allowed 17s. per annum for a child's clothes, a little over half the amount for an adult's (£1. 7s.).[67] Parish overseers in Bedfordshire paid 10s. 7½d. for a girl's gown in the early eighteenth century.[68] Sometimes charity clothing was distinctive in quality and colour, distinguishing the godly poor in rural parishes.[69] In addition to formal bequests, in rural parishes individual charity operated. In the 1790s, Eden's surveys of domestic economy among the poor revealed evidence of children clothed chiefly by the charity of neighbours.[70] Pious women donors usually reserved clothing for the virtuous poor.

Since buying new clothes was beyond the budgets of most poor parents, gifts of clothing were invaluable. Mothers handed down worn clothing and employed their needles to adapting, mending, and patching second-hand garments.[71] They could pawn any clothing in an emergency. Indeed, women ran a thriving trade in second-hand clothing, and even worn old clothing might be pawned or sold. In 1743, when Mary White stripped a 4½-year-old girl of her clothes, she managed to get 6d. for 'an old Pair of Child's Shoes, a little old Shift, a Flannel Petticoat, and an old Skirt'.[72] Poor mothers were always on the look-out for useful items, and some engaged in opportunistic theft. In 1626, Sollesy Axholl, a Devon labourer's wife, admitted taking a table cloth 'which she caused to be cutt to a smock for one of her children'.[73] The boundary between the second-hand clothing trade and theft could easily blur.[74] Shoes for children were a major item, especially necessary in winter. In the north of England, people wore clogs, which were far cheaper.[75]

Clothes mattered partly because contemporaries judged the quality of parental care by the appearance of their children, for which mothers were largely responsible. In 1687, one London free school's rules specified that the children were to be clean and neat, with their faces and hands washed, heads combed and polled.[76] Armstrong, who set up a London dispensary for 'the children of the industrious poor' in the 1760s, would attend only those whose mothers brought their offspring 'clean and decently dressed'.[77] The amount of maternal labour involved in keeping children clean and decent was considerable. If clothing was in short supply, then mothers would have kept children inside while their clothes were washed or mended. There may have been nothing but rags for children to wear if better clothing were pawned. Margaret Spufford judged that the barefooted children dressed in rags came from the section of the population who were so poor that no inventories of their goods were made at death.[78] Even so, some descriptions of the clothing of infants admitted to the Foundling Hospital speak poignantly of maternal care. Three-day-old Jane Cooper was wearing a dark cotton gown, a laced point cap, a biggin, forehead cloth and stays.[79]

It is not clear at what age mothers expected their children to look after their own washing and dressing. In 1766, Hanway asserted that children of 6 or 7 years of age should be taught to keep themselves clean and tidy (which he added required more teaching 'than is consistent with the ignorance and laziness of common nurses').[80] Poor mothers saved themselves time if they trained their children, or they may have enlisted the aid of older children, probably their daughters, to wash and dress the younger ones. Girls were probably not expected to be responsible for their own laundry; an 11-year-old London girl said she did not wash her own linen.[81] Observers increasingly distinguished between parents whom they considered clean, orderly, and sober, and the filthy, drunken, and wretched.[82] Hanway argued that care for clothing enhanced girls' self-respect; if they made and mended their own clothes, it 'has necessarily an influence on morals'.[83]

Parents were responsible for shelter and warmth. The rural poor were usually housed in a small cottage or hovel. Observers noted 'walls of earth, low thatched roofs', or walls of stone and clay, depending on the area and materials available.[84] Defoe told a story of meeting the wife and five children of a lead miner who lived in a cave in Derbyshire.[85] Legislation from 1589 restricted poor parents from building cottages on common or waste land without permission from the justices, or assizes, and landowners.[86] As always, parents who best succeeded were those able to enlist the support of their more prosperous neighbours. Even so, permissions to build were less likely to be granted as the number of poor increased; in Cheshire requests after 1660 were only half as likely to be granted as in the 1620s, and frequently cottages were allowed to stand only while all children in the household were under 16 years of age.[87] The loss of common rights in the eighteenth century further reduced the opportunities for poor families to survive in the countryside, especially in the Midlands.[88] Some impression of the poor living conditions of the rural poor emerges from preachers urging compassion: 'goe and see the miseries of our poore brethren', urged John Rogers in 1629, 'their ruinous & cold houses, poore fire...empty cupboards, thin clothing...; and to see what exceeding paines some take early and late'.[89] Later in the seventeenth century, Richard Baxter made similar observations.[90]

In towns and cities, poor families crowded into tenements in the suburbs rather than the centre. Urban rents were high, and formed a higher proportion of household expenditure than in the rural areas.[91] Many people migrated to London from the provinces and the British Isles in search of work, crowding into the spreading suburbs. London's population grew from around 200,000 in 1600 to over 500,000 in 1700, but slowed around the fourth and fifth decades of the eighteenth century, as the environment deteriorated and diseases spread.[92] In the suburbs of the seventeenth-century city, houses and households were small. Vanessa Harding's detailed analysis of the records of different parishes allows us to understand more about the lived experience of poor families in London. They crowded into alleys and closes behind the main streets; in the poorer parish of St Botolph Aldgate, the number of households in Ship Alley increased from 17 in 1638 to 23 in 1666 as the alley extended and subdivided. There were few lease or probate inventories for St Botolph's, but surveys implied that dwellings were cheaply built. Some people lived in cellars or converted stables, and shared privies and a water supply. A 1695 assessment for Tower Hill precinct, which included St Botolph Aldgate, revealed a mean household size of 3.34 persons, and analysis of housefuls (which included lodgers) showed that 75 per cent contained at least one child. Single parents, among whom were thirty-four women whose marital status was unclear and eleven men, were more likely to be lodgers than householders. Harding concluded that this was 'an extremely atomized society' and families in these crowded areas were fragmented and unstable.[93] Beier documented a similar picture in late sixteenth-century Warwick: in the 1587 census, the mean household size of 3.3 persons, which he termed 'fragments of families' headed by women, was more typical than nuclear families among the poor. Again, many poor households included lodgers.[94]

By the eighteenth century, when more than one poor family might share a single lodging room, a London physician judged this injurious to children's health.[95] Glimpses of family life in crowded London tenements emerge in incidental detail in eighteenth-century Old Bailey cases. In 1789, Mary Ryley lodged in a single room with her husband, a plasterer whose health was 'very bad', and five children. The family went to bed early, 'for we had very little candle or coals, and were much distressed', 'the children so heavy upon me'.[96]

Another mother, Sarah Batty, admitted that sometimes her 15-year-old son and 9-year-old daughter shared a bed: 'They being brother and sister, I did not think any harm'.[97] A shoemaker, John Williamson, his second wife, and three children crowded into one room with a closet, up three flights of stairs.[98]

Historians have tried to estimate how food, clothing, and fuel prices related to labourers' wages and the cost of living at specific times and in specific places. Wrightson and Levine calculated that the total income of an ordinary labouring family in Terling in the seventeenth century was around £15. 12s., assuming that the husband worked six days a week all the year. Underemployment was of course common. Some such figure seems reasonable: Gregory King estimated that a labouring family had a total income of £15 per annum. In the 1690s, Wrightson and Levine calculated that the cost of food for a couple with three children was £9. 4s., clothing £2, rent and fuel £2, amounting in total to £13. 14s. per annum. None of this left any margin for unemployment or sickness.[99] Obviously, costs and opportunities for work varied around the country as well as over time. Boulton calculated that in seventeenth-century London, which was probably atypical—rent may have been a more significant component of household budgets—consumers had to rely on purchased bread rather than grains, and imported coal for fuel. Prices fluctuated, and some decades were harsher than others. Overall, Boulton concluded that difficulties for poor families increased over the seventeenth century.[100]

It is almost impossible to put a figure on the annual cost of a child to parents. No doubt parents budgeted, as did parishes or charities, according to children's ages. In 1589, a Norwich parish paid 1s. 8d. for a week's nursing of 'a yong infant left in the parish'; to mothers, feeding their babies appeared to cost nothing.[101] In the seventeenth century, parishes paid sums varying between £3 and £6 per annum for the care of children, sometimes allowing extra sums for clothing and medical care; parents too were liable for such expenses.[102] In the late seventeenth century the costs for a parish of placing a child under 3 years in the proposed Royal Hospital was at the rate of roughly £5 per annum. Proposed charges for redeeming any child aged from 7 to 10 years was £50, with an extra £10 per annum for a child over 10 years.[103] (These rates may of course have been influenced by the calculation that the labour of a child over 10 years was more valuable.) A later seventeenth-century Cumberland yeoman boarded out children at between 1s. 4d. and 1s. 6d. weekly.[104]

From probate accounts, Amy Erickson estimated that annual costs for children maintained by the parish were not dissimilar from those in more prosperous households: in the seventeenth century costs were around £5 per annum. Rates varied regionally; in Westmoreland boys were boarded for only £4 per annum.[105] Ben-Amos suggested, on the basis of wills and payments by parish authorities, that in the early seventeenth century the cost was £4–£5 per annum for a child, £6 for a youth in their teens.[106] At the end of the eighteenth century, Eden calculated that Westminster parishes paid 3s. or 3s. 6d. weekly for children to be nursed in the country (amounting to round £7. 16s.–£9. 2s. per annum). Mary-le-bone allowed a similar amount, £7. 19s. 4d. per annum for children under 2 years, much more than any labourer with four or five children could expend.[107] Nutt's estimates for around the same date are somewhat lower: parishes paid for childcare, often at a rate between 1s. 6d. and 2s. 6d. per child.[108] Clearly rates varied, but the parish paid the same amount whether a child was legitimate or a foundling. However, if poor parents had three or four children, spending over £3 per annum on any one child was impossible. If either parent had to pay for childcare while working, then the sums involved were high compared to labouring wages, especially to those of women. Thus the childcare provided by relatives in some early eighteenth-century London parishes was invaluable.[109]

When we consider the costs of children, it is important to remember that not all had similar needs; children could be healthy, or chronically ill, deaf, blind, or incapacitated.[110] In the late seventeenth century, when parishes paid around £5 per annum for the upkeep of a child, Middlesex made allowance for the extra care required for 'a poore, lame, impotent child' by paying a woman 5s. per week (amounting to £13 per annum), a sum close to the total budget for the year for some poor families.[111]

Children were subject to a range of ills, as nutrition levels were poor, clothing scant, and housing damp and overcrowded.[112] They may have fared better in the countryside than in towns and cities, as health was adversely affected by poor accommodation.[113] Breast-feeding could spread syphilis and tuberculosis (although the poor may not have known this), and rickets was a disease of weanlings, children aged 6 months to 2 years.[114] Child mortality in London was seasonal, and usually peaked in August. In winter, children were liable to respiratory infections, in summer to bacterial ones. Infantile diarrhoea was one of the greatest causes of death after 1660, and smallpox increased child mortality in the first half of the eighteenth century, declining thereafter.[114] In towns and cities, after mid-eighteenth-century industrialization, air quality was bad, and working children had little time to recover from infections.[115] For chronic chest infections, popular remedies, such as Daffy's Elixir, often involved opiates, which contributed to respiratory problems and were a drain on the family budget.[117] In addition, there were outbreaks of plague, and the death rate of children under 5 was greater than that of older children.[118] Levene found that in the period 1741–99, the main causes of deaths of children aged 1 to 5 years in the care of the London Foundling Hospital were smallpox, fevers, measles, consumption, convulsions, whooping cough, and fits.[119]

Health care and medicine were additional burdens, especially for mothers, who were usually charged with nursing their sick children. Stories told of devoted mothers spending their savings on treatments. A widow, who sold fruit near Covent Garden and plied her needle mending, spent most of her earnings on physicians' attempts to cure her son's sores: in 1681 a woman's healing touch had cured him.[120] (Elements of this tale may be apocryphal, because belief in magical healing was widespread.)[121] Children's chronic illnesses and special needs further drained the family's savings and resources, as well as impeding mothers from undertaking gainful employment.

As in medieval times, society's attitudes to children with disabilities were generally harsh: the child's defect may have been a punishment for parental sins.[122] Even Newgate's chaplain preached of the Greeks and Romans who exposed maimed or infirm children, while trying to explain that such bloodshed was wrong.[123] Despite negative attitudes, some evidence suggests that mothers and fathers could be devoted to their unfortunate offspring. In the 1660s, the widowed Mary Lapworth applied to Christ's Hospital for a place for her second child so that she could care for her elder child whose disability required her constant attendance: he was 'dumb, and hath such violent convulsions that she dare not absent her selfe from him because he throws himself in the fire and burnes himselfe'.[124] Around the same date, Elizabeth, the second wife of John Bunyan who was in prison for Nonconformity, had four small stepchildren 'that cannot help themselves', the eldest of whom, Mary, was blind. This child, Bunyan wrote, 'lay nearer my heart than all I had besides'.[125] A 1725 rape case, before the Old Bailey, described the 17-year-old Elizabeth Harvison as 'a Dwarf, and an Idiot', who so lacked the use of her limbs that her family had to carry her around 'like an Infant'. Her mother, who discovered Elizabeth's rape when she 'undress'd her to put her to Bed', had been caring for her daughter's physical needs for years.[126]

A child's deafness required special management. When in 1796, William Burrams was on trial at the Old Bailey for theft, his mother explained that her son 'was born deaf and dumb', but she could make him understand by signs.[127] In a bastardy deposition in 1789, Hannah Samuel, the grandmother, had to give evidence on her daughter's behalf, since Catherine Nathan was 'deaf and dumb'. Mrs Samuel said that she could converse with her daughter 'by sign', and that Catherine understood the oath.[128] Older children with a disability were an ongoing concern, because they could not be indentured, unless in some version of apprenticeship according to ability.[129] Aged parents, especially mothers on their own, had particular difficulties in caring for children who were 'insane'. In 1761, a London widow's daughter was kept at the expense of a parish in a private madhouse.[130] However, in some of these cases the families may not have been poor.

The refounded London hospitals of the sixteenth century were willing to treat very young children, as Margaret Pelling has shown.[131] Although the voluntary hospital movement of the eighteenth century seemed to ignore children, Alysa Levene found from an examination of the registers of five eighteenth-century provincial hospitals that they did treat them, although more often as outpatients. The hospitals favoured the children of the industrious poor, whom they hoped to cure so they could return to work.[132]

During the eighteenth century, physicians were increasingly critical of maternal health care. Like other medical practitioners, Armstrong scorned the popular belief 'that the best doctor for a child, is an old woman'.[133] Although middling status fathers may have been more involved in overseeing the health of their families,[134] there seems no evidence that poor fathers were either more domesticated or more active in the work of caring for sick children. Indeed, the demands of the imperial British state for manpower may have removed even more poor fathers from their families.

Although upper-class observers claimed that the poor 'express great thankfulness, when any of their Children have died',[135] mothers' and fathers' feelings were more complex and ambivalent. They could include grief at their wasted efforts to sustain a child's fragile life, and relief that there was one less mouth to be fed. A widespread belief in providentialism—the religious interpretation of events as messages from God—during the seventeenth century especially cast a shadow over parental misfortunes.[136] Just as the birth of deformed babies, monsters, was generally seen as a punishment for sins, a portent of God's wrath, so children's injuries and deaths could convey a harsh reprimand for sins.[137]

TRAINING FOR LIFE AND FOR WORK

'Children were better unborne than untaught', pronounced Thomas Tusser in 1580,[138] and while poor parents may have agreed, their ideas about what it meant to bring up a child properly may have differed from those of their social superiors. First, how did they respond to the view that it was the duty of parents to raise their children as Christians? Secondly, how did they prepare their sons and daughters to be self-supporting?

Parental teaching of Christianity was the basis on which the church depended, but one theme during the sixteenth century was of youth rebellion; contemporaries were shocked at children rejecting the faith of their parents. Historians have found only limited evidence of ordinary people's involvement in the major religious changes of the early modern period. During the late Elizabethan period, the pro-scription of Catholic worship and beliefs affected all the laity. Some were prosecuted because they refused to attend church where there was 'neither priest, nor altar, nor Sacrifice'.[139] Undoubtedly some of those prosecuted were wealthy, but what of the social status of those who prayed with beads?[140] A horror at the sacrilege of communion in both kinds was not confined to the more prosperous. Still, the Angli-can church expected the laity to attend church and to participate in its ceremonies. There is evidence of compliance; in one London parish in the 1630s, 93 per cent of mothers attended for churching after the births of their children.[141] Petitions on the eve of the Civil Wars suggest that even the poorest laity on parish relief may have actively supported the prayer book and episcopacy.[142]

Mothers in daily contact with their young children played a signifi-cant role in teaching them about the Christian faith. Indeed, the Non-conformist minister Richard Baxter thought that this teaching was 'the most eminent service that women can do in the world'; 'mean gifts . . . may serve to speak to Children'.[143] Outcomes depended on parental commitment and levels of piety, notoriously difficult to discover in the case of poor labourers and husbandmen. However, Margaret Spufford's study of how people learnt to read, based on the spiritual autobiogra-phies of poor men and women, has shown both the importance of maternal instruction in teaching reading, and the widespread availabil-ity of small, cheap religious publications. Hornbooks cost 1d. or ½d. and taught children the catechism and the Lord's Prayer. In seventeenth-century Cambridgeshire, Spufford found that small schools taught by women and unlicensed by the ecclesiastical authorities were never far away, and such dames' schools usually taught an elementary catechism. Even labourers' wives might teach reading. The written word was influential among ordinary people, so that even those too poor to pay taxes inhabited a culture familiar with religious discussion.[144]

Children of the poor encountered Christianity in many contexts. If parents had taken their children to Anglican worship, as by law they should have done until 1689, then they familiarized them with the teachings of sermons and catechizing.[145] Against this we should set evidence of ministers' complaints about people's absence from worship.[146] Poverty may have kept some away from public worship 'because they had not cloaths'.[147] In the seventeenth century especially, Christianity was spread by godly women who visited the poor as part of their pious regime.[148] Popular broadsides illustrating Scriptural stories were designed for walls,[149] making biblical stories familiar even to the illiterate. The tradition of recording the exemplary words of the dying revealed that many children, including some very poor, breathed pieties at the last. Indeed, Janeway's collection of their joyful deaths revealed stories of spectacular conversions, such as that of a notoriously wicked beggar boy, an orphan rescued by a Christian and reformed, so 'that all the Parish that rung of his villainy before, was now ready to talk of his reformation'.[150]

Some ministers in the seventeenth century deliberately evangelized among the poor. Richard Baxter, a Nonconformist minister in Kidderminster, tried to adapt his teaching to the very different abilities of poor men, some of whom understood 'the Body of Divinity', and many of whom 'could pray very *laudably* with their Families'. Baxter commended a Southwark minister, Thomas Wadsworth, who distributed catechisms, testaments, and suitable books 'to the poor people of his Parish'. Once a week in winter, Wadsworth rented a house where he catechized the illiterate children and servants who lived in the alleys.[151] Similarly, catechizing by the Anglican clergy was widespread, supplementing parental instruction.[152]

Religious nonconformity was often believed to appeal especially to the socially dispossessed. From Elizabethan times onwards, separatist religious groups met in out-of-the-way places, and in the 1640s and 1650s, separatist churches were established in many parts of England. Such churches appealed not just to the poor, although adherents from the top social groups were few. Studies of social status of Quakers in Buckinghamshire in the 1670s suggest that over half (54.4 per cent) were labourers, husbandmen, or craftsmen. Regions differed, but clearly Quakerism was a rural agrarian movement as well as an urban one.[153] The Quakers managed the social relief of their own poor people on similar principles to the parish, supporting misfortune, making the poor work, and by assisting parents who had 'more [children] than they can maintain'.[154] From the 1650s, Quakers emphasized parents' duties to raise their children 'in the nurture and fear of the Lord'.[155] Later, in the eighteenth century, John Wesley and his followers directed their mission to the poor in areas where the power of the parson was weak, such as in regions of rapid urban expansion.[156]

Church attendance may have declined by the end of the seventeenth century. Furthermore, witnesses in church courts admitted to not taking communion for several years, although before the Civil Wars, communion at least at Easter had been nearly universal.[157] Nevertheless, in the eighteenth century some poor parents allowed their children to attend the charity schools which the Anglicans had established to counter Nonconformity.[158] Even if the emphasis on addressing children's spiritual development lessened during the eighteenth century, it was still widely agreed that religious instruction was fundamental to the raising of all children.[159] From the widespread popularity of magic, astrology, and popular healers we know that orthodox religion had a limited hold on some sections of the population.[160] The silence in the records does not mean that poor mothers and fathers did not value faith and spirituality; we can speculate about faith only from fragments and hints. In the 1670s, Baxter thought that poverty affected religious practice among poor labourers: they were so desperate that they had no time to read the Bible or to pray.[161] Sometimes religion seems formulaic: a respect for the Sabbath was demonstrated in a shoemaker's family in 1767 when Anne Williamson whispered an offer to read 'a book called Moll Flanders' to her stepdaughter, Mercy. Her husband said that it was not a book 'fit to be read on a Sunday'.[162] Children testifying in the Old Bailey were asked what would happen to them if they lied on oath, and most replied that they would go to hell.[163]

Anecdotal evidence about deep piety among ordinary poor women in later seventeenth-century Bedford suggests that such women would have reared their children in godliness. Faith shone from the talk of three or four poor women 'sitting at a door in the sun' whom John Bunyan overheard talking of 'how God had visited their souls with his love in the Lord Jesus', and who spoke 'with such pleasantness of Scripture language' 'about the things of God'.[164] Observers' hostile

observations about poor and mean people in the separatist churches
of the 1640s and 1650s can be read as evidence of religious commitment among the labouring poor.

After the Restoration, when religious Nonconformity was perse-
cuted, many Quakers were reduced to poverty by the seizure of their
goods and imprisonment. The Society of Friends kept records of
their Sufferings for the Truth, and credited children with sustaining
meetings after adults were imprisoned.[165] In 1682, when most of the
members of one congregation were in prison, 'the meetings were
mostly kept up by children', who were in turn punished in the stocks
or imprisoned in Bridewell.[166] In the seventeenth century, children
became Quakers by personal conviction, but in eighteenth century,
children were entitled to membership of the Society of Friends by
father-right. For the purposes of poor relief, in 1737, the Quakers
deemed that children were members of the meeting to which their
fathers belonged.[167]

In addition to raising their children as Christians, many poor
parents accepted a duty to educate them, although they could provide
only limited formal education. Some enrolled their children in informal schools for basic literacy and some religious instruction; in 1644
in one Buckinghamshire parish 'only 2 or 3 poore families' had not
bred up their children to reading.[168] The fees of a few pence for petty
schools may have deterred others.[169] In 1661, Charles Hoole observed that poor parents 'will not spare their children to learne if
they can but find them any employment about their domestick or
rureall affairs, whereby they may save a penny'.[170] Baxter made a
similar comment.[171] However, parental attitudes to education varied.
In 1742, a poor mother testified on behalf of her son: 'He has had a
good Education in reading and writing, and what I could afford to
give him.'[172] James Lackington (b. 1746), the eldest of eleven children, attended a day school 'kept by an old woman' for two or three
years until his father's drinking, and the family growing, meant that
his mother could no longer afford the two pence per week for his
schooling, and the boy became 'nurse' to several of his brothers and
sisters.[173] Boys who had the opportunity to attend school even for a
short time had usually learnt to read by 7 years of age. Writing was
a skill taught later.[174] Stories from the ordinaries (chaplains) of
the Old Bailey show that some parents struggled to provide their
offspring with some schooling, while others were unable to provide
any at all.[175]

Figure 12 *May Morning* (*c.*1760). Children at this May Morning celebration around 1760 seem unaccompanied by parents. The boy on the right in ragged clothing is carrying a younger child. An older girl, looking after a younger girl who holds a toy, seems more prosperous.

Parents did not think that their offspring should have all work and no play. Sarah Trimmer, evangelical promoter of education, told a story in 1787 about a mother who did not want her son at Sunday school: the mother 'rudely said "that she would instruct him herself, and did not chuse to have her child shut up from his recreations on Sunday"'.[176] The story can be read against the grain to see the mother's desire to protect her child's enjoyment.

While it was assumed that children under 7 years of age were unable to work, they could beg. Parishes tolerated begging by children still deemed too young to be apprenticed.[177] Tim Hitchcock argues that although unlicensed begging was legally prohibited by the 1697 Begging Act, in practice Londoners gave to beggars as part of the obligation of the rich to care for the poor. Begging was gendered; a London survey at the end of the eighteenth century estimated that of 15,000 beggars working the streets, the vast majority (90 per cent) were women with children. Mothers found a baby an asset, while fathers appealed to the stereotype of 'a wife who lay in and was starving'.[178]

Parents who failed to teach their children to work were thought to perpetuate poverty, and were increasingly vulnerable in the seventeenth century to the magistrates' statutory powers to apprentice their children.[179] Thus fathers and mothers who were able to demonstrate that they had taught their children how to earn their own livelihoods, were considered good parents, and were typically allowed to keep their children under their own supervision for longer. Another means by which authorities distinguished the worthy poor who deserved relief, was by the pains they had taken with their children's education.

Charity schools were widely available in the eighteenth century, but poor people were often unimpressed with the utility of such education. In 1773, the employer of one servant, Mary Pleydell, explained that her 16- or 17-year-old servant, Amelia Powell, had been reared in the charity school, and was so ignorant 'I question whether she knows how long a woman should go with child'.[180] Benjamin Shaw's wife Betty, likewise a charity-school girl, 'had no Shift . . . [or] management about her, as a poor woman ought to have'.[181]

What men and women could teach their offspring depended on the opportunities their society offered and the differential rewards of male and female labour. In the late sixteenth and early seventeenth centuries, parents in Ipswich, Norwich, and Salisbury could pay as much as 6d. per week for boys and girls to be trained to knit in 'knitting schools'.[182] Mothers taught children to plait straw. Later, in the eighteenth century, in some of the home-based textile industries (which were a more important source of employment for women and children than agriculture), mothers taught skills to children as young as 6 or 7 years and set them to work in cotton and wool weaving.[183] William Radcliffe, born around 1761,[184] who became an improver of cotton machinery, remembered his early training: 'my mother taught me to earn my bread by carding and spinning cotton, winding linen or cotton weft for my father and elder brothers at the loom.'[185] Whereas boys usually went on to receive more systematic industrial training, girls continued in low-status and low-paid work in their fathers' households.[186] Scraps of evidence point to parental aspirations for their daughters. Richard Hutton, the steward of the Quaker workhouse at Clerkenwell in the early eighteenth century, recorded parental disdain of an offer 'to bring up [a girl] to housewifery', 'esteeming their children qualified for better business (as shop maids, seamistry &c)'.[187]

Parents found that their illiterate sons had a wider range of occupations available to them than had illiterate daughters: sailor, waterman, soldier, coachman, blacksmith and butcher, to name a few compared with char-ring, laundry work, spinning, and silk winding.[188] Fathers often brought their sons up in the same occupation as their own, which in some cases, such as in mining, carried occupational risks.[189] Apprenticeships normal-ly required a premium which would have been beyond the reach of most ordinary labouring people. However, if fathers had a formal trade, they could apprentice their sons (and sometimes their daughters) to them-selves, and thereby gain additional authority over them. A father signed indentures, although if he were absent or dead, a mother could sign.

Later in the eighteenth century, when the charitable Marine Society was recruiting boys aged between 12 and 15 years, most of those selected were still living at home with their parents and engaged in a variety of casual occupations, though a few were at school. Boys worked for their fathers, a few for their mothers, and others with weavers, plasterers, and on brickfields and rope grounds. They ran errands, sold fruit, watercress, matches, and ballads. They hawked milk, fed horses, and drove cattle.[190] These sons of the industrious poor contributed to the household generally; any work, paid or unpaid, helped. Boys accompanied their fathers to labour, and girls assisted their mothers in housekeeping and childcare. Poor parents and their children inevitably spent much of their time together.

The informal education parents gave children was crucial to their futures. Mothers and fathers taught their children survival skills: how to work, how to beg and scrounge a living, how to secure their Poor Law entitlements, and how to gain charity.[191] John Clare's father took his young son to work with him, so that the boy was never idle. The neighbours had a poor opinion of John's learning to read, jeering that reading would qualify 'an idiot for a workhouse'.[192] Fathers taught their sons how to get a living; mothers, such as James Lackington's mother who took him from school to care for his younger siblings, taught both daughters and sons how to look after other younger children. Young women who became mothers outside mar-riage knew that mothers had a duty of nurture. Furthermore, parents had to teach children how to survive in a world that would view them negatively because they were poor; children had to learn to show deference but without internalizing images of themselves as inferior. Stories of resistances by the poor testify to parental success.

The transition to work, social adolescence, began early for many poor children. By the early nineteenth century, a legal treatise declared 7 years to be the age of adolescence: 'independent of any statutable regulation, seven years is at common law the age of puberty'.[193] Of course the adolescence of the sons and daughters of the middling sort and above, in the sense of a transition from childhood to the semi-independent state before social adulthood, was prolonged well into the teenage years. Puberty, associated with bodily changes, was likewise generally thought to occur at around 12 for girls and 14 for boys. But for the children of the poor, while social independence began earlier, bodily maturation, which depended on nutrition levels, was probably later than for those better fed. Menstruation and physical maturity would be delayed for poorly fed girls.[194] Nevertheless, the parish could remove poor children as young as 7 years from their parents' supervision, deeming them to be adolescent.

In practice, ages at which poor children left home and entered the households of others as workers depended on parental circumstances and geographical location. Nearly thirty years ago, Richard Wall established that young people left home at different points in the family life cycle.[195] Ages were affected by gender and birth order; girls were more likely to be kept at home than boys.[196] By the nineteenth century, the employment of adolescent girls outside the family was condemned.[197] Snell and Millar suggest that the average age at which children of the labouring classes left home was around 14 years,[198] but Sharpe has shown that in the west country children were usually bound out around 8, 9, and 10 years.[199] Although Wrigley et al. suggest that few children left home before the age of 10, and that two-thirds of adolescents aged between 15 and 19 lived at home while they worked, their estimates were based on family reconstitution studies;[200] the poorer the family the less likely it was that their 'data' could be found in any single area to be reconstituted, and the less likely that those in their teens lived with their parents.

Faced with destitution, some fathers and mothers ignored the distinction between the legal and illegal expedients.[201] They allowed their children to 'wander up and down the Parish, and parts adjacent, and between begging and stealing get a sorry living', complained Thomas Firman in the later seventeenth century.[202] Children's errands could shade into opportunistic theft. Another commentator lamented that the poor were 'brought up to Pilfer, and encourage their Children to do the like, as hath been found by great Experience'.[203] London Bridewell records noted that one mother was 'a common pilferer and teacheth her daughter the same', and a loitering father enticed his daughter to prostitution, and 'to pilfer and

picke'.[204] A mother's request for charring work might offer an opportunity for small thefts.[205] Parents would try to protect their children
from the consequences of their offences. One Yorkshire father, Henry
Trot, begged the woman his child had robbed to 'make no more noise
about it', and promised to satisfy her loss, and be her friend for life.[206]
Elizabeth Newton, whose son was on trial for theft, professed that she
took 'honest Care to get my Bread; my Child did the same, when it
was in his power'.[207]

The boundary between poverty and criminality could blur. An
urban environment with shops offered different opportunities for
casual theft. In 1743, the widowed Eleanor Carr, charged with theft
in the Old Bailey, said that she did not design to steal, but 'was
distressed to pay for my Child's Nursing'. Witnesses gave sympathetic
testimony: she had been virtuously educated in the family of her
grandfather, a minister, 'but now she is poor, and her Money is
gone'.[208] Servants were involved in thefts of food and clothing.
When times were bad, and many men were enlisted, more women
resorted to theft.[209] In the countryside, parents' usual means of
turning any opportunity to advantage could similarly shade into
crime. Women stole wood, milked other people's cows, or gleaned
and poached illegally.[210] A 28-year-old London father admitted in
1742 that he had stolen bread 'and pieces of Flesh the last hard
Winter, for the Support of his Family, when he was out of Business'.[211] In the countryside, sheep stealing, a capital felony, was
often equated with hunger and poverty, although other factors such
as gang theft could be involved. In 1781, one father was said to be
driven to steal by hunger and the cries of his family.[212]

A theft case prosecuted in the Old Bailey in 1752 against a widow
and her three children can be read as the story of how a mother's
poverty led her children to crime. Mary Edwards had once kept a
school, and her neighbours, who had known the family for many
years, viewed them as 'very honest, but very poor'. For a couple of
years, the household depended on loans from pawnbrokers, but the
goods they pawned were not their own; Ann Edwards had 'borrowed'
the small items of gold and silver and the clothes from the widowed
Elizabeth Griffis, in whose house she was in service. When the
Edwards family was in dire distress, Ann's unemployed sister,
Millicent, begged for more items which Millicent and her mother
pawned, but the theft was discovered when Mrs Griffis wanted her
plate collected for cleaning. A constable apprehended Ann Edwards,
who admitted the theft before a justice. Ann cried, 'and said had it not

been for her sister's persuasion she should not have done it; and said, she feared it would come to this at last, that she never should get the things again'. Her admission suggests that when she had pawned the goods before—one pawnbroker had lent 2 guineas on a silver saucepan three times over two years—she had managed to return them, but the sum of £10. 7s. on the last occasion was too large for a poor household to repay. The sentence fragmented the family further: the son Benjamin was acquitted, Ann's offence was downgraded, but Mrs Edwards and her two other daughters were sentenced to transportation.[213]

Children's roles in such a family economy as the poor possessed will be discussed further in the next chapter, but here it should be noted that whatever education and training was on offer, poor parents preferred to have their children, and perhaps their earnings, under their own care and control. Catherine Cappe, a social reformer in York, assumed that poor mothers and fathers, like other parents, wanted to keep their children, especially their little daughters, under their own roof.[214]

PROTECTION AND DISCIPLINE

Historians have discussed how the élite reared their children, but questions about the practices and aspirations of poor fathers and mothers have been less considered, understandably because of the limited evidence. This next section attempts a reading of various sources to assess the quality of parenting: could mothers and fathers protect their children from physical harm or from family violence? And how did they discipline their children?

Poor mothers, whether married, deserted, widowed, or single, were torn between providing adequate childcare and earning money. Childcare could be minimal. A physician thought that poor mothers left their children lying on their backs, or sitting upright 'pinned in a chair',[215] but we know from coroners' inquests that some children minded others: Ann Furneaux, a small child left with a 12-year-old girl, was killed by a fall from a window; 3-year-old John Dixon was accidentally burnt to death when he was left in the care of a young girl and his clothes caught fire.[216] Fourteen-year-old Ann Lowther was looking after three children aged 5, 4, and 2 years when she was pursued by a man and subsequently raped.[217] Mothers left babies in cradles while they were out: a 5-year-old child fell through a window when left alone rocking two infants in a cradle.[218] Accidents occurred while children played. In 1596, a 3-year-old girl in London drowned in a ditch; in 1592, another girl drowned in a well; a 7-year-old boy drowned in a pond.[219] Girls and boys were injured in accidents involving falling timber or masonry; they tumbled into cellars, or even drowned in privies.[220] Accidents occurred in crowded lodgings. A mother who was a washerwoman shared a bed with her infant child and a lodger; her infant drowned when she fell out of bed and into a washing tub.[221]

Very poor mothers in towns, who were perhaps charwomen, hawkers, or simply looking for casual employment, may have carried their younger children to work with them. Similarly, in the countryside, mothers would probably have carried their infants and taken children under about 3 years along with them. A woodcut depicting a vagrant woman showed one child in her arms, another at her skirts.[222] In 1626, Norwich's mayor's court ordered that Kathleen, the wife of a vagrant, Francis Tomson, should be punished and sent to Cambridge with a pass for herself and her two children: a boy of 6 years and a 'sucklinge childe' of 3 months.[223] Coroners' inquests show that children were frequently with their working parents when fatal accidents occurred.[224] Nevertheless, poor mothers may have shared childcare, watching out for each other's offspring.

One form of work which mothers could combine with their own maternal duties, although at some harm to their own offspring, was wet-nursing. While there was no organized national network of wet-nurses, we know that women were employed privately. From 1741, the Foundling Hospital employed 'foster mothers', who Alysa Levene found often had larger families than their local peers: 4.6 children baptized compared with 2.6. Perhaps, like other country women, foster mothers lacked other work options. The pay of 2s. 6d. weekly was comparable to relief allowances, and nurses received a bonus of 10s. if they kept the infant alive for a year.[225]

Mothers tried to supervise their children, and protect them from harm. In a seventeenth-century Cheshire marital dispute, one mother of thirteen children claimed that she needed to look after her children who were still at home, since their father could not supervise them while he was working.[226] In an eighteenth-century child rape case, Sarah Batty was surprised that her 9-year-old daughter Mary had a venereal infection, 'because she was never from under my care'.[227] Even allowing a small daughter to go upstairs to play with another lodger's child could expose her to sexual molestation.[228] But it was virtually impossible for mothers or fathers to watch their children all of the time. Children played outside in the country, and in the towns, boys and girls played in the streets. Crime reports claimed that London streets exposed deserted children 'to the black Guard Boys and Girls' bent on mischief.[229] However, girls on errands or working in the streets more likely faced dangers from others rather than posing a threat themselves.[230]

Poor boys and girls enjoyed a degree of independence. In later eighteenth-century London, Francis Place noted that they were 'permitted to run about their filthy streets' and mix with anyone.[231] A great festival for boys was Guy Fawkes' day, 5 November, and on Palm Sunday morning thousands of young people enjoyed a holiday.[232] Older boys engaged in collective public riots, such as traditional Shrove Tuesday riots, and breaking out of Bridewell. (Bridewell boys were notorious for attending all the fires in London, causing disorder in the streets.)[233] But even girls sometimes rioted. In 1719, they were part of a mob of about 100 boys and girls objecting to the effects of cotton goods on the weaving trade: they tore Elizabeth Price's calico gown shouting 'Callicoe, Callicoe; Weavers, Weavers'.[234]

Contemporaries disliked seeing disorderly children on the streets, contrasting 'the unnurture'd Crew, that lark about the Streets, either to Beg, or to Steal' with the orderly parades of charity school children all neatly clothed and badged.[235] The late seventeenth-century social reformer, Thomas Firman, complained of 'the Rudeness of young children' on London streets who could be found in gangs, fighting, whipping horses, and throwing dirt or stones. Such boys (it seems that Firman did not include girls) he considered unemployable; take one as a foot-boy for errands, he'd be off with his playfellows. Boys, he said, enjoyed games like push-pin and hide-farthing 'neither of which, nor twenty others now in use, are any ways conducing to the health of their Bodies, or to the improvement of their minds'.[236]

Home could be a place of threats and fear, not a place where children were protected. This was not specific to the poor, as Elizabeth Foyster has shown. In some instances, fathers deliberately involved children as a means of further cruelty to their wives.[237] However, poverty may have increased the daily stress under which families lived, as people were starving, sick, or cold. In the Brinsden case before the Old Bailey in 1722 discussed earlier, children saw verbal violence between their parents escalate into their mother's murder. One daughter, seeing her mother's blood flowing so fast, 'ran and took the Child from her [mother's] Breast' while the elder girl cried 'Lord Father, you have murder'd my Mother'. The father threatened his daughters with a violent imprecation: 'D—n, ye Bitches, hold your Tongues, or I'll stick you too'.[238] The testimony of the neighbours, that Matthias was 'often abusing and beating his Wife, and using her barbarously upon the least provocation', evokes a picture of an environment harmful to children. There was no mechanism for anyone to intervene in the marital household; contemporary discourse deemed it a private sphere for which a husband and father was responsible.

Within the household, as children grew up, mothers observed their bodies, assessing their children's general health, and their fitness for work. They kept an eye on girls' and boys' personal linen for suspicious discharges which they read variously as indications of menstruation, sexual activity, or sexually transmitted diseases. Thus in 1733, when Susan Faucet found 'a Disorder in my Child's Linen', she concluded that her 9-year-old daughter had reached puberty and started to menstruate, boasting to her neighbour, Mary Bishop, that her daughter was 'very Forward'. 'It can never be That', retorted Mary Bishop, 'at 9 Years of Age; it must be something else'. The Old Bailey brought in a conviction of rape.[239] Another mother was changing her 9-year-old daughter's shift, and noticed it 'had like corrupted matter upon it'. She then examined the child, and later gave details to the court.[240] A lodger who shared a bed with an 11-year-old girl told the child's mother of her suspicions of rape: as the girl explained, 'she found it out by my Linnen; and told my Mammy.'[241]

Despite maternal surveillance, child rape made up 20 to 25 per cent of sexual crimes tried before the Old Bailey in the eighteenth century.[242] Girls were at risk of sexual abuse in their families, households, or at work. Girls' and boys' roles as employees could expose them to danger, for which the Old Bailey court, more sensitive in the eighteenth century to childhood as a state requiring protection, censured the parents.[243] Eleven-year-old Mary Homewood, who was raped when her father sent her to deliver beer to a nearby dyer, did not initially tell her mother what had happened, for fear of a beating. The mother admitted that she was 'very passionate . . . and sometimes gave her [daughter] a very heavy blow', for which she was reprimanded by the court: 'You see what you have brought upon the child by your passion; I hope it will be a warning to you.'[244] Mothers were quicker to be angered at the abuse of their daughters than fathers, though fathers' prosecutions of assaults were more success-ful.[245] In 1779, 4½-year-old Sarah Poultney told her mother of a coachman who had taken her clothes up: Mrs Poultney said to her husband 'what does the fellow mean by playing tricks with my child, I'll go and kick up a dust with him; he [her husband] said pho, pho, the coachman is always playing with the children'.[246]

Although parents or employers were expected to protect children, court proceedings themselves placed girls in an ambiguous situation, for the court demanded that girls both understood the charges, and also were innocent of knowledge of sexuality.[247] Social status was not always clear, as in the case of a 14-year-old apprentice, Paul Oliver, who was sodomized by his master: 'as soon as he could get out, he went Home to his Mother, and made his Complaint to her.' It was she who took him to a justice, who sent for a surgeon, and the case came to court.[248] Court records may under-represent the very poor, as they could not afford the proceedings.[249]

The language in which girls and boys spoke of sexual abuse and rape at trials before the Old Bailey suggests that parental cautions, if they had indeed been given, had been in such unspecific terms that their offspring had failed to comprehend. A 10-year-old servant girl, Susannah Mitchel, confessed that an apprentice, Edward Fox, 'put something to the Bottom of her Belly, which hurt her very much'.[250] Girls and boys lacked vocabulary, and, as Laura Gowing pointed out, used a less legally conventional language.[251] (Fifteen-year-old Sarah Evans did not even understand the idea of resistance, although a witness did say that she was childish: 'she is not over burthened with Sense, but was always more for playing with Children, and Baby's [dolls], than keeping Company with Men.')[252]

Parental responses to the sexual abuse of children differed. When Frances Moses learnt from her 3-year-old daughter that her teacher 'Aaron [Davids] hurted her in her private parts', she could not speak to Davids about it 'my heart ached so'. Another mother, Sarah Jacobs, a necklace-maker and the wife of a tailor, whose 7-year-old daughter had been infected with a venereal disease, took direct action: 'I went to the school, and beat the prisoner well.'[253] (Mrs Jacobs may have found this more satisfactory than appealing to the courts, for when the case went before the Old Bailey, 7-year-old Sarah was examined, but not on oath, presumably because she was deemed too young, so Davids was acquitted.) Sometimes parents' economic circumstances delayed their reporting abuse. A Colchester mother of a girl aged 8 or 9 years explained that 'she did intend to complain but that she hath been out a nursing and could not'.[254]

In cases of incest, no script allowed daughters to disobey their fathers. The small number of prosecutions suggests that incest was rarely reported; it was one of the abuses of patriarchy with which early modern law and culture was unable to deal. Mary Doe's story came to the Old Bailey in 1733 because she was charged with the murder of her 'male bastard infant'. She said that her child was born dead, her father had taken the child away, and the midwife and others at the lying-in concluded from his behaviour that 'he was father to the child, as well as grandfather'. Mary told the midwife examining her 'that her father had lain with her'. Susan Glover declared that she had known Mary for two or three years as a 'good-natured, inoffensive, modest girl . . . she complained of her father for deluding her'. Mary was acquitted of infanticide, and the constable reported that her father was in Reading gaol.[255] In 1739, Mary Marsland seemed unaware that her father's actions were wrong. She told the surgeon who examined her of many 'unnatural Circumstances [. . . particularly, That it was what all Fathers did, &c]'.[256]

Another contentious issue between the élite and parents of poor children was the appropriate level of discipline. Many observers condemned poor parents as foolishly tender-hearted: the poor were 'carelesse' of their children and did not punish them sufficiently.[257] In the 1970s, some historians viewed all early modern parental discipline very negatively, and judged poor parents as the worst of all: they were 'often indifferent, cruel, erratic and unpredictable' because they themselves were reared 'in a tradition of education by physical brutality', and viewed their offspring as 'unproductive mouths', and 'an unmitigated nuisance'.[258] Others challenged such arguments, and took a more nuanced view.[259] The records of autobiographers suggested that only a minority of children were harshly treated before the nineteenth century.[260] Nevertheless, much of the evidence cited in the debate was class specific, resting as it did largely on diaries, letters, and autobiographies, and reflected more of the views of parents than of the children themselves.

Other records suggest a widespread acceptance of violence towards children; child-rearing treatises usually advocated physical punishments as a religiously directed parental duty. Quaker women's meetings urged mothers to discipline their children while they were young, though they did not specify the methods: 'Keep a watchfull eye over them', urged the York Women's Meeting in 1696, 'before they grow high and stubborn'.[261] In 1690, the Meeting urged mothers to restrain their children 'from all foolish and unnecessary things', especially clothes and food, because the 'Ordering and Governing' of children was especially mothers' responsibility, 'it may be more then Fathers, because they may be absent'.[262] The religious roots of punishments showed a widespread parental belief in the importance of both physical beatings and threats of damnation to break the child's will.[263] Court records suggest that in many households, aggression, and violence were routine.[264] Although both Plumb and Stone have argued for a softening of attitudes to discipline during the eighteenth century, they were not concerned with the poor.[265] Greven speculated about the damaging effects of punishments which he considered amounted to child abuse; children grew up with a lack of empathy with others, and demonstrated violence and aggression.[266] I have not found any evidence of poor parents training their children by rewarding them, but praise and approval may have mattered more than tangible gifts, yet left no trace in the records.

Individual fathers and mothers could differ about physical punishment. An eighteenth-century vagrant, Mary Saxby, claimed that her father was the tender one, who spoilt her because she was his only child; he 'could hardly bear to see me chastised, even when I well deserved it'.[267] Usually, mothers were the more lenient. Charles Conyer (the sawyer mentioned earlier) on trial at the Old Bailey in 1735 for murdering his wife Isabel, claimed that he was simply correcting 'his' 6-year-old son at his wife's request 'for calling her Bitch'. When Conyer struck the boy with a shoe, Isabel intervened, and unfortunately, Conyer said, when he took a cat-of-nine tails, she 'still endeavouring to save the Boy' received some blows which he conceded might have occasioned her death. In this case, the recent birth of another child and worries over how the family was to manage fuelled household tensions. The neighbours had heard Isabel calling her husband 'Dog, and Son of a Bitch, and bid him Murder her and the Child at once, and be hanged for them both'.[268]

Francis Place (1771–1854) wrote a memorable account of his father's brutal beatings of him and his brother, though he believed that his father intended to promote his children's good. His father, a baker by trade who ran a sponging house (a place of preliminary confinement for debtors), used threats 'accompanied by an oath or imprecation or both', and denied the children food, though his mother usually contrived to give them some.[269] (A factor in the different parental attitudes may have been that Francis was illegitimate, a detail he omitted in his autobiography.)

Outsiders thought some parents punished too harshly. In 1622, Norwich authorities removed a child from its mother who was beating it and ordered her to pay for someone else to maintain it.[270]

Bystanders reacted adversely to unkind handling of children: in 1714, when people in London streets saw Mary Vaughan carry a crying girl, and using her 'very roughly', they intervened, and found that the woman was trying to steal the child's gold necklace.[271] Witnesses in Old Bailey cases judged some parents unduly cruel. In 1777, a land-lady, Sarah Pearce, confessed that she had tried to protect 10-year-old Anne Mayne from parental punishment after the girl truanted from school. The parents 'used to beat the child unmercifully . . . I could not bear to hear it, so I did not tell them the last time. I told her [Anne] she must go to school.'[272] Catharine Cappe, writing in 1800 of the diffi-culties with devising punishments at the girls' charity schools at York, observed that parents beat the girls constantly at home.[273] Contemporaries conventionally judged that suicides of young people were attempts to escape harsh punishments from parents or masters. A 1653 poem warned 'the woful Childe of Parents Rage' to remember the 'everlasting Torments' of hell.[274]

Girls and boys were often too afraid of their parents to tell them that they had been sexually abused. In assize records in the sixteenth and seventeenth centuries, children spoke of their fears of parental punish-ment.[275] As we have seen, accounts of abuse sometimes emerged only after the signs of venereal disease led to questioning and threats. Thus in 1678, the 'friends' (family) of 8-year-old Elizabeth Hopkins threatened that 'she would be in danger of hanging in Hell' unless she confessed what had happened to her. (Her father's apprentice, Stephen Arrowsmith, was convicted of having raped the child regular-ly over a period of six months.)[276] In 1748, 13-year-old Hepzibah Dover did not initially confess to being raped because 'I was afraid of my father-in-law [stepfather]'.[277] Twelve-year-old Elizabeth Larmond feared her mother's response: 'I was asham'd, and I was affrighted; for when she finds any thing amiss she is ready to kill me.'[278] In 1753, a 9-year-old girl admitted what a man had done to her only after her mother promised that she 'would not let her be beat'.[279]

Parental beatings could be so severe as to lead to death, but because parental discipline was lawful, this was legally excusable as misad-venture. Coroners' juries found such cases difficult to judge, but the publicity surrounding a young person's death would bring shame to the parent who had so punished the child, a form of posthumous revenge.[280] Parents might hit their children, but they usually resented any outsiders' attempts to discipline them. In Oxford in the 1580s, another woman's beating of a child led to two church court cases.[281] Schoolteachers were also abused by parents.[282]

Parents threatened children with fears of hell and other torments to terrify them into behaving. In court, when questioned about their understanding of the oath to tell the truth, children spoke of their fears of eternal damnation. In the Old Bailey in 1755, 13-year-old John Travilian said that if he lied upon oath, 'the d—l will have me'.[283] Ten-year-old Mary Sherwin confusingly denied knowing how to read and write, but claimed that she could read in her spelling book, and knew from her catechism that if she lied she would go to hell.[284] Contemporaries were unsure at what age children knew about God, heaven, and hell.[285] Stories of ghosts and goblins were probably common: mothers of higher social status were warned not to let the servants terrify their children with such tales.[286] Nursery stories worked on discipline through fear.[287]

Adults who testified in Old Bailey trials spoke freely about bluffing children with lies. In 1759, the abusive schoolteacher of 7-year-old Sarah Jacobs threatened that if she complained to her mother, 'the rats and mice would eat me up'.[288] An apothecary pretended to write a note to the beadle of the hospital so that a 10-year-old girl who refused to confess the name of her abuser would go under the care of the surgeon there 'and be cut and slashed as he thought proper'.[289] Similarly, in a more prosperous family, William Read, a clerk to skylight and fan-light manufacturers, tried to force his 10-year-old son Thomas, who had allegedly been sodomized, to confess: Thomas said his father threatened that 'I might have something that might rot me all away or might swell me up as big as a tub, that I might not be able to walk'.[290]

Deprivations of food were another form of punishment. It emerged at a trial for the rape of 9-year-old Phillis Holmes in 1766, that she had been put on a diet of bread and water for a month because she gave away 4 shillings. A sick-nurse in the household thought the punishment too severe, and admitted she gave the child food 'by stealth'. When the nurse discovered that the girl's linen was foul, Phillis insisted that her injury was caused by a kick from her uncle, an innkeeper, who was her guardian. Finally, on a continuing diet of bread and water, Phillis confessed to the nurse what her uncle's servant, Edward Brophy, had done to her. (Ned had threatened 'that if she told any body, her uncle would kill her, and she would be hanged'.)[291]

Parents might threaten to deny affection to their offspring. In 1779, Philip Sherwin was tried and acquitted for the rape of his daughter. When asked in the Old Bailey 'had any body played any tricks with you?', 10-year-old Mary replied 'Only my daddy'; 'he put his cock up into my body'. Mary lived in the workhouse, and her father, who had lodgings outside the workhouse with his wife, had taken her and some other children for an outing to Bartholomew Fair. When Mary threatened to tell her mistress what her father had done, he retaliated by declaring 'if I did he would never come and see me any more'.[292] Presumably, Sherwin left his daughter confused between affection and fear. Although the paucity of evidence about paternal sexual abuse seems striking to some historians, there were, as there still may be, constraints upon daughters and sons in reporting their fathers.[293]

CONCLUSIONS

Labouring parents were not impervious to discourses about the godly household; the administration of the Poor Laws subjected them to men who promoted such ideals. But economic circumstances played a large part in what poor labouring mothers and fathers could do, and made many of the élite's ideals of child-rearing largely irrelevant.

The material worlds in which fathers and mothers attempted to maintain their families gave them little support. Inherited poverty made them more vulnerable to misfortune, and they were more likely to lack effective kin help. The state, which required men to serve in armies, navies, and colonies abroad, failed to provide forms of child-care which allowed women to work as well as to care for their children.[294] Poor families were more subject to fragmentation than those of their social superiors. Poor parents were less able to protect their children. Boys and girls left home younger, though the ages at which children were required to leave varied according to their position in the family as well as the general state of the parents' economy. Parish and charitable relief was insufficient to prevent boys and girls growing up with few skills, so that they perpetuated cycles of poverty when they became parents in turn.[295]

Whereas 'family' implies a shared economy of parents and children, this kind of family functioned intermittently for the poor. The extent to which there was a 'family economy' is questionable.[296] Fathers' wages were crucial, but poor mothers were more likely to be single parents, as many labourers migrated to find work. Indeed, in some families, men were never there in the first place: single mothers managed alone. Within a family, resources were distributed unevenly. Mothers shared inadequate material goods between their own offspring and any other children for whom they were responsible. Poor mothers faced decisions over which child's need was greatest, and they might be forced to sacrifice one child, so as to give more food, care, or nurture to another. To preserve one, it may have been necessary to place another in institutional care. Mothers and fathers who could envisage little better in their own lives may have found it difficult to plan better futures for their children.

A culture in which fathers were supposed to exercise authority over their families placed a heavy responsibility on men. A poor father's failure to provide for his children undercut his personal and social authority; he was only nominally head of his family because he was subject or potentially subject to the Poor Law authorities. As Steedman argues of working-class men at a later date, fathers were agents of the system, not the ones with power.[297] Subjection could cause fathers to lose self-respect, Francis Place thought, as 'adverse circumstances force on them those indescribable feelings of their own degradation which sinks them gradually to the extreme of wretchedness'.[298] Masculinity was compromised by poverty.

Later in the eighteenth century, a poor man's failure to control his family could destroy his position as a citizen. For centuries, the right to the franchise had rested in property; as an MP argued in the 1680s, if a man had the misfortune to be a pauper, and did not pay towards the cost of government, 'he ought not to have liberty of Choice of Representatives'.[299] But by 1774, James Burgh argued that for the franchise, a wife and children might count as property: 'Every man has what may be called property ... many men, who [live] in a state of dependence upon others, and who receive charity, have wives and children, in whom they have a right.'[300] If children were taken away, a father lost his paternal status on which his citizen's rights depended. Furthermore, subjection to the civic fathers reduced him to the status of a child.

A poor mother's reliance on the civic fathers rather than her own husband did not necessarily diminish her maternal status; since women were expected to be dependent, asking for relief was less demeaning than for men. Nevertheless, her husband's inability to maintain his family brought her maternity under the economic, religious, and moral scrutiny of outsiders. A deserted wife or a widow with young children differed little in practice from a single mother. While she was legally entitled to relief in her parish of settlement, she may have been unable to keep her children with her while they grew up.

4

SEVERE POVERTY

I have heard some people babble, saying 'You'l come into
* trouble,*
You must expect a charge come on,
When you are wed and brought to bed': those things I'de
* have you think upon!*[1]

Once couples were married, it was too late to 'think upon' the
consequences. Popular ballads told of how a poor father could
work day and night 'Yet will his labour not suffice, | His wages are
so small and slender.'[2] Parents knew that children themselves could
cause poverty. When troubles came to poor mothers and fathers, they
sought by various means to keep their children with them, but outside
forces as well as families' own dynamics could threaten the unit with
disintegration.

As we have seen, being a parent exposed men and women to one
stage of what has been termed life-cycle poverty.[3] Their social superiors frequently moralized about how precipitate marriage was a first
step to crime and the gallows: 'entering into Matrimony, before he
was well able to provide for himself' was a classic story of the fatal
consequences of too early marriage.[4] How much a couple had been
able to save before they married was frequently crucial, because
children followed fast. In some cases, labourers' wages were so
meagre that on or even before the birth of a first child, parents needed
assistance.[5] Subsequently, as children were born, a mother was
restricted in work, there were extra mouths to feed, and poverty
deepened as limited resources were shared. Mothers' time was taken
with caring for a number of children, most of whom were too young
to contribute, and limited mothers' own engagement in paid work.
By the time mothers were in their early thirties, fathers in their
mid-thirties, the family was frequently in serious poverty.

Gillray's satirical image of a quarrelling couple with 'six squalling
brats' invites multiple readings. The viewer might identify with the
beleaguered father threatened by a virago of a wife, a pathetic figure

Figure 13 'Les plaisir du mènage' (1781). James Gillray (1756–1815) presented a caricature of family life. A satirical verse accompanied the handcoloured etching:

> A smoky house, a failing trade
> Six squalling brats, and a scolding jade.

However, the husband who is menaced by his wife, and whose children are so ill-behaved, has failed in his fatherly duty.

who was not even properly shod. But he has failed in his role as a husband; he has not exercised his authority, nor has he provided for his family. He has also failed to maintain authority over his squabbling children, as a good father should.

In addition to individual and life-cycle poverty, poor parents faced general economic fluctuations. Wages were low, and unemployment and under-employment for the unskilled was chronic. Many pauper parents were partial wage earners and depended on composite sources of income.[6] Women as well as men had to adapt their lives to capitalism in different localities and regions; paid work was not always available.[7] Families moved from place to place seeking work, though any wanderers were liable to be charged as vagrants. Sickness, death, and desertions could soon transform a mother or father into a sole parent.

Included in this chapter are parents who were never married. The boundaries between married and *de facto*, legitimate and illegitimate children were often unclear; neighbours often assumed that a couple were married, but did not really know.[8] The household of a legally married couple could contain the illegitimate children of either. The children's legal status mattered only when parents applied to the parish for relief; parish authorities could dispatch any illegitimate children to the parish of their birth, which was legally liable to support them.

This chapter examines more closely how mothers and fathers coped with the crises and destitution of severe poverty. Whereas the previous chapter discussed how ordinary labouring people brought up their children in a state of chronic poverty, this focuses on parents' strategies for managing long-term economic change, as well as immediate crises such as poor harvests and fires, and problems caused by personal misfortunes, including sickness and deaths. It first discusses how parents were affected by the local administration of the Poor Laws. This parochial welfare system, created and modified by state legislation, defined the context in which poor fathers and mothers raised their children, and a high proportion of ordinary parents came into contact with the Poor Laws at one stage or another. These laws were framed and adapted around the domestic patriarchal ideals of the civic fathers: husbands and fathers were responsible for maintaining their wives and children, and wives and mothers were to look after the children and household.[9] Although ordinary women worked at both childcare and the economy of makeshifts, élite discourse made mothers' labour invisible, and increasingly encouraged mothers to think of themselves as dependents.

Secondly, the chapter considers the resources of poor parents, and whether they had a 'family' economy to help tide them over tough times. Parish relief was always limited, in some parishes more than others. Since not all the poor could be relieved, parents who were judged to be lazy, or immoral, or insufficiently godly might be denied relief. Such fathers and mothers still had to try to bring up their children. Did older children's labour have a role in assisting their parents? If the family was broken by desertion or death, did surviving parents remarry or informally repartner? And what was the role of charity in the makeshift economies of poor parents? Finally, stories from the Old Bailey illustrate the consequences of the multiple difficulties in which fathers and mothers found themselves. While we cannot generalize from such examples, they do nevertheless give some insight into the lives of parents in desperate straits.

The overall picture of what I have termed 'severe poverty' is a dismal one. Partly this is an effect of the sources, as petitions for parish or charitable relief inevitably emphasize miseries. But not all the bleak picture can be attributed to the nature of the sources. Old Bailey stories in the eighteenth century were directed to questions of innocence or guilt; poverty did not extenuate crime, although economic adversity was frequently part of the context in which crime was committed. This chapter argues that for those parents who were extremely poor, poverty meant hunger, cold, poor health, and incessant toil: a life spent in poverty was hard on the body. Desertions and deaths reduced families to fragments and exposed them even more to misfortunes. The children of such parents were likely to inherit poverty as well as experiencing life-cycle poverty.

THE PARISH

The context in which poor parents brought up their children was shaped by the Poor Laws which established a framework of legal entitlements to assistance. It is important to remember that parish relief, when it came, was usually inadequate and involved outside interference in families. Furthermore, if a father lacked a settlement, he and his family were ineligible for parish relief.

The parish was not necessarily the first place parents turned to when they were destitute. Indeed, historians have questioned the role of parish relief and charity in the 'mixed economy' of the poor.[10] Those with dense kinship connections based on blood, rather than marriage, often turned to their relatives as a first rather than a last resort. Such kinship links depended upon there being work available in a particular area.[11]

Nevertheless, over the early modern period, increasingly, many poor parents required and expected parish relief; up to 41 per cent of a local population could be involved in a bad year, such as 1796.[12] Agricultural change brought more ordinary labouring families under the jurisdiction of the Poor Laws. Initially, families who owned a little land and had rights to the commons enjoyed some independence. Their economy was varied, and family members had multiple employments. Men may have worked for wages at times, but their access to land allowed them to make a living. Wives and children gleaned and collected wood. They picked fruit and berries from hedgerows and heaths, caught hares, and gathered birds' eggs. Spinning, weaving, and other by-employments all contributed to the household economy. But when land was enclosed from the seventeenth century onwards, men lost their independent livelihoods, and both parents were forced to work as farm labourers. Encroachments onto uncultivated lands by the poor themselves further depleted common resources.[13] By the end of the eighteenth century, live-in service in husbandry declined, and more farmers preferred to hire labourers as needed.[14] The diminution of women's employment opportunities in some regions made families more dependent on the Poor Law authorities, and individuals within a family more dependent on each other.[15]

Many historians have contributed to our understanding of how these Poor Laws changed over the seventeenth and eighteenth centuries, and they have documented how administration varied in different regions.[16] Lynn Bothelo's recent study of how two parishes in the county of Suffolk administered poor relief is a brilliant demonstration of how the local outcomes of national welfare policies were affected by the economic and social conditions in particular parishes. In the poorer community of Poslingford those who were marginally poor died at earlier ages than those in more prosperous Cratfield.[17] In the late sixteenth century, attempts to promote hospitality and ideas of sharing proved inadequate to solve problems of poverty, so legislation attempted to regulate begging and vagrancy. Although ideas of general charity persisted, legislation established a more organized form of poor relief, and over the early modern period many poor parents looked to the parish for assistance.[18] Nevertheless, relief depended upon the resources of the parish, and since pensions were never intended to provide total relief, poor parents had to manage with a mixture of forms of assistance.

Because parishes and justices made moral judgments about the worthiness of those needing relief, patterns of relief were bound to vary in different places and over time. The practices in different counties, and between the north and south, varied; relief was less generous in the north. How much relief individual parents could call upon depended on temporal and individual factors as well as geography.[19] The Poor Laws were never simple, but poor parents developed a working knowledge of their complex and changing provisions, and an understanding of how the parish officers would administer the law, so they could present themselves in as favourable a light as possible.[20]

In particular, the petitions of those who had settlement entitlements but worked in other parishes show their rhetorical skills in balancing deference and threats: if the parish did not send relief, then the whole family would be back in the parish.[21]

Widows and orphans, classic objects of Christian charity, were most likely to receive aid. In addition to small sums for immediate relief, justices awarded parish pensions to supplement whatever people could earn themselves. Because wives were expected to be dependent, a poor widow with children was more likely to receive a pension than a widower in the same plight. Women generally were more likely to ask for assistance than men, and in the seventeenth century, as Tim Wales has shown, they and their children received a substantial share of parish relief.[22] When children reached an age when they could be put out to work, mothers' relief was reduced.[23] The age at which authorities deemed children might be placed in a pauper apprenticeship, usually to husbandry or housewifery, could be from 7 or 8 years. Jeremy Boulton has estimated various ways of calculating the value of pensions to recipients in the seventeenth century: by comparing them with minimum subsistence costs, with the full cost to the parish of boarding out the needy, and in relationship to male labouring wages. He concludes that whatever the parish paid to board out children, the amount it paid in pensions to parents was less. Furthermore, the pension compared poorly to labourers' wages: in 1621, the pension was 20 per cent of labourers' wages, in 1644, only 10 per cent. In relation to the household income of a labouring family, the pension was worth about 27 per cent in 1707.[24] Bothelo's study confirms the picture of the inadequacy of parish pensions. These were never intended to provide total relief, and the poor were expected to work and call on any family or charity to assist them.[25] Besides, in a poor parish with many poor, limited relief was all that the rates could supply.

During the Civil Wars of the 1640s and 1650s, widows and wives whose husbands were maimed or injured made claims, considering themselves entitled to relief on the basis of their husbands' service to the state.[26] Between 1652 and 1661, Essex quarter sessions granted some relief to widows; they were roughly a third of 123 petitioners for pensions.[27] The demands of the fiscal-military state and Britain's empire meant that many men were enlisted in armies and the navy to serve abroad: such service never gave them or their families a parish settlement. However, if husbands had settlement rights, then their wives and children were entitled to be 'on the parish' if the men were impressed into service. In such circumstances, the parish as well as wives and children had an interest in the men's return. There were widows' pensions and schemes for men disabled in the service of the state.[28] Obtaining such assistance was not easy, and contemporary newsbooks echoed with the cries of poor widows and orphans.

A deserted wife or widow had legitimate rights to relief in the parish where her husband had his Poor Law settlement, if she knew where this was, but she and her children could be even less welcome there than the mother of a 'bastard'. Her larger family would cost more than a single mother and her child, and whereas the 'father' of an illegitimate child could contribute to maintenance, there was little prospect of help for a widow and children. Although in principle, the kin of the widow could be asked for assistance, they were usually unable to help because of their own poverty. If children were orphaned, parishes sometimes found it cheaper to give small sums of money to relatives to care for them, rather than assume entire responsibility. In 1755, the overseers of St Katherine Cree paid a grandmother 1s. 6d. weekly to allow her 4-year-old grandchild to continue with her.[29]

The parish was not a safety-net for all; some remained outside the system.[30] If fathers had migrated from Ireland or Scotland, they lacked a parish entitlement to give to their children. Some children simply did not know their settlement. Ann Godfrey, aged 12 years, examined in Exeter in 1784 'saith she has neither father nor mother, nor knows where she was born or where her father was settled' nor had she done anything to gain a settlement.[31] In the later seventeenth century, settlement rights were clarified. Children derived their entitlement from their father's settlement. Illegitimate children, who lacked a legal father, derived theirs from their place of birth. Apprentices and servants could gain their own settlement by a year's labour; others could secure one by renting a house worth more than £10 per annum.[32]

Bypassing the parish, parents who were Nonconformists may have received relief from their own churches. Quakers, who were probably furthest from the established church, resisted parish relief, but shared the general assumptions about poverty: the worthy were to be relieved, but the idle were to be made to work. Quakers experimented with workhouses, and even stopped relief in order to compel people to enter. Again, parents had their own views of acceptable relief. One

Bristol mother refused to allow her children to go to the workhouse and 'be bred so slavish'.[33]

One reason why parents might seek alternative sources of aid was that they could lose control over their children, depending on the discretion of parish authorities. The overseers could order their children to be boarded out, placed in parish apprenticeships, or in the eighteenth century, be admitted to a workhouse.[34] If parents were hard-working, and rearing their children to work, then overseers might grant small sums of money for temporary relief. But if fathers and mothers kept their children at home, in what the parish authorities judged to be idleness, then the Poor Law authorities could authorize the removal of any children over 7 years of age into parish apprenticeships which subjected youngsters to labour discipline.[35] In practice, many of the children apprenticed had only one parent; the other was of unknown whereabouts or dead.[36]

Although apprenticeships are generally thought of as providing training and skills, pauper apprenticeships provided little of either, and less to girls than to boys. Parents saw sons and daughters indentured into poorer trades, at younger ages, and for longer periods. Most pauper apprentices were in agriculture and services as well as in the primary stages of manufacture.[37] Whereas parents usually consulted youngsters before binding them, the parish overseers acting *in loco parentis* had no such obligation. Parents knew that this 'training' was for a lifetime of comparatively unskilled labour; indeed, without a premium to secure training in a skill, parish apprentices would engage in similar work to servants, under harsher conditions.[38] In the eighteenth century, such children were concentrated in fewer trades, some of which were unhealthy, such as brick-laying and hat-making, and even dangerous ones, such as chimney-sweeping.[39]

Ironically, although being the father of a family gave a man social status, if he were poor, then children added to his poverty, and too many children could bring him to the hostile notice of the civic authorities who could bind out any children over 7 years (39 Eliz. I c. 30). Reading the administrative records of the Poor Law authorities against the grain allows us some insight into parental attitudes. Justices' manuals directed that any father who was unable to maintain his children, yet refused to allow them to be bound apprentice, was to answer for his default.[40] Some parents did resist the removal of their children. One reason was that they feared lest masters, especially those who were reluctant to receive the young children as apprentices, would maltreat them so that they fled.[41] In the 1630s, when Charles

I's Privy Council ordered the justices to enforce the Poor Laws, the Wiltshire justices reported 'the unwillingness of foolish poor parents to part with their children'.[42] In 1638, the assize judges in Somerset ordered that children who lived idly should be bound apprentices, 'and yf the parents of poore children shall refuse to have their children bound forth apprentices', the justices should send them to the House of Correction.[43] Yet parental resistance continued for, as some reformers acknowledged, 'our poor' did not 'think it good for their children to work hard during their youth'.[44] In 1703, the respectable parishioners of Brill complained to the Buckinghamshire justices that 'the children of severall poore people of the parish . . . that are fitt and able to goe out and hire att service refuse soe to doe, and doe live and cohabitt with theire parents whoe are not of ability to maintayne themselves or theire said children'. The justices threatened to withdraw parental allowances.[45]

Poor fathers and mothers had different objectives from those of the civic fathers. They wanted assistance so they could bring up their children themselves, while civic authorities, believing that idleness was an inherited disposition, aimed to remove the children and subject them to labour discipline.[46] Parents preferred to have their children under their own control, and tried to manipulate the system so that they could protect their offspring from ill-treatment in the households of others or in the workhouse.[47] In Somerset in 1623, a mother expressed solidarity to the death with her apprenticed daughter, Frances Hill, whose master Christopher Haddon had complained that Frances did no work and ran away. Frances affirmed that her daughter would hang or drown herself rather than live with Haddon; the mother threatened to hang herself if the justices punished her daughter.[48] Some parents tried to reclaim their offspring from pauper apprenticeships. Thus in 1633, the Somerset justices resolved that if the parents should 'intice them [their children] away, themselves not being able to mayntein them', the parents were to be punished: 'let them be committed to the house of correction.'[49]

After the 1690s, renewed interest in apprenticing poor children brought the scheme under more critical public scrutiny, no doubt adding to parental anxieties about parish apprenticeships. Widely publicized cases before the Old Bailey in the eighteenth century showed that some children were ill-fed and hungry: witnesses in one case spoke of 'a poor emaciated creature'.[50] In 1733, at the trial of John Bennet, a fisherman, for his apprentice's murder, the court heard that he beat the boy because he ate more victuals 'than he [Bennet] intended to let him'.[51] A witness had remonstrated with Bennet when the boy was clad only in a waistcoat and breeches in a hard frost: 'How can you use the poor Boy so, he is ready to perish with Wet and Cold, he'll never live to see London again?'[52] In many of these cases, an overseeing parent was actually absent. Since severe poverty and mortality frequently disrupted families, many abused children were isolated, lacking any effective adult to support them. In 1736, James Durant, a wig-ribbon-weaver, was tried for beating his 13- or 14-year-old apprentice, a 'very little Boy', to death for not working. A neighbouring woman had thought that the child was starved: 'No, says the Child, I can't say he starves me, for there's Bread and Cheese if I could eat it.' The apprentice was ill, unable to walk, and after the parish beadle carried him to the workhouse, surgeons testified to his emaciation, consumption, cough, fever, and diarrhoea.[53] In another case in 1784, William Rolls told how he watched Constance Frost, a young apprentice, come bare-footed three or four times a day to fetch water in the bitter cold: 'I thought every time she came she looked more miserable, and more like an object of pity.' As she seemed 'very dirty and nasty', he questioned her: 'little girl, what makes you go in that way?'[54] Since parents were aware that masters were often reluctant to receive poor children as parish apprentices, and were potentially or, as the Old Bailey cases demonstrated, actually abusive, when times were easier, parental resistance to apprenticeships may have increased.[55]

Apprenticeships may have been more easily found for boys than girls, but Pamela Sharpe suggests that in Colyton widowed parents sought to keep girls at home as they were more of an asset to the domestic economy.[56] Daughters also required protection from the dangers of illicit sexuality. Illiterate poor parents had limited opportunities to complain of their children's treatment in the households of others, but in 1774 in Coventry, the mothers of two chimney-sweeps (a notoriously dangerous occupation) petitioned on the boys' behalf against the masters.[57] Joanna Innes suggests that by the end of the eighteenth century, parents probably organized most apprenticeships themselves, rather than parishes and charities, so that they could monitor their children's welfare.[58]

Parents might resist the parish's attempts to control their children, but find that their position was a weak one. Thomas Turner, overseer in East Hoathly, told the story in his diary of two daughters of Richard Brazer, Ann and Lucy, who were boarded out to 'Dame Trill' in May 1756 at 18d. weekly. Within a couple of months, Trill was complaining that 4s. per month was insufficient. The two girls, aged 10 and 12 years were troublesome, 'very saucy and impudent', so William Elphick 'corrected' one at the vestry's order. Her father was outraged, and took her home, where she stayed for three months. When Brazer demanded relief for the cost of keeping his daughter, the parish had him summoned before the local justice, who reprimanded him severely, and directed him to beg the parish officers to return his daughter to the same place.[59]

After the end of the seventeenth century, parents were more and more forced to choose between total institutional dependence, or relying solely on their own resources.[60] Instead of boarding young children out or apprenticing them, overseers might insist that parents and children enter one of the institutional workhouses built by groups of parishes. A key feature of workhouse training was bodily discipline. Workhouse food was spare; bread with either butter or cheese featured largely among the items of expenditure.[61] Children could be admitted while their parents worked outside. Schemes to make children work varied from corporal punishment to shame and the withholding of privileges. Thus children would not be fed until they had completed tasks, nor allowed to see their parents until they had performed their religious duties. Girls would be kept in until they had learnt their collect for the week, and would only be 'suffer'd to go Home, and see their Parents, after the Evening Prayers are over'.[62] Some parents resisted the civic fathers' attempts to make children work. In 1725, the Bicester workhouse trustees planned to employ poor children in some useful labour 'but this Design was then laid aside, thro' the Mistake or Obstinacy of the Children's Parents'.[63] Parents doubted the utility of workhouse training: they saw their children engaged in endless repetitive drudgery that would never command any but the lowest rates of pay.

Hostile observers attributed bad motives to fathers and mothers who objected to civic authorities' attempts to train and discipline their children. In 1700, when Bristol parents opposed the establishment of a larger workhouse, the civic fathers dismissed their objection as trivial: a larger institution would restrain 'fond Parents, who upon frivolous Pretences would take their Children from the Parochial Work-house'.[64] Bristol philanthropist John Cary thought that the parents' opposition was economic, rather than affectionate: 'we had a great deal of trouble with their Parents, and those who formerly kept them, who having lost the sweetness of their Pay, did all they could to set both the Children and others against us.'[65] Other unsympathetic observers made a different argument about parents' attitudes: parents were glad to be relieved of their children because they did not love them. As one wrote in 1760,

> PARENTAL AFFECTION does not hinder Poor Parents from giving up their Children to Parish Officers, to be put out Parish Apprentices to Families always averse to 'em, and from whom consequently the best of Usage cannot be expected, but the hardest Servilities.[66]

Poor parents may have had few options but to juggle so as to do their best for all their children.

When parish officials did visit their apprentices in manufacturing areas later in the eighteenth century, they took seriously comments about the adequacy of diet, but were unsympathetic to the children's cries of homesickness. Children wanted to see their mothers and fathers, their families and friends, and many of those who absconded were making for 'home'.[67] Parish officials were largely unmoved by such emotional complaints, which suggests that in a society which deeply valued parents' bonds with their children, the officials saw poor parents as different from themselves.

Some parents aspired to better futures for their children. In 1691, a parish withdrew a widowed mother's relief, because 'she hath taken him [her son] from his worke and sent him to the schoole'.[68] Elizabeth Newton complained that the parish had thwarted her attempts to train her son, so that he ended up on trial for theft: 'I always was a very poor Woman, and took an honest Care to get Bread; my Child did the same, when it was in his Power. I applied to Coleman-street Parish to put him Apprentice, or fit him for the Sea, but they would do nothing for him.'[69]

Poor parents learnt to use parish relief over the early modern period. Determined parents might appeal over the head of the parish; justices could be allies against the overseers.[70] As early as 1621 Richard Frye complained to the Somerset quarter sessions that he was very poor with six small children who were fit to be bound apprentice, yet they still remained on his hands and he could get no relief.[71] The poor knew their rights, as the 'famous old song' declaimed:

> Hang sorrow! and cast away care!
> The parish is bound to find [for] us.[72]

A mid-eighteenth-century observer, Thomas Alcock, criticized the poor for their sense of entitlement: 'He has a right to it, he says, by

Law, and if I won't give, he'll go to the Justices, and compel me.'
Alcock observed much mutual abuse between rich and poor.[73]

Letters written by or on behalf of Essex paupers from the mid-
eighteenth century show both fathers and mothers engaging in a
variety of rhetorical ploys.[74] In 1770, George Oliver appealed to the
overseers of West Thurrock as fellow fathers: 'gentleman you have
got a family and you must now than [know then] a little how to keep a
family.' Oliver had been ill for fourteen weeks. Of the six in his family,
'there is nare a one of them able to bring anything in'.[75] As Sokoll
explains, many petitioners found themselves in a 'strategic position'
in appealing for temporary assistance, knowing full well that the
parish would find it cheaper to send some money rather than have
the whole family 'throw' themselves 'on the parish'.[76]

Thus the humble petitions of distressed and obedient fathers and
mothers should not be taken at face value: behind the 'facade of
deference', animosity could well lurk.[77] The tone might be deferential, as it was in one woman's petitions to the Cumbrian authorities
over a twenty-year period from the late seventeenth to early eighteenth century, but the content itself was 'truculent and embittered'.[78]
Libels mocking churchwardens, constables, bailiffs, justices, mayors,
and aldermen were prosecuted in the Jacobean court of Star Chamber,
so we know that poor parents were surreptitiously critical of their
superiors' fatherhood. In 1622, an Essex ballad mocked a councillor
and notable citizen accusing him of harshly beating his daughter.[79]
Men were vulnerable to shame and ridicule for allegedly fathering
bastards, and for being cuckolds whose children were the product of
the adultery of their wives.[80] However, since the civic fathers demanded respect, and punished those who abused them as seditious,
grovelling was strategic.

Initially, people were ashamed to be on parish relief, and their
relations and friends would do all they could to prevent such humiliation. Seventeenth- and eighteenth-century parishes demanded that
pensioners wore a badge, and even distinctive clothing, thereby
demonstrating dependence; the policy was enforced when ratepayers
felt most overburdened.[81] By the mid-eighteenth century, some
observers complained that shame had evaporated, and even badging
had little effect.[82] More sympathetically, others judged it cruel that a
poor man received relief 'with a mark of infamy'.[83] In the eighteenth
century, when many parishes sent their poor to workhouses rather
than provide 'outdoor' relief, shame attached to parents' failures to
provide for their families. Around 1800, Catharine Cappe considered

that a father was humiliated by admission to a workhouse: 'His wife and children look up to him no longer . . . [he] is sunk in the eyes of others and is altogether degraded in his own.'[84]

Settlement rights were nevertheless important to poor people, and parents carefully instilled into their offspring knowledge of their entitlements to relief. Over and over, men and women cited their inherited rights: a widow testified that her husband had never gained any settlement 'other than in the right of his Father';[85] a man 'maketh oath that he was informed, by his parents, that he was born and bred up'; 'she hath often heard her father [who was a soldier in Flanders] declare'.[86] If parents and their children stayed outside the parish welfare system, a marginal existence exposed the family to punishments under the vagrancy laws.

All parish relief depended on temporal and geographical factors as well as the local reputation of individuals. In the seventeenth century, those whom neighbours identified as the respectable rural poor would be treated sympathetically, especially if the parish as a whole was not 'overburdened' with poor. Similarly, in prosperous towns and city parishes, mothers and fathers with settlement entitlements would be relieved. By the eighteenth century, assistance was probably more formulaic and potentially harsher. Throughout the period, parents seeking relief had to negotiate. They did best if they had established a good reputation within their communities and behaved with deference to the authorities.

Thus, while parish relief created a framework within which parents could gain assistance, it was not parents' sole resource when they were in difficulties. Indeed, since many of the provisions for parish relief were demeaning and designed to discourage applications, especially in the eighteenth century when parents and children could be forced into the workhouse, generally fathers and mothers preferred to help themselves by taking advantage of any economic opportunities, and adapting their labour strategies.

THE 'FAMILY ECONOMY' AND CHILD LABOUR

When parents were in difficulties, a 'family economy', by which we might understand a sharing of roles and resources which would tide them over, was of limited assistance: not all families had an economy in which family life and production were inseparable. When Tilly and Scott originally argued that there was a change from a 'family economy' to 'the family wage economy', when families pooled their wages, they made an important exception: not all lower-status families had a 'family wage economy'.[87] As Pamela Sharpe has argued in the case of Colyton, particular factors such as the sex ratio in rural areas (which affected a woman's chance of marrying) and the economic structure (which created a demand for labour) meant that the 'family economy' was comparatively unimportant for many poor individuals who depended on wages and on charity.[88] The poor turned to their kin and neighbours for assistance, as well as appealing to specialized charities where their reputation as good hard-working parents affected the support others might offer. Deserted or widowed parents sought new partners, or remarried.

Historians have rightly shown that the collapse of parents' fragile economies led to their need for relief; what we have seen so far is the extreme vulnerability of families to any mishaps. Most families depended on both parents working. As Alice Clark pointed out nearly a century ago, poor mothers were always expected to work and keep themselves and at least one child.[89] A wife, argued Richard Dunning in 1698, might maintain herself and one child, 'which is the most a Woman can, and *what few will do*' (emphasis mine).[90] Even Dunning acknowledged the impossibility of a mother maintaining more than one child as well as herself by her own efforts. During the seventeenth century, social reformers grudgingly recognized that wages were inadequate. Healthy working parents, Locke claimed, could keep themselves and two children under three years;[91] but both parents were not always healthy and able to work, and besides, many had more than two young children. In one unhappy case, Anne Philmore, mother of four, was convicted in 1686 of drowning her 9-week-old baby. One report alleged that she and her husband worked hard for their four children, but each new child interfered with her work washing linen.[92] In an earlier case, the motives of a grandmother who drowned her 2-year-old granddaughter were variously canvassed. Some said that the grandmother was trying to improve the older children's chances of survival, threatened by the birth of another baby, and her son-in-law 'would not endeavour to maintain them'.[93]

Of course not all fathers did devote themselves to maintaining their children, and their wives had limited employment options. Eden, surveying the state of the poor in the 1790s, judged that the welfare of the humblest families was more at risk from men than from women. Many problems stemmed from husbands' ownership of their wives' wages, he argued, which militated against mothers providing for their children, and any form of self-help such as a benefit society. Furthermore, Eden considered that coverture was bad for domestic relations: when a man saw that the family depended on him, he became 'imperious and tyrannical'.[94] Yet many fathers were losing their roles as chief provider as economic change and new forms of labour meant that some women could earn more than men. In 1784, one observer grieved to see a strong young fellow at a loom 'where a woman will generally earn as much, what a sight, what a perversion of masculine strength!'[95]

The stereotype of fathers maintaining and exercising authority over their households could be meaningless for poor families: there was no marital household, only fragments. In 1770, Lydia Jones petitioned for her baby's admission to the London Foundling Hospital because 'the unavoidable misfortune of her husband leaving her' six months earlier meant that she could maintain herself only by going into service in another household.[96] Furthermore, although live-in service and marriage have been seen as incompatible,[97] there are instances of husband and wife working separately in the households of others. Jane Pollard petitioned the Foundling Hospital to take her child in 1773, explaining that she could not get by even with wages due from her service and the 'little assistance' from her husband who worked with a farmer in the country.[98] In the same year, Jane Howard, also married, begged the Hospital to take her second child because she and her husband were servants, with 'another child which they can scarce maintain'.[99] In the later eighteenth century when Poor Law authorities built shared housing for paupers, again there may have been no family household.[100] In the seventeenth century, some couples worked itinerantly as petty chapmen, though wives could be found searching for their husbands; Spufford suggests that among the very poorest the marriage tie may have sat very lightly, and families could lose members along the way. All wanderers were liable to punishment as vagrants.[101] Poverty could precipitate the breakdown of marriages, as merely lodging in one room where men struggled to work and mothers to care for infants was 'to live in great discomfort'.[102]

Labour migration was common among the poor, and easier for fathers than mothers and children. Agricultural distress in the late sixteenth and early seventeenth centuries prompted men from the dispossessed rural poor to take to the road in search of work. London was a magnet, and its growth in the early modern period was spectacular by European standards. Wrigley estimated that during the eighteenth century one in six adults in England had some contact with the capital.[103] Elsewhere, various opportunities for employment opened up as industries developed and Britain expanded overseas, but many of the paying jobs—in the colonies, in overseas trade, and in wars—were for men only, which created numerous difficulties for their families. Troop numbers at the peak of the War of the Spanish Succession in 1711 were 186,000. In the War of the Austrian Succession, numbers peaked in 1746 at 120,000.[104] Press gangs and recruiting officers lured or pressed an estimated 48,000 men into the navy during the War of the Spanish Succession, when the mortality rate may have reached 50 per cent or even higher (seven out of ten men in the service of the Dutch East India Company around the same date never came home).[105] High mortality levels continued after demobilization, mainly from smallpox and fevers.[106] Young men, labourers, and the casually employed were disproportionately represented among the recruits. Many were fathers, whose wives and children lacked the support of their wages.

Migration could shade into desertion as fathers (and less often mothers) simply departed, leaving their children 'on the parish', despite statutes threatening punishment.[107] Poor Law records over the seventeenth and eighteenth centuries document various kinds of desertion. In 1655, Portsmouth authorities acted against a man who merely threatened to abandon two of his children to the parish, and ordered that he be whipped.[108] In 1710, a father who had enlisted as a seaman, leaving his wife and three children chargeable to the parish, was reported to the Buckinghamshire sessions.[109] In the 1730s, a Hackney Justice, Henry Norris, committed men to gaol for refusing to maintain their families; on 5 February 1733, he sent Lionel Theed to hard labour at the house of correction for leaving his wife and child 'without making provision for them'. (Theed subsequently escaped.)[110] Norris also granted a warrant against John Wheeler whose wife had complained that he neglected 'to provide for the Support of his wife & 2 Children'.[111] Fairly typical stories tell of debt precipitating men's flight; in 1687, a year after Elizabeth Gardner's indebted husband fled, she petitioned for the admission of her children to Christ's Hospital.[112] Sometimes a father simply vanished: no one had heard any news of Jeremy Tyrrell for seven years.[113] In the eighteenth century, men who deserted and left their families on the parish were increasingly prosecuted under the vagrancy laws.[114] We do not know what percentage of families was affected by desertion. From settlement examinations in the south-eastern counties, Snell found that fathers who deserted usually had married earlier than other poor men, and had larger families. Frequently they deserted around harvest time, when their pay gave them the means to do so.[115] In a study of three rural agricultural counties, Bailey found that 78 per cent of deserting husbands left children as well as wives.[116] Long-term absences and desertions left many parents, usually mothers, managing alone. In some cases, deserting fathers established another family. Around 1759, Rebecca Edmunds married John Webber and bore five children. Subsequently, when John was found to have married her bigamously, all her children were bastardized, and her 11-year-old son was settled separately from her, sent to the parish of his birth.[117]

In the absence of their husbands, whether from enlistment, desertion or death, mothers had to negotiate with civic authorities and other bodies—especially Poor Law authorities, the military, the British East India Company and large merchant companies—for maintenance. Some mothers used their children instrumentally, as did seamen's wives in 1652 when they threatened a London merchant, John Paige, that 'they will bring their children and lie at my doors by reason they cannot receive their husbands' wages'. Paige considered it was nothing to do with him, 'but those kind of people will not understand reason'.[118] In the later seventeenth and eighteenth centuries, sailors' wives developed skills in negotiating with the navy bureaucracy for their share of their husbands' pay, and appealing to the courts to make financial claims against their husbands.[119]

Ill health in any family member was a burden, but if it were the father who was ill, this not only deprived the family of income, but might necessitate expenses in an attempt to cure him. Reverend Richard Baxter claimed that he acted as a physician for a few years among the rural tenant farmers because they could not afford the fees of physicians and apothecaries which could amount to £2.[120]

Death broke up families. Laslett calculated on the basis of life tables that if life expectancy at birth were 35 years, and if a man's first child was born when he was about 35, then 9 per cent of children aged 5 years would lack a father, 17 per cent aged 10, and 27 per cent aged 15. Nearly half the girls—46 per cent—who reached marriageable age around 25 years would be fatherless.[121] I know of no figures calculating the percentages of children who would be motherless. In 1977, Laslett speculated about the emotional impact of parental mortality. He offered a rosy view of 'orphans', those lacking one parent, brought up 'with a bevy of other children, caressed and attended to by a knot of other mothers and other adults, too, as is known to be the situation in many primitive societies today'.[122] The situation for poor children lacking parents in early modern England was not so happy. Poor children were more vulnerable than any others to the fragmenting of their families. Parents could deliberately farm them out for what they hoped would be the temporary care of relatives. In 1766, Mary Rycroft, a deserted London wife, left her two boys, aged 5 years and 18 months, with 'friends' in Yorkshire.[123] Kin might take in children but demand that they earn their keep. In 1709, John Kete took in his nephew for four years as a cheap source of labour requiring no wages.[124] Later, in 1800, a grandmother took in her granddaughter to do the work of the household for four years; the young woman left when she was pregnant.[125]

Widowhood presented poor parents with different issues from those faced by middling and élite parents. Instead of problems about property and inheritance, poor parents grappled with survival, with finding both economic subsistence and caring for their partially orphaned children. A widow might inherit nothing 'but extream poverty and want', as did Grace Penny in Somerset in 1662, who had 'many children, most of them sickly and feeble'.[126]

As we have seen, women on their own were likely to head households containing remnants of families. Even in late Elizabethan England, in Warwick such fragmentary families were far more typical than nuclear families among the poor.[127] The number of female-headed households increased in early modern times. In 1576, women headed 6 per cent of households in Rye; in 1660, over 11 per cent.[128] Snell and Millar found that around two-thirds of single-parent households were headed by women.[129] Such households were likely to be poor. The division of labour affected mothers' availability for paid work; work had to be something they could combine with childcare, such as spinning, lace-making, or agricultural tasks. Since women were paid less for their work, they were usually unable to manage to be the sole provider for their families. However, some industrial developments, such as those in textiles, offered employment, and in some industries the lower wages women and children could command meant they were more employable than men.[130]

Overall, the relative standing of such female-headed households deteriorated during industrialization, although children had higher labour-force participation rates.[131] Women heading households had less time for tasks involving the preparation of food and family hygiene. Living as they did in some of the worst accommodation, the combination of work, disease, and poverty adversely affected their children's health and height, as Horrell, Humphries, and Voth found in their study of early industrial Britain.[132] Sick children required mothers' nursing. Widows were usually financially worse off than widowers. Parishes might view them more sympathetically, but actual relief depended upon the wealth of the parish, the general economic situation, how successfully widows were able to negotiate, and what other assistance they could find.[133] Their situations varied according to their own ages and the number and ages of their children. If they were young and able-bodied, widows could work, provided they could arrange childcare. Sometimes a widow might ask the parish for a small one-off payment. Thus in 1731, Justice Henry Norris ordered churchwardens to pay 10s. to Katherine Browne, a very poor widow with two children, 'to put her in a way to get her living she having promised not to ask for any assistance for three years to come'.[134] The parish of St Katherine Cree, London, granted Alice Saxton, presumably widowed, a guinea 'to set her up in some Business whereby she may maintain her self and two Children'.[135] In other instances, parishes provided not money but relief with rent, or coals or bread.

Poor widowers similarly struggled to provide for their children. In 1739, St Katherine Cree, London, granted John Drury 20s. to buy tools for his trade of whip-making; he promised in return that 'he would use his Endeavour to Maintain his Family'.[136] Widowers and deserted fathers could usually look after older children, but were at a loss over feeding and caring for newborn infants and very young children. Finding a suitable and affordable nurse was difficult. Around 1790, a widowed father, Page, placed his 16-month-old daughter, Mary, with a London nurse, Lucy Acor, and visited two or three times each week. The nurse's landlady, Barbara Cass, believing that Acor was starving 'and ill-using' the child, advised the nurse 'to ask the father to take it to the workhouse'. The widowed father may have judged that the workhouse offered even less acceptable care. However, the child died, and although Acor was charged with murder in the Old Bailey, she was acquitted on a surgeon's testimony that the child was born of diseased parents.[137]

Both contemporaries and subsequently historians considered that children's work was a part of the poor family's economy, but were children able to help their beleaguered parents? Historians have debated the ethics of employing children, the economic value of their labour, and the role of child workers in the economy generally.[138] The earlier picture of child labourers in early industrialization has been modified by accounts of the varied work children performed in their families. Much of this discussion about child labour assumes that children were of an age where they could do something. Although contemporaries thought that poor children could be apprenticed out as young as 7 years, the key period for the transition to work was probably 10 to 16 years.[139] A significant variable may have been whether children were employed at the behest of their parents, or of the parish. There is evidence that in the north and the west, plebeian parents sought to retain the labour of their older children and did not want them to marry.[140]

There was a sharp distinction in the age at which boys and girls were believed to be ready for work at different social levels. Whereas élite and middling fathers and mothers took a keen interest in the education and training of their adolescent sons and daughters, and protected them as long as possible, in some cases into their twenties, poverty forced labouring parents to relinquish the supervision of their children at much earlier ages. In poor families, the care of young children kept mothers out of the workforce. Small boys and girls could do little more than contribute a meagre amount towards their keep. In the rural economy, such children were probably more use, as they might scare birds, care for poultry, gather firewood, or help to glean; in the towns and cities, their utility was more limited, but they might run errands or hawk small items. If children attended any of the charity schools in the eighteenth century, then parents frequently withdrew them in summer so that the family could work together in agriculture, or when some other low-skilled employment offered.[141] Usually, children would be in their teens before they could contribute to the parental budget.[142]

In some regions, young children worked in textiles. The 1570 Norwich Census of the Poor recorded poor parents working with young children. Agnes Harison, a 40-year-old Norwich widow, spun white warp with a child of 8 years 'that spyn also'.[143] In 1719, Defoe argued that poor boys 6 or 7 years old could earn 2s. to 4s. 6d. weekly at silk work 'which is a great Help to their poor Fathers and Mothers'.[144] Industrialization provided more opportunities for small, dexterous fingers. In the silk and cotton manufacture, children were employed at around 6 or 8 years of age 'because their fingers are supple and they learn the skills more easily'. Children could manage the new mechanized spinning machines, which required an awkward posture from adults.[145]

Figure 14 'Long Threed Laces Long & Strong' (1711). Young children in towns and cities might earn a few pence hawking goods on the streets.

Availability of work was a factor. Horrell and Humphries argue that as older children in labouring families gained independence at a younger age in the eighteenth century, so the ages of the children recruited as industrial workers dropped. (Parents needed their wages for the family economy.)[146] Although child labour was valued in the new textile technologies, the story in agriculture was different. Parents might still keep children out of schools in the summer, to take advantage of their labour, but by the late eighteenth century, children in agricultural families had relatively low participation rates in the labour force, contributed less to the household budget than in industrial families, and consequently were more dependent on their parents.[147] Although some historians have argued that in the eighteenth century the development of domestic industry made child labour profitable to poor parents, this seems mistaken.[148]

If the family were intact, then any financial or labour contribution of older children assisted the survival of the family unit. In the 1750s, James Lackington was one child who helped his mother by minding his younger siblings.[149] But families were not always intact, since a common strategy when a parent died or deserted was for the survivors to leave children with relatives, a charity, or the parish. Such children would be apprenticed out at any age from seven upwards. As we have seen, any parent who accepted parish assistance could have their children leave home for a pauper apprenticeship. Although fathers and mothers could be harsh taskmasters of children working at home, the children had bonds to a family and a locality. Those sent as apprentices or servants into other households might be treated even more harshly, and they lacked connections with anyone.

In the debate over child labour, one element has been neglected: what did parents want for their children? We know that this was a society in which fathers especially were expected to prepare their sons and daughters to be able to support themselves, and that they had a duty to see their daughters suitably married. Contemporaries judged that parents wanted their offspring's pay, or to be relieved of the cost of supporting them, but other evidence suggests that parents wanted their children to remain under their own supervision. The only way they could manage this was for the children to contribute something to their own upkeep. Many parents kept their children at home as long as they could. Only when the family was reduced to destitution, fragmented by desertions, ill health, and deaths, did parents allow their children to leave home and go into the households of others to work.

Again, a methodological point should be remembered: age at 'leaving home' implies that there *was* a family home.[150] For many children, orphans as well as illegitimate children, there was no 'home' offering a sense of security and familiarity. Even legitimate children may have been adversely affected by sickness and parental misfortunes; they had been nursed out, put in the workhouse, or experienced a series of temporary abodes. By the time poor children reached about 12 years, many of their families had disintegrated. Thus the Royal Philanthropic Society, founded in late eighteenth-century London to 'rescue' potentially criminal children, found many homeless young people. Some had fled apprenticeships, while others had been 'turned into the Streets', one girl by her stepfather.[151] The very poorest children were likely to be working in the households of others or on the streets at the youngest ages.

REMARRIAGE AND STEPPARENTING

Since a fragmented family headed by a widowed parent, especially a mother, was likely to be poor, and had limited choices, one option for the surviving parent was to recreate a semblance of a nuclear family by re-partnering, through remarriage, or *de facto* or bigamous marriage. In late sixteenth-century Norwich, the ages of many of those remarrying were more than ten years apart, suggesting that survival balanced abilities and disabilities.[152] In Clayworth in 1676, over a third of the couples in the village had been married before.[153] The families created by remarriage or *de facto* marriage were complex; the new couple had different relationships with the children, whether stepchildren or children of the new marriage.

Contemporaries believed that the stepparent relationship was difficult. 'Well, here is a second marriage, and there is one come to be a stepfather or stepmother. Such an one ought to be verie carefull, to doe the office of him in whose stead he is come', wrote an anonymous author in 1616. Even though remarriages could ensure that children were better cared for—it 'is euerie way better for the children, as I haue seene'[154]—stepparents, especially stepmothers, were widely feared. From medieval times, there were popular ballads about stepmothers resenting their charges, and proverbs about the harsh discipline of a stepfather: 'He that will not be warned bi his owne fader, he shall be warned bi his step fader.'[155] Stepparents complicated family dynamics, as the usual sibling rivalries were exacerbated and siblings related to different sets of kin. People suspected that conflicts between parents and children would be intensified when 'outsiders' were involved.

Over the period 1599 to 1811, widowed mothers who remarried were more likely to have their children living with them than remarrying fathers: 12.5 per cent of partially orphaned children lived with a widowed mother and stepfather, only 7.5 per cent with a father and stepmother.[156] However, these figures were for the whole society, not just the poor. Too much should not be deduced about the fates of poor children solely on the demographic evidence about residence. Children may have already left home; after a parent died a household may have disintegrated.

If the family were poor, remarriages might fragment children's relationships with their surviving parent. Relatives might facilitate a widow's remarriage by taking care of children. In early eighteenth-century London, one Westminster widow had an 8-year-old daughter by a previous husband, 'now with her Grandmother Elianor Morgan at Marlborough'. The child of another Westminster widow lived with her grandmother in Shrewsbury, while a very poor grandfather in Kingston, Surrey, kept his 4-year-old granddaughter.[157]

The assistance of the Poor Law authorities might allow a family to be re-formed. In 1756, St Katherine Cree assisted the widowed Amy Tedmarsh and her two children to leave the workhouse and remarry by providing some clothing, and a payment of 5s. to fetch a gown and blanket out of pawn.[158] Another widow, Prudence Erle, applied for weekly assistance after her remarriage to a hatter allowed her to reclaim her daughter Rose aged 7 years and her son Will aged 4 years from the workhouse. The overseers granted the children some clothes, but refused the new family any allowance.[159]

In other cases, the Poor Laws divided mothers and children: remarrying mothers might not be able to keep the children of their first husband with them because on remarriage they acquired a settlement in their new husband's parish, while their children by previous marriages retained their father's settlement. Legally, stepchildren were not properly a part of the new family. As Richard Burn explained, the reason was 'because it is not her [the mother's] family, but her husband's; and she cannot give the children any sustenance without the husband's leave'.[160] The children could not inherit a settlement from a stepfather, nor from a remarried mother, since a wife was 'under Coverture, and having a Settlement there herself only as Part of her Husband's Family'.[161] When the family needed relief, a woman's children by her earlier marriages or partnerships would be moved to their place of legal settlement. Thus in the mid-seventeenth century, when a widowed stepfather moved parishes with his three stepchildren, the justices ruled that he 'being father in Law [stepfather] only to the said Children cannot by Law bee charged with their maintenance'. Since the children were young and required relief, they were to be separated from their stepfather and returned to their late father's parish.[162] Burn's authoritative pronouncement in 1755 was that a husband should maintain his wife's children by a former husband during his wife's lifetime, but not after her death.[163] This meant that many orphaned children were left without any parent, for unless the widowed stepfather and his new wife were able to care for them, the orphaned children had to be boarded out, apprenticed, or, in the eighteenth century, placed in a workhouse. Thus, when Mrs White remarried in 1789, the guardians of the poor in the parish of St Clement Danes stopped her allowance and ordered her children into the workhouse.[164]

Remarriages and stepparents raised basic questions: how thinly would resources be spread? Would more children be born? Which sons and daughters would fare best? Historians have discussed the effects of being a stepparent, or having a stepparent largely on the basis of literary sources which inevitably related to the wealthier sections of society, and involved the recollections of adult children. Among the more prosperous, children's concerns related to inheritances, focusing not just on how their parent and the new spouse would consume the family's resources, but also on jealousies and fears of the stepmother's 'own' children receiving bequests.[165] For remarrying poor parents, the number of children could itself be a problem. In 1626, the churchwardens presented a Sussex couple for living apart; 'the reason is they have children on both sides and he is poore and aged and much controversy grew betwixt them because of theire children'.[166]

Even in poor families, there were fears about the dispersal of any small inheritances on remarriage. Despite a widespread belief that a father's remarriage and stepmothers were the danger, a widow's remarriage had potentially more adverse effects on her children, because a widow's property became that of her new husband. Some mothers tried to protect their children's inheritances, however small these may have been, by marriage 'settlements'. Erickson found that in about 10 per cent of married men's probate accounts, there were such settlements. While the status of men was from yeoman down, some were below median status labourers, so she concluded that efforts to preserve small amounts of personal property were not unknown at the lower levels of society.[167] Erickson argued that women managed negotiations for themselves, although O'Hara's sixteenth-century evidence suggests that widows might benefit from the assistance of male kin.[168] The level of involvement of ordinary parents in the marriages of children, as well as in the remarriages of widows, is not clear.

Legally, when a widower remarried, his children by earlier marriages remained under his care. But fathers might not want their older children to live with them. In 1748, the Newgate Ordinary, giving an account of 20-year-old Sarah Kenigem who had been sentenced to death for the theft of 27 guineas, explained that she fell into debauchery 'immediately upon her being turned adrift after her father's second Marriage'.[169]

New sexual dynamics could destabilize families. There are instances of stepfathers being attracted to their stepdaughters.[170] In a case of incestuous rape before the Old Bailey, John Marsland (in Chapter 3), who protested angelic innocence, claimed that his daughter Mary had been prompted to accuse him by his late wife's two brothers-in-law. Certainly the two uncles had been active in bringing Marsland before the court, after the girl had turned to her aunt, Hannah Dewsberry, for help. Mrs Dewsberry had asked Mary 'if some nasty Person, had not meddled with her', to whom she confessed 'it was her Father'.[171] Sentenced to death, Marsland left his second wife responsible for Mary and any other children he may have had.

Church and secular court records offer further negative evidence of orphans' experiences with a remarrying parent.[172] Contemporaries considered that second husbands resented their wives' first children as 'intruders', and neglected and ill-treated them so that they were thrown onto the parish.[173] Nevertheless, there is evidence of some stepfathers accepting responsibility. Thus in 1611 in Southampton, there was a complex case of a stepfather rescuing his stepson from his master who was in gaol; the master refused to release the boy, and the master's wife refused to feed the apprentice. The stepfather subsequently had the boy apprenticed to himself.[174] Hostile views of stepmothers were fed by fairy stories and folk tales. Stepmothers favoured their 'own' children in the competition for food,[175] but stepchildren's stories about hunger can be read as symptomatic of deeper losses. Small children especially were at risk after their mother had died, although studies of nineteenth-century Italy suggest that the presence of a grandmother could favourably affect their mortality.[176] All the children whose parents remarried had experienced bereavement.

Relationships between stepparents and their children looked different from their respective perspectives. A widowed stepmother prosecuted her stepdaughter, Mary Nace, for theft. Mary claimed in her defence that she was a servant to her stepmother, saying 'that her Mother had used her money often times before, so she thought now she might make bold with hers'.[177] Elizabeth Battison, who in 1686 was found guilty of killing her 11-year-old stepdaughter, Elizabeth Kell, by giving her a mortal wound from a kick or blow to her belly, protested 'that though she was Mother in Law [stepmother] to the Deceased Kell, yet she loved her very well, and always gave her moderate Correction'.[178] The harsh discipline of a stepmother could precipitate conflict between the parents. The Old Bailey court censured Ann Thacker's stepmother for her cruelty, and admonished the father to take care of his daughter: 'it will be very necessary for her

[Ann's] safety that she [the stepmother] should treat the child better in future.' The father said that he had applied to an attorney to draw up articles of separation.[179]

Despite all the negative evidence about stepmothers, casual evidence in some criminal trials suggests that in practice some stepmothers did the best they could. In 1776, a notorious case before the Old Bailey can be read as a 'good stepmother' story. A couple of years after one widowed father remarried, he fled, leaving his wife with a young stepdaughter and no means of survival. Mrs Clifford went from London to Cambridge to work for two years, leaving her stepdaughter on the parish. The parish apprenticed 13-year-old Mary Clifford to Elizabeth Brownrigg, from whom she experienced ill-treatment and sadistic punishment. Other apprentices and neighbours knew of Mary's sufferings, but dared not intervene. Only when Mary's stepmother returned from Cambridgeshire around Midsummer 1767, and started enquiring after her stepdaughter, did the neighbours tell her that Mary was being 'sadly used'. When Mrs Clifford's own attempts to investigate failed, she went to the parish officers of St Dunstan in the West, who eventually succeeded in finding and removing Mary. The parish sent the girl to St Bartholomew's hospital, where she died from her terrible injuries on 9 August 1767.[180] No neighbours had the power to override the authority of James Brownrigg and intervene. The parish had the power but did nothing until driven into action by the persistence of Mary's stepmother.

The responsibility for young children may have prompted their widowed parent to remarry so that they could bring up their children themselves rather than put the remnants of their family on the parish. We have few literary sources from ordinary people describing the emotional effects of a stepparent, only the odd glimpse from autobiographical records of poor individuals. The hints about family dynamics turn on jealousies and resentments: who was sitting by the fire and who was out in the cold; who was better fed or better clothed. New stepsiblings intensified sibling rivalries, and a new parent, especially a new stepfather who was entitled to authority over his family, could destabilize familial relationships. Elizabeth Ricketts, aged 22 years, was prosecuted before the Old Bailey by her stepfather James Walker for the theft of three of her mother's gowns.[181] Elizabeth claimed that she was 'distressed and had neither house nor home, and drove by necessity to do it'. She thought she might make herself welcome with her mother's things: 'I did not think that my mother would have brought me to such a place as this.' It is unclear whether her stepfather was prosecuting because he and Elizabeth's mother found her behaviour impossible, or whether they were acting, as they claimed, 'to save her from Tyburn'. Her mother, asked by the court 'Did you ever do for her as a mother ought to do?', answered yes, she had clothed her daughter with her own clothes, and had put her to school, 'but she would keep to nothing; sometimes she would be gone for two or three years and never let us hear from her; then she would come again all rags, and keep wicked company'.

Poverty could separate stepmothers from their charges. In 1626, in Essex, an 8-year-old girl whose father had died was to be taken from her stepmother who was returning to live with her own father. The proceeds of the sale of the goods of the child's deceased father, William Thorne, were to be employed for the girl's education.[182] This probably meant that the parish would pay someone to take charge of the girl who was by this stage bereaved of her mother, her father, and her stepmother.

Failing remarriage, a widow or widower might cohabit and 'pass' as married. Such *de facto* arrangements made families even more vulnerable to fragmentation as they were inherently unstable. Any need for poor relief, especially in the eighteenth century, would lead to a routine investigation of the legal status and the settlement rights of the couple and any children in the family. Such investigations revealed many complex parent–child relationships. Judith Rideout, who was examined in Southampton in 1773, had an illegitimate son thirteen or fourteen years before. When she married around 1763, her sister took the boy, but then married in her turn. The boy, who had lost the use of one of his legs, was found apparently alone in Devon.[183]

Kin might take in orphaned children. A factor which may have affected a rural orphan's experience was whether they were heir to any property or goods. If there was something to inherit, then those who would benefit by the orphan's death may not have been kindly guardians.[184] Guardians do not feature very often in the records relating to poor parents, perhaps because in general they chose wisely. One mother in 1687, chose a particularly unsuitable guardian when she asked an unmarried sail-maker, William Webb, to take charge of her 8-year-old daughter. Webb was subsequently tried for the rape of the child, but not convicted because although the girl had a venereal infection, the evidence of rape was unclear.[185]

Occasionally both the father and mother had died, and by a process of serial remarriage, two stepparents were responsible for any surviving children.[186] In a 1749 rape case, Susannah Tabart had two such unrelated stepparents. The prosecution, which depended upon whether or not Susannah was under 10 years of age, failed partly because her stepmother was vague about Susannah's birthday, thinking that the girl had been born in South Carolina in 1739.[187]

Remarriages did not necessarily solve the problems of parents in providing care for their children. Remarriages could create tensions and further fragmentations of families. Some children were lucky, finding unrelated foster parents. In 1608, Richard Anderson, who was kept by the town of Southampton for ten years, was apprenticed, but ran away from his master back to the house 'where he had benn formerlie kept & brought upp'.[188]

PUBLIC AND PRIVATE CHARITY

Parents in difficulties could appeal to the charity of their neighbours or of institutions. In the late sixteenth and seventeenth centuries, begging, both formal and informal, kept many families alive. In addition, there was a multitude of charities across England. Many charities, founded in the late seventeenth century by subscriptions, specialized in particular groups of the poor. Children were a popular target for social reformers, but the rules and sanctions of charities created relationships of power which the children's parents negotiated and resisted.

Mothers were more likely to appeal for charity on the basis of their parenting responsibilities than fathers. In public advertisements in the London press appealing for assistance from the 1740s to 1790s, only 12 out of 265 men who asked for aid did so for themselves and their offspring, unlike mothers, 159 of 349 of whom appealed for compassion for themselves and their children.[189] A common strategy employed, particularly by mothers, when approaching a charity was deference combined with flattery. One girl's mother attended the board meeting of a London charity 'and return'd the Gentlemen thanks for her child's Education and Cloathing, praying for leave to take her out of the School, and that her Books and Cloathes might be given her'. Since her daughter had behaved well, this was granted.[190] Men too could behave submissively. Thus when Christ's governors expelled their porter, with potentially ruinous consequences for his family, other employees petitioned for his reinstatement, acknowledging the governors' power: 'such Rulers are to a Common wealth fathers, seeking ye publique good.'[191]

Figure 15 'The London Begger' (1711). Parishes could license people to beg, but in larger cities begging was less controlled. Mothers were frequently accompanied by their children.

The London Begger
Le Gueux de Londres

Any charitable educational regimes demanded control; governors and teachers rivalled fathers and mothers for authority over the children. Clothes, discipline, and work were all contested issues.[192] The governors' minutes of Peter Joye's London Charity School show disputes over the children's attendance. Parents kept their children away; in June 1729, presumably when summer work was available, the governors recorded their resentment at three boys being absent 'by their Parents knowledge'.[193] At other times, parents strategically promised compliance: in July 1761, when girls were truanting and coming late to school; the committee ordered that their parents should appear and they 'were reprimanded, and they promised their Children should attend better for the future'.[194] If parents attended and pleaded, children were usually allowed another chance. Intercession from a mother rather than a father might be strategic, as humble behaviour was more appropriate for her than her husband. James Collins' mother let him go from place to place 'as Errand-boy'. On examining the matter, 'it appearing that poverty & a large Family was the occasion of her so doing', the governors allowed the boy to continue, provided he attended school when 'out of Place'.[195]

Poor parents might have been stern disciplinarians, but they resented anyone else disciplining their children. In 1718, the governors of one London charity resolved to exclude the children of any parent who should abuse the teacher 'in discharge of their Duty by way of Correction'.[196] In a school established by the Society for Promoting Christian Knowledge at Bath, the mistress had been 'as it were hector'd by the Barbarian mothers of the Children & has no body to stand by her, or to appeal to'. The governors resolved to expel children whose parents insulted the teachers and to deny the children their clothes.[197]

Contests which ostensibly occurred around the profits of the children's labour may be read as assertions of parental authority. The trustees' system of payment of the teachers in the charity schools encouraged the masters and mistresses to employ their scholars gainfully. However, at Attleborough school, the profit from the children's labour was sent to the parents 'who are thereby excited to send them to School'.[198] Governors of charities wanted to direct children's future employment, again threatening parental authority. No books or clothes were allowed for Margaret Misslt in 1778, 'her Mother having placed her out at Service without the consent of the Trustees'; another mother was told that her husband could remove his 9-year-old if he insisted, but the boy would be refused his clothes and books.[199]

Although the training offered by charities was generally of limited value, an exception was the mathematical education that Christ's Hospital offered clever boys from 1673. Christ's placed forty of 'their' boys in their special maths school for seven years so they might serve the king and 'the Publick Weale' in navigation.[200] The governors were affronted when those on whom they had expended so much time and effort ran away, or made their own contracts to serve masters, in 'manifest contempt of the Government of the House'.[201] In 1702, Benjamin Herne fled on the eve of his determined voyage. The governors raged, seeking the advice of the Attorney General, but failed to find the boy despite suspecting the complicity of 'his friends'; a year earlier, they had denied his mother's petition that her son should not go to sea.[202] Poor parents' powers were limited but sometimes very effective.[203]

Desperate parents could appeal to an institution or a charity for what many hoped would be temporary assistance. Putting children, usually the youngest, into the care of others was not unique to England.[204] London offered a wider range of charities for the care of children than other areas, of which the most important were Christ's Hospital (refounded in the mid-sixteenth century) and the Foundling Hospital (which received children from 1741).

Christ's Hospital initially accepted only the orphaned children of freemen, and usually only one child per family. In the Elizabethan period it was not difficult for parents or kin to reclaim children.[205] In 1596, Anne Perrine who was admitted as an infant, was apprenticed to a tailor, then discharged to her father, who sent his 18-month-old daughter Emme in her place.[206] In 1596, Thomas Bennit, a fishmonger, placed his 6-year-old daughter at Christ's. In 1602, when she was 12 years old, he reclaimed her, and the Hospital granted him 8d. per week to provide her with shoes and stockings as other children were at Michaelmas and Christmas.[207] Grace Maior aged 11 years was discharged to her uncle; a 13-year-old girl to her grandmother.[208] The registers do not record motives: parents or relatives may have wanted the young people's economic or material assistance; or they may simply have improved their own circumstances and been in a position to reclaim the children.

Christ's admission registers (which changed over time as admission policies altered) witness to some widows' efforts to cope by themselves for as long as they could. In 1571, Christ's accepted John Ratfford aged 4 years because his mother was 'withoute howse or anie comphert'.[209] Occasionally, the governors acknowledged a poor mother's devotion and granted her relief so that she could care for her child herself.[210] A child whom the governors had put out for three years was placed with his mother in 1580 when he was 10 years old, and again in 1583, for which she was allowed 8d.[211] The registers occasionally allow us to trace a mother's relationship with her child. In 1576, Steven Holforde, the 6-year-old son of a citizen and clothworker, was admitted and soon discharged to the care of Margaret Holford, presumably his mother. A year later, in 1577, the entry 'Home' indicates that Steven was returned to Christ's. He was then with a foster mother for several months, until in March 1578, he was back in the Hospital. There he remained until November 1581, when his mother was finally able to provide the Hospital with her bond and sureties that she would keep the child 'for ever'.[212]

From 1661, Christ's offered places to one child per family aged over 7 years. The governors required parents or those responsible to fill in a printed form confirming that the child was no foundling, was not maintained at the parish charge, and that those leaving the child relinquished their authority over the child, leaving it 'to the Dispose of the Governors of the said Hospital'.[213] These petitions offer further evidence about the material circumstances of poor London parents. Mrs Catesbee petitioned for temporary admission of her 2-year-old son, John, because her husband's business had failed; they could not buy bread. John had been at wet-nurse until he had 'almost peryshed in the limes [limbs] for want of a cleanly good nurse by reson I had not whear with to pay her'. Mrs Catesbee hoped to reclaim her son.[214] In 1675, Anne Draynor, whose husband had not been heard of since he went on a voyage four years earlier, petitioned for the admission of one of her three children, selecting her 11-year-old son John.[215] The widowed Lidia Marshall was trying to support her aged mother as well as her own three children when she applied for a place for Obadiah, who was nearly 9 years old.[216]

While most of the petitioners to Christ's were widows, in a few cases fathers applied. John Carter, a weaver, had remarried after his wife's death, but with the charge of five small children, he could not maintain his 7-year-old son William.[217] Even through the formulaic petitions there are tiny glimpses of some men's efforts to look after their children. In 1675, Thomas Butt, who had been caring for his bedridden wife and five children for fifteen months, sought a place for his 8-year-old son: he had been looking after the children for all that time.[218] After his wife's death, a weaver, Thomas Franklin, had struggled for a decade with six small children. In 1675, he sought admission for his 10-year-old son Ralph: institutional care for one child would help the others to survive.[219]

The opening of the London Foundling Hospital in 1741 offered another option to married parents for the care of very young children; one third of the infants admitted in the years of the general admission 1756–60 were legitimate.[220] Deserted wives, widows, and widowers all applied, a number of these with the assistance of their parishes.[221] Some stated explicitly that they hoped that the assistance would be temporary, as did Mary Morris in 1756. Her husband was abroad when she put in her twelfth child, Charlotte: 'I have suckle the child for this month and I hope the Child will fall into som good Nurses hands who will use it well I hope god enable me to take it out in two years time.'[222] In 1772, a poor widowed charwoman explained that 'The Father ran away & left her & the [two] Children & is since Dead'; the widowed Samuel Norbury could not afford to pay for care of his 3-year-old child as well as a younger one.[223] Another widower, Zaccheus Thor, petitioned for the admission of his youngest child; he was 'at present encumbred' with three children, aged from around 2 years to 2 months, and the costs of nursing defeated him, for although he could earn 16s. weekly as a mason, he was unemployed during the winter. His landlady supported Thor's application: he was a hard-working, honest poor man who simply could not afford a nurse for his youngest child.[224] Although contemporary propaganda for the establishment of the Hospital castigated married parents together with single mothers for their cruel and heartless 'abandonment' of their children, the evidence in the petitions shows mothers and fathers making difficult decisions in adverse circumstances.

In severe poverty, parents might surrender their children to a form of informal adoption. In 1591, a mother and father freely and voluntarily gave their 5-year-old son to a member of the Grocers' company, promising to have nothing to do with him other than pray for adoptive father and son.[225] Other desperate mothers and fathers left their children where they hoped others would find them and informally adopt them. As Chapter 1 argued, this 'abandonment' of children should be viewed as a strategy for the children's survival. In 1751, Mary Walker told a fellow lodger, Mrs Jane Harrad, that she 'had Dropped & left' her 6-week-old daughter near the workhouse door of St Botolph's. Unsurprisingly, the parish authorities did not want to be responsible for the infant, and a week later they caught up with Mrs Walker, who confirmed the legitimacy of her child; her husband was in the workhouse of St Margaret's.[226] In other cases, informal temporary arrangements for childcare might become long term, amounting to informal adoptions.

All of these charitable institutions, as well as the parish, depended upon ordinary mothers accepting the care of children who were not 'their own'. Wet-nurses undertook nurture of babies for individuals, the parish, and charities. Many charitable hospitals recalled the children after they were weaned, and placed them in institutional settings, thereby disrupting any emotional bonds. Fatherless children or orphans could be treated similarly. The surrogate motherhood that ordinary mothers offered their charges varied; some may have been forced to accept such children as the price of parish relief. Older children unhappily placed could run away, ending up in the world of beggars, vagrants, and street children.

PARENTAL STORIES

In the complex families of poor mothers and fathers, it was not always clear who was responsible for children. Nor was the boundary between legitimate children and 'bastards' so sharp as in legislation and law. Stories from the Old Bailey records, incomplete and tantalizing though they may be, offer some qualitative evidence about the lives of poor parents.

The first story relates to the tangled family of William Patmore, a London staymaker whom we met in the previous chapter. In 1789, he was tried before the Old Bailey for the murder of his wife Mary.[227] Patmore's trial revealed complex marital relationships and a constellation of differing views about parental responsibilities for children. The story was briefly as follows. The couple married around 1775, but separated after Mary bore a child. Mary then married (bigamously) one Harwood, an ivory turner, by whom she subsequently bore eleven children while William, a journeyman staymaker, lived with another woman, Rachel Walters, who passed for his wife.

Eventually, Mary left Harwood and their children. She lived in lodgings while she tried to run a school, which suggests that she was literate and capable, but returned to her parents when her school failed. Subsequently, after her mother died, she took lodgings again. In 1788, when Mary was destitute and pregnant, the parish officers where she lodged returned her to William, her lawful husband, whose parish of settlement would be responsible for the family's relief. Patmore pretended Mary was his sister, or a poor vagrant woman whom he had charitably taken in, and tried to persuade neighbouring women to help him get her into a workhouse, or a lying-in hospital; failing those expedients, Patmore vowed to send her to Bridewell. Mary subsequently gave birth on 3 January 1789 and died around three weeks later in an upstairs garret. Patmore was acquitted of her murder.

Mary and William argued over who married bigamously first, leading a bemused witness to tell Patmore: 'I thought it was a comical sort of mess of marrying'. In this 'comical sort of mess of marrying' who considered themselves responsible for the children? The Old Bailey never investigated the fate of the eleven children Mary allegedly bore in her bigamous marriage; presumably as 'bastards' they would be 'on the parish' unless their father, Harwood, was willing and able to accept responsibility, which seemed unlikely as the couple had separated. Patmore was their legal father, but the issue was academic, since he was, as one witness observed, 'a poor man'. The court asked 'Was he very poor?—He was very poor.' At the trial, the prosecution called on Mary, the 13-year-old daughter of the couple: 'it is painful task upon me to call a child against a parent; it is what nature shudders at.' Mary's chequered childhood included living for eight or nine years with her maternal grandparents, then subsequently with her father and his *de facto* wife Rachel, eating at the same table and presumably being treated as a daughter. Yet Mary had known her mother as long as she could remember and seemed aware of her parents' complex marital situation.

Witnesses declared that the 'pretty baby' Mary bore in the back garret looked 'likely to live', but died sometime within the next three weeks. Patmore denied paternity, saying after the birth, 'I suppose it is the paper bag man's; I must go and get a paper bag to put it in'. (The baby's paternity was never resolved, but Patmore could have been the father, as he had been visiting Mary early in the previous summer.) He told a neighbour he had 'got a young bantling', an ambiguous statement since the word 'bantling' at this date could imply bastardy, but 'got' could have meant 'begotten'.[228] Whether the child was of his begetting or not, Patmore horrified the neighbourhood by trying to sell the bodies of both his wife and the infant. A surgeon's pupil gave him 4s. for the child's body, but after he rejected Mary's because of its filthy and verminous state, Patmore threatened to throw it into the Thames, because he could not afford a burial.[229] In this story, the boundaries between legitimacy and illegitimacy seem relatively unimportant and emotional attachments are difficult to chart.

The 'comical mess of marrying' of William and Mary Patmore seemed extraordinary to neighbours, but bigamy and *de facto* marriages were not uncommon in eighteenth-century London. Bigamy cases from assize records and the Old Bailey suggest many such uncertain unions were accepted as valid marriages, because no one knew to the contrary: 'they call one another my Dear and my Wife, and if you ask whether they are married, yes to be sure, they'll tell you.'[230] Couples who had separated could plausibly claim that their spouses were dead; geographical distances and poor communications even between London parishes made confused marital situations difficult to clarify.[231] One suspicious employer went to check the parish register. His journeyman, Robert Hussey, who had lived with him for two years with a wife and children, said he was leaving, because he was not really married. While the marriage was certainly registered, Hussey claimed it was invalid as he had another wife living at the time.[232] Emotions drove some illegal unions: Lewis Hussar, condemned to death for murdering his wife after he had 'married' another, was unrepentant about killing his wife, but shed tears over the fate of his second, having 'such a Concern and Tenderness for his Second Wife and his Child ... at the Consideration of their being left without a Sufficiency to support them'.[233]

Stories of infanticide and child murder suggest that poverty and mental disturbance may have affected mothers more than did their marital status. Sometimes it was the physiological experience of giving birth and the deaths of children that left mothers vulnerable. At higher social levels, we know that people suffering disturbing grief for the deaths of their children in the early seventeenth century consulted the physician Richard Napier; though the fee could be as low as 12d., it was as high as a labourer's daily wage.[234] Nevertheless, poor mothers especially may have been deeply disturbed by deaths of children.

Since people expected that mothers naturally loved their offspring, they were always deeply shocked at murdering mothers, frequently viewing them as mentally disturbed.[235] A popular genre of literature was the pamphlet or broadside recounting terrible stories of maternal murders and wickedness.[236] Some explained maternal failings in terms of the supernatural.[237] Thus a 1675 pamphlet recounted the unhappy tale of a widow, who had hoped that her son would be some comfort 'after some trouble and cost in bringing him up', but the little boy proved peevish with ill health, continually crying at nights. The devil tempted her, saying that she would never remarry 'as long as this froward child is with you'. She killed him, remarried, but confessed thirty years later.[238] By the 1720s, infanticidal mothers may have been viewed with more sympathy, but even so, those who killed children as distinct from infants were always viewed with horror.[239] When Judith Defour, a single mother who worked spinning silk while her 2-year-old daughter was cared for at the parish workhouse, confessed to her fellow workers that she had left her child out on a January night, they were horrified: what, said Susan Jones, 'in such a dismal cold Night! How can you be so cruel?' The women rushed out to rescue the girl, who was found with a rag tied around her neck. John Wolveridge, a bystander, asked Defour 'how she could be so

Figure 16 *Natures Cruell Step-Dames* (1637). Newsbook pictures of murderous mothers drew upon the view that such deeds were unnatural and particularly horrifying. Here the pamphlet told of a mother who had pacified her child with raisins, then when her daughter fell asleep, she cut the child's throat.

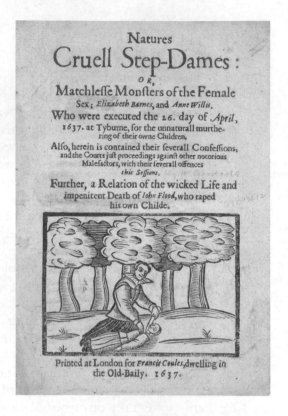

Natures
Cruell Step-Dames:
OR,
Matchleffe Monfters of the Female
Sex; *Elizabeth Barnes*, and *Anne Willis.*
Who were executed the 26. day of *April*,
1637. at Tyburne, for the unnaturall murthe-
ring of their owne Children,
Alfo, herein is contained their feverall Confeffions,
and the Courts juft proceedings againft other notorious
Malefactors, with their feverall offences
this Seffions.
Further, a Relation of the wicked Life and
impenitent Death of *Iohn Flood,*who raped
his own Childe.

Printed at London for *Francis Coules,*dwelling in
the Old-Baily. 1637.

barbarous as to murder her own Infant?' Defour's mother, her only supporting witness, alleged that her daughter was mad: 'She never was in her right Mind, but was always roving.'[240]

Another child-murder story relates to a widow, Mary Hindes, who was twice indicted before the Old Bailey for killing two infants to whom she was not related. In 1761, she was acquitted of drowning 5-month-old Edward Mulby in a pond, but in 1768 she was sentenced to death for drowning Joseph Smith, aged about 17 months, in the Serpentine in Hyde Park.[241] Hindes's circumstances were dismal. Her husband had disappeared around 1758, 'gone to sea or was dead', and after five years, poverty reduced Mary to living in St George's workhouse, doing plain sewing. In 1761, Mary, who described herself as a laundress earning 3s. per week, shared lodgings with the Mulbys. She thought that Sarah Mulby was almost starved, 'and her child too'. As Sarah Mulby explained, Mary 'took my child (being seemingly fond of it)'; 'We were not enemies, nor over great. She seemed to be fond of the child.'[242] Mary claimed that while she was carrying the baby Edward to her sister's to beg some silk to make him a cap, she rested on a bridge in Hyde Park and 'the child gave a jump out of her hands into the water'. No one was around to help, and although Mary said that she strove to rescue Edward, 'but being with child could not . . . I was affrighted, and did not know what to do.'[243] In the second case of 1768 the court suspected that Mary was out of her wits—had the moon affected her?—and her defence was madness: 'it was owing to a disturbed mind through a bad husband.' The dead child's father too was at a loss as to motive; Mary 'always used to be fond of this child,' he said, adding significantly, 'but the child was not fond of her'. Mary interjected: 'He used to call me Mad Moll.'

Mary Hindes's history, as told in these two court cases seven years apart, suggests deep derangement, which may have been linked to her own failed maternity. She had lost her own children; her husband 'had taken a couple of children from her, and put them into the Foundling-hospital'. If she were pregnant, as she pleaded in 1761, this was illicit; nothing more was recorded of that pregnancy or child. In 1768, she saw that her fellow-lodgers' child Edward was nearly starved, but her pathetic attempts to attach him to her failed, for he 'would struggle against her, and would never come to her arms'.[244] Mary Hindes said she wanted to die, but when the court asked why she did not drown herself rather than the child, her reply astonished observers: 'I know the difference between that and self-murder.'[245]

Although we lack first-person statements from poor women about their grief at the deaths of children, we should not assume indifference. If children died, many mothers experienced deep emotional disturbance, even to the extent of believing themselves insane.[246] The utterances of some mothers who killed their infants suggested that they saw no boundary between the lives of their infants and themselves. Thus Mary Cooke, the mother of eight children who had recently given birth and then killed her 'beloved Child', her 2-year-old daughter Betty in 1670, was so concerned about Betty's future that she concluded 'that she had better rid that of life first, and then all her fears and cares for it would be at an end'.[247] In 1708, a pamphlet recounted the unhappy story of 'The Cruel Mother', Elizabeth Cole, the newly delivered wife of an absent sailor, who threw her 5-year-old daughter into the Thames. The pamphlet reported that Elizabeth was viewed with pity, though she declined to plead 'as if she were Lunatick', insisting that she had 'sent my dear Child to Heaven, and am resolv'd to go after her'.[248]

Some of the issues which confronted poor fathers emerge in the Old Bailey trial of John Williamson for the murder of his second wife in

1767.[249] Williamson was a journeyman shoemaker, living and working in lodgings in an alley, up three flights of stairs. Williamson, who
had married Anne eight months earlier, lived with her and three of his
children in a single room with a closet, to which he confined his wife
much of the time. The details that emerged—of Williamson tying up
his wife with handcuffs and securing her to a staple in the closet,
feeding her little, and letting her sleep there covered in lice, under rags
and a single sheet—sound cruel and even sadistic. Certainly the
Tyburn Chronicle and the *Full and Authentic Account* of his execution portrayed him in such terms.[250]

But Williamson could be seen as a man at his wits' end. A tall thin
man, aged about 46 years, he was a widower with three children. He
had known Anne, who was aged 25 or 26 years, all her life and knew
that she was subject to fits, sometimes four or five a day, in which she
turned up her eyes. There was evidence of mental disturbance: 'she
was like a mad woman.' Williamson's children told him that they
were afraid to stay with her: she had thrown a knife at his 15-year-old
daughter Mercy who said she was 'afraid she was going to do something to me'. Contemporaries thought that his 'sole motive' for marrying Anne was the £60 portion in the hands of her guardian.
Williamson was certainly poor, at times 'in great poverty', and after
he received the £60 from her guardian, went into the country to pay
some debts. The neighbours could not understand why he did not put
his wife in the workhouse. Clearly, the idea had occurred to him: he
said that he and the committee could not agree. Another account
claimed that her guardian offered to take Anne from him and put her
in the workhouse, provided he, her husband, received only £30 of her
money.[251] Parishes were troubled at the cost of the sick poor; London
parishes were at considerable expense to send the 'insane' poor to
private madhouses, and would have required some money with
Anne.[252]

Poverty compounded the Williamsons' problems. Anne complained that her husband denied her food: if she asked for more
bread than the single slice she was given each day, Williamson refused
her, saying 'she should have no more, for she works for none'.
A fellow lodger thought her body looked 'like a skeleton'. Williamson
was angered at her complaints to fellow lodgers of hunger, which
reflected badly on him as family provider: she said 'what a rogue
I have, he will not give me a bit of dinner, and his children and he sit
there'. Williamson himself wrote to the coroner's jury explaining that
her death was not caused by starvation but was the consequence of

her fits, which were caused by a menstrual disorder: 'she had not the custom of women in the natural way; for they flew into the head.'[253]

Other witnesses spoke strongly in support of Williamson as a 'good man to his first wife and his family': 'he had a great family of children to bring up'. The terms in which witnesses praised him as a good father related to his working and providing for his family. Henry Cole, a fellow shoemaker, said that Williamson had 'five or six children, and worked very hard for them day and night'.

Evidence in the case was contradictory. Some witnesses suggested that relationships between the stepmother and stepchildren were bad, and that the children found fault with their stepmother, yet others told of Anne playing cards with her stepdaughter, and of their reading books together, such as *Moll Flanders* and Aesop's fables. Mercy said that her father made her throw water over her stepmother, which she disliked doing, because it was intended as a punishment, not as a cure for fits. When Anne was dying, Mercy urged that someone should stay with her, but her father had said 'No, no, never mind'. After Williamson was convicted and sentenced to death and dissection, he declared that 'my death is owing to that wicked d—l my daughter, notwithstanding she gave her evidence with trembling and tears'.[254] At 15 years of age, Mercy may well have had an ambivalent relationship with her stepmother.

In the Williamson family, the stepmother was ill and the children, who were bereaved of their mother and other siblings, had witnessed quarrels, violence, and a further death. Presumably after their father was executed, the parish workhouse had to take responsibility for the children and put them into apprenticeships or service.

CONCLUSIONS

Whereas the élite distinguished between the poor by misfortune and the idle and improvident, the good poor and the bad, the poor themselves calibrated their poverty on a scale of misery and hopelessness. Some poverty was manageable; mothers and fathers could cope by turning to relatives and friends, pawning goods, borrowing, and making do so that their children did not suffer actual hunger. Other poverty they judged as hopeless, producing states of disappointment and abjection: 'their hearts sink as toil becomes useless.'[255] Stories were told of parental misery. In 1765, when John Huddlestone cut his own throat, his wife cried 'my husband is dead at last hard fate and misfortunes drove him into despair'.[256] Such severe poverty was likely to weaken vulnerable family units further.

For parents who were on the poverty line all their lives, little changed over the period 1580 to 1800 despite the momentous social and economic changes in their society. The wages of agricultural labour had declined in relation to the cost of living, and work in the newly emerging industries was likewise poorly paid. In the face of economic adversity, which affected health and resilience, mothers and fathers generally did their best to care for their children and to keep them with them. Fathers were more likely than mothers to desert their families. Men who were unemployed or underemployed had the opportunity to migrate in search of work, or to join the army or navy; over time, their bonds with their families were eroded by their physical separation. They may even have started new families in other places. Mothers on their own with children struggled on as best they could. If they travelled to search for absent husbands, they and their children were likely to be punished as vagrants, subjected to whipping earlier, and incarceration in a workhouse later.

Perhaps what did change for the poorest parents was their social position. In the late Elizabethan period, they were still neighbours, members of the parish, subject to misfortune or life-cycle poverty. Over the period, the gap between 'the poor' and the rest of society increased. By 1800, those in severe poverty were almost a sub-class, the undeserving poor, who were least likely to receive either welfare or charity.

5

CIVIC FATHERS OF THE POOR

Preaching a charity sermon for the London Foundling Hospital in 1770, Robert Bromley put words into the mouths of grateful children: 'You were my father and my mother: You took me up . . . and raised me by your care: You taught my tender fingers, as soon as they were capable of use, the arts of honest industry, and showed me how to live.'[1]

The Hospital, he continued, generously cared for children whose parents, despite nature, had relinquished them. A dejected mother showed joy as 'she resigns the infant of her affliction into the arms of nursing fathers and nursing mothers *more able to protect it than its own*!' (emphasis mine).[2] Look on the children, Bromley urged: 'you see them in the way to be made useful citizens and members of society.' This in a nutshell was the public face of civic fatherhood towards the end of the eighteenth century: 'nursing fathers' and 'nursing mothers' had come to supplant and surpass the parenting by 'natural' fathers and mothers who were poor.

How had this come about? How could men, for whom their own roles as fathers of families were central to their manhood, intervene, in the name of the state and of Christian charity, in the families of the poor? How, over the early modern period, did these men come to understand their public fatherhood as superior to that of their social inferiors in making better and more useful citizens of the English nation and British empire? These are the questions with which this chapter is concerned. It extends the discussion of who the 'civic fathers' were, then, by examining their fatherly ideals and practices, and by linking their public fatherhood with specific groups of poor parents and their children. It shows how 'civic fathers', acting in the name of the state, articulated ideas about fatherhood and motherhood which they sought to impose on poor parents and colonized peoples.

The main sources are the administrative records created by statutory poor relief in a diffuse range of parishes throughout England, and the records of charitable institutions, particularly Christ's Hospital (founded 1552) and the Foundling Hospital (founded 1739).

Historians' excellent studies of welfare over the early modern period have established a broad narrative structure, although they dispute whether the Poor Laws were generally benevolent in their operations, or had adverse effects on poor families. Focusing on the rhetoric and practice of civic fathers, I argue that they disempowered poor parents by attempting to impose the domestic patriarchal ideals of late Tudor and early Stuart society.

WHO WERE CIVIC FATHERS?

The term 'civic fathers' has been used here for men who undertook public roles as fathers of poor children, substituting adequate fathers for inadequate or absent ones. As we have seen, from medieval times patriarchal ideals, so fundamental to families and society generally, required that a father maintained his wife and children and exercised authority over them. From around the mid-sixteenth century, Protestant reformers emphasized a father's responsibility for godly order in his family, a microcosm of society as a whole.[3] 'The dominion of a Parent in his Family, is a true representation of the government of a Virtuous prince, who is the Father of his Country.'[4] As has been argued, the legislators framed the Poor Laws at a particular moment in the history of the family, and assumed that the poor should emulate their ideals of the domestic patriarchal family, irrespective of their material circumstances.

The relationship between patriarchy and political authority was deeply embedded in early modern political thought as well as in families. Domestic patriarchy was strongest in the period before the Civil Wars of the 1640s. However, even in this period, as Alexandra Shepard has persuasively argued, men's opportunities to gain status in their society as domestic patriarchs were limited. Many men, unable to be heads of household, looked to alternative sources of masculine authority in their economic activities and credit-worthiness.[5] In addition, I argue that civic fatherhood provided men with another source of authority. Even single men could share in the public exercise of paternal authority over poor men, their wives and children.

During the Civil Wars, patriarchal authority was challenged, especially by the public execution of the king, the father of his people, the earthly representative of God's fatherhood. Although contractual theories of the state displaced patriarchalism by the end of the seventeenth century, the power of the domestic patriarch in the family nonetheless remained strong.[6] Furthermore, the state continued to uphold the power of fathers as heads of household over women, children, and servants inconsistently, as Mary Astell pointed out: 'is it not then partial in men to the last degree, to contend for, and practise that Arbitrary Dominion in their Families, which they abhor and exclaim against in the State?'[7] Some men were well aware that supporting the king's absolute power assisted their own domestic authority: in November 1687 Anne, the unhappily married wife of an Oxfordshire gentleman, Robert Dormer, wrote that her husband was 'violent in maintaining the K[ing']s absolute power, (thereby the better to countenance [his] owne)'.[8]

From Elizabethan times, men's involvement in national and local government was strengthened by a sense of Christian responsibility. Discourses justified their public exercise of paternal authority. As a 1616 treatise on parents explained, the magistrate was 'Pater patriae, the Father of the country'.[9] This was a new role for laymen, challenging both the monarch and the church. By the 1640s the monarch's exercise of patriarchal authority was disputed, and by the end of the century shared with members of Parliament. Even in 1642, John Milton hailed the Parliament as 'the Fathers of their countrey', receiving petitions from aggrieved subjects.[10] During the Commonwealth, in 1655, a catechist included, in answer to the question—who are our parents, whom the fifth commandment orders us to obey?— 'Our Civill Parents, magistrates, Governours, and all in Authority', and also religious and moral authorities, 'Our spirituall Parents, pastors, Ministers, and Teachers'.[11] Hugh Peters, in 1651, termed magistrates 'the civil Fathers of the fatherless',[12] while the social reformer Samuel Hartlib urged parishes 'to be the Father' to those who lacked father and friend.[13] Ideas about fatherhood and the nature of children crucially affected state policies: fathers were to exercise authority and children were to obey.[14] Increasingly, poor parents themselves as well as their children became part of the fatherly responsibility of civic authorities, which reduced their status accordingly.

In the earlier period, up to about 1660, there was fierce debate about how far duties to the poor extended. 'A Christian indeed cannot but take care of Gods familie, as well as his own family', urged a minister, John Moore, in 1653. Answering the objection, 'I [Aye] but there are so many wicked poor!', Moore insisted that God made all, poor as well as rich.[15] Interestingly, most of the radical reformers in the 1640s and 1650s, with a few exceptions including

Gerrard Winstanley and Abeizer Coppe, accepted conventional divisions of the poor into those deserving relief and the idle. Even Winstanley assumed that in a reformed society a father would continue to be the ruler and master of his family.[16]

After the restoration of the monarchy in 1660, the language of fatherhood was still employed to refer to public authorities.[17] Sir Josiah Child used it in proposing a scheme for employing the poor; Parliament should establish an incorporated body for London, Westminster, and Southwark to be called 'the Fathers of the Poor' who would oversee relief and employment.[18] In the eighteenth century, the reformer Jonas Hanway urged that obedience was not restricted to 'your natural parents alone' but was due to 'the *king*, and all that are put in *authority* under him'.[19] Richard Burn, a widely quoted eighteenth-century legal authority on the Poor Laws, referred to those who should care for the poor as 'fathers'.[20] Additionally, throughout the period, the clergy enjoyed special status as spiritual fathers. Ordained ministers were 'Fathers to all that would be Gods Children'[21] and an eighteenth-century archbishop of York bore the character 'of being the common Father of all people in distress'.[22]

The terms 'civic paternalism', 'civic fatherhood', and 'civic fathers' all draw attention to public fatherly activity undertaken for the benefit of the poor. (Although contemporaries spoke of 'the civil Fathers of the fatherless',[23] the meaning of the term 'civil' has so altered that the term 'civic' seems preferable.) Other historians have used comparable phrases for a similar concept: Grossberg referred to 'judicial patriarchy';[24] Bardaglio prefers the term 'state paternalism'.[25] As I explained in the Introduction, I have used the term 'civic fathers' to refer to the men engaged in both statutory and charitable poor relief. To exercise a public role as a civic father it was not necessary to be the father of a family: single men could participate. There were marked differences in social status and ideas between these public fathers. Some men worked voluntarily, others were paid. At the top were the legislators and policy makers, members of Parliament, justices of the peace, and judges, men of wealth and social distinction. Magistrates were gentlemen, and made policies through their local administration. Judges—paid officials who had undertaken legal training and reached the higher echelons of their profession—interpreted the Poor Laws when entitlements became more complex and were contested between parishes.[26] Although magistrates' practices were diverse, and subject to appeals to the assize judges and ultimately to the court of King's Bench, in the counties they acted largely on their own initiatives, working without too much outside intervention, apart from a brief period in the 1630s when the justices were subject to the active scrutiny of the Privy Council.[27] After the Restoration, men at the top of the social élite gradually withdrew from the active magistracy, which from then on depended more on the political power of the state rather than the personal pre-eminence of individuals.[28]

Below the legislators and magistrates were the local parish authorities in both urban and rural areas who became churchwardens and overseers of the poor. They could include the more prosperous members of their local communities, the 'middling sort' who included those who paid poor rates, larger farmers in the rural areas, prominent tradesmen in the towns and cities, and the 'chief inhabitants' who aspired to greater social distinction. They were often younger men, whose experience as administrators was direct and frequently face-to-face with the poor.[29] Slack noted that, although the overseers were sometimes young men new to office, they had limited freedom of action because they were accountable to the vestry, who in turn had to report regularly to two justices of the peace.[30] Overseers served for a year only, although in the eighteenth century the greater complexity of the laws of settlement required a more professional approach from all those involved in administration,[31] and some parishes paid their overseers, and administrators of workhouses.[32] However, while they were in office, overseers too were urged to regard themselves as civic fathers sharing in public fatherly authority, and acting as 'the parent or guardian of those who are in an infant state, and whose parents or friends have deserted them, *or are unable to provide for them*' (emphasis mine).[33] Churchwardens were involved in the administration of charities as well as the Poor Laws. The poor were not anonymous: they were people whom the overseers knew.

In addition to the men involved in statutory poor relief were the founders, governors, and administrators of charitable and philanthropic organizations devoted to the relief of poor children. Again, they ranged from men of high social status to those of middling status. Governors could be of similar or higher social status to justices of the peace. Many drew their wealth from economic activities rather than land, and were urban rather than rural. Governors of the great London hospitals were drawn from the élites of London companies, who often saw the position as the first step to important civic office. Typically, the first governors of Christ's Hospital in 1552 included London aldermen mainly from the twelve great companies.[34] Leading citizens usually served on several hospital and city committees, and some had links to the court; by 1579, Henry Campion, the queen's brewer, had served on a number of committees of the Court of Alderman, and as a governor of Christ's Hospital, St Thomas's hospital, and later of Bridewell.[35] In other cities, prosperous men engaged in city government and charitable foundations. In sixteenth-century Norwich, an ex-mayor, Thomas Anguish, founded a hospital for children.[36] In eighteenth-century London, endowed hospitals elected governors for life; they were self-perpetuating oligarchies.[37] During the later seventeenth and eighteenth centuries, as more people, both women and men, became active in philanthropy, wider social networks were involved in charity. The number of paid administrators of institutions erected both by local government and by charities amounted to thousands.[38] In the eighteenth century, being a governor of a hospital or of any charitable foundation was a public statement of civic virtue, which Burt argues was exercised in a space between the public world of the state and the emotional attachments of the family.[39] In addition to these large institutional charities, across the parishes and towns of early modern England men administered a multitude of small bequests and endowments. In some parishes, the prominent men coordinated the administration of rate-raised and charitable relief.[40]

Thus the 'civic fathers' were not a homogenous social group. They ranged from the monarch and the titled peers to men of lower middling status, and wide disparities of wealth separated them. We know that legislators, private philanthropists, and administrators were deeply divided in religion and politics.[41] They disputed among themselves about rates and payments. Furthermore, as nationalism, empire, and war increasingly demanded men for the navy and army, the parish overseers and ratepayers resented the demands of the fiscal-military state.[42] The parish had to bear the burden of the families of soldiers and sailors, while the government defended impressment as necessary 'to assert our empire of the sea' and protect our dominions.[43]

Despite all of the social, economic, and political differences between these 'civic fathers', their common public enterprise of disciplining the poor developed a sense of corporate identity and civic consciousness in this diverse group.[44] The governors of a medical charity in eighteenth-century Bath had sharp political differences, but their shared attitudes towards the sick poor gave them a symbolic unity.[45] Public fatherhood was a bond. By the eighteenth century, these civic fathers ranged themselves all on one side of a great moral

Figure 17 *Captain Thomas Coram* (late 18th cent.). Governors of London's hospitals, like Thomas Coram, were prosperous men. Coram was a successful colonial merchant who was active in the foundation of the London Foundling Hospital.

divide between the dependent labouring poor and those, like themselves, who were independent.

Over the early modern period, society was partly reconfigured on the basis of wealth rather than of estates. While birth, or 'blood', and ownership of land distinguished the peers and gentry from the rest of society, money and urban wealth were increasingly sources of social status. People's social position was partly determined by their relationships with the welfare authorities. Among the ordinary people, to be respectable and esteemed in towns and parishes of England was to be independent of the deliberations of the Poor Law authorities. A distinction between the worthy and unworthy poor became increasingly important, although this distinction dated back to the thirteenth century at least.[46] One guarantee of a man's own worth was to be one of the authorities who dispensed poor relief and charity to others. Men of middling and higher social status established a discourse about citizenship which asserted their own independence and their power to coerce others. Neither poor men nor those deemed disorderly could engage in this public sphere of civil society; their subjection to other men, their lack of independence, like that of all wives, increasingly excluded them.[47]

Public fatherhood was above individual men's weaknesses as fathers. In his own family, a man could try to present himself as a stern, and manly authority figure, but his own attachments, fears, and hopes affected his performance. He could record what he wanted remembered in a memoir or autobiography; preachers could be briefed for funeral sermons; but the boundaries between his household and public world were permeable. Badly behaved children and a disorderly household subjected him to censure, and publicly dishonoured him as a failure, less of a man.[48] Thus élite men were obsessive about their authority in their families. In the early seventeenth century, John Holles, earl of Clare, was not prepared to allow even a dog to come into his house without his permission: 'be assuring, what dogg cums into the hows is at no mans disposing, but at myn', he wrote to his son in 1623.[49] In contrast to a man's vulnerability over the conduct of his whole family, in the public performance of his role as a civic father he escaped personal criticism, and could be part of the collective public fatherhood lauded in sermons and treatises.

Although manhood was fundamental to civic fatherhood, wives and daughters of the civic fathers had a place in the discourses and practices of civic paternalism. While women were not legislators, did not administer the Poor Laws, nor serve as justices, judges, or governors of major charities, nevertheless, they supported the civic fathers in the dispensation of charitable welfare.[50]

Part of the godly duty of Christian women was to relieve the unfortunate. Even upper status women were expected to be active in charity. Initially, after the abolition of the monasteries, no collectives of religious women relieved the poor, unlike their counterparts in Catholic countries who had a strong role in charity. In Protestant England, part of the work of a godly pious woman was to offer individual charity, such as did the wife of the rector George Herbert who purchased a pair of blankets for a poor old woman in the parish.[51] In the 1650s, some women's religious groups worked to relieve the poor. Separate Quaker women's meetings for charitable purposes began, and were more formally established around the country in the late 1660s.[52] Women's moral authority as mothers was central to the Quaker movement, and the Women's Meetings determined who was to be relieved.[53] Like the civic fathers, Quaker women believed in the benefits of work, and that poor children should be trained to labour; the London Women's meeting exhorted others to help poor parents to 'put their Children to some Imployment, as soon as they are capable'.[54]

By the late sixteenth century, women's role in public charity was less prominent than earlier, as their involvement in charitable bequests was subjected to the advice of churchwardens and overseers.[55] However, from the later seventeenth century, women were involved in more public charitable work, especially with institutions supporting maternity.[56] The development of subscription charity allowed a wider range of women to participate in more secular philanthropic work. Women, as well as men of middling social status and above, were involved in charitable collections and determinations about the objects of relief. Their civic-minded activity was increasingly important in the emerging public sphere. Ladies subscribed to charities, although they did not attend the committee meetings.[57] The support of aristocratic women for the establishment of the Foundling Hospital was urged as an example to others: 'Ladys of Quality and Distinction' were touched with concern for the treatment meted out to 'poor Miserable Children...by their cruel Parents', who abandoned them in the streets, put them out to barbarous nurses, or directed them into the streets to steal.[58] At a more practical and lower social level, in eighteenth-century Berkshire wives of non-executive governors supervised the foundlings whom the Hospital placed out at nurse.[59]

Like their male counterparts, ladies and women of middling status sought to reinforce the gender order and to teach the children of the poor their class and gender position. They initiated and subscribed to charities designed to turn poor girls into either good servants or good wives.[60] Some undertook civic reform agendas, publishing on the subject of social ills. Thus at the end of the eighteenth century, Priscilla Wakefield, a woman of Quaker descent married to a London merchant, promoted the education of poor boys and girls, echoing the widely held view that the labouring poor were unable to provide for themselves because of their moral failings: 'The misery of the poor, like that of other ranks, chiefly originates in their vices.' Wakefield advocated training the children, girls particularly, so that they would be able to find work as 'useful servants' and become virtuous wives who would keep good homes to which men would return after work.[61] (This was no new refrain: 'Certainly wife and children are a kind of discipline of humanity', Francis Bacon had observed nearly two centuries earlier.)[62]

Throughout the period, the civic fathers spoke respectfully of motherhood; but they believed that paternal discipline was essential to counter maternal tenderness. By the eighteenth century, though they increasingly venerated and sentimentalized motherhood, civic fathers more commonly emphasized that women's weaknesses required male oversight. Thus the charitable work of women was always subject to the supervision of men who would substitute manly discipline for maternal indulgence which failed to check children in wickedness.[63] In the eighteenth century, the chaplains of Newgate frequently commented on how maternal failures to discipline had brought children to the gallows. Even though most of these stories demonstrated that parents had tried hard to rear their children properly, crimes were blamed on mothers: Barbara Spencer had come to the gallows because of the 'too great indulgence' of her widowed mother.[64] Thomas Taverner confessed that 'by the Death of my Father, in my Infancy, I was deprived of that paternal Care which might have been the Means of regulating my future Life and Actions more agreeable to the Laws of God and Man'.[65]

Of course civic fathers strongly disapproved of any motherhood outside marriage, so ladies had to be careful in supporting charities which seemed to condone immorality lest they be deemed immoral in turn: a father's printed advice to his daughter in 1774 advised *secret* compassion to ruined women.[66] By speaking of unmarried mothers as 'whores', or 'bastard bearers', the civic fathers obscured single women's maternity; in 1624, a Somerset justice contemptuously referred to women before him as 'idle whores that have had 1, 2, 3 and 6 bastards'.[67] Good mothering and sexual immorality were thought incompatible. It was argued that prostitutes rarely produced offspring—that wicked manner of life 'is commonly void of natural Affection'[68]—and in the eighteenth century some thought that a 'bastard' was hated by its mother as 'the Witness of her Folly and Ruin'.[69] All that a single mother could teach her daughter was vice, 'It being no uncommon Thing for Whores to prostitute their own Daughters, and breed them up to their own infamous Profession'.[70] Ironically, although the civic fathers censured 'bastard bearers', they assisted single mothers relatively generously, as we saw in Chapter 1, and during the eighteenth century attributed the plight of the unmarried mother to villainous male seducers. Even so, the civic fathers disliked female-headed households and were suspicious of their disorderly potential. Over time, they modified the Poor Laws to place poor women and their children under public paternal authority. A statute of 1719 permitted overseers to seize any assets of a deserted wife or widow; without anything to sustain independent livelihood, mothers and children were forced into workhouses where they would be subject to male authority.[71]

The policies the legislators developed to solve 'the problem' of the poor were grounded in their understandings of their society and their shifting beliefs about the causes of poverty. Whereas in medieval times, there was an acceptance of poverty, involving Christians in duties towards the unfortunate, the sick, the old, the widowed, and the orphaned, in the sixteenth century, reformers began to think of poverty among the able-bodied as a 'problem' that could be solved.[72] By representing the problem of poverty in such terms, they devised 'solutions', policies to care for those who were unable to work, and to make the able-bodied work.[73] Even though there were always competing discourses about the causes of poverty, and contemporaries recognized that some impoverished people 'eate the bread of carefulness', there was a sense that all who were poor, however virtuous, wasted the labours of others.[74] The civic fathers would replace parents who failed to teach their children to work. This view of the Poor Laws as a means of reforming society faded over the seventeenth century, as the poor rates were used to supply temporary relief rather than to set the poor to work.[75] Over time, the kinds of action undertaken by the civic fathers for the public good changed, as Paul Slack has shown, from emphasis on 'the common weal' to public welfare. Sometimes they sought reformation, a comprehensive change, while at others they espoused the more gradual policy of improvement.[76]

Thus through the Poor Laws, the state (though it was no clear, coherent whole) authorized the exercise of public fatherly power in localities. Overseers of the poor in parishes, and justices in their quarter sessions, asserted their superior masculine authority through the multitude of their day-to-day decisions. They assumed a gendered division of labour in families: fathers were to provide maintenance and mothers nurture. When poor fathers could not maintain their families, their social superiors judged them adversely as failures. Male dependence was no source of honour, and husbands who relied on their wives' economic contributions had failed to live up to the patriarchal ideal of independent manhood.[77] Indeed, to deter applications, the civic fathers intended that men should be shamed by asking for relief. Badging the poor[78] and making recipients enter the workhouse were all designed to humiliate, although as earlier chapters have argued, poor parents asserted their entitlements, and resisted the assumptions of their social superiors about their failings.

The civic fathers exercised their authority over a society in rapid social and economic change. The population grew, agriculture became more structured by capital, and urbanization increased. By-employments became industries, and there was what Wrightson has termed 'a huge increase in the numbers of the population primarily dependent on wage labour'.[79] Inevitably, poverty increased. Over the period 1580–1800, men disputed the causes of poverty, and the remedies. Some of the earlier idealism about the possibility of eradicating poverty lost ground, as the civic fathers came to accept that 'the poor' would always be a problem. In all the debates about poverty, there were few criticisms of the social structure and the gender divisions of labour which increased the likelihood of poverty for ordinary women and their children. Early modern welfare policies were designed to leave the social and gender orders intact and to transform the lower orders into productive members of society. The administration of the Poor Laws involved a large section of the male population in exercising the paternal authority of the state over poor men, women, and children. The poor themselves could be forced to acknowledge the state's authority by their deferential behaviour towards the men who exercised it.[80] While a common purpose bound the civic fathers together, they distanced themselves from the poor.

RHETORIC AND PRACTICES

The terms in which the civic fathers analysed the causes of poverty had implications for poor parents. Some poverty they recognized was caused by misfortune, such as deaths: widows and orphans were objects of Christian charity. However, they judged that much poverty was a consequence of moral failings, so they distinguished between the 'deserving' and the 'undeserving' poor. As we have seen, poor mothers and fathers claimed an entitlement to relief on the basis of their having worked hard and successfully raised their children, and the civic fathers generally recognized that such poverty deserved assistance.

However, the civic fathers judged that poor parents were irresponsible. They had married precipitously, without thought for the maintenance of their children: thus in 1601, it was observed that 'commonly the poor do most of all multiply children'.[81] One town in 1653 wanted to enclose the lands to prevent the poor from overwhelming them: 'the poor increase like fleas, and lice, and these

Figure 18 'The Orphans Cry, We perish, we die' (1650). Orphans who lacked fathers were a classic object of the Christian charity of civic fathers. Public fatherhood was to substitute for children's own absent parents.

vermine will eat us up unless we inclose'.[82] Was there 'no mean between eating up the poor, and being eaten up by them?', complained Joseph Lee in 1653.[83]

Civic fathers berated poor fathers and mothers as heartless. They cruelly abandoned their children at the doorsteps of worthy citizens, at church porches, and in the streets. Preachers made maternity precarious: giving up a child, as did Moses' mother, was 'an Act of Unnatural Cruelty', unless prompted by necessity, which would forfeit a woman 'the title of a Mother, which belong'd to her, as having conceiv'd, and born him'. Children owed more to Christians who remedied the neglect of 'their natural Parents' and who thus became 'their Better, Spiritual Parents'.[84]

Although from the late seventeenth century, philanthropists advocated the foundation of hospitals specifically to care for foundlings,[85] as in other European countries, not until 1739 did campaigners led by Thomas Coram succeed in obtaining a charter for a foundation for the 'abandoned' children of London. The rhetoric of the 1739 Royal Charter for the establishment of the Foundling Hospital indicted parental care, citing 'the frequent Murders committed on poor miserable Infants, by their Parents, to hide their Shame, and the inhuman Custom of exposing new born Children to perish in the Streets, or training them up in Idleness, Beggary, and Theft'.[86]

Rather than leave such infants to fend for themselves, it was far better, according to an anonymous author of 1740, 'to see the Public become the *avowed Parent* of them, and authorized to take Care both of their Maintenance and Education'.[87] Those who had 'the Name of a Father' and 'the Heart of a Mother' should take on the duties of parents to those who had 'properly become the Children of the Public'.[88] Such public criticism of 'indigent and inhuman parents' represents the view of civic fathers, although as we saw in earlier chapters, so-called abandonment might be a careful parental strategy to ensure that their child survived; so far from being parents barbarously rejecting a child, 'abandonment' was a complex decision.[89]

The poor would not work, chorused those who paid rates. In 1699, the King's speech to Parliament labelled all the poor as a burden to the kingdom, and declared 'their loose and idle life' a contributory cause. One pamphleteer referred to their 'extravagance and idleness', another to 'domestic improvidence and misconduct'.[90] In words which have become chillingly familiar, Defoe declared that no man could be poor, 'merely for want of work'.[91] Forcing the poor to labour would remedy the problem of poverty.

Not only did the poor refuse to work, they trained their children in idleness and crime. As William Lambarde wrote in his manual for justices published in 1594, such parents would transmit poverty to the next generation:

> the poor are exceedingly much multiplied because for the most part all the whole children and brood of the poor be poor also, seeing that they are not taken from their wandering parents and brought up to honest labour for their living, but, following their idle steps . . . , as they be born and brought up so do they live and die, most shameless and shameful rogues and beggars.[92]

The able-bodied poor roamed around, begging and vagrant; migration was not a search for work, but a symptom of an irresponsible and work-shy disposition. As a 1601 treatise for overseers explained, poor parents 'by nature much inclined to ease and idleness', were therefore incapable of training their children properly.[93] Parents in these poor families, a Hertfordshire clergyman explained in 1636, brought their young people up idly, 'many of them getting their living more by begging & stealing then by any honest labour'.[94] Parents set a bad example: 'And how sad is it to consider how many thousand poor Children, by the folly, the negligence, the vitiousness, or ill example of their Parents' spend their time 'either idly in playing and wandring up and down, or what is worse, Begging or Pilfering, as Hedge-breaking, Wood-stealing, or the like'.[95] Such representations of poor parents assumed that the problem of poverty could be rectified by the better training of unemployed children.[96] Implicit was the assumption that work was a virtue: 'Idleness in Youth is the Seed–plot of the Hangmans Harvest.'[97]

Public assistance to parents was counterproductive. In 1616, John Downame complained that the poor were 'now adaies so unthankfull, that all is lost which is bestowed upon them'; they did not work.[98] In 1636, a Hertfordshire clergyman argued that no honest man would take poor children into his household, because 'they have bynne so ill & unprofitably brought up'.[99] Welfare efforts which focused on bringing up children to work would prevent what nineteenth-century historians termed 'the cycle of deprivation'.[100]

Poor fathers and mothers wasted money, especially on drink. There was no point in giving fathers money for their children, said John Locke, since 'it is not seldom spent at the ale-house, whilst his children are left to perish at home'. Any food would have to be given directly to children at the 'working-schools'.[101] In 1698, Richard Dunning of Exeter argued similarly: men as heads of households received money in respect of their wives and children, 'and having got the Money, soon spend it', leaving their families to beg.[102] The availability of cheap spirits by the early eighteenth century led to growing censure, especially of mothers. *Gin Lane*, Hogarth's particularly shocking picture of 1751, depicted a drunken mother whose infant slipped head-first from her grasp. In the background are other images of maternal failure.[103] Since drink and opiates were destructive of children, little wonder that some religious authorities thought that the best policy was to have children removed from such parents 'and placed at a safe Distance from the contagious Influence of their wicked example'.[104]

From the sixteenth century, the civic fathers were prepared to remove children from their parents and board them out or apprentice them. As Michael Dalton's 1635 handbook for justices explained, poor children should be apprenticed 'while they are young and tractable (so as they be above the age of seven years) otherwise by reasons of their idel and base [low, inferior] educations, they will hardly keep their service or imploy themselves to work'.[105] By the later seventeenth century, it was thought that children would be better off in 'a working-hospital' subject to discipline rather than left at home where they had 'onely an over-fond Parent to keep them to it'. A child of 4 years of age would be able to work in a workhouse as well as one of 6 years elsewhere.[106] Newly emerging demands for labour increased the reforming imperative in the eighteenth century. Thus the 1737 petition to establish the London Foundling Hospital promised to make those children 'now a Pest to the Publick' into 'good and faithfull Servants'.[107] Parental unwillingness to subject their offspring to labour discipline thus justified policies which fragmented rather than sustained families.

The rhetoric of the civic fathers made poor men 'other', irresponsible, failures, and ultimately dependents, lacking the masculine virtues of independence and autonomy. Implicitly and explicitly, the civic fathers devalued poor fathers as well as mothers, treating them all as children who required paternal supervision. They knew that interference in another man's family was deeply offensive; taking his children away undercut a father's common-law rights. However, an endless litany of critical comment on the failings of poor fathers eased

Figure 19 *Gin Lane* (1751). Hogarth claimed that 'the Subjects of those Prints are calculated to reform some reigning Vices peculiar to the lower Class of People'. In this famous engraving, with its particularly horrifying central figure of a drunken mother, he depicted the evil consequences of gin drinking in the notorious parish of St Giles. To reach a wide audience, cheap versions of the print were sold at 1s.

troubled thoughts. Paternalist rhetoric justified intervention and allowed the civic fathers to feel themselves morally superior.

The civic fathers' responsibilities extended from newborn infants to 'adolescents'. Elizabethan legislators divided poor children into different categories according to age and status. Usually, they thought that children under 7 years were best cared for by a mother, or surrogate mother, but at 7 years both boys and girls were old enough to be apprenticed out. Legislators classified children on the basis of their father's status. In 1531, Parliament passed the first of a series of statutes to punish vagrants.[108] Children were to be removed from vagrants and beggars even if they were the child's parents: if such a child were brought up by its parents, idleness would be so rooted that the child would never learn to labour.[109] Thus in Norwich, authorities removed a child from its mother, because she was a fortune-teller.[110] Legislation exempted young children from corporal punishment; nevertheless, in 1698, the inhabitants of Stewkley complained that the constables of the parish of Wing had whipped two children aged 2 years and 4 years as vagrants, and sent them to Stewkley.[111] Generally, local authorities were reluctant to provide for vagrant children. The Tudor and early Stuart authorities feared the potential disorder from vagrancy, especially in periods of economic crisis, such as the 1590s, 1620s and 1630s,[112] but by the mid-seventeenth century, Beier estimates that as real wages improved, vagrancy was less feared. Authorities redefined wanderers as transient paupers.[113] Irish and gypsy children fared badly throughout the period because they were outside the parochial system; they had no place of settlement because they were not members of local communities.[114]

Fatherless children, referred to as orphans, and customarily termed some of the 'true poor', had been part of the charge of the civic authorities from medieval times. Some parishes provided a widow with immediate relief, others with a small pension to look after her children under 6 years of age; practices varied. Pensioners were never more than about 5–6 per cent of those on relief; amounts varied from place to place and over time. Widows often received over half the parish relief funds.[115] After the outbreak of the Civil War in 1642, Parliament passed several ordinances for the relief of widows and orphans. Initially, money was set aside for their maintenance, but by 1643, ordinances shifted the burden to parishes, whereby, as Amanda Whiting observes, relief became 'a matter of neighbourly charity enforced by state legislation rather than a national matter that was administered locally'.[116]

If both parents were dead, by statutory authority the parish overseers were to try to find kin who could care for the children or at least contribute financially to their upkeep. Failing relatives, in the seventeenth century, the child might be placed in a family with a nurse paid by the parish, or boarded into households where they would learn to be useful, just as were other children for whom the civic fathers were responsible. The 1597 statute gave the overseers power to compel ratepayers to take needy children.[117] Southampton authorities granted outsiders permission to settle provided they accepted a poor child as their apprentice. Thus in 1577, Charles Poyntdexter and his wife had to undertake to keep the orphaned Elizabeth Darvall for one year for 6d. per week, then to accept her as their apprentice for twelve years. In return, the Southampton Assembly permitted Poyntdexter to set up as a cobbler.[118] In the eighteenth century orphans were sent to a workhouse or a charitable foundation.

One of the most startling responsibilities of the civic fathers involved a new kind of intrusion into poor families. As medieval civic authorities attempted moral regulation of the population, public intrusion into domestic space was not itself new in the later sixteenth century.[119] But this new intervention involved men's roles as fathers of families and heads of household. If authorities judged that a poor father had too many children, they could take them away at an early age either to be boarded out in the households of others or, by the Act of 1601 (43 Eliz. I c. 2), bound as parish apprentices.[120] Ironically, such policies further undermined the viability of poor families by removing the very children who were least burdensome and might be old enough to make some economic contribution, or whose assistance might free up a mother to undertake some economic activity.

Over a couple of centuries, the administration of the laws became more bureaucratic. Increasingly, the use of printed forms meant that individual stories were lost.[121] Variations between regions and even parishes remained, but the civic fathers ignored the different status of children—vagrants, foundlings, 'bastards', orphans—and treated them all in similar ways. The practices of either paying pensions to mothers or boarding out of infants to nurses gave way to institutional arrangements which were cheaper and offered better opportunities for supervision and discipline. From the mid-seventeenth century, reformers advocated the building of workhouses in which poor children would be taught to labour.[122] Between 1696 and 1712, fifteen towns built workhouses, and in London from the 1720s, eighty-six workhouses were built before 1776.[123]

Optimists always believed that with proper discipline and supervision, poor children could earn their keep. In a workhouse, poor children would 'be put very early into a Capacity' of earning their Livings' and be better provided for 'than Children usually are, who are put forth by a Parish as Apprentices'.[124] In 1725, Artleborough workhouse in Northamptonshire was commended for its fifty-six spinning wheels where the mistress could see all the children at the same time, and direct them at her pleasure.[125] Authorities continually affirmed that workhouses offered better discipline than individual families: 'there are Rules and Methods for the better Breeding up of those Children which are sent thither.'[126] A 1725 account of several workhouses explained that all the children were to be reared in religion and instructed 'in civil and good Behaviour'.[127] In the eighteenth century, if poor parents refused to enter the workhouse with their children, they were denied relief.[128]

Rhetorical justifications of workhouses employed the language of 'family': 'One great and chief design' of sending people—parents and children—from all parts of the county to one place was 'the maintenance of good government; by which the *whole family* may be instructed in good manners' (emphasis mine). Ideally, a godly minister would be appointed 'for the better education and instruction of *this great Family*' (emphasis mine).[129] The patterns of institutional care in the 'workhouse as family household' reflected the gendered divisions of labour in the ideal family; men acting in the name of public fatherhood exercised authority, and women provided physical care.

Workhouses trained boys and girls for different work. In many workhouses, girls concentrated on routine sewing. In 1686, in the Middlesex college of infants, a seamstress taught all the girls to 'work' (meaning to sew) to make all the linen used in house.[130] Published reports on various workhouses across the country in 1725 indicated gendered attitudes to training. At Stroud, girls knitted, made caps, aprons and shifts, as well as learning to clean the house, make beds, wash, look after clothes, and prepare food.[131] Boys at St Albans workhouse made horsewhips for jockeys, while the girls spun both linen and wool.[132] At St James Westminster, the aim was to train girls 'as may prepare them to be good servants'.[133] In Cambridgeshire, women and children were employed to spin and knit; men and boys to plough, and feed cattle.[134] The girls kept at reading and sewing schools made and mended linen for boys and themselves. Other girls knitted stockings.[135] Similar gendered training was reported in 1758: boys learnt to read, write, and cast accounts, girls to read, knit, and work with a needle.[136]

Like any good father responsible for his children's futures, the civic fathers undertook the training of boys and girls. Legislation as early as 1536 authorized placing 'single' children in some form of training, and from 1572, parish authorities were authorized to bind out all beggars' children to farmers and others, while other children aged 5 to 14 years could be bound as parish apprentices.[137] In the previous chapter, pauper apprenticeship was discussed from the perspective of the parents. Here, the focus is on the objectives of the Poor Law authorities acting as public fathers to the children of unsatisfactory poor parents.

Pauper apprenticeship differed from the older types of apprenticeships, as we have seen. First, they were usually to 'husbandry' or 'housewifery', not to a specific trade; if a trade, it was a poorer one, especially for girls. Secondly, pauper apprentices were considerably younger than others; in 1716, one London parish bound a girl aged 3 years.[138] Generally, overseers bound children before they were 12 years of age, but ages varied in different regions. In the southwest of England, justices sometimes apprenticed children as young as 7 or 8 years, although in other areas 8 to 10 years was more normal.[139] By the eighteenth century, 7 years was more typical, and historians have judged that children were not usually bound before aged 6.[140] In 1755, Burn observed that whereas a legitimate child formerly had the right to stay with its parents 'as a nurse child' until the age of 8 years, it was generally agreed that a child shared the settlement of its parents only until 7 years.[141] The nomination of 7 years reflects legislators' view that seven was a significant life stage: the classics divided all life stages into multiples of seven and at 7 years, boys from wealthier families were thought capable of reason and were moved from the nursery under the government of women, to the discipline of men. Sometimes these élite boys' rite of passage was marked by a ceremonial change of clothing; they put off their 'coats' and wore breeches for the first time.[142] By the end of the eighteenth century, the legal interpretation of the Elizabethan law 5 Eliz. I c. 2 (which allowed the churchwardens to select children for service 'whom they [the churchwardens] shall think their parents are not able to maintain') was that girls might be bound younger than

10 years; the age of 10 referred to husbandry, 'where greater strength may be required, than in a girl bound in housewifery'.[143]

Civic fathers judged that adolescence began early for poor children; as a legal commentator explained in 1805: 'independent of any statutable regulation, seven years is at common law the age of puberty.'[144] The civic fathers conflated physical and social maturity for poor girls and boys, although ironically poor girls' diet may have delayed the onset of puberty, making it later than for others of higher economic status. In contrast, their own children's adolescence as a stage of physical maturing and semi-independence was prolonged into their late teens and even twenties.

Thirdly, the justices or overseers usually bound poor boys and girls for longer periods than the customary 7 years of trade apprenticeships. (Ages fluctuated over the period, but in some cases boys were bound till 24 years, girls to 21. The terminal age was reduced in the later eighteenth century.)[145] Overseers' practices were always influenced by local factors, and were not necessarily consistent, except in seeking the maximum period of controlled service for poor children.

How many poor children civic authorities placed in apprenticeships is difficult to calculate. In the early Stuart period, the judges attempted to put pressure on the overseers to apprentice poor children. Norfolk justices reported that 500 children had been bound; Suffolk none.[146] During the 1630s, when Charles's Book of Orders required regular reporting by the justices, several counties reported numbers of apprentices bound. From an analysis of the magistrates' returns to the Privy Council in the 1630s, Steve Hindle found that in five counties in one year, 2,292 pauper children were bound apprentice.[147] The number of children ultimately affected was considerable, as Pamela Sharpe's study has shown.[148] Employers may have preferred to accept boys; Hindle calculated that over two-thirds of pauper apprentices were boys in the 1630s.[149] Proportions of boys and girls fluctuated in individual parishes; in Enfield, as many girls as boys were bound up to 1640, but from then until 1690, boys predominated.[150] There was a similar pattern of decline in the number of poor girls apprenticed in Southampton over the seventeenth century.[151] Numbers of children apprenticed may have declined during the eighteenth century; by 1800, it seems that parish officials did not apprentice out more than a tiny fraction—around 5 per cent—of the relevant age group.[152]

In the seventeenth century, employers as well as parents resisted the apprenticeship scheme.[153] Masters did not welcome children whom they believed had been badly educated and were potentially of criminal dispositions.[155] Illegitimate children may have been especially unwelcome in households as apprentices, because contemporaries assumed that 'bastards' were the products of unworthy parents and inherited 'bad blood'. Thus a Devon pauper apprentice who was convicted of murdering her master was described, in popular reports, as being born 'of sensual Parents' and lacking any knowledge of Christianity.[155] Magistrates could force reluctant employers to receive apprentices, and from 1697 could fine them for refusing.[156] If a master, who was in theory *in loco parentis*, hoped for the financial advantage of another premium, he could drive the apprentice to flight by ill-usage.[157]

Magistrates could bind over parents who refused to allow their children to be apprenticed.[158] Exercising this power required the justices to use discretion. Indeed, Hindle and Herndon argue that the legislation was so vague that the judges were forced to clarify the justices' powers, thereby reinforcing a discretionary element which allowed them to separate the good poor from the bad.[159] Although the Poor Laws did not insist that parents surrender their children, the parish could coerce them by withholding relief.

Financial considerations underpinned parish attitudes to pauper apprenticeships. By the eighteenth century, overseers of the poor had realized that for a fixed sum of money, they could move a child off the parish books, since, by the Act of 1692 (3 Will. & Mary c. 11), a child apprenticed outside the parish would gain a settlement elsewhere. Parish overseers in early eighteenth-century Kent paid £4 to £5 and as much as £20 to apprentice children outside the parish.[160] The older the child, the smaller the premium required. Indeed, the child's labour might return a profit to the child's parish of origin; in 1758, the parish of Biddenden agreed to clothe a girl, and in 1759, her master agreed to keep her for another year 'and he is to pay to the parish 12 shilling for her wages'.[161] By the later eighteenth century, parishes and also charitable foundations saw opportunities for placing their pauper children in manufacturing industries chiefly in the north of England.[162] In 1792, Chatham parish sent two of their members to inspect the cotton mills of Manchester to see 'how the children there are treated'. On their favourable report, the parish resolved to bind the children 'apprentice to the proprietors of such manufactories', 'with the consent of those persons who ought legally to be consulted'.[163] However, studies suggest that a majority of children were apprenticed into textiles in their own areas.[164] In the later eighteenth century, a growing public concern was articulated about the apprenticeship of poor parish children from the south of England to the manufacturing areas of the north, far away from the support of friends and family. Critics argued that the parish could not supervise and the children were distant from their parents.[165] Honeyman has shown that parish officials who visited were prepared to intervene if the children complained of being ill-fed, but were less sensitive to complaints of working conditions and exploitation. Nor did they heed the children's cries of misery and homesickness. In general, they thought that parish children should accept hard work and discipline.[166] A parliamentary report of 1814 recommended that children should be bound apprentice within a distance which allowed 'occasional intercourse with a parent and the superintendence of the officers of the parish by which they [children] were bound'.[167]

Even when pauper apprentices were in the same geographical parish in London, parish supervision was limited. Supervision was a new area of responsibility for the parish overseers, who were preoccupied with keeping people off the poor rates. Unlike the guild system, which had a time-honoured system of oversight and remedies,[168] the overseers' supervision proved arduous, and in practice the formal procedures—individuals might complain to a parish committee—proved ineffective in protecting children and young people from abuse. Not until 1747 was the statute of Artificers amended so that applications could be made to the justices if there was ill usage.[169] Parish officers intervened only occasionally, and even then only after the apprentice had died. Murder cases before the Old Bailey publicized the failings of parish supervision. In 1681, Elizabeth Wigenton, a coat-maker, was convicted of beating her 13-year-old apprentice so severely that the child had died.[170] In 1745, a 14-year-old orphan, Thomas Salter, was placed in Newington workhouse, then apprenticed out to Edmund Gilbert, a weaver, who was subsequently convicted of beating the boy to death.[171] Thomas was not friendless. His godmother fruitlessly attempted to remonstrate with Gilbert, and a neighbouring woman tried to restrain Mrs Gilbert, who told her that 'I had no business to trouble my head with it, for the more I spoke, the more she would beat him'. Thomas had complained to his uncle and aunt, that 'I am perished and starved and beat to death'—other witnesses testified to his poor clothing, poor bedding, and generally emaciated condition—but even his uncle's attempts to restrain the Gilberts proved ineffectual. Only the parish officers could have removed the boy. Likewise, the notorious Elizabeth Brownrigg's brutal treatment of one of her apprentices, Mary Clifford, was investigated only because her step-mother insisted.[172]

Furthermore, parish officials could not even prevent the substitute mothers in the workhouse from abusing the children, as again Old Bailey trials show. In 1755, Mabell Hughes was sentenced to death for brutally beating a workhouse boy to death. Hughes was a poor widow whose own two children had died. In the hard winter of 1739, unable to provide for herself by silk-spinning, she was admitted to the Aldgate workhouse where, to earn her keep, she was given charge of the working boys. The Newgate ordinary (the prison chaplain) judged that she was ill-suited to such work, 'being not much used to children, who are apt to be unlucky, where there is not that authority over them, which ought to be, they would often play tricks with the old woman'. Hughes, who was allegedly ignorant, and of a peevish temper, managed the boys by beating them: she was 'as unfit to have management of children, as to tame lions'.[173] Nevertheless, other witnesses testified to Hughes' kindness and earlier experience in caring for children.[174] These cases were extreme, but the wide publicity about individuals' cruelty diverted attention from the civic fathers who made the workhouse policies and were responsible for their oversight.

The rationale for the state's authorization of the intervention of the civic fathers into the families of the poor was that they could do better than the children's own parents. And in some instances, parents thought that they could, because they petitioned the authorities to apprentice their children. But public fatherhood had limited goals for poor children. Whereas fathers of the middling sort and above were concerned to provide their own sons with an economic future, and to marry their own daughters as well as they could, their aims for the children of the poor were to turn them into productive labourers. Poor children were to earn their own keep so that the ratepayers might be relieved of supporting them. Pauper apprenticeships disciplined children's bodies to labour and their spirits to servility and obedience. While the parish apprenticeship scheme may have provided some form of welfare for poor children, the civic fathers' failures to oversee the welfare of the boys and girls surely conveyed to the children the sense that they were worthless, and reinforced their emotional deprivation.

By the later eighteenth century, parish apprenticeship came under more critical scrutiny as children were employed in emerging industries. Critics alleged that those acting with the authority of public fathers had failed their charges. Too many parishes who apprenticed children out did not concern themselves 'about the temper of a Master, the Goodness of his Profession, or his Skill in it', wrote one in 1700.[175] In 1738, another alleged that the overseers of the poor did not care.[176] But there were other voices and, as Joanna Innes has shown, the Health and Morals of Apprentices Act of 1802 was in part a product of public concern over the fate of poor children during industrialization.[177]

In both their public and individual capacities, civic fathers were concerned with providing for 'their' children, exercising authority, and being respected and obeyed. They considered that women should do the physical work of caring for the children, under their rule. Their own fatherhood was remote, and they did not themselves nurture the children; they were not swayed by 'womanish' tenderness. However, as 'fathers of the poor', their protective roles were compromised by their desire to save the ratepayers' money. While they may have been moved by Christian compassion, by the end of the period routine administration dominated. Furthermore, under a rhetoric of benevolence, they intruded into the lives of poor families. By 1800, when the boundary between those who received some form of welfare and the rest of society had widened, poor parents and children were viewed with a certain contempt. Negative attitudes to 'bastards' had not lessened, even though their 'fallen' mothers were to be rescued.

CIVIC FATHERS AND CHARITIES

During the early modern period, informal and voluntary welfare continued as well as statutory relief for the poor. Charity and philanthropy involved men and women of the middle and upper classes. Together with those who made and administered the Poor Laws, they operated a 'mixed economy' of welfare; they shared similar values.[178] At parish level, an élite could coordinate both rate-raised and charitable relief.[179]

After the religious changes of the sixteenth century, although Protestant leaders' attitudes to poverty differed in some ways from those of Catholics, they continued to promote private charity and alms giving. The Elizabethan homily on 'Almsdeeds and mercifulness toward the poor and needy' commended 'works of mercy and pity shewed upon the poor, which be afflicted with any kind of misery' as highly acceptable to God, and profitable to the Christian; such good works did not undermine the Protestant doctrine of salvation by faith alone.[180] Nevertheless, as Keith Thomas argued, voluntary neighbourly charity declined, although religious beliefs continued to motivate many men and women to individual charitable giving.[181] Begging could be licensed, and people continued to give alms at their doors. In some parishes, churchwardens collected alms in cash and in kind.[182]

Over the early modern period, new forms of charity developed, supplementing the multitude of charitable bequests administered by parishes, towns, and cities. From the mid-seventeenth century, philanthropists were more likely to be engaged in charity during their lifetimes, rather than leave bequests.[183] Furthermore, the concept of charity was affected by the compulsory collection of rates to relieve the poor: private charity became more discerning in selecting objects of relief.[184] At the end of the seventeenth century, new charities for particular purposes developed. They depended on a system of subscription so that many women of middling status as well as men could participate in public charitable work. This created what Donna Andrew has termed a 'world of charitable concerns' whose objectives changed over the eighteenth century.[185] Andrew has constructed an impressive list of major donors, prominent men and a few ladies who subscribed to more than three significant charities.[186] Children were always popular objects of voluntary charities.

Preachers promoted the work of charities to attract supporters. Their rhetoric is familiar: poor parents were idle and would not work; they disregarded their children's welfare by wasting their money on drink; they failed to teach their children how to work. By contrast, charities would do a much better job: 'You therefore, little Children, who are born of meane Parents, rejoice in this, that God provides you friends *better than your Parents*' (emphasis mine).[187] Civic fathers would earn the eternal gratitude not just of children but parents as well: 'With what grateful Hearts would poor Parents embrace these Opportunities of having their Children taught, not only how to live, but how to be for ever happy?'[188] Such sermons promoted an idealized construction of public fatherhood.

Eighteenth-century charitable institutions shared several common features, despite a variety of social and economic conditions across the country. Some were residential, and included over a hundred children among their inhabitants, others only a few.[189] In other cases children resided at home with their parents. But in all the institutions focused on children, there was a gender division of labour: the men, who were governors, determined policies, while women cared for the children, subject to surveillance. Such charitable institutions promoted specific constructions of fatherhood and motherhood as the examples of the refounded Christ's Hospital, the charity school movement, and the London Foundling Hospital show.

In practice, the charitable interventions of civic fathers favoured particular class and gender constructions of identity, as a brief account of the refounded Christ's Hospital shows. In 1552, governors were selected from London's social and economic élite. The 'innocent and fatherless' were to be 'trained up in the knowledge of God and some virtuous exercises, to the overthrow of beggary'.[190] These public fathers were urged to be 'as carefull for the vertuous bringinge up of theis children as well in good qualityes apt & fitt for Children *as if they weare their owne*' (emphasis mine).[191] In 1688, writing to the wardens of Trinity House about the progress of 'their' boys, the governors spoke as fathers:

> The Governours of our House esteem themselves charged wth a *Parentall care of ye Children* yt are bred under them; & wee all know, *how natural it is for Parents*, not onely to be inquisitive, but even very sollicitous, about the weale & prosperity of their offspring, cheifly after they are passed their Nonage & minority.[192]

Here the governors claimed a 'natural' paternal responsibility with mutual obligations continuing even after 'their' offspring were adult.

Christ's governors constantly reviewed admission policies. Initially, they favoured fatherless children, but in the 1580s and 1590s about 10 per cent of the sixty to ninety children admitted annually were foundlings. Sometimes the governors gave parents money to help them keep their children, but on other occasions they removed a child.[193] On 23 February 1572, they took in Dorothy Brooker, whose mother was 'frantic and hath six children more and not able to keep them'.[194] In 1607, they required that the fathers of any children admitted were freemen of the city, and certainly not 'aliens'.[195] Like fathers in families, the governors determined poor children's futures, arranging for placements and apprenticeships. Infants placed with Christ's were moved around, initially to wet-nurses, subsequently to other carers. The governors required that the children be brought 'home' each year so they could inspect them. In 1624, they restricted the intake to children over 4 years of age so that they could focus on training and education.[196] Later in the seventeenth century, Christ's admitted one child from impoverished London families to be trained, and then placed in work.

A key feature of charitable education, for which Christ's serves as an example, was that it reinforced gender and class positions. The governors of Christ's treated boys and girls differently, physically separating them, including, from 1703, at meals. They regulated the children's dress, boys in blue coats, girls in skirts. In 1724, they allowed the girls high-heeled shoes.[197] Boys might have a career path, proceeding to grammar schools, to Christ's mathematics school, or even attend one of the universities, some with scholarships.[198] Former scholars of Christ's might be taken into the service of the Hospital.[199]

Class considerations shaped Christ's educational curriculum. In the sixteenth century, the governors determined that girls whose parents were 'of good abillitye although now in pouertie' were not to be taught spinning, the work of ordinary women, for that would find them no husbands. Rather, such girls were to learn embroidery, 'soinge [sewing] in silke siluer & goulde, in workinge of sondrye kinds of laces and suche other thinges'.[200] Over time, such 'nice' distinctions were abandoned: the poor were the poor, whatever their social origins, and girls were to sew and knit, as befitted their impoverished status.[201] Charity children learnt the class status of occupations.

Unlike 'natural' parents, the governors of Christ's were not bound to accept all those children whom God had given, nor to be responsible until their deaths. They inspected every child before admission; in 1578, they refused any who were 'lame blind or an innocent' (mentally deficient), a policy reiterated in 1689 and 1748.[202] When the governors placed children out as servants or apprentices, they always rejected any further applications for assistance from masters, deeming them obliged 'to provide as well for Physick as all other necessaries, especially in a case of service without wages'.[203] Sometimes the governors intervened when apprentices were maltreated,[204] but if parents disliked their child's apprenticeship, and reclaimed their child, the governors refused to readmit them.[205] The governors disowned children. In 1571, a lad was returned to his parents for abusing a 'wench' in the house.[206] In 1687, Christ's expelled a boy who had been readmitted for a second trial: where such a child was to go is not clear from the letter book.[207]

Christ's governors rarely acknowledged any claims of affection. Suspicious of parental indulgence, they sent children out of the City to a branch of the Hospital at Ware, in Hertfordshire: children were forbidden 'to stay in London with their parents or others, who may suffer the said Children to runn up and downe streetes in this Citty, dirty and nasty, to the great discredit of this Hospital'.[208] If any children should 'lie out of the Wards', suggesting that they had gone home to their parents, then the governors expelled them.[209] In 1710, the reverend Dr Moss begged the governors to readmit Charles Hosey who had slept out twice; the boy's mother was poor, and Charles himself only 12 years of age. The governors sternly resolved to consider an expedient other than expulsion to deter boys from committing 'the like crimes'.[210] Even a request that children might 'go home for the holidaes'—'home' here meaning to their families, not Christ's—was rejected as contrary to ancient precedent, and 'very prejudicial to the good order and Government of this House'.[211] The governors made no attempt to keep siblings together or to protect the very young; Christ's own rules prohibited the admission of more than one child from a family.[212] Nor did the governors welcome requests to adopt their children. In 1661, Christ's steward, William Wickens, petitioned that a boy whom he had cared for at 2s. per week might stay with him 'in regard he hath an affection to the child'; permission was granted, but was not to be a precedent for anyone else.[213]

Towards the end of the seventeenth century, philanthropists were increasingly preoccupied with the education and training of poor children. Locke proposed that in all poor families, children aged between 3 and 14 years should be sent to working schools where they would be instructed in how to maintain themselves.[214] An alternative approach was undertaken by Anglicans. In 1699, the Anglican bishops, lower clergy and laity joined to form the Society for Promoting Christian Knowledge (SPCK). They collected funds by subscription and established schools where boys and girls would learn Christianity and habits of industry.[215] The promoters' rhetoric was familiar: they would take the children 'out of, the Condition of meer Brutes almost . . . to all the Purposes of Humanity and Usefulness'.[216] Everyone who contributed £30 could nominate a child, which encouraged a quasi-parental relationship; the subscriber could take a particular interest in the child they put in.[217] The SPCK established nearly 900 charity schools before 1720; it was an enormously influential social experiment.[218] The schools were to combine work with basic education, and provided more places for boys than girls.[219]

Unsurprisingly, the charity school curriculum, like that of Christ's, was gendered: boys were for trained for husbandry or the sea, girls for service. Such schools were more suitable for poor boys than grammar schools which were deemed 'too high for meaner Boys, born to the Spade and the Plough',[220] although the SPCK did further the careers of some poor boys as scholars at the University.[221] Generally, the charity schools taught boys to read, write, and cast accounts, girls to read, 'and to sew, knit, make their own Cloathes, and do such other work as children of their rank are or ought to be taught'.[222] Schools disciplined by a combination of punishments and rewards. A girl who stole spoons was deemed very hardened, and expelled 'for an Example to the rest of ye Children'.[223] On the opposite principle, Hannah More's schools encouraged children's attendance with gifts of 1d. or gingerbread.[224]

Promoters of educational schemes for children always hoped to reform entire families. In matters of morality they treated poor adults as children.[225] The SPCK wanted the boys' and girls' access to their schools to be dependent on parental good behaviour, although they found this impossible to secure.[226]

Charity schools attracted controversy. Critics complained that children would be educated 'above their station' and so undermine class hierarchies.[227] Supporters insisted that boys and girls would not receive advantages which the children of honest labourers were unable to secure.[228] A 1723 sermon promised that the schools would not teach 'either to puff the Children up, and set them above their Proper Rank and Order, or to make them disdain any the lowest kind of Work or Service, such as they are born to'.[229] The bishop of Chester hailed the schools' transformative powers, turning poor families which were 'too often Nurseries of idle Persons, Beggars, and Villains' into 'Nurseries of honest and industrious Servants, ... profitable Members of our Common-wealth'.[230] The schools' training was simply to break the patterns of poverty. Supporters hoped that education and training would allow poor children to triumph over nature. Children in charity schools were like plants that had been 'cultivated and removed', wrote Zinzano in 1725.[231]

Annual sermons lauded the superiority of the charities' governors to the children's parents. Thus in 1706, White Kennett (later bishop of Peterborough) urged the children to rejoice, 'that God provides you Friends *better than your Parents*' (emphasis mine).[232] The children

Figure 20 *London charity school children in the Strand, on the occasion of the National Thanks giving for the Treaty of Utrecht, 1713 (1715).* The spectacle of massed charity school children was directed to supporters so that they would be impressed with the good work performed by reformers. The orderliness of these children could be contrasted with images of the disorderly offspring of poor mothers and fathers.

owed more to those who had educated them, 'their Better, Spiritual Parents', than to 'their natural Parents', preached George Smallridge in 1710.[233] However, the charity school movement waned in the 1730s and 1740s, riven by religious differences between High Church and Low Church supporters.[234] A labour shortage offered poor parents the option of putting their offspring to work, and the schools did not revive until the later eighteenth century.[235]

Charity schools were concerned with godly education as well as with training poor children to work. Likewise, the movement to establish Sunday schools throughout England led by Robert Raikes at the end of the eighteenth century was intended to turn children into industrious citizens, or into good wives of the industrious. Initially, religion was seen as a way to inculcate a work-discipline in areas where child labour was important.[236] The basic Sunday school curriculum for boys usually included reading, writing, and perhaps casting accounts, while for girls sewing, and perhaps reading, formed the staple curriculum. Hannah More's Sunday schools taught the children

to read the Bible and the catechism but not to write. As Sarah Lloyd concluded, 'Virtues taught in all of the public institutions for the poor, working schools, and charity schools, included self-reliance, cleanliness, piety, and obedience.'[237]

The charity school governors believed in display: to attract supporters, their work had to be seen to be believed. Many of the charity school children in towns and cities wore distinctive dress and 'badges'.[238] Supporters claimed that children were educated 'much beyond the Imaginations of any Persons that do not go to see them, and to the great Satisfaction of all that do'.[239] Parades of charity children were lauded as part of civic life. In 1715, the Prince of Wales was impressed at the spectacle of 4,000 children of the charity schools at St Paul's where they sang verses from the 21st psalm: 'the Charity Children was one of the finest sights he ever saw in his Life.'[240] Such performances were the best public statements that civic fathers organized, but they were more for their supporters, rather than the children's parents, who may have felt somewhat resentful of the civic fathers' usurpation.[241] If the children still had living parents, regulations prevented them from appearing with their offspring: the civic fathers were the only parents to be acknowledged.[242]

Of all the institutions concerned with children in the early modern period, the London Foundling Hospital most captured public imagination and that of subsequent historians. The arguments for its establishment have been read as a damning indictment of the parenting of

A PERSPECTIVE VIEW OF THE FOUNDLING HOSPITAL, WITH EMBLEMATIC FIGURES.

Figure 21 *A Perspective view of the [London] Foundling Hospital, with Emblematic Figures* (1749). The London Foundling Hospital was an impressive building. Single and married mothers (and sometimes even fathers) looked to the Hospital to provide care for their infants. The Governors sent the children out to nurse, then educated them at the Hospital until they were old enough to be apprenticed out. However, less than half the children survived so long.

the poor, and the superiority of public fatherhood: those '*deserted* and exposed by their *natural Parents*, are properly become *the Children of the Public*'.[243] Discourse and visual propaganda focused on failures of parenting, especially that of absent and even murderous mothers, although as we have seen, mothers gave up their children to the care of others because of desperate poverty. Women did not choose to erase their maternity; rather, as Toni Bowers has argued, their social conditions made maternal failure inevitable.[244] Around the mid-eighteenth century, attitudes to prostitutes had shifted from seeing them as lewd and promiscuous to women driven by economic necessity. Such views allowed pity, and promoted schemes to reform the mothers.[245]

Having taken on the public role of exemplary fatherhood, what kind of fathering did the Hospital governors and administrators

Figure 22 *The Foundlings* (1739). This print presents an idealized view of the work of the Foundling Hospital. Desperate mothers who abandoned, or even killed their infants—there is a knife in front of the penitent mother— were offered the hopeful transformation of their children under the benign fatherhood of the Hospital governors. Girls and boys were trained in gender-appropriate occupations, girls to sweep and spin, while boys were sent to sea.

offer? If the basic task of parents was to keep children alive, then these fathers failed. Although the governors appointed inspectors to supervise the foundlings at nurse, mortality rates were high; only about a third of the children survived.[246] Between its opening in 1741 and 1756, the London Foundling Hospital took in about 1,500 children under six months of age. In 1756–60, when admissions were unrestricted, 14,934 children were admitted, of whom 10,389 died.[247]

Like other charity governors, those at the Foundling Hospital were determined to replace the children's own parents. Although receipts were given to those, usually mothers, leaving children so that they might be returned, the governors deliberately severed any links with the children's mothers and fathers, routinely renaming the children, 'at their own will and pleasure', and refusing to divulge the whereabouts of any children apprenticed.[248] Their reasons for separating the children from any kin were not stated; the governors may have been determined that the Hospital would not serve as a source of temporary childcare for indigent parents, or that their educational schemes would proceed uninterrupted. Their policies involved moving the foundlings around. Children under 7 years were generally nursed in the country, after which those who survived were returned to the Hospital. Although many nurses did not wish to part with their charges,[249] the Poor Laws militated against the children staying in parishes lest they acquire the right of settlement. (In the absence of any mechanisms for informal adoptions, the only means by which nurses could keep the children was by apprenticing them to their husbands.) By 1803, Hospital admission policies favoured the children of living mothers rather than orphans; fallen women could be rescued and returned to the labour force.[250] The governors opposed any specific emotional bonding, abandoning their early practice of giving their own names to the children because they found that their namesakes were making demands of them; the children 'were apt to lay claim to some affinity of blood with their nomenclators'.[251] The governors as fathers in their own families may have allowed themselves to express affection, but public fatherhood had its limits.

Fatherhood in the public domain and in the household were strongly linked, as the story of one single mother, Mary Gance, illustrates.[252] In 1790, Mary petitioned the London Foundling Hospital for the admission of her child whom she claimed 'legetimate' although she did not know where the father was. For two years she had lived in the household of Crisp Molineux (1730–92), MP for King's Lynn, at Garboldisham in Norfolk, 'in quality of a Ladies Woman' to her friend Miss Molineux. Miss Molineux was happy to take Mary back into her service, but her father refused to allow Mary to return. Molineux himself had come to England in 1754 from the West Indies, 'Blessed . . . with a very ample fortune at home and abroad',[253] and was of the same class from which the Governors of the Foundling Hospital were drawn. Yet he considered that his own position in Norfolk as an MP and a householder demanded he tolerate no hint of misrule. Were he to have readmitted Mary Gance to his household, as his daughter wished, he might appear to condone immorality. Since single mothers were widely viewed as 'fallen' women, a source of moral contagion, the servant's illicit sexuality might touch his daughter and perhaps even himself. Lord Chief Justice Mansfield of King's Bench considered that to keep such women 'in a family where there are young persons, both scandalous and dangerous'; his fellow judges agreed that 'if the master had daughters, it would not be fit that he should keep such a servant'.[254] The purpose of the Foundling Hospital was to 'rescue' such women by taking their children and raising them. The alternative, that Molineux permitted Mary Gance to resume her service, pay for childcare, and retain contact with her child, was unthinkable.

The Hospitals' governors took advice about the health of the children from male medical practitioners, although the hands-on physical care was provided by women.[255] Medical men published scornful treatises about female care of infants (again, some points of which have been accepted uncritically by subsequent historians).[256] In 1740, the governors rejected the use of opiates although it was an almost 'universal Custom among Nurses'.[257] The governors wanted the children kept in order, cleanliness, and decency. They ordered a spare diet suitable for those expected to labour, since it was generally thought that too much food would increase blood and spirits, and enflame the mind, 'so that Pride and Fulness of Bread commonly go together'.[258]

Again, boys and girls were to be trained in gender- and class-specific skills. As one of the Hospital's preachers, Isaac Maddox, bishop of Worcester, declared, the boys' plain hard education suited them for 'the Hazards of the Sea and the Labours of the Plough', necessary work for 'this happy Island, assigned by Providence for the Arts of Commerce and Husbandry'. Girls were 'educated in the meanest and most laborious Employments', and fitted to be servants.[259] In 1757, the governors decreed that no children should be educated 'in such a manner as to put them upon a Level with the Children of Parents who have the Humanity and Virtue to preserve them, and the Industry to support them'.[260] Training in manufacturing, they declared unsuitable for boys: 'Manufactures in general seem improper for the Employment of Boys, very likely to incline them to a way of Life not intended for them.'[261] Like the philanthropists of the Society for Promoting Christian Knowledge, the Hospital governors fended off critics who alleged that the children were educated beyond their station in life, declaring in 1765 that they never intended to instruct the children in French, drawing, or even in how to write.[262]

Acting as surrogate fathers, the governors of the London Foundling Hospital signed the children's apprenticeship indentures. The boys and girls were usually around 11 years of age, slightly older than the age at which parishes apprenticed children out. Some foundlings may have been apprenticed even younger; in 1760, a 2-year-old girl was apprenticed to 'household business'.[263] New manufacturing industries in the north provided further employment. In 1764, a Leeds clothier took forty-two girls for woollen textile work, and a year later asked for fifty more girls, at or near 7 years of age. The governors paid employers £5 per annum to feed, clothe, and house the young workers.[264] They may have been more vigilant in supervising apprenticeships than parish overseers, sending an official to check the credentials of those requiring apprentices. They declined to apprentice foundling girls to single men, and objected to households where they thought that girls would simply perform the drudgery required by a large number of children. They attempted to weed out other unsuitable masters, such as one who 'seem'd rather shy, when I told him that there was no fee Given with the Children'.[265] Subsequently, although the governors tried to monitor the apprentices' welfare, the numbers involved made this difficult. In the 1760s alone, 4,000 indentures were signed; in one year, 1769, 1,430 children were apprenticed out.[266] In March 1770, the governors prosecuted a couple for ill-using a girl, but much of the governors' time was spent on answering their critics.[267]

Critics of civic fathers came from within their own social ranks. Jonas Hanway (1712–86), merchant and philanthropist, was a powerful voice opposing the removal of children from their parents.[268] Hanway could not see 'how we can, consistently with liberty, detain them [the children], under a notion that they [the parents] will breed them up improperly'. Putting the poor into leading strings, he argued, 'seems to be almost as absurd as dictating to the rich, how they shall dispose of their children'.[269] Hanway criticized the economic rationale for the actions of parish officers, 'worthy men', who nevertheless promoted schemes to relieve the parish of expense.[270] He argued that the 'bond of parental affection' should be sustained because a son's love for his parents would prevent him from disgracing them: '*Parental Love* and *filial Obedience* are the main Pillars of Religion and Government'.[271] Hanway criticized Parliament for the misguided effects of their 'tenderness', which led them to vote £50,000 for the maintenance of the Foundling Hospital: 'Every body meant well', but the effect was a disastrous breaking of the strongest tie of all, 'that of blood'.[272] Other critics claimed that the Foundling Hospital, by receiving all children, undermined 'the affection of parents and the virtue of women'.[273]

Such criticisms of the policies of intervention in families were a radical departure from the dominant discourse of the period, which emphasized the inadequacies of poor parents and the need to remove their children so as to subject them to labour discipline. There had been critics of policies towards the poor earlier, but even the reformers in the mid-seventeenth century, who criticized the distinctions between the rich and the poor, were still in favour of labour discipline. By the end of the eighteenth century, the public face of civic fatherhood could involve an element of compassion for pauper children.

Later eighteenth-century philanthropists interested themselves in special groups of poor children, such as those who were blind. In 1790, they established the School for the Indigent Blind to train such children so that they could contribute to their own support. A similar purpose lay behind the Asylum established in Bermondsey in 1783 'for the Deaf and Dumb Children of the Poor'. Perhaps most interesting of all, in 1788 the Philanthropic Society was established to reform the nation's criminal poor by rehabilitating the children.[274] Earlier, as we have noted, ideas about 'bad blood' and inherited bad qualities meant that children of criminal parents were to be restrained from crime; but were not thought reformable. Ideas changed, and the Philanthropic Society believed that with proper education, children could be rehabilitated. Reformers would use the authority of the state to remove the children from the care of their parents, using 'the sword of justice to sever those cords of paternal authority, which are used only to drag the child to ruin'. Like early seventeenth-century reformers, they judged that boarding the children in other families would be more effective than institutional care, and they claimed as their authority the state itself, as 'a common parent over all competent individuals'. As Donna Andrew has argued, such charity was to promote national regeneration.[275]

Governors of charities, like those who framed and administered the Poor Laws, espoused the ideal of a father who was remote from the difficult work of bringing children up. Such a gendered ideal, which they imposed in their own families, they promoted through their public philanthropic work.

IMPERIAL PATERNALISM AND CHILDREN

The extension of state power in early modern England involved a wider empire as well as intrusion into the families of the poor. Tudor social reformers' concern over the 'explosion' of population, the apparent multiplication of the poor, prompted overseas ventures to solve population problems.[276] Before the 1640s, private enterprise drove the quest for trade and empire; thereafter the state was involved. Between 1580 and 1800, England became a major imperial power. At the end of the eighteenth century, although the North American colonies were lost, Britain was still a significant presence in Africa and India, and was founding new colonies in Australia. Here I want to outline very briefly two related patterns involving the settlers, administrators, and governors of colonies acting as 'imperial fathers': the first, using colonies as a solution to England's own population problems, especially that of 'idle children' on the streets; and the second, developing 'civilizing' policies towards the indigenous peoples, and their children, who were to provide labour.

Attempts to establish colonies in North America extended the geographical boundaries of English thinking about population problems. Although the interests of traders, adventurers, and planters were diverse, all believed that colonies had a role in solving England's problems of trade and surplus population. Typically, early promoters argued that it would be 'most profitable for our state, to rid our multitudes of such as lie at home, pestering the land... and infecting one another with vice and villainy worse than the plague itself'.[277] In particular, one important promoter, Richard Hakluyt, argued in 1584, in words echoing the Poor Law legislation of the period, that colonies would ensure that the children of wandering beggars would be 'better bredd upp... to their owne more happy state'.[278]

The activities of the members of the Virginia Company in the early Stuart period may serve as an example of how colonizing policies developed from perceptions of England's social problems, particularly the 'problem' of the idle poor and their untrained children. From 1609, the London promoters of the Virginia Company knew that the colony was struggling for labour. In 1616, John Smith tried to enlist support from English parishes: if they would fit out 'fatherless children of thirteen or fourteen years of age, or young married people that have but small wealth to live on', such people would prosper in the colonies.[279] In 1617, Sir Thomas Smythe, observing that the streets of London were swarming with idle and apparently parentless children, persuaded the Common Council to support a forcible migration scheme. The Company would transport 100 'idle' children aged between 8 and 16 years of age from London's streets to Virginia where each child (they probably meant boy) would be given fifty acres of land after serving an apprenticeship. In 1618, the Lord Mayor instructed the constables to apprehend all boys and girls 'as they shall find in the streets and in the markets or wandering in the night', and assemble them in Bridewell, the customary place for confining vagrant children.[280] Additionally, the churchwardens of every parish were instructed to 'resort to all the poor inhabitants within their several precincts and require of them that are overcharged and burdened with poor children' to nominate any of their offspring 10 years and upwards to sail to Virginia. Ninety-nine children were collected and in 1619, the Company shipped them to Virginia to 'be put in a condition to be of use and service to the state'.[281] Subsequently, the Virginia Company restricted the emigration to children over 12 years, and reduced the proffered benefits.

Unsettled male labour troubled the colonizers, so in 1619, Sir Edwin Sandys proposed that the Virginia Company send 100 young women, 'Maids', 'to become wifes; that wifes, children and families might make them [the labourers] less moueable and settle them, together with their Posteritie in that Soile'.[282] Again in 1621, the governors urged that it would be Christian charity to attach labourers to the colony 'by the bonds of wives and children'.[283] Families would discipline male labourers.

However, in January 1620, the children assembled in Bridewell protested. Since the City and the Company believed that their rebellion was abetted by people outside (presumably parents and friends), they persuaded the Privy Council to compel the children to migrate, on threat of further imprisonment in Bridewell.[284] In 1621, the Company turned to Parliament, where Sandys pleaded for legislation to dispatch the unemployed poor to Virginia at the expense of their parishes. Before the bill could be drawn up, Parliament dissolved, and subsequently the colony passed from private to royal control.[285] Even after news of the massacre of the Virginian settlers arrived in England in 1622, the Company continued to petition for labour and the City agreed to dispatch 100 boys. Fatality rates among the child migrants were high: of the sixty-six children forcibly emigrated in 1620, only five were alive in 1625.[286]

Despite the North American colonizers' rhetoric, which emphasized opportunity and betterment for the young, in practice, they needed labour and were none too scrupulous about how they secured it. The idea of child migration retained a firm hold on imperial thinking. Children were sent aboard the *Mayflower* in 1620, and London congregations continued to raise money for child migration. In 1636, St Giles Cripplegate collected funds, and in 1643, Governor Winthrop in Massachusetts recorded the arrival of twenty children 'sent by money given one fast day in London'.[287] Even kidnapping for the North Americas continued.[288] In June 1643, a woman was prosecuted at the Middlesex sessions 'for taking of diverse little children in the street and selling them to be carried to Virginia'.[289] Parliament passed an ordinance in May 1645 against those who went up and down the London streets 'and in a most barbarous and wicked Manner steal away many little Children', but still there were incidents.[290] In 1657, a ship's master accused a London woman of receiving two of his sons; another woman was accused of enticing away a boy, a covenanted servant, to transport him.[291] The records of the Middlesex quarter sessions show further prosecutions related to the forced emigration of young servants, but the penalties were slight, such as fines of 12d.[292] In the later seventeenth century, the abuse was the subject of petitions to the Privy Council: parents complained that their children were enticed onto ships and they could not pay to reclaim them.[293]

Tales of 'spiriting away' young people to the colonies continued to surface during the next two centuries, resonating widely with parental anxieties.[294] Stories told of fathers who threatened or actually sent their children away, believing them the products of adulterine bastardy.[295] In 1734, when Matthew Pilkington was separating from his wife Laetitia, she was horrified to hear a rumour that Matthew, abetted by his mother, had sold their two younger children for slaves to New York.[296] However, by the eighteenth century, workhouse life could be made so unpleasant to children that transportation seemed preferable. In 1702, the governors of one Nonconformist workhouse claimed that of 400 boys and girls, 100 had agreed to go to Virginia and other plantations. The governors of the London Corporation for the Poor explained that 'spiriting' children away would be impossible.[297]

Another scheme to rid England of surplus population and provide the colonies with workers involved transporting prisoners to the North American colonies as indentured labour. Although this ceased at the American Revolution, Britain subsequently sent convicts to the Australian colonies.[298]

There was a precedent for the policies of the North American colonists and their promoters. Subjugating, Christianizing, and 'civilizing' the native population had characterized the earlier English colonizing of Ireland in the sixteenth century. Such a mission created some corporate sense of identity among the colonizers, and, as Nicholas Canny has argued, 'was almost a laboratory experiment for the colonization of North America'.[299] Thus from the earliest period of contact with North America, the invaders had plans for the indigenous population. In 1608, Smith wanted to compel the 'rebellious Infidels' to work.[300] Indigenous children captured in war might be apprenticed, and others sent to England for education.[301] Later, according to a treaty of 1646, 'Indians' under 12 years of age could be placed in English households in the colony. Although 'Indians' could be enslaved between 1670 and 1691, the Virginian Assembly forbade the enslavement of 'Indian' children.[302]

Initially, some Englishmen expressed benevolent intentions towards the North American 'Indians'. Adults as well as children were to be educated and Christianized. In 1588, William Kempe argued that 'the children of Adam' required learning.[303] In 1612, Robert Johnson urged the Virginian colonists to 'Take their [the native Americans'] children, train them up with gentleness, teach them our English tongue and the principles of religion'.[304] By treating the indigenous inhabitants well, 'Their children, when they come to be saved, will bless the day their fathers saw your faces'.[305] In 1617, there were plans for a college for the education of children at Henrico and the Virginian Company promoted special collections for the work of converting 'Indian' children to Christianity.[306] An anonymous donor gave £500 in 1620 to erect a school in which 'a convenient number of young Indians' aged from about 7 to 12 years might be educated in Christianity, after which they were to be taught a trade, but the scheme foundered. Most of the invaders' educational plans came to nothing, partly because they could not 'obtain' indigenous children 'with the consent and good liking of their parents, by reason of their tenderness of them, and fear of the hard usage by the English'.[307] Intermittently, efforts continued. In the 1690s, Sir Robert Boyle's legacy for an Indian college began with twenty boys attending.[308] Thomas Coram, who subsequently led the scheme for the London Foundling Hospital, made much of his money in North America; he was eulogized for his hopes to draw 'the Indians in North America more closely to the British interest, by an establishment for the education of Indian girls'.[309]

Unsurprisingly, 'Indian' parents wanted, like the English parents of the labouring poor, to keep their children with them, and were suspicious of civic fatherhood. Furthermore, conflicts over land led to hostilities, and relations between the indigenous inhabitants and the colonizers deteriorated. Some colonizers spoke of 'Indians' as if they were to be hunted as 'wolves, tigers, and bears'.[310] Aside from deliberate violence, European diseases decimated indigenous populations, so that by 1705, observers were writing with sentimental regret about 'what had happened' to the 'Indians'.[311]

Just as men of the élite judged poor fathers in England as failures, so they judged North American 'Indian' men as inadequate. Colonizers were especially troubled because Indian men did not exercise paternal authority over their families; in fact, many of their cultures were matrilineal in that men neither disciplined their wives or children, nor did they supervise the training and marriages of their children.[312] Increasingly, colonial legislators sought to prohibit marriages between the two groups, which led to the isolation of indigenous households from the colonies' public life.[313] During the eighteenth century, indigenous Americans were marginalized, and, as Ruth Herndon has argued, came to occupy the same moral space in the townships as the poor in England. Town leaders in Rhode Island, called 'fathers of the town', acted as surrogate fathers to households which failed to function according to the patriarchal ideal.[314] They judged that households headed by 'Indian' and coloured women were disorderly; they 'warned out' women of colour from towns, and indentured their children into labour service.[315]

Englishmen also addressed the labour shortage in the North American colonies by trading in slaves. For most of the eighteenth century, Britons transported over 23,000 slaves per annum to North America and the West Indies.[316] Slaves were 'owned' by a patriarch, and children born to slave mothers were automatically enslaved in turn. The powers normally given to fathers did not apply to slave fathers;[317] masters could buy and sell their children in total defiance of slave fathers' rights and feelings.

Thus in the eighteenth-century colonies, there were children of colour descended both from slaves and indigenous Americans, as well as white children whose parents seemed incapable of teaching them to labour. Forms of pauper apprenticeship were widespread, under a variety of terms. In New England, the elected 'town fathers' took over the duties of apprenticing out any children who were poor.[318] In the mainland North American colonies, as in England, publications decried as unnatural any poor parents who were unwilling to let the magistrates train their children, thus condemning their offspring to 'Ignorance and Want'.[319]

Imperialists were also prepared to seize children from other countries. On a return voyage from the East Indies in 1622, Terry reported that two young 'savages' came aboard, and the commander resolved to bring them home, 'thinking that when they had got some English [language] here they might discover [reveal] something of their Country which we could not know before'. One died, but the other, Cooree, was brought to London, where all he would do was weep, and cry 'Cooree home goe'.[320] In 1651, the Guinea Company instructed an agent to journey to Africa to 'buy for us 15 or 20 young lusty negers of about 15 years of age, [and] bring them home with you for London', presumably to serve as pages and servants.[321] By the time of the colonization of Australia at the end of the eighteenth century, indigenous peoples were viewed almost as trophies, akin to the native flora and fauna, to be exhibited to the audience back at home. At Sydney Cove in 1789, one of the local tribesmen, Bennelong, was captured, and accompanied Governor Philip to England in December 1792.[322]

In colonizing Australia from 1788, the British took possession of the lands, and colonial authorities intervened in the families of indigenous people. In both North America and the Australian colonies, traders, missionaries, and colonists judged indigenous societies as lacking any concept of family, because they could not detect their own assumptions about the duties of fathers and mothers. Colonial authorities regarded indigenous parents as childlike and incapable of educating their children and so attempted to remove children from their parents. In 1814 in New South Wales, Governor Lachlan Macquarie opened a school to train indigenous children 'either as labourers in agricultural employ or among the lower class of mechanics'. Similarly, in the Swan River Colony in 1842, Governor Hutt promoted educational schemes for Aboriginal children 'to combine discipline of the body with cultivation of the mind'.[323]

Inherent in the expansion of the British empire was an oppressive creed of racism. By their policies towards indigenous peoples, participating in the slave trade, and the systems of plantation slavery, imperial patriarchs denied the parental rights of those who did not possess the privileges of white skins. Britons shared a view that their whiteness was normative, and non-Europeans were racialized 'others'.[324] By 1764, *The London Chronicle* was deploring the number of 'blacks' who were taking work from 'our native population' thereby favouring 'a race, whose mixture with us is disgraceful'.[325]

Britons looked on themselves as protectors of an empire, responsible for the well-being of its indigenous inhabitants.[326] They frequently conceptualized empire in the language of family. England was referred to as 'our dear Mother',[327] and the establishment of new colonies was equated with the formation of new families: 'what are new families but petty colonies'? Colonies had a warrant from God; the sons of men who inherited the earth had the duty of peopling it.[328] By the later eighteenth century, Englishmen thought that a large population was an advantage rather than a drain on the kingdom's wealth, for 'manpower' was needed for wars, as well as colonial ventures.[329]

There were direct links between the policies of civic authorities towards poor children in England and those of imperialists and colonizers towards indigenous peoples. In both cases, men acting publicly and under the authority of the state became fathers to those they viewed as children. Just as the rule of fathers was fundamental to men in their families, so it was in the public ordering of the state, and to England (later Britain) as an imperial power.

CONCLUSIONS

The welfare system established in England was unique in Europe in the early modern period, and for many who belonged to parishes, it provided essential assistance. Initially, the civic fathers saw the Poor Laws as an opportunity for social engineering; they intended to transform the poor, especially the children of the poor, into productive workers and so eradicate poverty.[330] Over time, these reformist goals gave way to a system of welfare for those the civic fathers deemed deserving. During the seventeenth century, the power of poor parents to negotiate for relief declined, and less informal relief was offered as more people paid poor rates.[331] The civic fathers to whom they were subjected frequently demonstrated the worst elements of paternalism: authoritarian, self-righteous, and unbending. The civic fathers assumed the moral superiority of their discourse, their civilization, and their religion. Poor mothers and fathers and colonized peoples might resist, but could not avoid being affected by systems of welfare, in which the abstract state itself became a public father through the administration of legislative policies.

The civic fathers' thinking about the effects of heredity and environment, nature and nurture, fluctuated. Sometimes they thought that a child's propensity to idleness, its bad disposition, was inherited; at other times, they thought that heredity could be overcome by education. Policies were always in tension, but in all instances, civic fathers promoted specific understandings of fatherhood and motherhood as well as particular class values. Exercising their paternal roles in the public eye, these fathers were stern and manly; pity and tenderness, characteristic of women, they checked. As good Christians, civic fathers reflected the benevolent fatherhood of God over unruly and improvident children. But public fatherhood increasingly lacked flexibility. Although churchwardens and overseers often knew those petitioning for relief, and had considerable discretion, bending the rules could expose them to legal challenges. Civic fathers professed benevolence, but unlike the children's own fathers and mothers, they lacked affection for 'their' children.

6

CONCLUDING REFLECTIONS

In well-ordered families, as preachers and moralists never tired of reiterating throughout the early modern period, a father was given authority over his wife and children. His power was buttressed by the law, and by the institutional church and its teachings based on the Bible. Within this 'familial patriarchy', a husband's and father's privileges were greater than those of a wife and mother. In the period 1580 to 1800, these Elizabethan Protestant ideals about domestic patriarchy were enshrined in the Poor Laws, and civic authorities took on public roles as fathers, first of poor children, later of wider social groups. Men of élite and middling status extended the power of the state into the family lives of a sizeable proportion of the population.

Public fatherhood gave Elizabethan domestic patriarchy a new lease of life. The poorer parents were, the more likely their families were to be subject to the authority of the state through its agents, the framers and administrators of the Poor Laws, who subscribed to the ideals of familial patriarchy. A key social distinction became that between parents whose families were apparently outside the state's intervention, and those who lost control of their offspring. The men whom I have collectively referred to as 'civic fathers' applied the ideals of domestic patriarchy in their own families and households then reified the image of public fatherhood as stern, manly and remote. Their ideals affected the definition of national identity consequent upon Britain's acquisition of empire. Just as the structure of authority in families was intimately connected with the history of the nation-state,[1] so too it affected Britain's sense of paternal responsibility for a wider empire. Fatherly authority in a family was intimately related to public fatherhood.

POOR MOTHERS AND FATHERS COMPARED
WITH OTHERS

Not all families were alike across social and economic divisions in early modern England, although élite fathers tended to assume that all fathers faced the same difficulties: Thomas Wentworth, later earl of Strafford, wryly alluded to the 'common fortune' of parents in a letter commiserating with another father about difficulties with sons.[2] Certainly there were some universal elements about being a parent. Not least, labouring fathers and mothers lived in a world influenced by the domestic patriarchal ideals promoted by élite discourse and enshrined in the Poor Laws.

Almost universal was the expectation of married couples that they would be parents, and that they would spend most of their resources on the care and rearing of their children. Childlessness in a couple was a social stigma and frequently deemed the woman's 'fault'. From the highest to the lowest, any barren wife was deemed unfortunate; Queen Catherine of Braganza, the wife of Charles II, who failed to bear and rear a son suffered profoundly in public esteem.[3] Giving birth to a child was *prima facie* evidence of womanliness, with all the attendant stereotypes, and in the eighteenth century motherhood was more closely tied to femininity.

Married men usually wanted children too, and in popular culture childless men were subjected to ridicule.[4] At all social levels, husbands insisted on their genetic fatherhood; children born to their wives should be men's 'own', although they had, of course, no means of being sure. An adulterous wife undermined a man's public reputation.[5] All husbands were vulnerable to gossip and rumours about being cuckolded, which placed the blame for a wife's infidelity on the inadequacies of her husband.[6] If children were the product of a wife's adultery, a husband was not expected to love the child. Charles Drew, condemned to death for the murder of his father, claimed in his dying speech that evil counsellors had made him believe 'that my Father thought me a Bastard, ... and that he did not love me upon that Account'.[7] If men engaged in illicit sexual activity themselves, and begot a child liable to be chargeable to the parish, they risked the public humiliation of other men imposing a bastardy order against them. For wealthier men, this may have been more a matter of honour than of financial hardship, but for poor men it was both. If alleged fathers were poor and single, the justices or overseers could order them to marry, something they had not planned when they engaged in illicit sexuality.

While there were many shared attitudes across social levels, a closer look at mothers and fathers as parents reveals many differences in both attitudes and practices. As we have seen, 'blood' was the metaphor widely used to explain the bonds between parents and children,[8] and most people distinguished between children of 'their own', those of their own 'blood', and others, such as stepchildren, sons- and daughters-in-law, and foster children. Such distinctions were more frequently encountered in poor families because they were more liable to fragmentation, and to remarriages or casual cohabitation. Even so, in practice, people often cared for and developed emotional attachments to children to whom they were not biologically related.

Poverty prevented the poor from realizing even the basic desiderata of parenting, of father providing, mother nurturing. Both mothers and fathers had to work. Unlike élite and middling level fathers, those of the labouring poor never earned sufficient to maintain a whole family, so in addition to caring for their children, poor mothers usually worked for pay. Poor parents expected older children to contribute to their keep, although they knew that younger children could do little. Even though the poor lacked the means to provide for their children's basic needs, their commitment to their children's welfare usually kept them working.

The births of children were not necessarily welcome to poor parents, which is not to say that children were unloved or neglected when they did come along, only that more children required that scarce resources be shared even further. Men of the labouring poor had no reason to share élite fathers' preoccupation with having many sons. Indeed, whether poor fathers shared the élite and middling preference for boys is unclear, although some demographic evidence suggests that throughout society there was a favouring of sons over daughters.[9]

Economic circumstances could force poor mothers, whether single, deserted, married, or widowed, to 'abandon' their children to the care of others. While upper-class observers publicly criticized such mothers as failures, in many cases destitution left them little choice, though they might hope that relinquishing their children would be a temporary measure. Poverty rather than maternal failings led to children being left to the care of others.

Unlike wealthier women, poor mothers lacked servants to assist them with their tasks of keeping children clean and fed. They themselves carried water for washing clothes and bedding, and kept fires for cooking and heating, all the while keeping an eye on their children. Babies might be relatively easily carried or left in cradles; but soothing crying children, rocking them to sleep, while simultaneously caring for other young children, was difficult. Girls and boys of about 6 or 7 years were easier; mothers and sometimes fathers could take them to work with them, leave them to the supervision of neighbours, or even expect them either to earn a few pence or provide childcare for younger children.

Poor women used the positive stereotypes of motherhood to speak out and to claim authority. Motherhood could authorize labouring women's participation in collective actions, including grain riots, and bread riots.[10] 'Being in pou[er]tie and wanting victual for Children' was one mother's reason for protesting over shipping grain away from Maldon in 1629.[11] During the Civil Wars, women demonstrated for peace, and widows petitioned for relief for orphans. Women sometimes appeared with their children to reinforce their claims to cheaper bread.[12] The defence of their children from a whipping was the reason some mothers alleged for their involvement in an anti-enclosure protest. They had sent their children with the cows to the town's cow pasture, where enclosure led to conflict.[13] When in late eighteenth-century London a magistrate acquitted a man charged with raping two charity school girls, women acted collectively to punish him.[14]

In both rural and urban contexts, poor fathers lived in close proximity to their young children, and sometimes worked in the same confined physical spaces. They slept in the same room with their wives and children; all might even share a bed. Labouring fathers were of necessity involved with family life. Court records give us a glimpse of father cutting up bread for his children while his wife sat on the bed and suckled their youngest: this was not the scene in an élite family where children were tended by nurses, and did not eat at the parental dinner table.[15] Thus the actual amount of contact which labouring fathers had with their younger children was different from that of socially superior fathers. Although élite and middling fathers might amuse themselves with the merry prattle of youngsters, they had more to do with children over 7 or so years of age, and more with sons than with daughters. In some cases, they continued to treat their sons and daughters as children even after they had grown up and married in their turn.[16]

Poor fathers, like others, were expected to maintain their families; seeing their families hungry caused them distress. Threats to their families' subsistence, they claimed, justified their participation in riots. Cloth-workers in Gloucestershire in 1586 attacked barges transporting grain, alleging that 'they were dryven to feede their Children with Catts, doggs and roots of nettles'. Wiltshire weavers in 1614 averred they would rather die than see their wives and children starve.[17] Such pleas were common throughout the period.

Poor fathers were also expected to see their children able to provide for themselves, which usually meant some training or education for boys, and preparation for marriage for girls. They did what they could to teach their sons to work, often taking them along with them to labour, but by the time sons reached 12 or 14 years of age, they were usually employed, frequently as servants in husbandry, or had migrated in search of work. Employment subjected youths to the discipline of a master rather than that of a father. In contrast, among the more prosperous, when sons reached adolescence at around 14 years of age, fathers were usually active in arranging education or apprenticeships to prosperous trades.[18]

Lacking property and status, poor fathers were less concerned than their social superiors about sons inheriting. They rarely made wills, since they had little land, cash, or goods to bequeath to their offspring. Pauper inventories showed that goods were valued at around £3 in one Lincolnshire parish over the period 1648–1766.[19] Being a successful father was more about seeing that children survived, less about transmitting wealth and 'blood' to the next generation. Contemporaries believed that 'supplying their real Wants' preoccupied the poor: 'And they have no Views for the Children after them, but to gain a plain and honest Subsistence.'[20] Yet as we have seen, some poor parents certainly aspired to better lives for their children.

Even though labouring fathers were dependent on wages, they attempted to secure to their children shares in whatever property and possessions they had.[21] Sixteenth-century evidence from Kent suggests that they attempted to bequeath some dowry to their daughters although inflation of dowries made this increasingly difficult.[22] Elsewhere, even fathers who were landless commoners made wills to dispose of leaseholds, or animals, to help their widows and under-age children.[23] However, by the time children reached their mid-twenties, the age at which most married, fathers and mothers were likely to be needing some assistance themselves. No parish welfare would be provided until they had disposed of any assets.

Unlike aristocratic fathers, poor fathers showed little interest in sacrificing individual wants to familial ends. Survival rather than inheritance and 'the continuance of the line' was the key matter.[24] Poor people's sense of family differed from that of the élite, and could turn on common physical characteristics: 'All our Family are pot-belly'd', claimed Hannah Butler, a young single woman suspected of illicit pregnancy.[25]

When sons and daughters came to marry, labouring fathers had limited involvement, unlike fathers at the middling and élite levels. Although the importance of seeking 'good blood' and lineage in their children's marriages may have waned for the aristocracy and gentry during the seventeenth century, élite fathers were still concerned to see their children well married, and were closely involved in overseeing the process and arranging marriage settlements.[26] By contrast, poor fathers lacked economic power over their sons' and daughters' marriages, so the state's attempt in 1753 to support parental control of marriages in Hardwick's Marriage Act had little relevance to them. The Act's greatest effect was on aristocratic fathers because it made void the marriages of minors under 21 years without paternal consent.[27] Members of Parliament opposing the marriage bill argued that it was ridiculous to enact 'that a servant-maid who was turned out of her father's family almost as soon as she could crawl, shall not marry against the consent of her father or mother'.[28]

Most young women who worked as servants in households or in husbandry amassed a marriage portion from their own savings, supplemented by the contributions from parents and other kin.[29] A labourer in a Cambridgeshire village left his daughter a small monetary dower of 26s., but added gifts of household goods such as flaxen sheets, and a new brass pan.[30] In rural Yorkshire over a long seventeenth century, husbandmen's bequests to unmarried daughters were £15 or less; in the market town of Selby, around £10 from husbandmen, labourers, and poorer craftsmen. In 1671, one linen weaver's daughter received a heifer, a pot, and two pewter dishes, while her sister inherited a colt, a pot, two pewter dishes, and a swarm of bees. In Westmoreland, labourers' daughters married with only £1–£5, although the really poor probably had no portion at all.[31] In the earlier period, some maidservants who lived in their masters' households received marriage gifts or bequests, but these dwindled in the later seventeenth and eighteenth centuries, as live-in service declined.[32] Yet even though labouring fathers did not arrange their children's marriages, evidence from spousals litigation in the church courts in the sixteenth and early seventeenth centuries—where litigants did not include the very poorest, but included some poor—shows that parental lack of support or opposition could prevent marriage promises being fulfilled.[33] However, many poor parents were dead by the time their children reached their mid-twenties, a common age for marriage. Probably half the young women who married were effectively fatherless.[34]

The absence of lands and worldly goods did not necessarily make labouring fathers less authoritarian. Nor did the economic contributions of wives and children seem to have altered power relations in the family. Manliness demanded that fathers exercised authority. Indeed, men who were not the sole providers may have been even more insistent on their authority; although they could not discharge their duty of maintaining their families, they could assert their masculinity by exacting obedience. Fathers disciplined their children, and equated tenderness with motherly weakness: spare the rod and spoil the child was a widely heeded injunction. In 1712, Benjamin Coole advised fathers that 'Softness and Effeminacy in Education . . . will degenerate into such a state of Corruption'.[35] In practice, however, degrees of paternal harshness varied. At home with their families, even the sternest fathers could show affection towards their offspring.

Disobedience by wives and children undermined a father: how could a man command others, if he had no rule in his own family? As Lord Burghley observed of the bad behaviour of his eldest son Thomas in 1581, 'The shame that I shall receive to have so unruled a son grieveth me more than if I had lost him by honest death.'[36] Even a poor father was thought to be disgraced by the sexual misdemeanours of his daughter, as the petitions of single mothers to the London Foundling Hospital attest. A poor father's authority over his family was his only opportunity to command others, for in society at large he was forced to show deference to achieve his objects.

Most theorists in the seventeenth century grounded a father's authority in his begetting of children; but not all concluded that paternal power was absolute. At the end of the seventeenth century, John Locke argued that a father's power was conditional. When his children (Locke later referred to 'his son') came of age and no longer required his care, 'The father's empire then ceases'.[37] In practice, in families of the poor, a father's empire could cease quite early, when children were apprenticed out. In contrast, middling and élite fathers may have faced greater challenges from their sons, because sons depended on their fathers to achieve adult status.[38] Many father–son conflicts in élite and middling families related to property and inheritances, and relationships between many fathers and their heirs were unhappy.[39] Analysing the patriarchal family in early modern France, Jonathan Dewald has argued that writers in 'high culture' showed an awareness of the murderous conflict at its heart. Conflict was the norm rather than 'an unhappy accident', and many recognized that implicit in such families was the 'sacrifice of personal wants to political and familial ends'.

Patriarchal ideology, Dewald concluded, was unstable and created resistances.[40] The absence of wealth and physical separation removed this tension from the relationship between labouring poor fathers and their sons.

It can be argued that at all social levels emphasis on the duty of obedience to a father was dysfunctional. Paternal demands authorized the excessive use of physical violence and punishments. While not all fathers and masters were cruel and brutal, if they were violent towards children, a patriarchal culture had limited means of restraining them. Only after a child's death would society intervene, charging a father with murder; in their defence, men usually pleaded that they were simply exercising their paternal authority and administering due correction. Mothers, whose nurture of children might have given them authority over their upbringing, were themselves expected to be obedient.[41]

Some observers considered that élite and middling fatherly behaviour softened over the early modern period. By the end of the seventeenth century, John Locke (himself a bachelor) urged fathers to behave in a more friendly fashion towards their sons as they grew up. Locke's own father had followed this method: severe when John was a boy, but increasingly conversing in a familiar way.[42] It was a fine balancing act, as an early eighteenth-century Quaker father, Thomas Thompson, recalled in commendation of his own father: he was 'very free and open towards me; yet not so as thereby to lessen his Authority, but kept me in that Subjection, as he could aw[e] and bring down my Spirit with a Look'.[43]

Historians have argued about the decline of patriarchal power and whether more egalitarian families emerged in the early modern period.[44] While Gillis has argued that 'fatherly presence varied by class', his view that it was weakest at the highest and lowest levels, and most prominent at the middling, needs more testing.[45] Little evidence suggests that poor fathers relinquished authority over their offspring. Authoritarian fathering could be found at all social levels: although some fathers were kindly disposed, others were indifferent or brutal. Neighbours, confronted with a cruel or abusive father, hesitated to interfere because of the widespread belief that children were a father's property. A father's rights took priority over any rights of his children.

Being a mother may have mattered more to poor women than being a wife. In élite discourse, being a parent took second place to the marital relationship. The eighteenth-century legal theorist, William

Blackstone, rated parental love highly—it was for life, and so strong that not even the wickedness or rebellion of children could extinguish it—but the relation between parent and child was 'the most universal relation in nature' *after* that between husband and wife.[46] Among the poor, the relationship between husband and wife may not have been the primary one; many marriages and *de facto* relationships were unstable, and many mothers had a series of male partners. At the lowest levels of society, maternal bonds with children may have been more lasting than those with men. Perhaps mothers of élite status shared something of this commitment to their children with their poorer counterparts: it was fathers at different social levels who had least in common.

MEANINGS OF MOTHERHOOD AND FATHERHOOD TO POOR PARENTS

Being a mother or a father had both social and personal meaning to poor parents. A reputation for being a good parent was a marker of public worth. Aged widows petitioning for charity justified their claims with formulaic representations of themselves as successful mothers. At Bruton in Somerset in the later seventeenth century, Elizabeth Bone declared that she was 'very well knowne . . . to bee a paynfull woman for the breeding up' of ten children.[47] Elizabeth Lawlane was 'well knowne always to bee a hard labouring woman in the worke to breed up her children'.[48] Another had 'bred up and mainteined a great family in this towne, as is very well known to the Inhabitants'.[49] Similarly, nearly a century later in London, the widowed Christine Whittle appealed for assistance claiming that for sixteen years 'with great difficulty & Industry [I] have brought up three Children'.[50]

Fathers too argued that, as they had worked all their lives and maintained their children, they were entitled to assistance. In the reign of Charles I, Richard Savage of Lewes sought a place to end his days: he had dwelt in Lewes all his life, 'and by his painfull endeavours brought up many children is now become aged helpless & destitute'.[51] Again in Bruton, Thomas Hilborn's petition claimed that he was well known 'to bee Loyall faithfull & a painestaking man in the world for the breeding up of his family of children', which were seven small ones, he added, apart from one placed in apprenticeship by their worships.[52] Richard Edwards, aged over 80 years, had 'by his labour and industrie bred up & mainteyned a great family (vizt) twelve children'.[53]

Heading a household was a key social marker, as parish authorities deemed men who were never householders as less worthy. In 1738, admissions to St Katherine Cree's workhouse were to distinguish between 'Antient Housekeepers, that have lived in good repute, and those who have not been Housekeepers or are become poor by Vice or Idleness'.[54] A man who lodged with his family in one room may still have defended his patriarchal authority over his wife and children, especially since misfortunes might soon subject him to the adverse judgment of parish authorities. So long as he could maintain his family, he retained his self-esteem, but the corollary was that failure destroyed him. As Francis Place observed, 'when the evil day' of extreme poverty came upon such men, they kept on working 'steadily but hopelessly, more like horses in a mill, or mere machines than human beings', seeing their families lacking 'the common necessaries of life, yet never giving up until "misery has eaten them to the bone"'.[55] In the 1780s, the boys with whom Place associated would not keep company with those whose fathers were not householders.[56] A poor man who went into the poor house 'is sunk in the eyes of others, and is altogether degraded in his own', observed Catharine Cappe in 1805.[57]

Poor fathers and mothers whose neighbours endorsed their claims to be good parents were likely to receive charity as well as parish relief. Unlike their social superiors, neighbours evaluated parents according to criteria which took account of the stresses created by poverty. Thus in a murder case before the Old Bailey in 1766, the court enquired what kind of father the accused, James Field, a day-labourer, had been. Mary Duck, who had known James as a child, considered him a responsible father: the children were 'hearty and clean, *for a poor man's children*; they looked as if they had been taken care of' (emphasis mine).[58] As in twentieth-century Britain, observers differentiated between those who could not cope with the demands of parenting and those who did not try.[59] A Staffordshire parish complained that a mother who had been imprisoned, leaving four children on the parish, was 'so unnatural to her children' that she neither visited them nor enquired after their welfare on her release.[60]

Ironically, a 1790 trial for the murder of a child offers some comments about good parenting. The judge was puzzled when Thomas Hewett Masters confessed that he had kicked and beaten to death his 6-year-old *de facto* stepdaughter, Mary Lovedon: there was no history of ill usage, 'there has been the greatest good usage and tenderness'. A fellow lodger explained that Masters and his wife were good parents: they showed 'as tender usage as any parents could use a child with; to outside appearance, more so than most parents: I never saw them strike the child, or even heard the child cry, without it was playing with the children.' Clearly this couple managed their daughter without recourse to noisy beatings. Masters was sentenced to death for murder, but the court cleared the mother on the basis of her demonstration of appropriate maternal feelings: 'this woman, [was] affected with all the affection of a mother, and shewed all that distress which was expected in a mother.'[61] While the mother's grief at the death of her child seems a universal human response, her expression of emotion was judged according to specific cultural norms.[62]

Poor Law records show indirectly that parents supported their adult children when they could. In 1744, when 19-year-old Mary Waple petitioned St Helen's parish in London for admission to the workhouse, she explained that she had worked as a hired servant for three years, but for the previous year had lived with her mother and father, 'she being in a bad State of health'.[63] Other evidence confirms that parents, especially mothers, were the ones young people turned to when they were in difficulties. In 1653, the London Weavers' court instructed one mother not to take in her son without the consent of his master, but he 'did constantly go away from his master to his mother'.[64] (In this instance, the mother was probably widowed but not necessarily poor.) In a mid-eighteenth-century rape trial before the Old Bailey, 12-year-old Martha Chalkley complained that her master, Richard Knibb, had sexually abused her and subsequently she had 'a great running' (a venereal disease). Although her mistress was in bed in the house at the time, Martha confided in no one until she went home to her mother.[65]

Poor parents' reputations could also be affected by the behaviour of their children, including how they assisted their ageing parents. As we have seen, the practical operation of the Poor Laws made it difficult to sustain family bonds because the settlement laws discouraged poor children from remaining in the parish of their parents, lest they secured an entitlement to relief.[66] Many adolescents and adults who could have helped their aged parents were prevented from providing live-in care. In the century 1650–1750, 33 per cent of the poor who were over 60 years of age had no children living nearby.[67] Ottaway argues that a decline in the economic situation of the working poor meant that the community had to take up support which the family was unable to provide.[68]

Poor parents might hope that their children would take them in, but it was not a right to be assumed. Elderly mothers were more likely to be on their own than aged fathers. In the 1570 Norwich census, only 5 per cent of elderly men were on their own without wives or daughters; 3 of 10 men lived with children under 16.[69] Margaret Spufford admits that it is a mystery how retired yeomen and labourers lived in old age, but she too found examples of fathers sojourning by sons' fires. In 1649, a 92-year-old yeoman, a widower with grown-up children, lived with one of his sons.[70] Census-type listings from the later seventeenth century revealed very few elderly parents residing with their children. Studies of co-residence among the poor in the eighteenth century suggest that the legal obligation on children to provide housing for their parents was not enforced. Prosecutions were rare.[71] It was difficult for adult children to support their aged parents, for at the same time as their parents were declining physically, young people in their thirties had become parents in turn. As a labourer in Puddletown explained, he 'thought it his Duty to assist her [his mother] if he could without injuring his family'; poor parents were caught between the demands of the new generation and the old.[72]

Accommodation was not the sole measure of children's support for their aged parents, although other assistance is hard to measure. Even today there is very little systematic recording of what Pat Thane has termed 'intimacy at a distance', close and supportive relationships which do not involve house sharing.[73] Such support from children could be complex but leave few records. Scattered incidental references hint at children's sense of responsibility for their parents. In 1666, after Alice Jenkins went to Weston-super-Mare with her illegitimate child to obtain maintenance from the reputed father, she returned to Curston 'to be a helpe to her Aged parents'.[74] Thirty-year-old Elizabeth Brooks mentioned health care specifically. She had been in service since she was 14 years of age, but left her place in London around 1770 to nurse her blind mother, the wife of a Sussex day-labourer.[75] Family bonds among the poor were in many cases sustained in despite of the Poor Laws.

What of the emotional content of the relationships between poor parents and their children? Other evidence points indirectly to children's bonds with their parents. Mary Graham, accused in the Old Bailey of perjury in 1785, told the court she had nobody 'belonging to me, but a poor mother...I have nobody to my character; I get my bread either by the silk business or weaving.'[76] As we saw in Chapter 1, many pregnant single women tried to shield their parents from shame. In 1649, Mary Gash, who was accused of infanticide in Southampton, confessed that she sought 'to keepe the greife & shame of it [her illicit maternity] from her friends'.[77] Unmarried mothers petitioning the London Foundling Hospital in the later eighteenth century were similarly protective. 'Shame prevented me from Applying to my friends', claimed Mary Edwards in 1770; it 'Might be a Means of Breaking my poor Mothers Heart if she knew of my Unhappy Situation'.[78] In 1772, 30-year-old Elizabeth Brooks dreaded lest her disgrace become known, for it would 'hasten ye Death of her poor Mother'.[79]

Labouring parents lived in greater physical proximity to their children than did the more prosperous. In 1777, Armstrong observed that 'persons in the lower station of life' spent more time talking with each other than those of higher rank 'and make their children a more frequent topic of conversation', which Armstrong attributed to 'want of other subjects'.[80] Sarah Trimmer imagined that children's 'innocent spats and prattle chear his [father's] hours of leisure'.[81] Popular literature depicted a man's satisfaction in fatherhood:

> By christning of my little lad
> I did in credit rise
> All this by my good wife I had,
> then 'tis not otherwise.[82]

An early eighteenth-century estate worker was overjoyed at the birth of his son, promising 'Honny thou's my Darlin and shalt want for nothing as long as I am able to worke for thee'.[83] One father was singing to his children while repairing a tub in his shop, when he died unexpectedly.[84] John Clare (b. 1793) wrote of his dread at leaving home for an apprenticeship: at home 'I had been coddled up so tenderly and so long'.[85] However, experiences varied: Francis Place remembered that his father never spoke to his children 'in the way of conversation', and answered questions with a blow.[86]

Some of the strongest evidence of maternal feelings comes from poor mothers' self-representations in a number of different contexts. As we have seen, mothers petitioned for places for their infants in the Foundling Hospital, participating in the shaping of narratives within the formula the Hospital prescribed. They asserted that they were good mothers, who put the welfare of their children first. Highly revealing of the subjectivity of mothers is Garthine Walker's analysis of texts from cases of infanticide and child deaths in coroners' and assize records.[87] Dorothy Hixon's story of her attempts to keep her baby alive after she found that the nurse had almost starved the child—'I took up the child and opened it [undid the swaddling] and held it to the fire and gave it suck. And I and the poor woman tended it all night'—drew on multiple cultural discourses. Through these, Dorothy constructed herself as a naturally nurturing mother, in contrast to the paid nurse who was indifferent.[88] Evidence about maternal fears and fantasies can be found in court cases involving unmarried mothers. In 1650, Susan Lay, a servant who had borne children to both her master and his son, told an Essex magistrate how she was haunted by the ghost of her dead mistress, Priscilla Beauty. Susan's illicit maternity disrupted the emotional bonds between members of the Beautys' household, and she turned to the supernatural to make sense of her disturbing experiences.[89]

Early modern people had limited control over a hostile environment, which some historians have argued led to severe, even psychotic, anxiety.[90] On this line of argument, the poor, who had least control over their environment and fewest resources to meet crises, suffered the greatest stress. There may be elements of truth in this, but material hardship did not necessarily intensify parental grief. Any mothers who had gone through pregnancy, childbirth, and breastfeeding could be traumatized by the ill-health and deaths of their infants and children.

Not all parents, rich or poor, did bond with their children, despite contemporary expectations that those who did not were unnatural. Perhaps society reserved the harshest judgment for mothers who declined nurture. In contrast, fathers who migrated in search of work, then took the opportunities offered to stay away, or to enlist in armies or the navy, attracted comparatively little adverse comment, and that chiefly from harassed parish authorities.

Unlike their social superiors, poor mothers and fathers were not involved with schemes for reforming other people's families; they were ordinary people with tasks to perform. Parents of poor children had to get through each day, doing the best they could. As this book has argued, their actions bear witness to their strong investment in the duties and responsibilities of parenthood. Hard labour speaks loudly of the work of being a father: a Durham wagon worker in the 1780s 'wrought at waggons and waggonery all day, and 3 or 4 nights a week...was down the pit, Erning to get money to bring up his family'.[91] Neighbours were favourably impressed by the self-denial of a poor father who had 'but a pennyworth of bread' which he left for his wife and children while he went 'to walk in the fields': he was 'a very tender husband and father'.[92] Similarly, a neighbour commended a single mother, Elizabeth Shudrick, who had a 5-year-old daughter: 'no Woman could ever be fonder of a Child than she is of that.'[93] Rachel Beacham, condemned to death for a murder, 'had no other Reason to desire to live, but for the Sake of her own Children, which are 4 or 5, whom she feared would not have that Care taken of them hereafter, as she had [given] heretofore'.[94] While some historians have debated insoluble questions about whether parents loved their children on the basis of literary texts, here we have seen from what poor parents actually did that they demonstrated affection as well as strong commitment to their children's welfare. Poverty, rather than lack of feeling, determined much of the behaviour of mothers and fathers.

NOTES

INTRODUCTION

1. GL, MS 10026/1, St Botolph Aldgate, Bonds of indemnity concerning parish poor children, 1587–1741, loose sheet.
2. Lawrence Stone, *The Family, Sex and Marriage in England, 1500–1800* (1977); Ralph A. Houlbrooke, *The English Family 1450–1700* (1984); Linda Pollock, *Forgotten Children: Parent-Child Relations from 1500–1900* (1993); see also James Casey, *The History of the Family* (Oxford, 1989); Rosemary O'Day, *The Family and Family Relationships 1500–1900: England, France, and the United States of America* (1994).
3. Roger North, *Notes of Me: The Autobiography of Roger North*, ed. Peter Millard (Toronto, 2000), 84.
4. University of Nottingham, Manuscripts Department, Clifton papers, Cl C 721, Thomas Wentworth to Sir Gervase Clifton, 8 Sept. 1638.
5. Stone, *Family, Sex and Marriage*.
6. E. P. Thompson, 'Happy Families', in his *Persons and Polemics* (1994), 307.
7. Britain was the name adopted after the Act of Union in 1707; *Oxford English Dictionary Online*: http://dictionary.oed.com. Note that this book remains focused on England alone.
8. Steve Hindle, *On the Parish? The Micro-Politics of Poor Relief in Rural England c. 1550–1750* (Oxford, 2004); see further Select Bibliography.
9. Richard Price, *British Society, 1680–1880: Dynamism, Containment and Change* (Cambridge, 1999), 1–16; Amy Louise Erickson, 'The Marital Economy in Perspective', in Maria Agren and Amy Louise Erickson (eds), *The Marital Economy in Scandinavia and Britain 1400–1900* (Aldershot, 2005), 5, argues that the term 'pre-industrial' was not applicable after 1750; Harvey and Shepard argue that the period 1500–1650 is dominated by social histories, 1650–1800 by cultural histories; Karen Harvey and Alexandra Shepard, 'What have Historians done with Masculinities? Reflections on Five Centuries of British History circa 1500–1950', *JBS*, 44 (2005), 277.
10. Lawrence Stone and Jeanne C. Fawtier Stone, *An Open Élite? England 1540–1880* (Oxford, 1984).
11. Jonathan Barry and Christopher Brooks (eds), *The Middling Sort of People: Culture, Society and Politics in England, 1550–1800* (Basingstoke, 1994); Margaret R. Hunt, *The Middling Sort: Commerce, Gender, and the Family in England 1680–1780* (Berkeley, CA, 1996). For women, see Amy Louise Erickson, 'Married Women's Occupations in Eighteenth-Century London', *Continuity and Change*, 23 (2008), 267–307.
12. Paul Slack, *Poverty and Policy in Tudor and Stuart England* (1988), 2–5; see also, Olwen H. Hufton, *The Poor in Eighteenth-Century France 1750–1789* (Oxford, 1974), 11–24.

13. Alan Everitt, 'Farm Labourers', in Joan Thirsk (ed.), *The Agrarian History of England and Wales*, vol. 4 (Cambridge, 1967), 399.
14. *Chelsea Settlement and Bastardy Examinations, 1733–1776*, ed. Tim Hitchcock and John Black, London Rec. Soc. vol. 33 (1999), p. ix. Cf. Dianne Payne who writes of 60% of the population as the poor; Dianne Payne, 'Children of the Poor in London 1700–1780' (PhD Thesis, University of Hertfordshire, 2008), 153.
15. Douglas Hay, 'War, Dearth and Theft in the Eighteenth Century: The Record of the English Courts', *Past and Present*, 95 (1982), 131–2.
16. E. A. Wrigley and R. S. Schofield, *The Population History of England 1541–1871: A Reconstruction* (Cambridge, 1989), 528–9.
17. Keith Wrightson, *Earthly Necessities: Economic Lives in Early Modern Britain* (New Haven, 2000), 36.
18. Tim Wales, 'Poverty, Poor Relief and the Life-Cycle: Some Evidence from Seventeenth-Century Norfolk', in Richard M. Smith (ed.), *Land, Kinship, and Life-Cycle* (Cambridge, 1984), 365, 375, 378; K. D. M. Snell, *Annals of the Labouring Poor: Social Change and Agrarian England, 1660–1900* (Cambridge, 1985), 28.
19. Smith (ed.), *Land, Kinship, and Life-Cycle*, 68–71.
20. Barry Stapleton, 'Inherited Poverty and Life-Cycle Poverty: Odiham, Hampshire, 1650–1850', *Social History*, 18 (1993), 339–55; see also B. Stapleton, 'Marriage, Migration and Mendicancy in a Pre-Industrial Community', in Barry Stapleton (ed.), *Conflict and Community in Southern England: Essays in the Social History of Rural and Urban Labour from Medieval to Modern Times* (Stroud, 1992), 51–91.
21. Slack, *Poverty and Policy*, 7, 73–80.
22. Robert W. Malcolmson, *Life and Labour in England, 1700–1780* (1981), 11–12.
23. Andy Wood, *The Politics of Social Conflict: The Peak Country 1520–1770* (Cambridge, 1999), 19–26.
24. See also Pamela Sharpe, *Population and Society: Reproducing Colyton, 1540–1840* (Exeter, 2002), 299–302.
25. Lyndal Roper, *Witch Craze: Terror and Fantasy in Baroque Germany* (New Haven, 2004), 8.
26. Patricia Crawford, 'Sexual Knowledge in England, 1500–1750', in Patricia Crawford, *Blood, Bodies and Families in Early Modern Europe* (2004), 55–63.
27. Wrigley and Schofield, *Population History*, 423–4.
28. H. J. Hajnal, 'Age at Marriage and Proportions Marrying', *Population Studies*, 7 (1953), 111–36; J. Hajnal, 'European Marriage Patterns in Perspective', in D. V. Glass and D. E. C. Eversley (eds), *Population in History* (1965), 101–43.
29. Pamela Sharpe, *Adapting to Capitalism: Working Women in the English Economy, 1700–1850* (Basingstoke, 1996), 140.
30. Keith Wrightson, 'The Family in Early Modern England: Continuity and Change', in S. Taylor, R. Connors, and C. Jones (eds), *Hanoverian Britain and Empire: Essays in Memory of Philip Lawson* (Woodbridge, 1998), 13–14.
31. Patricia Crawford, 'Introduction', in Crawford, *Blood, Bodies and Families*, 3–6.
32. Miranda Chaytor, 'Household and Kinship: Ryton in the late 16th and early 17th Centuries', *HWJ*, 10 (1980), 25–60.
33. Bridget Hill, 'The Marriage Age of Women and the Demographers', *HWJ*, 28 (1989), 144.

34. Margaret Spufford, 'The Cost of Apparel in Seventeenth-Century England, and the Accuracy of Gregory King', *Economic History Review*, n.s., 53 (2000), 685.

35. For further accounts, see Slack, *Poverty and Policy*; Paul Slack, *The English Poor Law 1531–1782* (Basingstoke, 1990); Hindle, *On the Parish?*.

36. See Penry Williams, *The Tudor Regime* (Oxford, 1979), 196–215.

37. Steve Hindle, 'Exclusion Crises: Poverty, Migration and Parochial Responsibility in English Rural Communities, c. 1560–1660', *Rural History*, 7 (1996), 125–49.

38. Richard Burn, *The History of the Poor Laws* (1764).

39. Sidney and Beatrice Webb, *English Poor Law History: Part 1: The Old Poor Law* (1927).

40. E. M. Leonard, *The Early History of English Poor Relief* (Cambridge, 1900); Dorothy Marshall, *The English Poor in The Eighteenth Century: A Study in Social and Administrative History* (1926, reprinted 1969).

41. Ivy Pinchbeck and Margaret Hewitt, *Children in English Society*, 2 vols (1969), vol. 1.

42. Ibid. 308–12.

43. Slack, *Poverty and Policy*; Paul Slack, *From Reformation to Improvement: Public Welfare in Early Modern England* (Oxford, 1999); Joanna Innes, 'The Mixed Economy of Welfare in Early Modern England: Assessments of the Options from Hale to Malthus (c. 1683–1803)', in Martin Daunton (ed.), *Charity, Self Interest and Welfare in the English Past* (1996), 139–80.

44. Margaret Pelling, *The Common Lot: Sickness, Medical Occupations and the Urban Poor in Early Modern England* (1998).

45. Hindle, *On the Parish?*.

46. M. G. Jones, *The Charity School Movement: A Study of Eighteenth Century Puritanism in Action* (Cambridge, 1938); Ruth McClure, *Coram's Children: The London Foundling Hospital in the Eighteenth Century* (1981); Donna T. Andrew, *Philanthropy and Police: London Charity in the Eighteenth Century* (Princeton, 1989); Tanya Evans, *'Unfortunate Objects': Lone Mothers in Eighteenth-Century London* (2005); Alysa Levene, *Childcare, Health and Mortality at the London Foundling Hospital, 1741–1800: 'Left to the mercy of the world'* (2007).

47. Snell, *Annals of the Labouring Poor*, 369.

48. [Jonas Hanway], *Serious Considerations on the Salutary Design of the Act of Parliament for a Regular, Uniform Register of the Parish Poor* (1762), 39, 43.

49. E[dmund] Bott, *A Collection of the Decisions of the Court of King's Bench upon the Poor's Laws* [1771], 47.

50. Mary E. Fissell, *Vernacular Bodies: The Politics of Reproduction in Early Modern England* (Oxford, 2004), 1–13.

51. Susan Dwyer Amussen, *An Ordered Society: Gender and Class in Early Modern England* (Oxford, 1988).

52. Sara Mendelson and Patricia Crawford, *Women in Early Modern England* (Oxford, 1998), 31–49.

53. Thomas Cobbet, *A Fruitfull and Useful Discourse touching the honour due from children to parents, and the duty of parents towards their children* (1656), sig. A3v.

54. See Naomi Tadmor, *The Social Universe of the English Bible: Scripture, Society and Culture in Early Modern England* (Cambridge, forthcoming). I am most grateful to Dr Tadmor for allowing me to read her book before publication, and for discussions.

55. Daniel Waterland, *Religious education of children: recommended in a sermon preach'd in the parish-church of St. Sepulchre, June the 6th, 1723* (1723), 4.
56. Patricia Crawford, 'Katharine and Philip Henry and their Children: A Case Study in Family Ideology', in Crawford, *Blood, Bodies and Families*, 182–3.
57. Rosemary O'Day, *Women's Agency in Early Modern Britain and the American Colonies* (Harlow, 2007), 152–84, and references.
58. Sylvia Walby, *Theorizing Patriarchy* (Oxford, 1990), 19–20.
59. Judith M. Bennett, *History Matters: Patriarchy and the Challenge of Feminism* (Philadelphia, 2006), 54–81 and *passim*.
60. R. W. Connell, *Masculinities* (Sydney, 1995), 242; Alexandra Shepard, *Meanings of Manhood in Early Modern England* (Oxford, 2003), 3.
61. Robert Cawdry (1617), quoted Shepard, *Meanings of Manhood*.
62. John R. Gillis, *A World of Their Own Making: Myth, Ritual, and the Quest for Family Values* (Cambridge, MA, 1997), 179.
63. Alan Bray, *The Friend* (Chicago, 2003); Randolph Trumbach, *Sex and the Gender Revolution* (Chicago, 1998); Elizabeth Foyster, *Manhood in Early Modern England: Honour, Sex, and Marriage* (New York, 1999); Tim Hitchcock and Michèle Cohen (eds), *English Masculinities 1600–1800* (1999); Shepard, *Meanings of Manhood*.
64. Thomas W. Laqueur, 'The Facts of Fatherhood', in Marianne Hirsch and Evelyn Fox Keller (eds), *Conflicts in Feminism* (New York, 1990), 205–21, quotation on 205.
65. Sara Ruddick, *Maternal Thinking: Towards a Politics of Peace* (Boston, 1995), 42–7; Sara Ruddick, 'Thinking about Fathers', in Hirsch and Keller (eds), *Conflicts in Feminism*, 222–33, quotation on 226.
66. Louis Haas, *The Renaissance Man and his Children: Childbirth and Early Childhood in Florence, 1300–1600* (New York, 1998); Anthony Fletcher, 'Men's Dilemma: The Future of Patriarchy in England 1560–1660', *TRHS*, 6th ser., 4 (1994), 61–81; Cynthia Herrup, '"To Pluck Bright Honour from the Pale-Faced Moon": Gender and Honour in the Castlehaven Story', *TRHS*, 6th ser., 6 (1996), 137–59; Bernard Capp, 'The Double Standard Revisited: Plebeian Women and Male Sexual Reputation in Early Modern England', *Past and Present*, 162 (1999), 70–100; Foyster, *Manhood in Early Modern England*; Bernard Capp, *When Gossips Meet: Women, Family, and Neighbourhood in Early Modern England* (Oxford, 2003).
67. Linda Pollock, 'Rethinking Patriarchy and the Family in Seventeenth-Century England', *Journal of Family History*, 23 (1998), 21–2.
68. For a valuable comparative study, see Megan Doolittle, 'Close Relations? Bringing Together Gender and Family in English History', in Leonore Davidoff, Keith McClelland, and Eleni Varikas (eds), *Gender and History: Retrospect and Prospect* (Oxford, 2000), 124–36.
69. Pollock, 'Rethinking Patriarchy and the Family', 3–27.
70. Stone, *Family, Sex and Marriage*, 4–9 and *passim*.
71. Houlbrooke, *English Family*; Ralph Houlbrooke (ed.), *English Family Life, 1576–1716: An Anthology from Diaries* (1988); see also James Casey, *The History of the Family* (Oxford, 1989); O'Day, *The Family and Family Relationships*.
72. Miriam Slater, *Family Life in the Seventeenth Century: The Verneys of Claydon House* (1984); Vivienne Larminie, *Wealth, Kinship and Culture: The Seventeenth-Century Newdigates of Arbury and their World* (1995); Susan

E. Whyman, *Sociability and Power in Late-Stuart England: The Cultural Worlds of the Verneys 1660–1720* (Oxford, 1999); John Broad, *Transforming English Rural Society: The Verneys and the Claydons, 1690–1820* (Cambridge, 2004).

73. Hunt, *The Middling Sort: Commerce, Gender, and the Family in England 1680–1780* (Berkeley, CA, 1996); Richard Grassby, *Kinship and Capitalism: Marriage, Family and Business in the English-speaking World, 1580–1740* (Cambridge, 2001).

74. For a recent critique of Stone, see Steve Hindle, 'A Cumbrian Family and the Poor Law Authorities, c. 1690–1730', in Helen Berry and Elizabeth Foyster (eds), *The Family in Early Modern England* (Cambridge, 2007), 126–57.

75. Stone, *Family, Sex and Marriage*, 470–8. Stone relied heavily on Ernest Caulfield, *The Infant Welfare Movement in the Eighteenth Century* (New York, 1931).

76. Lawrence Stone, *The Family, Sex and Marriage In England 1500–1800 Abridged* (New York, 1979), preface.

77. Houlbrooke, *English Family*, 254; see also a brief comment in Linda Pollock, 'Training a Child in the Way He/She Should Go. Cultural Transmission and Child-Rearing within the Home in England, circa 1550–1800', in Johan Sturm, Jeroen Dekker, Richard Aldrich, and Frank Simon (eds.), *Education and Cultural Transmission, Paedagogica Historica: International Journal of the History of Education*, supplementary series, 11 (1996), 79–103.

78. Stone, *Family, Sex and Marriage*.

79. Lloyd de Mause (ed.), *The History of Childhood* (New York, 1975).

80. Pollock, *Forgotten Children*; cf. Patricia Crawford, '"The sucking child": Adult Attitudes to Child Care in the First Year of Life in Seventeenth-Century England', in Crawford, *Blood, Bodies and Families*, 140–3.

81. Valerie Fildes (ed.), *Women as Mothers in Preindustrial England* (1990); Naomi Miller and Naomi Yavneh, *Maternal Measures: Figuring Caregiving in the Early Modern Period* (Aldershot, 2001); Hilary Marland (ed.), *The Art of Midwifery: Early Modern Midwives in Europe* (1993); Laura Gowing, 'Secret Births and Infanticide in Seventeenth-Century England', *Past and Present*, 156 (1997), 87–115; Laura Gowing, *Common Bodies: Women, Touch and Power in Seventeenth-Century England* (2003); cf. Elizabeth Foyster, 'Parenting was for Life, not just Childhood: The Role of Parents in the Married Lives of their Children in Early Modern England', *History*, 86 (2001), 313–27.

82. Mendelson and Crawford, *Women in Early Modern England*.

83. See Bray, *The Friend*, 2–3.

84. Crawford, 'Introduction', in Crawford, *Blood, Bodies and Families*, 3–7.

85. Connell, *Masculinities* (1995).

86. For a critique of men's history and gender history, see Toby L. Ditz, 'The New Men's History and the Peculiar Absence of Gendered Power: Some Remedies from Early American Gender History', *Gender and History*, 16 (2004), 1–35.

87. See Ruddick, *Maternal Thinking*, p. xi.

88. Peter Gay, *Freud for Historians* (New York, 1986).

89. Michael Roper and John Tosh (eds), *Manful Assertions: Masculinities in Britain since 1800* (1991), Introduction.

90. Linda Colley, *Britons: Forging the Nation 1707–1837* (1996), 5–6.

91. *The Office of Christian Parents* (Cambridge, 1616), 1.

92. Ibid. 1–3.

93. Ibid. 4.

94. Robert Cleaver, *A Godly Forme of Houshold Gouernment* (1630), sig. [z5].

95. Peter Rushton, 'Property, Power and Family Networks: The Problem of Disputed Marriage in Early Modern England', *Journal of Family History*, 11 (1986), 213–14.

96. John Child, *Industrial Relations in the British Printing Industry: The Quest for Security* (1967), 35.

97. [J. Dod and R. Cleaver], *A Plaine and Familiar Exposition of the Ten Commandments* (1606), 184, 216. For commentaries on the fifth commandment, see Ian Green, *The Christian's ABC: Catechisms and Catechizing in England c. 1530–1740* (Oxford, 1996), ch. 6.

98. Gordon J. Schochet, *Patriarchalism in Political Thought: The Authoritarian Family and Political Speculation and Attitudes Especially in Seventeenth-Century England* (Oxford, 1975), 79–81.

99. [Robert Openshaw], *Short Questions and Answeares, conteyning the summe of Christian Religion* (1681), sig. B3.

100. *Office of Christian Parents*, 1.

101. Ibid.

102. Samuel Brewster, *The Christian Scholar* (1703), 29.

103. Michael J. Braddick, *State Formation in Early Modern England c. 1550–1700* (Cambridge, 2000), 1; Steve Hindle, *The State and Social Change in Early Modern England, c. 1550–1640* (2000), 1–36.

104. John Moore, *The Crying Sin of England of Not Caring for the Poor* (1653), 2–4.

105. Naomi Tadmor, *Family and Friends in Eighteenth-Century England: Household, Kinship and Patronage* (Cambridge, 2001).

106. John Ball, *A Short Treatise Containing All the Principall Grounds of Christian Religion by way of questions and answers, very profitable for all sorts of men, but especially for housholders* (1650), 194–5.

107. John White, *A Way to the Tree of Life* (1647), 11.

108. Thompson, 'Happy Families', in *Persons and Polemics*, 301–11; Hindle, 'A Cumbrian Family', in Berry and Foyster (eds), *Family*, 126–7.

109. Tim Hitchcock, Peter King, and Pamela Sharpe (eds), *Chronicling Poverty: The Voices and Strategies of the English Poor, 1640–1840* (Basingstoke, 1997), 1–18 and *passim*; Tim Hitchcock, *Down and Out in Eighteenth-Century London* (2004), 233–40.

110. Peter Linebaugh and Marcus Rediker, *The Many-Headed Hydra: Sailors, Slaves, Commoners, and the Hidden History of the Revolutionary Atlantic* (Boston, 2000), 71–103.

111. See Chapter 4.

112. Joan Kent, 'The Centre and the Localities: State Formation and Parish Government in England, Circa 1640–1740', *Historical Journal*, 38 (1995), 390.

113. *Essex Pauper Letters 1731–1837*, ed. Thomas Sokoll (Oxford, 2001), 3–77; *Narratives of the Poor in Eighteenth-Century Britain*, ed. Alysa Levene, 5 vols (2006); see also Pamela Sharpe, 'Survival Strategies and Stories: Poor Widows and Widowers in Early Industrial England', in Sandra Cavallo and Lyndan Warner (eds), *Widowhood in Medieval and Early Modern Europe* (1999), 230; Hitchcock, *Down and Out*, 234–6.

114. Garthine Walker, 'Just Stories: Telling Tales of Infant Death in Early Modern England', in Margaret Mikesell and Adele Seeff (eds), *Culture and Change:*

Attending to Early Modern Women (Newark, NJ, 2003), 98–115, quotation on 112.

115. Tanya Evans, *'Unfortunate Objects': Lone Mothers in Eighteenth-Century London* (2005).

116. William Sloane, *Children's Books in England and America in the Seventeenth Century* (New York, 1955), 28–43.

117. William Gouge, *Of Domesticall Duties* (1626), sig. [A3v].

118. T. G. A. Nelson, *Children, Parents, and the Rise of the Novel* (Newark, NJ, 1995), 15.

119. See, for example, Dorothy Kilmer, *The Life and Perambulations of a Mouse* [1783?].

120. Marina Warner, *From the Beast to the Blonde: On Fairy Tales and their Tellers* (1955); Maria Tatar, *Off with Their Heads: Fairytales and the Culture of Childhood* (Princeton, NJ, 1992).

121. Thomas Tusser, *Five Hundred Points of Good Husbandrie*, ed. Geoffrey Grigson (Oxford, 1984), 180, 210.

122. 'The Widow of Watling Streete', *The Shirburn Ballads 1585–1616*, ed. Andrew Clark (Oxford, 1907), 2–19.

123. Lyndal Roper, 'Witchcraft and Fantasy', in her *Oedipus and the Devil: Witchcraft, Sexuality and Religion in Early Modern Europe* (1994), 202.

124. Annette Kuhn, *Family Secrets: Acts of Memory and Imagination* (1995).

125. Adam Fox, *Oral and Literate Culture in England 1500–1700* (Oxford, 2000), 190.

126. Benjamin Shaw, *The Family Records of Benjamin Shaw Mechanic of Dent, Dolphinholme and Preston, 1772–1841*, ed. Alan G. Crosby, Rec. Soc. of Lancashire and Cheshire, vol. 130 (1991), 1.

127. *OBP*, t16770601-6, Midwife (killing: infanticide, not guilty).

128. Rachel Weil, *Political Passions: Gender, the Family and Political Argument in England, 1680–1714* (Manchester, 1999); Crawford, 'Blood and Paternity', in Crawford, *Blood, Bodies and Families*, 113–39.

129. Cf. Arlette Farge and Jacques Revel, *The Vanishing Children of Paris: Rumour and Politics before the French Revolution*, trans. C. Miéville (Cambridge, MA, 1991), 104.

130. Laura Gowing, *Domestic Dangers: Women, Words, and Sex in Early Modern Oxford* (1996), 45–8; Steve Poole, 'Tales from the Old Bailey: Writing a New History from Below', *HWJ*, 59 (2005), 282–4.

131. See Hitchcock, *Down and Out*, 235–6 and notes.

132. Tim Hitchcock and Robert Shoemaker, 'The Value of the *Proceedings* as a Historical Source', see 'Witness Testimony', http://www.oldbaileyonline.org.

133. John H. Langbein, 'The Criminal Trial before the Lawyers', *The University of Chicago Law Review*, 45 (1978), 263–316; John H. Langbein, *The Origins of the Adversary Criminal Trial* (Oxford, 2003).

134. Peter Linebaugh, *The London Hanged: Crime and Civil Society in the Eighteenth Century* (1991), pp. xxi–xxii.

135. For printed examples, see *The Casebook of Sir Francis Ashley JP, Recorder of Dorchester 1614–1635*, ed. J. H. Bettey, Dorset Rec. Soc, vol. 7 (1981), 18 and *passim*.

136. Natalie Zemon Davis, *Fiction in the Archives: Pardon Tales and their Tellers in Sixteenth-Century France* (Stanford, 1987).

1. MOTHERS OF 'THE BASTARD CHILD'

1. LMA, A/FH/A/8/1/1/4, Petitions for admission to the London Foundling Hospital, 1773, Anne Newman.
2. Nicholas L'Estrange, *'Merry Passages and Jests': A Manuscript Jestbook of Sir Nicolas L'Estrange (1603–55)*, ed. H. F. Lippicott (Salzburg, 1974), 105–6.
3. 1662 An Act for the better Releife of the Poore of this Kingdom, http://www.british-history.ac.uk/report; Michael Dalton, *The Countrey Justice* (1618 edn), 31–2, 77; *The Westminster City Fathers (The Burgess Court of Westminster) 1585–1901*, ed. W. H. Manchee (1924), 105–6.
4. *The Book of Examinations and Depositions Before the Mayor and Justices of Southampton 1648–1663*, ed. Sheila D. Thomson, Southampton Rec. Soc. vol. 37 (1994), 136.
5. John March, *Actions for Slaunder* (1648), 91.
6. Peter Laslett, 'The Bastardy Prone Sub-Society', in Peter Laslett, Karla Oosterveen, and Richard M. Smith (eds), *Bastardy and its Comparative History* (1980), 217–46.
7. Peter Laslett, 'Long-term Trends in Bastardy in England', in Peter Laslett, *Family Life and Illicit Love in Earlier Generations: Essays in Historical Sociology* (Cambridge, 1977), 177, 147.
8. Carolyn Steedman, *Landscape for a Good Woman: A Story of Two Lives* (1986), 138–9.
9. Henry Fielding, *The History of Tom Jones, a Foundling* (1749), vol. 4, p. 26.
10. E. Wayne Carp, *Family Matters: Secrecy and Disclosure in the History of Adoption* (Cambridge, MA, 1998), p. xiii.
11. Laslett, 'Introduction', in Laslett, Oosterveen, and Smith (eds), *Bastardy*, 14–19.
12. Richard Adair, *Courtship, Illegitimacy and Marriage in Early Modern England* (Manchester, 1996), 25–7.
13. Laslett, 'Introduction', in Laslett, Oosterveen, and Smith (eds), *Bastardy*, 14–15; Laslett, 'Long-Term Trends in Bastardy', in his *Family Life and Illicit Love*, 119; Keith Wrightson, 'The Nadir of English Illegitimacy in the Seventeenth Century', in Laslett, Oosterveen, and Smith (eds), *Bastardy*, 176–91.
14. Roger Finlay, *Population and Metropolis: The Demography of London 1580–1650* (Cambridge, 1981), 149–50, 229–31.
15. Alysa Levene, 'The Origins of the Children of the London Foundling Hospital, 1741–1760: A Reconsideration', *Continuity and Change*, 18 (2003), 201–35.
16. *The Parish Register and Tithing Book of Thomas Hassall of Amwell*, ed. Stephen G. Doree, Hertfordshire Rec. Soc. vol. 5 (1989), 27; Gloucester RO, P344 in 1/1, Tytherington.
17. Adair, *Courtship, Illegitimacy and Marriage*, 39.
18. Ibid. 32–5.
19. Laslett, 'The Bastardy Prone Sub-Society', in Laslett, Oosterveen, and Smith (eds), *Bastardy*, 217–46; Steven King, '"The Bastardy Prone Sub-society" Again: Bastards and their Fathers and Mothers in Lancashire, Wiltshire, and Somerset, 1800–1840', in Alysa Levene, Thomas Nutt, and Samantha Williams (eds), *Illegitimacy in Britain, 1700–1920* (2005), 66–85.
20. Thomas Nutt, 'Illegitimacy and the Poor Law in Late-Eighteenth and Early-Nineteenth Century England' (PhD thesis, Cambridge, 2006), 209; King, '"The Bastardy Prone Sub-society" Again', in Levene, Nutt, and Williams (eds), *Illegitimacy in Britain*, 68, 72–5.

21. E. A. Wrigley, 'Marriage, Fertility and Population Growth in Eighteenth-Century England', in R. B. Outhwaite (ed.), *Marriage and Society: Studies in the Social History of Marriage* (1981), 155–6.
22. See, for example, Wrightson, 'The Nadir of English Illegitimacy', in Laslett, Oosterveen, and Smith (eds), *Bastardy*, 176–91; David Levine and Keith Wrightson, 'The Social Context of Illegitimacy in Early Modern England', in Laslett, Oosteveen, and Smith (eds), *Bastardy*; Adair, *Courtship, Illegitimacy and Marriage*.
23. Dalton, *The Countrey Justice* (1618 edn), 31; Walter J. King, 'Punishment for Bastardy in Early Seventeenth-Century England', *Albion*, 10 (1978), 134.
24. Samantha Williams, 'Poor Relief, Labourers' Households and Living Standards in Rural England c. 1770–1834: A Bedfordshire Case Study', *Economic History Review*, n.s., 58 (2005), 485–519, 506; Nutt, 'Illegitimacy and the Poor Law', 208–9.
25. *The Office of Christian Parents* (Cambridge, 1616), 2.
26. Ralph Houlbrooke, *Church Courts and the People during the English Reformation 1520–1570* (Oxford, 1979), 75–9, 278–81; Nutt, 'Illegitimacy and the Poor Law', 32–4.
27. William Sheppard, *An Epitome of all the Common and Statute Laws of the Nation* (1656), 179–80; John Ayliffe, *Parergon Juris Canonici Anglicani* (1726), 109; William Blackstone, *Commentaries on the Laws of England*, 4th edn (Dublin, 1771), vol. 1, pp. 454–6.
28. Marjorie Keniston McIntosh, *Controlling Misbehavior in England, 1370–1600* (Cambridge, 1998), 202.
29. R. H. Helmholz, 'Support Orders, Church Courts, and the Rule of *Filius Nullius*: A Reassessment of the Common Law' (1977), in *Canon Law and the Law of England* (1987), 169–86; Paul Slack, *Poverty and Policy in Tudor and Stuart England* (1988), 130.
30. 1733, 6 Geo. II c. 13, cited in Steven King, *Poverty and Welfare in England 1700–1850: A Regional Perspective* (Manchester, 2000), 274.
31. Poor Law legislation: 39 Eliz. I c. 3 (1597) and 43 Eliz. I c. 2 (1601).
32. King, 'Punishment for Bastardy', 130–51.
33. Dalton, *The Countrey Justice* (1655 edn), 41.
34. *Statutes of the Realm*; Martin Ingram, *Church Courts, Sex and Marriage in England 1570–1640* (Cambridge, 1987), 338; see also Ronald A. Marchant, *The Church under the Law: Justice, Administration and Discipline in the Diocese of York, 1560–1640* (Cambridge, 1969), 224.
35. *Quarter Sessions Records for the County of Somerset*, 4 vols (1607–77), ed. E. H. Bates, Somerset Rec. Soc., vols 23, 24, 28, 34 (1907–19), vol. 1, p. 297.
36. Garthine Walker, *Crime, Gender and the Social Order in Early Modern England* (Cambridge, 2003), 228.
37. *The Westminster City Fathers*, ed. Manchee, 105–7.
38. King, 'Punishment for Bastardy', 135–6.
39. Keith Thomas, 'Puritans and Adultery: The Act of 1650 Reconsidered', in Donald Pennington and Keith Thomas (eds), *Puritans and Revolutionaries: Essays in Seventeenth-Century History Presented to Christopher Hill* (Oxford, 1978), 256–82.
40. Stephen Roberts, 'Fornication and Bastardy in mid-Seventeenth Century Devon: How Was the Act of 1650 Enforced?', in John Rule (ed.), *Outside the Law: Studies in Crime and Order 1650–1850* (Exeter, 1982), 1–20.

41. J. M. Beattie, *Crime and the Courts in England 1660–1800* (Oxford, 1986), 614; King, 'Punishment for Bastardy', 140–51.

42. Wrigley, 'Marriage, Fertility and Population Growth', in Outhwaite (ed.), *Marriage and Society*, 155–6; Bridget Hill, 'The Marriage Age of Women and the Demographers', *HWJ*, 28 (1989), 152–5.

43. Peter Rushton, 'Property, Power and Family Networks: The Problem of Disputed Marriage in Early Modern England', *Journal of Family History*, 11 (1986), 205–19; Eric Josef Carlson, *Marriage and the English Reformation* (Oxford, 1994), 105–41; Diana O'Hara, *Courtship and Constraint: Rethinking the Making of Marriage in Tudor England* (Manchester, 2000), 45–6.

44. Martin Ingram, 'Spousals Litigation in the English Ecclesiastical Courts c. 1350–c. 1640', in Outhwaite (ed.), *Marriage and Society*, 45, 54–5.

45. Martin Ingram, 'The Reform of Popular Culture? Sex and Marriage in Early Modern England', in Barry Reay (ed.), *Popular Culture in Seventeenth-Century England* (1988), 149–50, 154.

46. Laslett, 'Introduction', in Laslett, Oosterveen, and Smith (eds), *Bastardy*, 17–18.

47. Ingram, *Church Courts*, 214–15; Steven Hindle, 'The Problem of Pauper Marriage in Seventeenth-Century England', *TRHS*, 6th ser., 8 (1998), 71–89; see further, Chapter 2.

48. Susan Dwyer Amussen, *An Ordered Society: Gender and Class in Early Modern England* (Oxford, 1988), 111, 117; Laura Gowing, *Common Bodies: Women, Touch and Power in Seventeenth-Century England* (2003), 7–9.

49. Pamela Sharpe, 'Poor Children as Apprentices in Colyton, 1598–1830', *Continuity and Change*, 6 (1991), 253, 256 and *passim*; see further discussion in Chapters 4 and 5.

50. Laura Gowing, 'Secret Births and Infanticide in Seventeenth-Century England', *Past and Present*, 156 (1997), 103–5; Gowing, *Common Bodies*, 159, 162.

51. David Harley, 'Provincial Midwives in England: Lancashire and Cheshire, 1660–1760', in Hilary Marland (ed.), *The Art of Midwifery: Early Modern Midwives in Europe* (1993), 37–8.

52. 21 Jac. I c. 7; Sara Mendelson and Patricia Crawford, *Women in Early Modern England* (Oxford, 1998), 44–5.

53. Gowing, 'Secret Births and Infanticide', 87–115; Gowing, *Common Bodies*; Mark Jackson, *New-Born Child Murder: Women, Illegitimacy and the Courts in Eighteenth-Century England* (Manchester, 1996); Mark Jackson (ed.), *Infanticide: Historical Perspectives on Child Murder and Concealment, 1550–2000* (Aldershot, 2002).

54. J. R. Dickinson and J. A. Sharpe, 'Infanticide in Early Modern England: The Court of Great Sessions at Chester, 1650–1800', in Jackson (ed.), *Infanticide*, 35. For the concept of blood guilt, see Patricia Crawford, ' "Charles Stuart: That Man of Blood" ', *JBS*, 17 (1977), 41–61.

55. Slack, *Poverty and Policy*; Lynn Hollen Lees, *The Solidarities of Strangers: The English Poor Laws and the People, 1700–1948* (Cambridge, 1998), 7; Steve Hindle, *On the Parish? The Micro-Politics of Poor Relief in Rural England c. 1550–1750* (Oxford, 2004).

56. Thomas Nutt, 'The Paradox and Problems of Illegitimate Paternity in Old Poor Law Essex', in Levene, Nutt, and Williams (eds), *Illegitimacy in Britain*, 104–6.

57. [J. Brydell?], *Jus Primogeniti* (1699), 3.

58. G. J. Barker-Benfield, *The Culture of Sensibility: Sex and Society in Eighteenth-Century Britain* (Chicago, 1992); Hugh Cunningham, *Children and Childhood*

in Western Society since 1500 (1995), 61–2; Toni Bowers, *The Politics of Motherhood: British Writing and Culture, 1680–1760* (Cambridge, 1996).

59. Ruth Perry, 'Colonising the Breast: Sexuality and Maternity in Eighteenth-Century England', *Journal of the History of Sexuality*, 2 (1991), 204–34.
60. Randolph Trumbach, *Sex and the Gender Revolution* (Chicago, 1998), 424.
61. Tony Henderson, *Disorderly Women in Eighteenth-Century London: Prostitution and Control in the Metropolis 1730–1830* (1999), 166–91.
62. Hugh Cunningham, *The Children of the Poor: Representations of Childhood since the Seventeenth Century* (Oxford, 1991); Cunningham, *Children and Childhood*, 41–78.
63. See Lisa Zunshine, *Bastards and Foundlings: Illegitimacy in Eighteenth-Century England* (Columbus, OH, 2005), 1–22 and *passim*; M. P. Tilley, *A Dictionary of the Proverbs in England in the Sixteenth and Seventeenth Centuries* (Ann Arbor, 1950), 31, B104.
64. Tilley, *Dictionary of the Proverbs*, 723, W353.
65. *The Diary of Henry Prescott LLB, Deputy Registrar of Chester Diocese*, 3 vols, ed. John Addy, Rec. Soc. of Lancashire and Cheshire, vols 127, 132, 133 (1987–97), vol. 3, pp. 766–7.
66. Punishments of bastard-bearers: 18 Eliz. I c. 3 (1576), 7 Jac. I c. 4 (1610); King, 'Punishment for Bastardy', 139.
67. Hindle, *On the Parish?*, 224–6.
68. Ruth McClure, *Coram's Children: The London Foundling Hospital in the Eighteenth Century* (1981), 91.
69. Interestingly, the term 'mother' was used to refer to the womb.
70. Patricia Crawford, 'Blood and Paternity', in Patricia Crawford, *Blood, Bodies and Families in Early Modern England* (2004), 113–39.
71. Ann Kussmaul, *Servants in Husbandry in Early Modern England* (Cambridge, 1981), 44; Adair, *Courtship, Illegitimacy and Marriage*, 88.
72. J. A. Sharpe, *Crime in Seventeenth-Century England: A County Study* (Cambridge, 1983), 60.
73. Levine and Wrightson, 'Social Context of Illegitimacy', in Laslett, Oosteveen, and Smith (eds), *Bastardy*, 164–6.
74. R. W. Malcolmson, 'Infanticide in the Eighteenth Century', in J. S. Cockburn (ed.), *Crime in England, 1500–1800* (1977), 192, 202.
75. *Nottinghamshire County Records: notes and extracts from the Nottinghamshire county records of the 17th century*, ed. H. Hampton Copnall (Nottingham, 1915), 68; cf. Kussmaul, *Servants in Husbandry*, 32.
76. LMA, A/FH/A/8/1/1/2, Petitions for admission to the London Foundling Hospital, 1770–1, 21 Feb. [1771].
77. Blackstone, *Commentaries on the Laws of England*, 5th edn (Oxford, 1773), vol. 1, p. 457; see, for example, petition of Margaret Currins to Foundling Hospital for return of a child: LMA, A/FH/A/11/2/3, Petitions for return of children, 1762.
78. James Stephen Taylor, *Poverty, Migration and Settlement in the Industrial Revolution* (Palo Alto, CA, 1989), 26–7.
79. See further, Chapter 4.
80. E. A. Wrigley, 'Marriage, Fertility and Population Growth', in Outhwaite (ed.), *Marriage and Society*, 156–7. Wrigley lowered Hair's figures of 20% and 40%; E. H. Hair, 'Bridal Pregnancy in Rural England in Earlier Centuries', *Population Studies*, 20 (1966), 233–43; E. H. Hair, 'Bridal Pregnancy in Earlier Rural

England Further Examined', *Population Studies*, 24 (1970), 59–70; Levine and Wrightson, 'Social Context of Illegitimacy', in Laslett, Oosterveen, and Smith (eds), *Bastardy*, 161–2. See also E. A. Wrigley and R. S. Schofield, *The Population History of England 1541–1871: A Reconstruction* (Cambridge, 1989), 254.

81. John Black, 'Who were the Putative Fathers of Illegitimate Children in 1740–1810?', in Levene, Nutt, and Williams (eds), *Illegitimacy in Britain* (2005), 60–1.

82. Adair, *Courtship, Illegitimacy and Marriage*, 79–83.

83. King, 'The Bastardy Prone Sub-society Again', in Levene, Nutt, and Williams (eds), *Illegitimacy in Britain*, 66–85.

84. Shannon McSheffrey, *Love and Marriage in Late Medieval London* (Kalamazoo, 1995); Carlson, *Marriage and the English Reformation*; O'Hara, *Courtship and Constraint*.

85. Gowing, 'Secret Births', 96–8, 103.

86. Patricia Crawford, 'Attitudes to Menstruation in Seventeenth-Century England', in Crawford, *Blood, Bodies and Families*, 34; Amussen, *Ordered Society*, 114–15.

87. *Women's Worlds in Seventeenth-Century England: A Sourcebook*, ed. Patricia Crawford and Laura Gowing (2000), 18–19; for another case, see David Cressy, *Birth, Marriage, and Death: Ritual, Religion, and the Life-Cycle in Tudor and Stuart England* (Oxford, 1997), 48.

88. Michael MacDonald and Terence R. Murphy, *Sleepless Souls: Suicide in Early Modern England* (Oxford, 1990), 285–9.

89. Laura Gowing, 'Giving Birth at the Magistrate's Gate: Single Mothers in the Early Modern City', in Stephanie Tarbin and Susan Broomhall (eds), *Women, Identities and Communities in Early Modern Europe* (Aldershot, 2008), 137–50; Jodi Mikalachki, 'Women's Networks and the Female Vagrant: A Hard Case', in Susan Frye and Karen Robertson (eds), *Maids and Mistresses, Cousins and Queens: Women's Alliances in Early Modern England* (Oxford, 1999), 52–69.

90. Claire S. Schen, 'Women and the London Parishes, 1500–1620', in Katherine L. French, Gary G. Gibbs, and Beat A. Kümin (eds), *The Parish in English Life 1400–1600* (Manchester, 1997), 262.

91. R. H. Helmholz, 'Harboring Sexual Offenders: Ecclesiastical Courts and Controlling Misbehavior', *JBS*, 37 (1998), 258–86.

92. Paul Slack, 'Vagrants and Vagrancy in England, 1598–1664', *Economic History Review*, n.s., 27 (1974), 360–79.

93. Gowing, *Common Bodies*, 158.

94. Steve Hindle, 'Beating the Bounds of the Parish: Order, Memory and Identity in the English Local Community, c. 1500–1700', 28–9 (forthcoming: I am most grateful to Steve Hindle for allowing me to read and cite).

95. K. D. M. Snell, *Annals of the Labouring Poor: Social Change and Agrarian England 1660–1900* (Cambridge, 1985), 106–7; Dave Postles, 'Surviving Lone Motherhood in Early-Modern England', *Seventeenth Century*, 21 (2006), 160–83.

96. Gowing, *Common Bodies*, 156–7.

97. Cressy, *Birth, Marriage, and Death*, 77–8.

98. Peter C. Hoffer and N. E. H. Hull, *Murdering Mothers: Infanticide in England and New England 1558–1803* (New York, 1981), 15–17.

99. Gloucester RO, Gloucs, Kingswood, P193 OU5/1/6, 28 Feb. [1720].

100. Cressy, *Birth, Marriage, and Death*, 76.

101. Adair, *Courtship, Illegitimacy and Marriage*, 34–5.

102. Malcolmson, 'Infanticide in the Eighteenth Century', in Cockburn (ed.), *Crime in England*; Beattie, *Crime and the Courts*, 113–34; Jackson, *New-Born Child Murder*; Alison Rowlands, ' "In Great Secrecy": The Crime of Infanticide in Rothenburg ob der Tauber, 1501–1618', *German History*, 15 (1997), 179–99; Gowing, 'Secret Births', 87–115; Marilyn Francus, 'Monstrous Mothers, Monstrous Societies: Infanticide and the Rule of Law in Restoration and Eighteenth-Century England', *Eighteenth-Century Life*, 21 (1997), 133–56.
103. Julie Wheelwright, ' "Nothing in Between": Modern Cases of Infanticide', in Jackson (ed.), *Infanticide*, 272–3.
104. Hilary Marland, *Dangerous Motherhood: Insanity and Childbirth in Victorian Britain* (2004), 9–15.
105. *OBP*, t16960227-18, M— S— (killing: infanticide, not guilty).
106. *OBP*, t17370216-21, Mary Shrewsbury (killing: infanticide, guilty).
107. Garthine Walker, 'Just Stories: Telling Tales of Infant Death in Early Modern England', in Margaret Mikesell and Adele Seeff (eds), *Culture and Change: Attending to Early Modern Women* (Newark, NJ, 2003), 98–115.
108. Gowing, 'Secret Births', 90.
109. *OBP*, t17310714-29, Martha Busby (killing: infanticide, not guilty).
110. Randall Martin, *Women, Murder, and Equity in Early Modern England* (2008), 194–5.
111. *OBP*, t16940711-23, Mary Maye (killing: infanticide, not guilty).
112. *OBP*, t16960227-18, M— S— (killing: infanticide, not guilty).
113. *OBP*, t17901027-78, Martha Miller (killing: infanticide, not guilty).
114. *OBP*, t17451016-19, Grace Usop (killing: infanticide, not guilty).
115. Walker, *Crime, Gender and the Social Order*, 155–8.
116. *Book of Examinations and Depositions . . . Southampton*, ed. Thomson, 27–9.
117. Sharpe, *Crime in Seventeenth-Century England*, 135–7.
118. Alan Macfarlane, *Witchcraft in Tudor and Stuart England: A Regional and Comparative Study* (1970), 61; Dickinson and Sharpe, 'Infanticide in Early Modern England', in Jackson (ed.), *Infanticide*, 35–51.
119. Amussen, *Ordered Society*, 115.
120. Beattie, *Crime and the Courts*, 119–24.
121. *OBP*, t17430413-36, Sarah Wilmshurst (killing: murder, guilty).
122. Gowing, 'Secret Births', 90.
123. Gowing, *Common Bodies*, 196–7.
124. *Quarter Sessions Records . . . Somerset*, ed. Bates, vol. 1, p. 52.
125. LMA, A/FH/A/8/1/1/1, Petitions for admission, 1768–9.
126. *Norfolk Quarter Sessions Order Book 1650–1657*, ed. D. F. Howell James, Norfolk Rec. Soc., vol. 26 (1955), 75.
127. LMA, A/FH/A/9/1/1, [Foundling Hospital] Billet book, 1741, 22M.
128. LMA, A/FH/A/8/1/1/2, Petitions for admission, 1770–1.
129. Keith Wrightson, 'Infanticide in Earlier Seventeenth-Century England', *Local Population Studies*, 15 (1975), 16.
130. Tim Hitchcock, ' "Unlawfully begotten on her body": Illegitimacy and the Parish Poor in St Luke's Chelsea', in Tim Hitchcock, Peter King, and Pamela Sharpe (eds), *Chronicling Poverty: The Voices and Strategies of the English Poor, 1640–1840* (Basingstoke, 1997), 77–8.
131. Rowlands, ' "In Great Secrecy" ', 179, 196–8.
132. Valerie Fildes, 'Maternal Feelings Re-assessed: Child Abandonment and Neglect in London and Westminster, 1550–1800', in Valerie Fildes (ed.), *Women as*

Mothers in Pre-Industrial England: Essays in Memory of Dorothy McLaren (1990), 150.

133. Alysa Levene, 'The Mortality Penalty of Illegitimate Children: Foundlings and Poor Children in Eighteenth-Century England', in Levene, Nutt, and Williams (eds), *Illegitimacy in Britain*, 40–1.

134. Gowing, *Common Bodies*, 194–6.

135. *County of Middlesex, Calendar to the Sessions Records*, ed. W. Le Hardy, 3 vols (1935), vol. 3 (1615–16), 89.

136. GL, MS 11280/6, St Dionis Backchurch, Churchwardens' vouchers and miscellaneous papers, 1766–72.

137. Personal communication from Alysa Levene.

138. GL, MS 3242/1, St Sepulchre Holborn, Minutes of the Guardians of the Poor, 1767–1806, 19 July 1767, pursuant to 7 Geo. III c. 29. Thanks to Alysa Levene for kindly sending me this information.

139. Westminster Archives Centre, Parish records: St Paul Covent Garden, Guardians of Poor Children minutes, 1768–95. (Again, thanks to Alysa Levene.)

140. Hindle, *On the Parish?*, 225, 337–42.

141. John R. Gillis, 'Conjugal Settlements: Resort to Clandestine and Common Law Marriage in England and Wales, 1650–1850', in John Bossy (ed.), *Disputes and Settlements: Law and Human Relations in the West* (Cambridge, 1983), 267, 270.

142. David Levine, *Family Formation in an Age of Nascent Capitalism* (New York, 1977), 127.

143. G. R. Quaife, *Wanton Wenches and Wayward Wives: Peasants and Illicit Sex in Early Seventeenth Century England* (1979), 59–64; Sharpe, *Crime in Seventeenth-Century England*, 60.

144. Adrian Wilson, 'Illegitimacy and its Implications in Mid-Eighteenth-Century London: The Evidence of the Foundling Hospital', *Continuity and Change*, 4 (1989), 103–64; Nicholas Rogers, 'Carnal Knowledge: Illegitimacy in Eighteenth-Century Westminster', *Journal of Social History*, 23 (1989), 355–75.

145. LMA, A/FH/A/8/1/1/24, Petitions for admission, 1799.

146. LMA, A/FH/A/8/1/1/4, Petitions for admission, 1773.

147. LMA, A/FH/A/8/1/1/6, Petitions for admission, 1775.

148. Black, 'Putative Fathers', in Levene, Nutt, and Williams (eds), *Illegitimacy in Britain*, 50–65.

149. Randolph Trumbach, *Sex and the Gender Revolution* (Chicago, 1998), 234.

150. Keith Wrightson and David Levine, *Poverty and Piety in an English Village: Terling, 1525–1700* (New York, 1979), 128.

151. For an excellent discussion of how to read the Foundling Petitions, see *Narratives of the Poor in Eighteenth-Century Britain*, ed. Alysa Levene, 5 vols (2006), vol. 3, *Institutional Responses: The London Foundling Hospital*, pp. vii–xviii.

152. Tanya Evans, *'Unfortunate Objects': Lone Mothers in Eighteenth-Century London* (2005), 6–9.

153. Garthine Walker, 'Rereading Rape and Sexual Violence in Early Modern England', *Gender and History*, 10 (1998), 1–25.

154. Patricia Crawford, 'Sexual knowledge in England, 1500–1750', in Crawford, *Blood, Bodies and Families*.

155. LMA, A/FH/A/8/1/1/2, Petitions for admission, 1770, loose petition.

156. LMA, A/FH/A/8/1/1/7, Petitions for admission, 1776.

157. LMA, A/FH/A/8/1/1/1, Petitions for admission, 1768–9.

158. GL, MS 10852, St Benet Paul's Wharf, Churchwardens' papers, 1672–1720, settlement papers.
159. GL, MS 2676/1, St Botolph Aldgate, Pauper examinations, 1742–50.
160. Pamela Sharpe, *Population and Society in an East Devon Parish: Reproducing Colyton 1540–1840* (Exeter, 2002), 282.
161. *OBP*, t17451016-19, Grace Usop (killing: infanticide, not guilty).
162. John Black, 'Illegitimacy, Sexual Relations and Location in Metropolitan London, 1735–85', in Tim Hitchcock and Heather Shore (eds), *The Streets of London: From the Great Fire to the Great Stink* (2003), 117.
163. Trumbach, *Sex and the Gender Revolution*, 235; Evans, '*Unfortunate Objects*', 37.
164. Sharpe, *Population and Society*, 285.
165. LMA, A/FH/A/8/1/1/10, Petitions for admission, 1779.
166. LMA, A/FH/A/8/1/1/1, Petitions for admission, 1768–9.
167. LMA, A/FH/A/8/1/1/7, Petitions for admission, 1776.
168. GL, MS 2676/18, St Botolph Aldgate, Pauper examinations, 1788–90, Hannah Gotschin, 1788.
169. Jeremy Boulton, '"It is Extreme Necessity That Makes Me Do This": Some "Survival Strategies" of Pauper Households in London's West End during the Early Eighteenth Century', *International Review of Social History*, 45 (2000), 60.
170. GL, MS 2676/2, St Botolph Aldgate, Pauper examinations, 1750.
171. John R. Gillis, *For Better, For Worse: British Marriages, 1600 to the Present* (Oxford, 1985), 128.
172. LMA, A/FH/A/8/1/1/6, Petitions for admission, 1775.
173. LMA, A/FH/A/8/1/1/1, Petitions for admission, 1768–9.
174. LMA, A/FH/A/8/1/1/2, Petitions for admission, 1770–1.
175. LMA, A/FH/A/8/1/1/10, Petitions for admission, 1779.
176. LMA, A/FH/A/8/1/1/2, Petitions for admission, 1770–1.
177. LMA, A/FH/A/8/1/1/4, Petitions for admission, 1773.
178. Postles, 'Surviving Lone Motherhood', 165–6; Helmholz, 'Harboring Sexual Offenders', 258–68.
179. King, 'Punishment for Bastardy', 138; Steve Hindle, 'A Sense of Place? Becoming and Belonging in the Rural Parish, 1550–1650', in Alexandra Shepard and Phil Withington (eds), *Communities in Early Modern England* (Manchester, 2000), 101.
180. Ian W. Archer, *The Pursuit of Stability: Social Relations in Elizabethan London* (Cambridge, 1991), 184–5.
181. *[Warwickshire] Quarter sessions order book*, 8 vols (1625–96), ed. S. C. Ratcliffe and H. C. Johnson (Warwick, 1935), vol. 2 (1637–50), 125.
182. Ibid. vol. 4 (1657–65), 153–4.
183. Claire S. Schen, 'Women and the London Parishes, 1500–1620', in Katherine L. French, Gary G. Gibbs, and Beat A. Kümin (eds), *The Parish in English Life 1400–1600* (Manchester, 1997), 262–3.
184. Lambeth Palace Library, VG 4/13, Vicar General archive, visitation returns for the diocese of Canterbury, 1786–1935, fo. 22v. June 1631 (thanks to Laura Gowing for this reference).
185. *John Clare's Autobiographical Writings*, ed. Eric Robinson (Oxford, 1983), 2–3.
186. Benjamin Shaw, *The Family Records of Benjamin Shaw Mechanic of Dent, Dolphinholme and Preston, 1772–1841*, ed. Alan G. Crosby, Rec. Soc. of Lancashire and Cheshire, vol. 130 (1991), 20.

187. Ibid. 89.
188. Ibid. 90.
189. Ibid. 56, 58, 90–1.
190. LMA, A/FH/A/8/1/1/3, Petitions for admission, 1772, Elizabeth Brooks, 30 Dec. 1772.
191. LMA, A/FH/A/8/1/1/4, Petitions for admission, 1773.
192. *Quarter Sessions Records...Somerset*, ed. Bates, vol. 3, p. 251.
193. Quoted in Pamela Sharpe, *Adapting to Capitalism: Working Women in the English Economy, 1700–1850* (New York, 1996), 146.
194. LMA, A/FH/A/8/1/1/4, Petitions for admission, 1773.
195. LMA, A/FH/A/8/1/1/1, Petitions for admission, 1768–9, Sarah Page.
196. Boulton, ' "Survival Strategies" of Pauper Households', 59, 63.
197. Trumbach, *Sex and the Gender Revolution*, 289–92.
198. *Norfolk Quarter Sessions Order Book 1650–57*, ed. James, 38.
199. Mendelson and Crawford, *Women in Early Modern England*, 193.
200. *The Norwich Census of the Poor 1570*, ed. J. F. Pound, Norfolk Rec. Soc. vol. 40 (1971), 36.
201. LMA, A/FH/A/8/1/1/4, Petitions for admission, 1773.
202. LMA, A/FH/A/8/1/1/12, Petitions for admission, 1781.
203. LMA, A/FH/A/9/1/1, [Foundling Hospital] Billet book, 1741, 26.
204. Ibid.
205. LMA, A/FH/A/8/1/1/2, Petitions for admission, 1770–1, Eleanor Richardson 19 May [1771].
206. Ibid. Elizabeth Turpin.
207. Ibid. Sarah Aviary.
208. Evans, *'Unfortunate Objects'*, 135.
209. Felicity A. Nussbaum, *Torrid Zones: Maternity, Sexuality and Empire in Eighteenth-Century English Narratives* (Baltimore, 1995), 27.
210. George Moore, *Esther Waters* (1894).
211. *OBP*, t17470909–11, Elizabeth Fletcher (killing: infanticide, not guilty). Thanks to Joanne McEwan for this case.
212. LMA, A/FH/A/8/1/1/1, Petitions for admission, 1768–9.
213. Peter Earle, *A City Full Of People: Men and Women of London 1650–1750* (1994), 291–2.
214. LMA, A/FH/A/8/1/1/4, Petitions for admission, 1773.
215. Alysa Levene, *Childcare, Health and Mortality at the London Foundling Hospital, 1741–1800: 'Left to the mercy of the world'* (2007), 108, 134.
216. GL, MS 613/1, St Augustine Watling Street, Vestry and precinct minute books (including some minutes of the joint vestry meetings of the united parishes of St Augustine Watling Street and St Faith under St Paul), 1744–81, Vestry minutes 1765–76, 348.
217. LMA, A/FH/A/8/1/1/1, Petitions for admission (1768–9). See also Evans, *'Unfortunate Objects'*, 127–44.
218. *Chelsea Settlement and Bastardy Examinations 1733–1766*, ed. Tim Hitchcock and John Black, London Rec. Soc., vol. 33 (1999), 146, 149–50.
219. D. A. Kent, 'Ubiquitous but Invisible: Female Domestic Servants in Mid-Eighteenth Century London', *HWJ*, 28 (1989), 122–3.
220. Kussmaul, *Servants in Husbandry*, 37.
221. Kent, 'Female Domestic Servants', 124–5.

222. LMA, A/FH/A/8/1/1/2, Petitions for admission, 1770–1; see also LMA, A/FH/A/8/1/1/1, Petitions for admission, 1768–9.
223. LMA, A/FH/A/8/1/1/1, Petitions for admission, 1768–9.
224. LMA, A/FH/A/8/1/1/24, Petitions for admission, 1799.
225. Gowing, *Common Bodies*, 202.
226. *A True Relation of the Most Horrid and Barbarous Murders Committed by Abigail Hill* (1658).
227. Dorothy Marshall, *The English Poor in the Eighteenth Century: A Study in Social and Administrative History* (1926; reprinted 1969), 98–9.
228. LMA, A/FH/A/8/1/1/24, Petitions for admission, 1799.
229. R. Campbell, *The London Tradesman* (1747), 208.
230. LMA, A/FH/A/8/1/1/17, Petitions for admission, 1787–91, 27 Nov. 1788.
231. LMA, A/FH/A/8/1/1/7, Petitions for admission, 1776, 10 April 1776.
232. Mendelson and Crawford, *Women in Early Modern England*, 292–8.
233. Levene, *Childcare, Health and Mortality*, 4–5.
234. Ibid. 24–5.
235. McClure, *Coram's Children*, 139; Levene, *Childcare, Health and Mortality*, 7–8, 20–1, 30.
236. McClure, *Coram's Children*, 141.
237. R. B. Outhwaite, '"Objects of Charity": Petitions to the London Foundling Hospital, 1768–72', *Eighteenth-Century Studies*, 32 (1999), 507.
238. Wilson, 'Illegitimacy and its Implications', 136.
239. Outhwaite, 'Objects of Charity'; Evans, '*Unfortunate Objects*', 98–126.
240. Outhwaite, 'Objects of Charity', 499–500; Evans, '*Unfortunate Objects*', 98–102; see also Levene, *Narratives of the Poor*, vol. 3, pp. xv–xviii.
241. LMA, A/FH/A/8/1/1/1, Petitions for admission, 1768–9.
242. LMA, A/FH/A/8/1/1/12, Petitions for admission, 1781.
243. LMA, A/FH/A/8/1/1/4, Petitions for admission, 1773.
244. R. H. Nichols and F. A. Wray, *The History of the Foundling Hospital* (1935), 39.
245. Gillian Clark, 'Infant Clothing in the Eighteenth Century: A New Insight', *Costume*, 28 (1994), 47–59. Some tokens are on display in the Foundling Museum, London.
246. LMA, A/FH/A/8/1/1/3, Petitions for admission, 1772.
247. Nichols and Wray, *History of the Foundling Hospital*, 186; Levene, *Childcare, Health and Mortality*, 18.
248. LMA, A/FH/A/11/2/5, Petitions for return of children, 1764.
249. Levene, 'Origins of the Children', 219.
250. LMA, A/FH/A/8/1/1/7, Petitions for admission, 1776.
251. LMA, A/FH/A/11/2/15, Petitions for return of children, 1789, 9 June 1789.
252. *Women's Worlds*, ed. Crawford and Gowing, 118–19.
253. Essex RO, Q/SR, 156–61, 16/17, undated.
254. Mendelson and Crawford, *Women in Early Modern England*, 285.
255. *Essex Quarter Sessions Order Book 1652–1661*, ed. D. H. Allen (Chelmsford, 1974), 90.
256. GL, MS 613/1, St Augustine Watling Street, Vestry minutes 1765–76, 348.
257. T. R. Forbes, *Chronicle from Aldgate: Life and Death in Shakespeare's London* (New Haven, CT, 1971), 199.
258. Fildes, 'Maternal Feelings Re-assessed', in Fildes (ed.), *Women as Mothers*, 164–6.

259. Daniel Defoe, *The Generous Projector, or a friendly proposal to prevent murder and other enormous abuses* (1731), 9–10.

260. [Jonas Hanway], *Serious Considerations on the Salutary Design of the Act of Parliament for a Regular, Uniform Register of the Parish Poor* (1762), 5; Jonas Hanway, *Letters on the importance of the rising generation of the laboring part of our fellow-subjects*, 2 vols (1767), vol. 1, pp. 12–13.

261. LMA, A/FH/A/12/1, Petitions to take apprentices, letter from Samuel Ginks of Worcestershire, 23 June 1761. Thanks to the kindness of Amy Erickson for this reference.

262. Peter Linebaugh, *The London Hanged: Crime and Civil Society in the Eighteenth Century* (1991), 148.

263. Levene, *Childcare, Health and Mortality*, 90–117.

264. Ibid. 94.

265. William Sheppard, *A Sure Guide for his Majesties Justices of Peace* (1663), 251, 257; see also Crawford, 'Maternity', in Crawford, *Blood, Bodies and Families*, 87.

266. *Essex Quarter Sessions*, ed. Allen, 32.

267. Joseph Keble, *An Assistance to Justices of the Peace* (1683), 196–7, 203.

268. Richard Burn, *The Justice of the Peace, and Parish Officer*, 14th edn, 4 vols (1780), vol. 1, p. 195; James Burrow, *A Series of Decisions of the Court of King's Bench upon Settlement Cases*, 2nd edn (1768), 2.

269. Nutt, 'Paradox and Problems of Illegitimate Paternity', in Levene, Nutt, and Williams (eds), *Illegitimacy in Britain*, 114.

270. *The Papers of Nathaniel Bacon of Stiffkey*, ed. V. Morgan, J. Key, and B. Taylor, Norfolk Rec. Soc., vol. 64 (2000), 290–1.

271. *Quarter Sessions Records . . . Somerset*, ed. Bates, vol. 1, p. 53.

272. Blackstone, *Commentaries on the Laws of England*, 1st edn (Oxford, 1765–9), vol. 4, p. 65.

273. Marshall, *English Poor*, 216–17.

274. Hitchcock, ' "Unlawfully begotten on her body" ', in Hitchcock, King, and Sharpe (eds), *Chronicling Poverty*, 73–6; Amy M. Froide, *Never Married: Singlewomen in Early Modern England* (Oxford, 2005), 40–1.

275. E. A. Wrigley, R. S. Davies, J. E. Oeppen, and R. S. Schofield, *English Population History from Family Reconstitution* (Cambridge, 1997), 207–8, 489–92.

276. E. N. Hampson, *The Treatment of Poverty in Cambridgeshire 1597–1834* (Cambridge, 1934), 169.

277. *Poor Law Records of Mid Sussex 1601–1835*, ed. Norma Pilbeam and Ian Nelson, Sussex Rec. Soc., vol. 83 (1999), 364.

278. Jennine Hurl, ' "She being bigg with child is likely to miscarry": Pregnant Victims Prosecuting Assault in Westminster, 1685–1720', *London Journal*, 24 (1999), 18–33, 24.

279. *The Court Leet Records of the Manor Manchester, from the Year 1552 to the Year 1686*, ed. J. Earwaker, 12 vols (1884–90), vol. 1, pp. 23, 27.

280. *The Westminster City Fathers*, ed. Manchee, 96–7.

281. LMA, A/FH/A/8/1/1/1, Petitions for admission, 1768–9, Mary Cole.

282. Boulton, ' "Survival Strategies" of Pauper Households', 54.

283. LMA, A/FH/A/8/1/1/1, Petitions for admission, 1768–9, letter [torn] at end.

284. LMA, A/FH/A/8/1/1/10, Petitions for admission, 1779.

285. Boulton, ' "Survival Strategies" of Pauper Households', 52–4.

286. *Chelsea Settlement and Bastardy Examinations*, ed. Hitchcock and Black, p. xvii.

287. Hitchcock, 'Unlawfully Begotten on her Body', in Hitchcock, King, and Sharpe (eds), *Chronicling Poverty*, 77.
288. Aylsa Levene, 'The Mortality Penalty of Illegitimate Children: Foundlings and Poor Children in Eighteenth-Century England', in Levene, Nutt, and Williams (eds), *Illegitimacy in Britain*, 47–8.
289. *OBP*, t17340227–32, Judith Defour (killing: murder, guilty).
290. See, for example, *Chelsea Settlement and Bastardy Examinations*, ed. Hitchcock and Black, 9–10.
291. LMA, A/FH/A/8/1/1/24, Petitions for admission, 1799.
292. Evans, *'Unfortunate Objects'*, 205.
293. Essex RO, Calendar of Records, vol. 17, pp. 67, 263–4.
294. Trumbach, *Sex and the Gender Revolution*, 242–5.
295. *[Warwickshire] Quarter sessions order book*, ed. Ratcliffe and Johnson, vol. 1, (1625–37), 19, 25, 60, 162, 172; vol. 2, (1637–50), 139, 141–2, 199–200, 251; vol. 3, (1650–7), 106. Thanks to Tim Wales for piecing this story together; see also Hindle, *On the Parish?*, 389.
296. LMA, A/FH/A/8/1/1/3, Petitions for admission, 1772, Margaret Smith 16 Sept. 1772.
297. LMA, A/FH/A/8/1/1/1, Petitions for admission, 1768–9, Mary Brown 1769.
298. LMA, A/FH/A/8/1/1/3, Petitions for admission, 1772.
299. LMA, A/FH/A/8/1/1/24, Petitions for admission, 1799, Maria Thomas, 1799.
300. Gowing, *Common Bodies*, 197.
301. LMA, A/FH/A/8/1/1/3, Petitions for admission, 1772.
302. LMA, A/FH/A/11/2/15/1, Petitions for return of children, 9 June 1789.
303. LMA, A/FH/A/6/1/11/47, Foundling Hospital Correspondence, 1758.
304. *OBP*, t17431012–20, Elizabeth Shudrick (killing: infanticide, not guilty).
305. *Poverty in Early-Stuart Salisbury*, ed. Paul Slack, Wiltshire Rec. Soc. vol. 31 (1975), 22.
306. A. L. Beier, *Masterless Men: The Vagrancy Problem in England 1560–1640* (1985), 54.
307. *Calendar of Bradford-on-Avon Settlement Examinations and Removal Orders, 1725–98*, ed. Phyllis Hembry, Wiltshire Rec. Soc. vol. 46 (1990), 14–15.
308. *Mitcham Settlement Examinations, 1784–1814*, ed. Blanche Berryman, Surrey Rec. Soc., vol. 27 (1973), 58, 81.
309. Burn, *Justice of the Peace* (1755 edn), vol. 2, p. 198.
310. GL, MS 2676/2, St Botolph Aldgate, Pauper examinations, 1750.
311. Sharpe, *Adapting to Capitalism*, 134–5; Carolyn Steedman, 'Lord Mansfield's Women', *Past and Present*, 176 (2002), 105–43.
312. Pamela Sharpe, 'The Parish's Women: A Reply to Steedman', paper delivered at the Australian Historical Association Conference, Newcastle, 2004. I am grateful to Professor Sharpe for permission to cite her unpublished paper.
313. Garthine Walker, 'Expanding the Boundaries of Female Honour in Early Modern England', *TRHS*, 6th ser., 6 (1996), 242–5; Walker, *Crime, Gender and the Social Order*, 227–37.
314. Laurence Fontaine and Jurgen Schumbohm, 'Household Strategies for Survival: An Introduction', *International Review of Social History*, Supplement 8, *Household Strategies for Survival 1600–2000: Fission, Faction and Cooperation* (Cambridge, 2000), 12.
315. Ingram, *Church Courts*, 310; Adair, *Courtship, Illegitimacy and Marriage*, 79–83.

2. 'FATHERS' OF ILLEGITIMATE CHILDREN

1. Naomi Tadmor, 'Women and Wives: The Language of Marriage in Early Modern English Biblical Translations', *HWJ*, 62 (2006), 14.

2. Richard Burn, *The Justice of the Peace, and Parish Officer*, 2 vols, (1755 edn), vol. 2, p. 198.

3. H. Pettit, 'Parental Control and Guardianship', in R. H. Graveson and F. R. Crane (eds), *A Century of Family Law* (1957), 58 n. 12, 62; see also Thomas Nutt, ' "There may be supposed something of natural affection": Fatherhood, affiliation and the maintenance of illegitimate children in eighteenth and early-nineteenth century England', NEER conference paper, Perth July 2007; I am grateful to Dr Nutt for permission to cite his paper.

4. Patricia Crawford, 'Blood and Paternity', in Patricia Crawford, *Blood, Bodies and Families in Early Modern England* (2004), 113–39.

5. William Blackstone, *Commentaries on the Laws of England*, 4th edn (Dublin, 1771), vol. 1, p. 458.

6. Robert Foulkes, *An Alarme for Sinners* (1679), 9.

7. Jonas Hanway, *Letters to the Guardians of the Infant Poor* (1768), 58.

8. Daniel Defoe, *The Generous Projector, or a friendly proposal to prevent murder and other enormous abuses* (1731), 12.

9. Crawford, 'Blood and Paternity', in Crawford, *Blood, Bodies and Families*, 113–39.

10. Thomas Nutt, 'The Paradox and Problems of Illegitimate Paternity in Old Poor Law Essex', in Alysa Levene, Thomas Nutt, and Samantha Williams (eds), *Illegitimacy in Britain, 1700–1920* (2005), 104.

11. *The Posthumous Works of Mr Thomas Chubb*, 2 vols (1748), vol. 1, p. iv.

12. Diana O'Hara, *Courtship and Constraint: Rethinking the Making of Marriage in Tudor England* (Manchester, 2000).

13. John Broad, 'Housing the Rural Poor in Southern England, 1650–1850', *Agricultural History Review*, 42 (2000), 151–70.

14. E. A. Wrigley and R. S. Schofield, *The Population History of England, 1541–1871: A Reconstruction* (Cambridge, 1981), 255.

15. See earlier discussion in Chapter 1.

16. [Jonas Hanway], *A Candid Historical Account of the Hospital for the Reception of Exposed and Deserted Young Children* (1759), 11.

17. Philippa Maddern, 'Between Households: Children in Blended and Transitional Households in Late-Medieval England', unpublished paper, Medieval Children Conference, Kent, 2006. I am most grateful to Professor Maddern for permission to cite this paper.

18. Quoted in Jeremy Gregory, 'Gender and the Clerical Profession in England, 1660–1850', in R. H. Swanson (ed.), *Studies in Church History: Gender and the Christian Religion*, vol. 34 (1998), 260–1.

19. John Black, 'Illegitimacy, Sexual Relations and Location in Metropolitan London, 1735–85', in Tim Hitchcock and Heather Shore (eds), *The Streets of London: From the Great Fire to the Great Stink* (2003), 113–14.

20. Richard Cooke, *A White Sheete, or A Warning for Whoremongers. A Sermon* (1629).

21. *The 'Bawdy Court' of Banbury: The Act Book of the Peculiar Court of Banbury, Oxfordshire and Northamptonshire 1625–1638*, ed. R. K. Gilkes, Banbury Historical Soc., vol. 26 (1997), 101–2.

22. Bernard Capp, 'The Double Standard Revisited: Plebeian Women and Male Sexual Reputation in Early Modern England', *Past and Present*, 162 (1999), 72–3.

23. *OBP*, t17861025–56, William Hodge (sexual offences: rape, not guilty). Thanks to Joanne McEwan for this case.

24. David Turner, ' "Nothing is so secret but shall be revealed": The Scandalous Life of Robert Foulkes', in Tim Hitchcock and Michèle Cohen (eds), *English Masculinities 1660–1800* (1999), 169–92.

25. Paul Griffiths, *Youth and Authority: Formative Experiences in England 1560–1640* (Oxford, 1996), 287, 249.

26. Alexandra Shepard, 'Manhood, Credit and Patriarchy in Early Modern England c. 1580–1640', *Past and Present*, 167 (2000), 75–106.

27. Cooke, *A White Sheete*, 22–4.

28. Somerset RO, Q/SR/ 114, fo. 104, 13 June 1670.

29. GL, MS 9083, St Sepulchre Holborn, Middlesex Division: Workhouse Committee Minutes and Orders, 1728–48, 8.

30. Clive Holmes, 'Law and Politics in the Reign of Charles I: The Case of John Prigeon', *Journal of Legal History*, 28 (2007), 161–82.

31. Martin Ingram, *Church Courts, Sex and Marriage in England 1570–1640* (Cambridge, 1987), 285–91; Dave Postles, 'Surviving Lone Motherhood in Early-Modern England', *Seventeenth Century*, 21 (2006), 170.

32. R. H. Helmholz, 'Harboring Sexual Offenders: Ecclesiastical Courts and Controlling Misbehavior', *JBS*, 37 (1998), 258–9, 262.

33. *Nottinghamshire County Records: notes and extracts from the Nottinghamshire county records of the 17th Century*, ed. H. Hampton Copnall (Nottingham, 1915), 123.

34. Oxfordshire RO, MS Archidiaconal papers, Oxon c. 118 c. 1616–20, fo. 35v. Sara Mendelson kindly shared her notes of this case when we were working on our book about women in early modern England.

35. *County of Buckingham: Calendar to the Sessions Records*, ed. William Le Hardy and G. L. Reckitt, vol. 3 (Aylesbury, 1939), pp. xvii, 263, 275–6.

36. Oxfordshire RO, Quarter sessions, Minutes Books, QSM/l/1 Easter (1710), 25, 26, 27 (in this case the sworn deposition was later shown to be false); *Women's Worlds in Seventeenth-Century England: A Sourcebook*, ed. Patricia Crawford and Laura Gowing (2000), 19.

37. Dana Rabin, 'Beyond "Lewd Women" and "Wanton Wenches": Infanticide and Child-Murder in the Long Eighteenth Century', in Jennifer Thorn (ed.), *Writing British Infanticide: Child-Murder, Gender, and Print, 1722–1859* (Newark, NJ, 2003), 48–9.

38. LMA, A/FH/A/8/1/1/2, Petitions for admission to the London Foundling Hospital, 1770–1.

39. LMA, A/FH/A/8/1/1/6, Petitions for admission, 1775.

40. LMA, A/FH/A/8/1/1/12, Petitions for admission, 1781.

41. Randolph Trumbach, *Sex and the Gender Revolution* (Chicago, 1998), 279; see also R. B. Outhwaite, ' "Objects of Charity": Petitions to the London Foundling Hospital, 1768–72', *Eighteenth-Century Studies*, 32 (1999), 504. Outhwaite likewise found that one third of his sample of 217 fathers (1768–72) had fled.

42. LMA, A/FH/A/8/1/1/10, Petitions for admission, 1779.

43. LMA, A/FH/A/8/1/1/12, Petitions for admission, 1781.

44. LMA, A/FH/A/8/1/1/24, Petitions for admission, 1799.

45. G. R. Quaife, *Wanton Wenches and Wayward Wives: Peasants and Illicit Sex in Early Seventeenth Century England* (1979), 95; see Crawford, 'Blood and paternity', in Crawford, *Blood, Bodies, and Families*, 127.
46. Postles, 'Surviving Lone Motherhood', 174–5.
47. Garthine Walker, *Crime, Gender and Social Order in Early Modern England* (Cambridge, 2003), 260.
48. LMA, A/FH/A/8/1/1/1, Petitions for admission, 1768–9.
49. *Deposition Book of Richard Wyatt JP 1767–1776*, ed. Elizabeth Silverthorne, Surrey Rec. Soc., vol. 30 (1978), 28–9.
50. Laura Gowing, 'Secret births and Infanticide in Seventeenth-Century England', *Past and Present*, 156 (1997), 103.
51. R. W. Malcolmson, 'Infanticide in the Eighteenth Century', in J. S. Cockburn (ed.), *Crime in England, 1500–1800* (1977), 192, 200–1.
52. Rabin, 'Beyond "Lewd Women" and "Wanton Wenches"', in Thorn (ed.), *Writing British Infanticide*, 52–3.
53. *OBP*, t16831212–2, Elenor Adams (killing: infanticide, guilty).
54. Frances E. Dolan, *Domestic Familiars: Representations of Domestic Crime in England, 1550–1700* (Ithaca, 1994), 121–70.
55. Keith Wrightson, 'Infanticide in Earlier Seventeenth-Century England', *Local Population Studies*, 15 (1975), 12.
56. Laura Gowing, *Common Bodies: Women, Touch and Power in Seventeenth-Century England* (2003), 196.
57. *OBP*, t16850826–18, Mary Aris, Mary Arrow, Dorothy Critor (deception: fraud, guilty); see also Gowing, *Common Bodies*, 202.
58. LMA, A/FH/A/8/1/1/4, Petitions for admission, 1773.
59. John Boswell, *The Kindness of Strangers: The Abandonment of Children in Western Europe from Late Antiquity to the Renaissance* (New York, 1988), 423; Dolan, *Dangerous Familiars*, 125 and notes to, 421–2.
60. LMA, A/FH/A/11/2/1, Petitions for return of children, 1759, 21 Aug. 1759.
61. LMA, A/FH/M/01/005, Documents and books collected by J. Brownlow, 1759, 77.
62. Ibid. 63.
63. LMA, A/FH/A/11/2/2, Petitions for return of children, 1760.
64. *Correspondence of the Foundling Hospital Inspectors in Berkshire, 1757–68*, ed. Gillian Clark, Berkshire Rec. Soc., vol. 1 (1994), 32–4.
65. Crawford, 'Blood and Paternity', in Crawford, *Blood, Bodies, and Families*, 121–4.
66. Gowing, *Common Bodies*, 195–6.
67. Oxfordshire RO, Quarter sessions, Minutes Books, QSM/l/1 Easter (1712), 146.
68. *The 'Bawdy Court' of Banbury*, ed. Gilkes, 103, 23 Mar. 1629.
69. LMA, P91/LEN/(1200), St Leonard Shoreditch, Settlement and Bastardy examinations, 1758–64, 188; John Black, 'Illegitimacy and the Urban Poor in London, 1740–1830' (PhD thesis, London, 2000), 137–8.
70. Quaife, *Wanton Wenches and Wayward Wives*, 94.
71. *The Book of Examinations and Depositions Before the Mayor and Justices of Southampton 1648–1663*, ed. Sheila D. Thomson, Southampton Rec. Soc., vol. 37 (1994), 42.
72. Oxfordshire RO, Quarter sessions, Minute Books, QSM/l/1 Easter 1714, 20 Jan. 1713/4.

73. Richard Adair, *Courtship, Illegitimacy and Marriage in Early Modern England* (Manchester, 1996), 72–4, 84; Capp, 'Double Standard Revisited'.

74. Penry Williams, *The Tudor Regime* (Oxford, 1979), 210.

75. Susan Dwyer Amussen, 'Elizabeth I and Alice Balstone: Gender, Class, and the Exceptional Woman in Early Modern England', in Betty S. Travitsky and Adele F. Seeff (eds), *Attending to Women in Early Modern England* (Newark, NJ, 1994), 231.

76. *The 'Bawdy Court' of Banbury*, ed. Gilkes, 169–76.

77. Devon RO, Chanter 878, February 1679, fo. 1; 5 Feb. 1679, witness 2. Thanks to Sara Mendelson for this case. Southcombe took the child about three weeks before Easter.

78. For examples, see Chapter 1.

79. Jeremy Boulton, ' "It is Extreme Necessity That Makes Me Do This": Some "Survival Strategies" of Pauper Households in London's West End during the Early Eighteenth Century', *International Review of Social History*, 45 (2000), 64 and n. 65.

80. Devon RO, Chanter 878, 21 Osbourn con Archer; Osbourn con Vallence [Nov. 1679?]. Thanks to Sara Mendelson for this record.

81. Ibid.

82. Tim Meldrum, 'London Domestic Servants from Depositional Evidence, 1660–1750: Servant-Employer Sexuality in the Patriarchal Household', in Tim Hitchcock, Peter King, and Pamela Sharpe (eds), *Chronicling Poverty: The Voices and Strategies of the English Poor, 1640–1840* (Basingstoke, 1997), 47.

83. *Women's Worlds*, ed. Crawford and Gowing, 142–6.

84. 'Rocke the Babie Joane', in Christopher Marsh et al., *Songs of the Seventeenth Century: The Ballads* (Belfast, 1994).

85. *[Warwickshire] Quarter sessions order book*, 8 vols, 1625–1696, ed. S. C. Ratcliffe and H. C. Johnson (Warwick, 1935), vol. 4 (1657–65), 26.

86. Ingram, *Church Courts*, 221–2.

87. Wrigley and Schofield, *Population History of England*, 254; E. A. Wrigley, 'Marriage, Fertility and Population Growth in Eighteenth-Century England', in Outhwaite (ed.), *Marriage and Society*, 156–7.

88. Quaife, *Wanton Wenches and Wayward Wives*, 95–7; John R. Gillis, 'Conjugal Settlements: Resort to Clandestine and Common Law Marriage in England and Wales, 1650–1850', in John Bossy (ed.), *Disputes and Settlements: Law and Human Relations in the West* (Cambridge, 1983), 267–70.

89. Benjamin Shaw, *The Family Records of Benjamin Shaw Mechanic of Dent, Dolphinholme and Preston, 1772 1841*, ed. Alan G. Crosby, Rec. Soc. of Lancashire and Cheshire, vol. 130 (1991), 29–32.

90. ['Jenny is poor'], *The Roxburghe Ballads*, ed. W. Chappell (vols 1–3) and J. W. Ebsworth (vols 4–9), 9 vols (Hertford 1872–99; reprinted New York, 1966), vol. 7, p. 129.

91. J. A. Sharpe, *Crime in Seventeenth-Century England: A County Study* (Cambridge, 1983), 60.

92. John Black, 'Who were the Putative Fathers of Illegitimate Children in London, 1740–1810?', in Levene, Nutt, and Williams (eds), *Illegitimacy in Britain*, 51.

93. Ibid. 63–4; *Chelsea Settlement and Bastardy Examinations 1733–1766*, ed. Tim Hitchcock and John Black, London Rec. Soc., vol. 33 (1999), p. xviii.

94. Griffiths, *Youth and Authority*, 5.

95. Frances Harris, *A Passion for Government* (Oxford, 1991), 24–5; Sara Mendelson, 'The Civility of Women', in Peter Burke, Brian Harrison, and Paul Slack (eds), *Civil Histories: Essays Presented to Sir Keith Thomas* (Oxford, 2000), 121.

96. Quoted in Patricia Crawford, 'Construction and Experience of Maternity', in Crawford, *Blood, Bodies and Families*, 92.

97. L. D. Schwartz, 'The Standard of Living in the Long Run: London 1700–1800', *Economic History Review*, n.s., 38 (1985), 24–41.

98. Pamela Sharpe, *Population and Society in an East Devon Parish: Reproducing Colyton 1540–1840* (Exeter, 2002), 299.

99. David Levine and Keith Wrightson, *The Making of an Industrial Society: Whickham 1560–1765* (Oxford, 1991), 303–4.

100. Peter Laslett, 'The Bastardy Prone Sub-Society', in Peter Laslett, Karla Oosterveen, and Richard M. Smith (eds), *Bastardy and its Comparative History* (1980), 217–46.

101. Steven King, 'The "Bastardy Prone Sub-society" Again: Bastards and Their Fathers and Mothers in Lancashire, Wiltshire, and Somerset, 1800–1840', in Levene, Nutt, and Williams (eds), *Illegitimacy in Britain*, 79–80.

102. Black, 'Illegitimacy and the Urban Poor', 176.

103. GL, MS 2676/5, St Botolph Aldgate, Pauper examinations, 1768.

104. *OBP*, t17971206-2, Thomas Wardropper (sexual offences: bigamy, guilty).

105. *OBP*, t17970111-30, Ambrose Rowe (sexual offences: bigamy, not guilty).

106. Lawrence Stone, *Road to Divorce: England, 1530–1987* (Oxford, 1990), 309–12.

107. GL, MS 2676/18, St Botolph Aldgate, Pauper examinations, 30 Sept. 1789 (thanks to Tim Hitchcock).

108. Ibid.

109. James Stephen Taylor, *Poverty, Migration and Settlement in the Industrial Revolution: Sojourners' Narratives* (Palo Alto, CA, 1989), 43–4.

110. Ibid. 27, 43–4.

111. Ibid. 28.

112. *The Justicing Notebook of William Hunt 1744–1749*, ed. Elizabeth Crittal (Devizes, 1982), 28.

113. Ibid. 55.

114. *The Diary of a Country Parson: The Reverend James Woodforde*, vol. 2, *1782–1787*, ed. John Beresford (Oxford, 1926), 82, 297–8.

115. Adair, *Courtship, Illegitimacy and Marriage*, 138–9.

116. Keith Wrightson and David Levine, *Poverty and Piety in an English Village: Terling 1525–1700* (New York, 1979), 80–1.

117. Ingram, *Church Courts*, 130–1, 214–15; Steve Hindle, 'The Problem of Pauper Marriage in Seventeenth-Century England', *TRHS*, 6th ser., vol. 8 (1998), 71–89; Steve Hindle, *On the Parish? The Micro-Politics of Poor Relief in Rural England c. 1550–1750* (Oxford, 2004), 337–52; see also Chapter 1 this book.

118. Keith Wrightson, *English Society 1580–1680* (1982), 78.

119. Garthine Walker, 'Expanding the Boundaries of Female Honour in Early Modern England', *TRHS*, 6th ser., 6 (1996), 235–45, 243–4.

120. Capp, 'Double Standard Revisited'.

121. *Poor Law Records of Mid Sussex 1601–1835*, ed. Norma Pilbeam and Ian Nelson, Sussex Rec. Soc., vol. 83 (1999), 364.

122. Nutt, 'Paradox and Problems of Illegitimate Paternity', in Levene, Nutt, and Williams (eds), *Illegitimacy in Britain*, 102–21.
123. Adair, *Courtship, Illegitimacy and Marriage*, 78.
124. Crawford, 'Blood and Paternity', in Crawford, *Blood, Bodies, and Families*.
125. Essex RO, Q/SR, 156–61, 153/29, 20–26 Feb. 1601.
126. Shropshire RO, QS/2/8, Salop sessions August 1700.
127. Gowing, *Common Bodies*, 162–3.
128. Ronald A. Marchant, *The Church under the Law: Justice, Administration and Discipline in the Diocese of York, 1560–1640* (Cambridge, 1969), 224–5.
129. Capp, 'Double Standard Revisited', 75–6, 79.
130. Thomas Nutt, 'Illegitimacy and the Poor Law in Late-Eighteenth and Early-Nineteenth Century England' (PhD thesis, Cambridge, 2006), 43–50.
131. Capp, 'Double Standard Revisited', 79–92.
132. *The Casebook of Sir Francis Ashley JP Recorder of Dorchester 1614–1635*, ed. J. H. Bettey, Dorset Rec. Soc., vol. 7 (1981), 66, 68–9.
133. Ibid. 66.
134. LMA, MJ/SP/1165 (68), Middlesex Sessions of the Peace, 24 Apr. 1657.
135. Dorothy Marshall, *The English Poor in the Eighteenth Century: A Study in Social and Administrative History* (1926; reprinted 1969), 208–9.
136. Adair, *Courtship, Illegitimacy and Marriage*, 152 (more common Somerset, Notts., Sussex, West Riding).
137. *Quarter Sessions Records for the County of Somerset*, 4 vols, 1607–1677, ed. E. H. Bates, Somerset Rec. Soc., vols 23, 24, 28, 34 (1907–19), vol. 1, p. 211.
138. Marchant, *Church under the Law*, 224–5.
139. Keith Wrightson, 'The Nadir of English Illegitimacy in the Seventeenth Century', in Laslett, Oosterveen, and Smith (eds), *Bastardy*, 180–1 and n. 22.
140. *Nottinghamshire County Records*, ed. Copnall, 122.
141. Giles Jacob, *The Modern Justice*, 3rd edn (1720), 51.
142. *Essex Quarter Sessions Order Book 1652–1661*, ed. D. H. Allen (Chelmsford, 1974), 33.
143. *Nottinghamshire County Records*, ed. Copnall, 123.
144. *Abstract of the orders made by the Court of Quarter Sessions for Shropshire*, vol. 1, *1638–1708*, ed. R. Lloyd Kenyon (Shrewsbury, 1901), 174.
145. Nutt, 'Natural affection', NEER paper, 7.
146. Walter J. King, 'Punishment for Bastardy in Early Seventeenth-Century England', *Albion*, 10 (1978), 130–51.
147. Michael Nolan, *A Treatise of the Laws for the Relief and Settlement of the Poor*, 2 vols (1805), vol. 1, pp. 182–3.
148. Peter King, 'The Summary Courts and Social Relations in Eighteenth-Century England', *Past and Present*, 183 (2004), 152.
149. Susan Dwyer Amussen, *An Ordered Society: Gender and Class in Early Modern England* (Oxford, 1988), 112.
150. *A Kentish Parson: Selections from the Private Papers of the Revd Joseph Price, Vicar of Brabourne, 1767–1786*, ed. G. M. Ditchfield and Bryan Keith Lucas (Stroud, 1991), 15.
151. James Lackington, *Memoirs of the First Forty-Five Years of James Lackington* (1794; facs. edn New York, 1974), 77–8.
152. Amussen, *Ordered Society*, 116.
153. Essex RO, Q/SR 107/44, Session Rolls Epiphany 1589. Thanks to Stephanie Tarbin for this reference.

154. *Quarter Sessions Records...Somerset*, ed. Bates, vol. 1, p. 303.
155. Ibid. 252–3.
156. For appeals, see E[dmund] Bott, *A Collection of Decisions of the Court of King's Bench upon the Poor's Laws*, [1771].
157. Nutt, 'Paradox and Problems of Illegitimate Paternity', in Levene, Nutt, and Williams (eds), *Illegitimacy in Britain*, 103–4.
158. *Quarter Sessions Records...Somerset*, ed. Bates, vol. 1, p. 250.
159. *The Papers of Nathaniel Bacon of Stiffkey*, ed. V. Morgan, J. Key, and B. Taylor, Norfolk Rec. Soc., vol. 64 (2000), 100–1.
160. Margaret Pelling, 'Child Health as a Social Value', in Pelling, *The Common Lot: Sickness, Medical Occupations and the Urban Poor in Early Modern England* (1998), 113.
161. *Borough Session Papers 1653–1688, Portsmouth Record Series*, ed. Arthur J. Willis and Margaret J. Hoad (Chichester, 1971), 133.
162. Bott, *Collection of Decisions of the Court of King's Bench*, 70.
163. Pamela Sharpe, 'Poor Children as Apprentices in Colyton, 1598–1830', *Continuity and Change*, 6 (1991), 253–7.
164. Burn, *Justice of the Peace* (1755 edn) vol. 1, p. 122.
165. *Quarter Sessions Records...Somerset*, ed. Bates, vol. 1, p. 38.
166. Oxfordshire RO, Quarter sessions, Minutes Books, QSM/l/1 Easter 1687, 21.
167. *Justice in Eighteenth-Century Hackney: The Justicing Notebook of Henry Norris and the Hackney Petty Session Book*, ed. Ruth Paley, London Rec. Soc., vol. 28 (1991), 99.
168. Borthwick Institute, PR S. H. 9, Maintenance Orders and Bonds, 1716–1800.
169. *[Warwickshire] Quarter sessions order book*, ed. Ratcliffe and Johnson, vol. 4 (1657–65), 158.
170. *Norfolk Quarter Sessions Order Book 1650–1657*, ed. D. E. Howell James, Norfolk Rec. Soc., vol. 26 (1955), 76.
171. *Quarter Sessions Records...Somerset*, ed. Bates, vol. 3, p. xxix.
172. *Norfolk Quarter Sessions Order Book 1650–1657*, ed. James, 25.
173. Oxfordshire RO, MS Archidiaconal papers, Oxon c.118, fos. 40–44v, Testamentary dispute Parratt c. Hinckes, 25 Jan. 1617.
174. *The Reports of Sir George Croke Knight* (1657), 337–8.
175. *Essex Quarter Sessions*, ed. Allen, 20.
176. *Quarter Sessions Records...Somerset*, ed. Bates, vol. 1, p. 53.
177. Charles II (1662): An Act for the better Releife of the Poore of this Kingdom, Statutes of the Realm: volume 5: 1628–80 (1819), 401–5. URL: http://www.british-history.ac.uk/report. Date accessed: 7 April 2008.
178. Nutt, 'Paradox and Problems of Illegitimate Paternity', in Levene, Nutt, and Williams (eds), *Illegitimacy in Britain*, 103 and n. on 222: 1733 6 Geo. II c. 31 An Act for the Relief of Parishes and other Places from such Charges as may arise from Bastard Child Born in the same.
179. GL, MS 18977, All Hallows Lombard Street, Bonds of indemnity for the maintenance of parish poor children bound as apprentices, 1668–1701.
180. *Poor Law Records of Mid Sussex*, ed. Pilbeam and Nelson, 365.
181. Black, 'Illegitimacy and the Urban Poor', 136–8.
182. Nutt, 'Natural Affection', NEER paper, 10–14.
183. Burn, *Justice of the Peace* (1755 edn), vol. 1, p. 122.
184. *The Westminster City Fathers (The Burgess Court of Westminster) 1585–1901*, ed. W. H. Manchee (1924), 114.

185. *County of Middlesex: Calendar to the Sessions Records*, ed. William Le Hardy, vol. 3, 1615–16, 26.
186. Ibid. 8.
187. *[Warwickshire] Quarter sessions order book*, ed. Ratcliffe and Johnson, vol. 4 1657–65, 311.
188. *Justicing Notebook of William Hunt*, ed. Crittal, 37.
189. Ibid. 52.
190. Bott, *Collection of Decisions of the Court of King's Bench*, 42–3.
191. LMA, A/FH/A/8/1/1/4, Petitions for admission, 1773.
192. *Nottinghamshire County Records*, ed. Copnall, 123.
193. Shropshire RO, P246/L/1, Warrant 5 Oct. 1680.
194. A. L. Beier, *Masterless Men: The Vagrancy Problem in England 1560–1640* (1985), 56.
195. King, 'Punishment for Bastardy', 131.
196. Nutt, 'Illegitimacy and the Poor Law', 173–5.
197. *Casebook of Sir Francis Ashley*, ed. Bettey, 74.
198. Adam Fox, *Oral and Literate Culture in England 1500–1700* (Oxford, 2000), 137.
199. LMA, A/FH/A/11/2/5, Petitions for return of children, 1764, 22 Aug. 1764.
200. *Essex Quarter Sessions*, ed. Allen, 55.
201. Gowing, *Common Bodies*, 194–6, 203.
202. Robert Moss, *The Providential Division of Men into Rich and Poor and the respective duties thence arising* (1708), 14.
203. Tanya Evans, *'Unfortunate Objects': Lone Mothers in Eighteenth-Century London* (2005), 137–8.
204. GL, MS 7674, St Alban Wood Street, Churchwardens and overseers' accounts, 1627–75.
205. *Accounts of the Churchwardens of the Paryshe of St Christopher's in London 1572 to 1662*, ed. Edwin Freshfield (1885).
206. Boswell, *The Kindness of Strangers*.
207. GL, MS 12818A/4, Christ's Hospital Presentation Papers, 1686–7, no. 96, Joseph Hobday, petition for Joseph Swetnam. (Thanks to Jeremy Boulton and Jacob Field for checking this for me.)
208. Joseph Maskell, *Collections in Illustration of the Parochial History...All Hallows Barking* (1864), 23.
209. *The Distressed Child in the Wood: Or, the Cruel Unkle*, [1709?], 4.
210. *Christ's Hospital Admissions, etc*, ed. G. A. T. Allan (1937), 55.
211. *The Distressed Child in the Wood*, 8.
212. *Records of the Borough of Nottingham*, ed. W. H. Stevenson, vol. 4, 1547–1625, 231.
213. GL, MS 18977, All Hallows Lombard Street, Bonds of indemnity.
214. Quoted in Alannah Tomkins, 'The Experience of Urban Poverty: A Comparison of Oxford and Shrewsbury 1740 to 1770' (DPhil thesis, Oxford, 1994), 262.
215. Taylor, *Poverty, Migration and Settlement*, 42.
216. Blackstone, *Commentaries on the Laws of England*, 4th edn (Dublin, 1771), vol. 1, p. 450.
217. Nolan, *Treatise of the Laws*, vol. 1, pp. 211–14.
218. Nutt, 'Natural Affection', NEER paper, 21.
219. Gowing, 'Secret births', 105.

220. Essex RO, Q/SR Sessions rolls, vol. 19, 1611–24, no. 99.
221. *OBP*, t16751013–2, L. O., L. T. (theft: housebreaking, guilty, death).
222. *Chelsea Settlement and Bastardy Examinations*, ed. Hitchcock and Black, p. x.
223. *Augustine: Confessions*, ed. A. C. Outler (1961), 72.
224. Burn, *Justice of the Peace* (1780 edn), quoted in Nutt, 'Illegitimacy and the Poor Law', 127–9.
225. Rabin, 'Beyond "Lewd Women" and "Wanton Wenches"', in Thorn (ed.), *Writing British Infanticide*, 47.
226. Peter Laslett, 'Long-Term Trends in Bastardy in England', in Peter Laslett, *Family Life and Illicit Love in Earlier Generations* (Cambridge, 1977), 133–47.
227. Karla Oosterveen and Richard M. Smith, 'Bastardy and the Family Reconstitution Studies of Colyton, Aldenham, Alcester and Hawkshead', in Laslett, Oosterveen, and Smith (eds), *Bastardy*, 120.
228. John T. Swain, *Industry before the Industrial Revolution: North-east Lancashire c. 1599–1640*, Chetham Soc., 3rd ser., vol. 33 (Manchester, 1986), 25–7.
229. Ibid. 26, 200.
230. Adair, *Courtship, Illegitimacy and Marriage*, 159–60.
231. Keith Thomas, 'Puritans and Adultery: The Act of 1650 Reconsidered', in Donald Pennington and Keith Thomas (eds), *Puritans and Revolutionaries: Essays in Seventeenth-Century History Presented to Christopher Hill* (Oxford, 1978), 256–82.
232. 1610, 7 Jac. I c. 4, For Due Execution of Laws against Rogues...and Other Lewd and Idle Persons.
233. William Hunter, 'On the uncertainty of the signs of murder in the case of bastard children' [speech delivered to Royal Academy of Sciences, Paris, 1784] (1812), 6–7 (thanks to Joanne McEwan for notes).

3. BRINGING UP A CHILD

1. Benjamin Shaw, *The Family Records of Benjamin Shaw Mechanic of Dent, Dolphinholme and Preston, 1772–1841*, ed. Alan G. Crosby, Rec. Soc. of Lancashire and Cheshire, vol. 130 (1991), 15.
2. Gervase Holles, *Memorials of the Holles Family*, ed. A. Wood, Camden Soc., 3rd ser., vol. 55 (1937), 31.
3. Kendal RO, WD/Ho, Box 44, file 4, Lady F. Dorset to her aunt, Lady Anne Clifford, 1 Aug. 1664.
4. Margaret R. Hunt, *The Middling Sort: Commerce, Gender, and the Family in England 1680–1780* (Berkeley, CA, 1996), 32.
5. Holles, *Memorials*, 34–5.
6. Kate Riley, 'The Good Old Way Revisited: The Ferrar Family of Little Gidding, c. 1625–1637' (PhD thesis, University of Western Australia, 2007), 213–14. Around the same date in Salisbury, a minimum family pension may have been around two shillings weekly; Paul Slack, *Poverty and Policy in Tudor and Stuart England* (1988), 81.
7. Steve Hindle, *The State and Social Change in Early Modern England, c. 1550–1640* (Basingstoke, 2000), 54; E. A. Wrigley and R. S. Schofield, *The Population History of England 1541–1871: A Reconstruction* (Cambridge, 1989), 341.
8. Jeremy Boulton, 'Welfare Systems and the Parish Nurse in Early Modern London, 1650–1725', *Family & Community History*, 10 (2007), 144–5 (St James

Westminster and St Giles in the Fields). I am very grateful to Professor Boulton for allowing me to read his paper prior to publication.

9. J. H. Plumb, 'The New World of Children in Eighteenth-Century England', *Past and Present*, 67 (1975), 64–95; Hugh Cunningham, *Children and Childhood in Western Society since 1500* (1995), 61–74.

10. Anne-Marie Kilday and Katherine Watson, 'Child Murder in Georgian England', *History Today*, 55 (2005), 44.

11. Wrigley and Schofield, *Population History of England*, 423–4.

12. P. E. H. Hair, 'Bridal Pregnancy in Earlier Rural England Further Examined', *Population Studies*, 24 (1970), 59; Wrigley and Schofield, *Population History of England*, 304–5.

13. Alysa Levene, Thomas Nutt, and Samantha Williams (eds), *Illegitimacy in Britain, 1700–1920* (Basingstoke, 2005), 6.

14. Wrigley and Schofield, *Population History of England*, 249–50.

15. Sir Frederick Morton Eden, *The State of the Poor*, 3 vols (1797), vol. 1, p. xviii.

16. Irvine Loudon, *Death in Childbirth: An International Study of Maternal Care and Maternal Mortality 1800–1950* (Oxford, 1992), 158–62; E. A. Wrigley, R. S. Davies, J. E. Oeppen, and R. S. Schofield, *English Population History from Family Reconstitution* (Cambridge, 1997), 307–15, especially table 6.29.

17. Graham Mayhew, 'Life-Cycle Service, and the Family Unit in Early Modern Rye', *Continuity and Change*, 6 (1991), 205.

18. Wrigley et al., *English Population History*, 352–3.

19. Tim Wales, 'Poverty, Poor Relief and the Life-Cycle: Some Evidence from Seventeenth-Century Norfolk', in Richard M. Smith (ed.), *Land, Kinship, and Life-Cycle* (Cambridge, 1984), 375, 378.

20. *John Clare's Autobiographical Writings*, ed. Eric Robinson (Oxford, 1983), 2. (Narrative written 1821–41; pp. vii–viii.)

21. Shaw, *Family Records*, 16.

22. Ibid. 21.

23. Ibid. 15.

24. *OBP*, t17350911–69, Charles Conyer (killing: murder, guilty).

25. Alice Clark, *Working Life of Women in the Seventeenth Century* (1919; 1968), preface.

26. Marjorie Keniston McIntosh, *Working Women in English Society 1300–1620* (Cambridge, 2005), 1–5.

27. Mayhew, 'Life-Cycle Service', 205.

28. Sir Josiah Child, *A New Discourse of Trade* (1693), 60.

29. Peter King, 'Pauper Inventories and the Material Lives of the Poor in the Eighteenth and Early Nineteenth Centuries', in Tim Hitchcock, Peter King, and Pamela Sharpe (eds), *Chronicling Poverty: The Voices and Strategies of the English Poor, 1640–1840* (Basingstoke, 1997), 178, 183.

30. Patricia Crawford, 'The Construction and Experience of Maternity', in Patricia Crawford, *Blood, Bodies and Families in Early Modern England* (2004), 94–5.

31. David Levine and Keith Wrightson, *The Making of an Industrial Society: Whickham 1560–1765* (Oxford, 1991), 321–2; David Cressy, *Birth, Marriage, and Death: Ritual, Religion, and the Life-Cycle in Tudor and Stuart England* (Oxford, 1997), 15–94.

32. Patricia Crawford, '"The sucking child": Adult Attitudes to Child Care in the First Year of Life in Seventeenth-Century England', in Crawford, *Blood, Bodies,*

and Families, 147; see also Mary E. Fissell, *Vernacular Bodies: The Politics of Reproduction in Early Modern England* (Oxford, 2004), 83–9.

33. R. H. Nichols and F. W. Wray, *The History of the Foundling Hospital* (1935), 39.
34. Wrigley et al., *English Population History*, 207–8, 489–92.
35. [M. Underwood], *A Treatise of the Disorders of Children; Adapted to Domestic Use*, 3 vols (1797), vol. 3, p. 11.
36. Fissell, *Vernacular Bodies*, 78–80.
37. Patricia Crawford, *Women and Religion in England 1500–1720* (1993), 101–2; Crawford, ' "The sucking child" ', in Crawford, *Blood, Bodies and Families*, 157–8: *Women's Worlds in Seventeenth-Century England: A Sourcebook*, ed. Patricia Crawford and Laura Gowing (2000), 26–7.
38. Jane Sharp, *The Midwives Book* (1671), 251–6.
39. William Buchan, *Domestic Medicine; Or, the Family Physician* (Edinburgh, 1769), 3–4.
40. *OBP*, t17220907-8, Matthias Brinsden (killing: murder, guilty).
41. Ian W. Archer, *The Pursuit of Stability: Social Relations in Elizabethan London* (Cambridge, 1991), 190–1.
42. Clark, *Working Life of Women*, 72.
43. Jeremy Boulton, 'Food Prices and the Standard of Living in London in the "Century of Revolution", 1580–1700', *Economic History Review*, n.s., 53 (2000), 468.
44. Peter Earle, *The Making of the English Middle Class: Business, Society and Family Life in 1660–1730* (1989), 280–1.
45. D. J. Oddy, 'Food, Drink and Nutrition', in F. M. L. Thompson (ed.), *The Cambridge Social History of Britain 1750–1950* (Cambridge, 1990), vol. 2, pp. 255–6, 269.
46. S[amuel] H[artlib], *London's Charity Inlarged, Stilling the Poor Orphans Cry* (1650), 13, 17.
47. Ruth McClure, *Coram's Children: The London Foundling Hospital in the Eighteenth Century* (1981), 198–204.
48. Joan Thirsk, *Food in Early Modern England: Phases, Fads, Fashions 1500–1760* (2007); see also Donald Woodward, 'Straw, Bracken and the Wicklow Whale: The Exploitation of Natural Resources in England since 1500', *Past and Present*, 159 (1998), 45–8.
49. John Komlos, 'The Secular Trend in the Biological Standard of Living in the United Kingdom, 1730–1860', *Economic History Review*, n.s., 46 (1993), 115–44.
50. Dianne Payne, 'Rhetoric, Reality and the Marine Society', *London Journal*, 30 (2005), 72.
51. Jessica Warner and Robin Griller, ' "My Pappa Is out, and My Mamma Is Asleep": Minors, their Routine Activities, and Interpersonal Violence in an Early Modern Town, 1653–1781', *Journal of Social History*, 36 (2003), 566.
52. Charles Varley, *The unfortunate husbandman* (1768; reprinted 1964), 40–1.
53. George Armstrong, *An Account of the Diseases Most Incident to Children* (1777), 193–5.
54. Catharine Capp, *An Account of Two Charity Schools for the Education of Girls* (York, 1800), 12.
55. Eden, *State of the Poor*, vol. 1, pp. 152, 496–7.
56. Keith Wrightson and David Levine, *Poverty and Piety in an English Village: Terling, 1525–1700* (New York, 1979), 39.

57. *The Reverend Richard Baxter's Last Treatise: The Poor Husbandman's Advocate* (1691), ed. F. J. Powicke (Manchester, 1926), 25.

58. *OBP*, t17890225–1, William Patmore (killing: murder, not guilty).

59. Dana Y. Rabin, 'Searching for the Self in Eighteenth-Century English Criminal Trials, 1730–1800', *Eighteenth-Century Life*, 27 (2003), 93–4.

60. Ibid. 86.

61. William Gouge, *Of Domesticall Duties* (1622), 506–7.

62. Thomas Granger, *The Tree of Good and Evil* (1616), 19.

63. [Underwood], *Treatise of the Disorders of Children*, vol. 3, p. 30.

64. Margaret Spufford, 'The Cost of Apparel in Seventeenth-Century England, and the Accuracy of Gregory King', *Economic History Review*, n.s., 53 (2000), 679–80.

65. Archer, *Pursuit of Stability*, 193.

66. Wrightson and Levine, *Terling*, 40; Boulton, 'Food Prices and the Standard of Living', 472.

67. GL, MS 613/1, St Augustine Watling Street, Vestry and precinct minute books (including some minutes of the joint vestry meetings of the united parishes of St Augustine Watling Street and St Faith under St Paul), 1744–81, Vestry minutes, 1765–76, 293–4.

68. Anne Buck, 'Buying Clothes in Bedfordshire: Customers and Tradesmen, 1700–1800', in N. B. Harte (ed.), *Fabrics and Fashions: Studies in the Economic and Social History of Dress* (1991), 232.

69. Dolly MacKinnon, ' "Charity is worth it when it looks that good": Rural Women and Bequests of Clothing in Early Modern England', in Stephanie Tarbin and Susan Broomhall (eds), *Women, Identities and Communities in Early Modern Europe* (Aldershot, 2008), 79–93.

70. Eden, *State of the Poor*, vol. 2, p. 148.

71. Beverly Lemire, *Dress, Culture and Commerce: The English Clothing Trade before the Factory, 1660–1800* (Basingstoke, 1997), 95–146.

72. *OBP*, t17430519–14, Mary White (violent theft: highway robbery, guilty lesser offence).

73. Dorset RO, QSB, Easter 1626, 8.

74. Penelope Lane, 'Work on the Margins: Poor Women and the Informal Economy of Eighteenth and Early Nineteenth-Century Leicestershire', *Midland History*, 22 (1997), 92.

75. Eden, *State of the Poor*, vol. 1, p. vii.

76. GL, MS 5841, Worshipful Company of Brewers, James Hickson's Charity (Ordinances for the Free School 1687), 1689–1751.

77. George Armstrong, *An Essay on the Diseases Most Fatal to Infants*, 2nd edn (1771), 182; Armstrong, *Account of the Diseases*, 214.

78. Spufford, 'The Cost of Apparel', 683.

79. LMA, A/FH/A/11/2/6, Petitions for return of children, 1765.

80. Jonas Hanway, *An Earnest Appeal for Mercy to the Children of the Poor* (1766), 94–7.

81. *OBP*, t17960914–12, David Scott (sexual offences: rape, guilty).

82. Eden, *State of the Poor*, vol. 1, p. 615.

83. Jonas Hanway, *Letters on the importance of the rising generation of the laboring part of our fellow-subjects*, 2 vols (1767), vol. 1, p. 144.

84. Alan Everitt, 'Farm Labourers', in Joan Thirsk (ed.), *The Agrarian History of England and Wales* (Cambridge, 1967), vol. 4, pp. 442–9.

85. Daniel Defoe, *A Tour through the Whole Island of Great Britain* (1724–7), ed. Pat Rogers, 3 vols (1983), vol. 3, pp. 34–6.
86. Slack, *Poverty and Policy*, 63.
87. Garthine Walker, *Crime, Gender, and Social Order in Early Modern England* (Cambridge, 2003), 237–9.
88. J. M. Neeson, *Commoners: Common Right, Enclosure and Social Change in England, 1700–1820* (Cambridge, 1993).
89. John Rogers, *A Treatise of Love* (1629), 224.
90. Baxter, *Last Treatise*, ed. Powicke.
91. Boulton, 'Food Prices and the Standard of Living', 477.
92. Vanessa Harding, 'Families and Housing in Seventeenth-Century London', *Parergon*, 24 (2007), 115; John Landers, *Death and the Metropolis: Studies in the Demographic History of London 1670–1830* (Cambridge, 1993), 352–3.
93. Harding, 'Families and Housing', 130–7.
94. A. L. Beier, 'The Social Problems of an Elizabethan County Town: Warwick, 1580–90', in Peter Clark (ed.), *County Towns in Pre-industrial England* (Leicester, 1981), 60–2.
95. Armstrong, *Account of the Diseases*, 196–7.
96. *OBP*, t17890225–1, William Patmore (killing: murder, not guilty).
97. *OBP*, t17490411–22, James Peneroy (sexual offences: rape, guilty).
98. *OBP*, t17670115–24, John Williamson (killing: murder, guilty).
99. Wrightson and Levine, *Terling*, 41–2.
100. Boulton, 'Food Prices and the Standard of Living', 455–92.
101. John Pound, *Poverty and Vagrancy in Tudor England*, 2nd edn (1986), 103.
102. Clark, *Working Life of Women*, 70–1.
103. Elizabeth Cellier, *A Scheme for the Foundation of a Royal Hospital, Harleian Miscellany*, vol. 4 (1744), 138–40.
104. Alan Macfarlane, *Marriage and Love in England: Modes of Reproduction 1300–1840* (Oxford, 1986), 89.
105. Amy Louise Erickson, *Women and Property in Early Modern England* (1993), 50–1.
106. Ilana Krausman Ben-Amos, 'Reciprocal Bonding: Parents and their Offspring in Early Modern England', *Journal of Family History*, 25 (2000), 308 n. 53. See also, Ilana Krausman Ben-Amos, *Adolescence and Youth in Early Modern England* (New Haven, 1994), 111; Alan Macfarlane, *The Family Life of Ralph Josselin, a Seventeenth-Century Clergyman: An Essay in Historical Anthropology* (Cambridge, 1970), 45.
107. Eden, *State of the Poor*, vol. 1, p. 450.
108. Thomas Nutt, 'The Paradox and Problems of Illegitimate Paternity in Old Poor Law Essex', in Levene, Nutt, and Williams (eds), *Illegitimacy in Britain*, 103–4.
109. Jeremy Boulton, '"It is Extreme Necessity That Makes Me Do This": Some "Survival Strategies" of Pauper Households in London's West End during the Early Eighteenth Century', *International Review of Social History*, 45 (2000), 64–6.
110. Sara Ruddick, *Maternal Thinking: Towards a Politics of Peace* (Boston, 1989; reprinted Boston, 1995), pp. xv–xvi.
111. Clark, *Working Life of Women*, 71 n.
112. Sara Horrell, Jane Humphries, and Hans-Joachim Voth, 'Stature and Relative Deprivation: Fatherless Children in Early Industrial Britain', *Continuity and Change*, 13 (1998), 73–115.

113. Landers, *Death and the Metropolis*, 156, 354.
114. Pamela Sharpe, '"The tender lungs of children", Infant and Child Morbidity and Short Stature in Nineteenth-Century England', NEER conference paper, UWA, Perth, July 2007. I am grateful to Professor Sharpe for allowing me to cite her paper.
115. Alysa Levene, *Childcare, Health and Mortality at the London Foundling Hospital, 1741–1800: 'Left to the mercy of the world'* (2007), 172–3 n. 68; Landers, *Death and the Metropolis*, 156, 228.
116. Sharpe, '"The tender lungs of children"'.
117. *OBP*, a17311208–1, Advertisements 8 Dec. 1731; Sharpe, '"The tender lungs of children"'.
118. Paul Slack, *The Impact of Plague in Tudor and Stuart England* (1985), 181–2.
119. Levene, *Childcare, Health and Mortality*, 150–1, 155–68.
120. *A true and wonderful account of a cure of the King's-evil, by Mrs Fanshaw*, [1681].
121. Crawford, '"The sucking child"', in Crawford, *Blood, Bodies and Families*, 157–8.
122. Elaine Clark, 'Mothers at Risk of Poverty in the Medieval English Country-side', in John Henderson and Richard Wall (eds), *Poor Women and Children in the European Past* (1994), 145; Crawford, 'Attitudes to Menstruation in Seventeenth-Century England', in Crawford, *Blood, Bodies and Families*, 30.
123. *OBP*, oa17241207, The Ordinary of Newgate's Account, Lovi Houssart.
124. GL, MS 12818A, Christ's Hospital Presentation Papers, 1674–5.
125. John Bunyan, *Grace Abounding to the Chief of Sinners* (1928 edn), 127–8, 98.
126. *OBP*, t17250827–14, Samuel Street (sexual offences: rape, not guilty).
127. *OBP*, t17960113–97, William Burrams (theft: simple grand larceny, guilty with recommendation).
128. GL, MS 2676/18, St Botolph Aldgate, Pauper examinations, 1787–9, 9 April 1789; accessed with thanks to the kindness of Tim Hitchcock.
129. Margaret Pelling, 'Child Health as a Social Value', in Pelling, *The Common Lot: Sickness, Medical Occupations and the Urban Poor in Early Modern England* (1998), 128–30.
130. Akihito Suzuki, 'The Household and the Care of Lunatics in Eighteenth-Century London', in Peregrine Horden and Richard Smith (eds), *The Locus of Care: Families, Communities, Institutions and the Provision of Welfare since Antiquity* (1998), 161–2.
131. Pelling, 'Child Health as a Social Value', in Pelling, *Common Lot*, 107.
132. Alysa Levene, 'Children and Hospitals Before Children's Hospitals', NEER conference paper, UWA, Perth, July 2007. I am most grateful to Dr Levene for permission to cite.
133. Armstrong, *Essay on the Diseases Most Fatal to Infants*, 3, 186–7.
134. Lisa Smith, 'The Relative Duties of a Man: Domestic Medicine in England and France, ca. 1685–1740', *Journal of Family History*, 31 (2006), 237–58.
135. [Underwood], *Treatise of the Disorders of Children*, vol. 3, p. 121.
136. Alexandra Walsham, *Providence in Early Modern England* (Oxford, 1999), 194–201.
137. Crawford, 'Sexual Knowledge in Early Modern England', and '"The sucking child"', in Crawford, *Blood, Bodies and Families*, 62, 144; Fissell, *Vernacular Bodies*, 64–9.

138. Thomas Tusser, *Five Hundred Points of Good Husbandrie*, ed. Geoffrey Grigson (Oxford, 1984), 180.

139. Crawford, *Women and Religion*, 54.

140. J. S. Purvis (ed.), *Tudor Parish Documents of the Diocese of York* (Cambridge, 1948), 150, 67.

141. Jeremy Boulton, *Neighbourhood and Society: A London Suburb in the Seventeenth Century* (Cambridge, 1987), 196–7.

142. Judith Maltby, *Prayer Book and People in Elizabethan and Early Stuart England* (Cambridge, 1998), 181–227.

143. Richard Baxter, *The Poor Man's Family Book* (1674), 309–11.

144. Margaret Spufford, *Contrasting Communities: English Villagers in the Sixteenth and Seventeenth Centuries* (Cambridge, 1974), 216–17; Margaret Spufford, 'First Steps in Literacy: The Reading and Writing Experience of the Humblest Seventeenth-Century Spiritual Autobiographers', *Social History*, 4 (1979), 407–53; Margaret Spufford, 'The Importance of Religion in the Sixteenth and Seventeenth Centuries', in Margaret Spufford (ed.), *The World of Rural Dissenters, 1520–1725* (Cambridge, 1995), 70, 78–85; Margaret Spufford, 'Women Teaching Reading to Poor Children in the Sixteenth and Seventeenth Centuries', in her *Figures in the Landscape: Rural Society in England, 1500–1700* (Aldershot, 2001), 249–64.

145. For catechisms, see Ian Green, *The Christian's ABC: Catechisms and Catechizing in England c. 1530–1740* (Oxford, 1996), 170.

146. Margaret Spufford, *Small Books and Pleasant Histories: Popular Fiction and its Readership in Seventeenth-Century England* (1981), 194–5.

147. Richard Baxter, *Reliquiæ Baxterianæ* (1696), 84–5; Thomas Wadsworth, *Last Warning to Secure Sinners* (1677), sigs. [b2v.–b4]; see also Eamon Duffy, 'The Godly and the Multitude in Stuart England', *Seventeenth Century*, 1 (1986), 40–8.

148. Crawford, *Women and Religion*, 79.

149. Tessa Watt, *Cheap Print and Popular Piety, 1550–1640* (Cambridge, 1991), 178–203.

150. James Janeway, *A Token for Children* (1676), 569 and *passim*.

151. Baxter, *Reliquiæ Baxterianæ*, 84–5; Wadsworth, *Last Warning to Secure Sinners*, sigs. [b2v.–b4]; see also Duffy, 'The Godly and the Multitude', 40–8.

152. Green, *The Christian's ABC*.

153. Bill Stevenson, 'The Social and Economic Status of post-Restoration Dissenters, 1660–1725', in Spufford (ed.), *World of Rural Dissenters*, 354, 357.

154. Arnold Lloyd, *Quaker Social History 1669–1738* (1950), 32–3.

155. Ibid. 166–74, quotation on 166.

156. Paul Langford, *A Polite and Commercial People: England 1727–1783* (Oxford, 1989), 252–6.

157. Boulton, *Neighbourhood and Society*, 281; Peter Earle, *A City Full of People: Men and Women of London 1650–1750* (1994), 158, 176–8.

158. See further Chapter 5.

159. Cunningham, *Children and Childhood*, 61–2.

160. Keith Thomas, *Religion and the Decline of Magic: Studies of Popular Beliefs in Sixteenth and Seventeenth Century, England* (1971).

161. Baxter, *Last Treatise*, ed. Powicke, 23.

162. *OBP*, t17670115-24, John Williamson (killing: murder, guilty).

163. For example, *OBP*, t17790113–96, Philip Sherwin (sexual offences: rape, not guilty); *OBP*, t17500711–33, Anthony Barnes (sexual offences: rape, not guilty).

164. Bunyan, *Grace Abounding*, 16.

165. William C. Braithwaite, *The Second Period of Quakerism*, 2nd edn (Cambridge, 1961), 226–7.

166. John Whiting, *Persecution Exposed*, quoted ibid. 102–3.

167. Braithwaite, *Second Period of Quakerism*, 459 n. 1.

168. Spufford, 'Importance of Religion', in Spufford (ed.), *The World of Rural Dissenters*, 47.

169. Earle, *City Full of People*, 21–2.

170. Charles Hoole, *A New Discovery of the Old Art of Teachinge School* (1661), 213–14.

171. Spufford, 'Importance of Religion', in Spufford (ed.), *The World of Rural Dissenters*, 68.

172. *OBP*, t17420428–26, Richard Cooley, Charles Newton (theft: burglary, guilty).

173. James Lackington, *Memoirs of the First Forty-Five Years of James Lackington* (1794; facs. edn New York, 1974), 30.

174. Spufford, 'First Steps in Literacy', 410–12.

175. Earle, *City Full of People*, 29, 31–2.

176. Sarah Trimmer, *The Oeconomy of Charity* (1787), 133–4.

177. Tim Wales, 'Work, Learning and the Fear of God: The English Poor Laws and the Young, c. 1570-c. 1700', unpublished paper, 26–36; I thank Tim Wales for permission to cite, as well as for many helpful conversations.

178. Tim Hitchcock, 'Begging on the Streets of Eighteenth-Century London', *JBS*, 44 (2005), 478–98; Hitchcock, *Down and Out*, 75.

179. Hindle, *On the Parish? The Micro-Politics of Poor Relief in Rural England c. 1550–1750* (Oxford, 2004), 222–6.

180. *OBP*, t17731020–75, Amelia Powell (killing: infanticide, not guilty).

181. Shaw, *Family Records*, 41.

182. Slack, *Poverty and Policy*, 82.

183. Maxine Berg, *Age of Manufactures 1700–1820: Industry, Innovation and Work in Britain*, 2nd edn (1994), 136–65.

184. David J. Jeremy, 'Radcliffe, William (1761?–1842)', *Oxford Dictionary of National Biography* (Oxford, 2004) [http://www.oxforddnb.com/view/article/22994), accessed 12 Sept. 2008].

185. Quoted by Berg, *Age of Manufactures*, 161.

186. Ibid. 157, 160.

187. *Richard Hutton's Complaints Book: The Notebook of the Steward of the Quaker Workhouse at Clerkenwell, 1711–1737*, ed. Timothy V. Hitchcock, London Rec. Soc., vol. 24 (1987), 71, 23, 28.

188. Earle, *City Full of People*, 37–8.

189. John Rule, *The Experience of Labour in Eighteenth-Century Industry* (1981), 87.

190. Payne, 'Rhetoric, Reality and the Marine Society', 72–8.

191. George R. Boyer, *An Economic History of the English Poor Law, 1750–1850* (Cambridge, 1990), 5.

192. *John Clare's Autobiographical Writings*, ed. Robinson, 5.

193. Michael Nolan, *A Treatise of the Laws for the Relief and Settlement of the Poor*, 2 vols (1805), vol. 2, p. 219.

194. Crawford, 'Attitudes to Menstruation', in Crawford, *Blood, Bodies and Families*, 33.
195. Richard Wall, 'The Age at Leaving Home', *Journal of Family History*, 3 (1978), 181–202.
196. Richard Wall, 'Leaving Home and the Process of Household Formation in Pre-industrial England', *Continuity and Change*, 2 (1987), 94–5.
197. Sara Horrell and Jane Humphries, '"The Exploitation of Little Children": Child Labour and the Family Economy in the Industrial Revolution', *Explorations in Economic History*, 32 (1995), 487.
198. K. D. M. Snell and J. Millar, 'Lone-parent Families and the Welfare State: Past and Present', *Continuity and Change*, 2 (1987), 391.
199. Pamela Sharpe, 'Poor Children as Apprentices in Colyton, 1598–1830', *Continuity and Change*, 6 (1991), 253–70.
200. Wrigley et al., *English Population History*, 210 and note.
201. Heather Shore, 'Crime, Criminal Networks and the Survival Strategies of the Poor in Early Eighteenth-Century London', in Steven King and Alannah Tomkins (eds), *The Poor in England 1700–1850: An Economy of Makeshifts* (Manchester, 2003), 137–65.
202. T[homas] F[irman], *Some Proposals for the Imploying of the Poor* (1681 edn), 5.
203. GL, MS 20484, Clayton and Morris, Papers concerning poor relief in the City of London, and the Corporation for the Poor of the City of London and its workhouse in Bishopsgate Street, 1698–1702.
204. Paul Griffiths, 'Overlapping Circles: Imagining Criminal Communities in 1545–1645', in Alexandra Shepard and Phil Withington (eds), *Communities in Early Modern England: Networks, Place, Rhetoric* (Manchester, 2000), 122–3.
205. Hitchcock, *Down and Out*, 75; Hitchcock, 'Begging on the Streets', 490.
206. North Yorkshire RO, North Allerton, typed list QSB 1696, 126.
207. *OBP*, t17420428-26, Richard Cooley, Charles Newton (theft: burglary, guilty).
208. *OBP*, t17430114-26, Eleanor Carr (theft: simple grand larceny, part guilty, theft under 1s.).
209. Lane, 'Work on the Margins', 92.
210. Ibid. 90.
211. *OBP*, oa17420113, The Ordinary of Newgate's Account, John Newman.
212. John G. Rule, 'The Manifold Causes of Rural Crime: Sheep-Stealing in England, c. 1740–1840', in John G. Rule (ed.), *Outside the Law: Studies in Crime and Order, 1650–1850* (Exeter, 1982), 105–29.
213. *OBP*, t17520914-40, Ann Edwards, Benjamin Edwards, Mary Edwards, Millicent Edwards (theft: receiving; theft from a specified place, part guilty, not guilty, guilty, guilty).
214. Catharine Capp, *Observations on Charity Schools, female friendly societies, and other subjects connected with the views of the Ladies Committee* (York, 1805), 34–5.
215. [Underwood], *Treatise of the Disorders of Children*, vol. 3, p. 126.
216. Westminster Muniment Room, Coroners' Inquests 1760 to December 1771, 3 December 1771, St Margaret (compiled by Tim Hitchcock).
217. *OBP*, t17790707-49, James Barrett (sexual offences: rape, guilty).
218. Westminster Muniment Room, Coroners' Inquests, 15 April 1768, St. Margaret.

219. Thomas R. Forbes, 'The Changing Face of Death in London', in Charles Webster (ed.), *Health, Medicine and Mortality in the Sixteenth Century* (Cambridge, 1979), 133–4.

220. Westminster Muniment Room, Coroners' Inquests, 20 Apr. 1762, St Martin in the Fields; 21 Apr. 1762, St George Hanover Square.

221. Westminster Muniment Room, Coroners' Inquests, 6 March 1769, St. James.

222. See Figure 6, 'Three Beggars met Together'.

223. Norfolk RO, Mayor's court book 1624–34, fo. 102.

224. See, for example, Norfolk RO, Coroners' inquests 1691–99, Ca/2/, 19, 21, 27.

225. Levene, *Childcare, Health and Mortality*, 118–44.

226. Walker, *Crime, Gender and Social Order*, 71–2.

227. *OBP*, t17490411–22, James Penroy (sexual offences: rape, guilty).

228. *OBP*, t17321206–69, Joseph Pearson (sexual offences: rape, not guilty).

229. *OBP*, oa17410731, The Ordinary of Newgate's Account, Richard Eades.

230. Capp, *An Account of Two Charity Schools*, 3.

231. *The Autobiography of Francis Place (1771–1854)*, ed. Mary Thale (Cambridge, 1972), 57.

232. Ibid. 65–7, 77.

233. A[nthony] Highmore, *Pietas Londinensis: The History…of Various Public Charities* (1810), 42; Jane Lane, *Apprenticeship in England, 1600–1914* (1996), 104–9.

234. *OBP*, t17190708–57, John Larmony, Mary Mattoon (violent theft: robbery, not guilty).

235. Robert Moss, *The Providential Division of Men into Rich and Poor and the respective duties thence arising* (1708), 14.

236. F[irman], *Some Proposals*, 3–8.

237. Elizabeth A. Foyster, *Marital Violence: An English Family History, 1660–1857* (Cambridge, 2005), 129–67.

238. *OBP*, t17220907–8, Matthias Brinsden (killing: murder, guilty).

239. *OBP*, t17330912–55, John Cannon (sexual offences: rape, guilty).

240. *OBP*, t17540530–1, John Grimes (sexual offences: rape, not guilty).

241. *OBP*, t17350911–90, Phillip Brown (sexual offences: assault with intent to rape, not guilty).

242. Julie Gammon, ' "A Denial of Innocence": Female Juvenile Victims of Rape and the English Legal System in the Eighteenth Century', in Anthony Fletcher and Stephen Hussey (eds), *Childhood in Question: Children, Parents and the State* (Manchester, 1999), 76.

243. Ibid. 78–80.

244. *OBP*, t17960914–12, David Scott (sexual offences: rape, guilty).

245. Anna Clark, *Women's Silence, Men's Violence: Sexual Assault in England, 1770–1845* (1987), 48.

246. *OBP*, t17790915–18, Charles Ketteridge (sexual offences: rape, not guilty).

247. Gammon, ' "A Denial of Innocence" ', in Fletcher and Hussey (eds), *Childhood in Question*, 74–95.

248. *OBP*, t17300828–24, Gilbert Laurence (sexual offences: sodomy, guilty).

249. Greg T. Smith, 'Expanding the Compass of Domestic Violence in the Hanoverian Metropolis', *Journal of Social History*, 41 (2007), 40.

250. *OBP*, t17230116–39, Edward Fox (sexual offences: rape, not guilty).

251. Laura Gowing, *Common Bodies: Women, Touch and Power in Seventeenth-Century England* (2003), 93–4.

252. *OBP*, t17351210–10, Edward Jones (sexual offences: rape, not guilty).
253. *OBP*, t17591205–25, Aaron Davids (sexual offences: rape, not guilty).
254. Martin Ingram, 'Child Sexual Abuse in Early Modern England', in Michael J. Braddick and John Walter (eds), *Negotiating Power in Early Modern Society: Order, Hierarchy and Subordination in Britain and Ireland* (Cambridge, 2001), 70–1.
255. *OBP*, t17331205–20, Mary Doe (killing: infanticide, not guilty).
256. *OBP*, t17390117–25, John Marsland (sexual offences: rape, guilty).
257. William Harrison, *The Description of England* (1587), quoted in Keith Wrightson, *English Society 1580–1680* (1982), 116.
258. Lawrence Stone, *The Family, Sex and Marriage 1500–1800* (1977), 159–78, 470–8. Stone relied heavily on Ernest Caulfield, *The Infant Welfare Movement in the Eighteenth Century* (New York, 1931) and Lloyd de Mause (ed.), *The History of Childhood* (New York, 1974).
259. Michael MacDonald, *Mystical Bedlam: Madness, Anxiety, and Healing in Seventeenth-Century England* (Cambridge, 1981), 75–85; Wrightson, *English Society*, 116–17; Ralph Houlbrooke, *English Family 1450–1700* (1984); Linda A. Pollock, *Forgotten Children: Parent-Child Relations from 1500–1900* (1983), 162.
260. Pollock, *Forgotten Children*, 162; Houlbrooke, *English Family*, 140–5; Ralph Houlbrooke (ed.), *English Family Life, 1576–1716: An Anthology from Diaries* (Oxford, 1988).
261. *York [from Women's Meeting]* (1696), 2.
262. *From our Yearly Meeting at York* (1690), 2.
263. Stone, *Family, Sex and Marriage*, 163–70, 176–8; Philip Greven, *Spare the Child: The Religious Roots of Punishment and the Psychological Impact of Abuse* (New York, 1991).
264. Foyster, *Marital Violence*.
265. Plumb, 'The New World of Children'; Stone, *Family, Sex and Marriage*, 434–5.
266. Greven, *Spare the Child*, 121–212.
267. [Mary Saxby], *Memoirs of a Female Vagrant written by herself*, Samuel Greatheed (preface) (1806), 3.
268. *OBP*, t17350911–69, Charles Conyer (killing: murder, guilty).
269. *Autobiography of Francis Place*, ed. Thale, 59–62; see also William Thomas, 'Place, Francis (1771–1854)', *Oxford Dictionary of National Biography* [http://www.oxforddnb.com/view/article/22349, accessed 18 Sept. 2008].
270. Pelling, 'Child Health as a Social Value', in Pelling, *Common Lot*, 118.
271. *OBP*, t17141209–16, Mary Vaughan (violent theft: robbery, guilty).
272. *OBP*, t17771015–1, Benjamin Russen (sexual offences: rape, guilty of one).
273. Capp, *An Account of Two Charity Schools*, 4.
274. William Denny, quoted in Terence R. Murphy, ' "Woful Childe of Parents Rage": Suicide of Children and Adolescents in Early Modern England, 1507–1710', *Sixteenth-Century Journal*, 17 (1986), 265.
275. Ingram, 'Child Sexual Abuse', in Braddick and Walter (eds), *Negotiating Power*, 71–2.
276. *OBP*, t16781211e–2, Stephen Arrowsmith (sexual offences: rape, guilty).
277. *OBP*, t17480907–50, William Garner (sexual offences: rape, guilty).
278. *OBP*, t17590711–6, Gilbert Wright (sexual offences: rape, not guilty).
279. *OBP*, t17530502–35, John Birmingham (sexual offences: rape, not guilty).
280. Murphy, 'Woful Child', 266–7, 269–70.

281. Jack Howard-Drake (ed.), *Oxford Church Courts: Depositions 1581–1586* (Oxford, 1994), 31, 37. Thanks to Sybil Jack for checking these cases for me.

282. CUL, SPCK, D2/11, Abstract Letter book, 1715–1716, no. 4443, 25 Aug. 1715.

283. *OBP*, t17550910–41, Mabell Hughes (killing: murder, guilty).

284. *OBP*, t17790113–36, Philip Sherwin (sexual offences: rape, not guilty).

285. Daniel Waterland, *Religious education of children: recommended in a sermon preach'd in the parish-church of St. Sepulchre, June the 6th, 1723* (1723), 10.

286. *The Accomplish'd Housewife; or the Gentlewoman's Companion* (1745), dedication.

287. Adam Fox, *Oral and Literate Culture in England, 1500–1700* (Oxford, 2000), 194.

288. *OBP*, t17591205–25, Aaron Davids (sexual offences: rape, not guilty).

289. *OBP*, t17660903–33, Edward Brophy (sexual offences: rape, guilty).

290. *OBP*, t17791020–5, Charles Atwell (sexual offences: sodomy, not guilty).

291. *OBP*, t17660903–33, Edward Brophy (sexual offences: rape, guilty).

292. *OBP*, t17790113–36, Philip Sherwin (sexual offences: rape, not guilty).

293. Ingram, 'Child Sexual Abuse', in Braddick and Walter (eds), *Negotiating Power*, 74–5.

294. Felicity Nussbaum, *Torrid Zones: Maternity, Sexuality, and Empire in Eighteenth-Century English Narratives* (Baltimore, 1995), 29.

295. Horrell, Humphries, and Voth, 'Stature and Relative Deprivation', 73–115.

296. This paragraph draws on ideas from Laurence Fontaine and Jurgen Schumbohm, 'Household Strategies for Survival: An Introduction', *International Review of Social History*, Supplement 8, *Household Strategies for Survival 1600–2000: Fission, Faction and Cooperation* (Cambridge, 2000), 1–17.

297. Carolyn Steedman, *Landscape for a Good Woman: A Story of Two Lives* (1986), 82.

298. *Autobiography of Francis Place*, ed. Thale, 172.

299. A. Grey, *Debates of the House of Commons 1667–1694*, 10 vols (1769), vol. 9, p. 127.

300. James Burgh, *Political Disquisitions* (1774–5), vol. 1, p. 37.

4. SEVERE POVERTY

1. *Toby's Delight* [1682/3], *The Roxburghe Ballads*, ed. W. Chappell (vols 1–3) and J. W. Ebsworth (vols 4–9), 9 vols (Hertford 1872–99; reprinted New York, 1966), vol. 7, pp. xi-xii.

2. *The Poor Folks Complaint* (later 17th cent.), quoted in L. A. Bothelo, *Old Age and the English Poor Law, 1500–1700* (Woodbridge, 2004), 89.

3. Tim Wales, 'Poverty, Poor Relief and the Life-Cycle: Some Evidence from Seventeenth-Century Norfolk', in Richard M. Smith (ed.), *Land, Kinship, and Life-Cycle* (Cambridge, 1984), 353.

4. *OBP*, oa17500207, The Ordinary of Newgate's Account, John Edwards.

5. Barry Stapleton, 'Inherited Poverty and Life-Cycle Poverty: Odiham, Hampshire, 1650–1850', *Social History*, 18 (1993), 339–55.

6. Wales, 'Poverty, Poor Relief and the Life-Cycle', in Smith (ed.), *Land, Kinship, and Life-Cycle*, 352; Sara Mendelson and Patricia Crawford, *Women in Early Modern England* (Oxford, 1998), 256–300; Samantha Williams, 'Poor Relief, Labourers' Households and Living Standards in Rural England c. 1770–1835: A Bedfordshire Case Study', *Economic History Review*, n.s., 58 (2005), 515.

7. Pamela Sharpe, *Adapting to Capitalism: Working Women in the English Economy, 1700–1850* (1996; reprinted Basingstoke, 2000).

8. Discussed in Chapter 1.

9. See Chapter 5.

10. See especially, Steven King and Alannah Tomkins (eds), *The Poor in England 1700–1850: An Economy of Makeshifts* (Manchester, 2003).

11. Sam Barrett, 'Kinship, Poor Relief and the Welfare Process in Early Modern England', in King and Tomkins (eds), *The Poor in England*, 199–227.

12. Williams, 'Poor Relief, Labourers' Households and Living Standards', 495–9.

13. Alan Everitt, 'Farm Labourers', in Joan Thirsk (ed.), *The Agrarian History of England and Wales*, vol. 4 (Cambridge, 1967), 400–12, 425–9; Bridget Hill, *Women, Work, and Sexual Politics in Eighteenth-Century England* (Oxford, 1989), 47–68; J. M. Neeson, *Commoners: Common Right, Enclosure and Social Change in England, 1700–1820* (Cambridge, 1993); Mark Overton, *Agricultural Revolution in England: The Transformation of the Agrarian Economy 1500–1850* (Cambridge, 1996), 147–9, 171.

14. Ann Kussmaul, *Servants in Husbandry in Early Modern England* (Cambridge, 1981), 120–9.

15. Pamela Sharpe, *Population and Society in an East Devon Parish: Reproducing Colyton 1540–1840* (Exeter, 2002), 310–11.

16. See Introduction.

17. Bothelo, *Old Age and the English Poor Law*, 155–7 and *passim*.

18. Steve Hindle, 'Dearth, Fasting and Alms: The Campaign for General Hospitality in Late Elizabethan England', *Past and Present*, 172 (2001), 44–86.

19. Steven King, 'Poor Relief and English Economic Development Reappraised', *Economic History Review*, n.s., 50 (1997), 360–8.

20. James Stephen Taylor, 'The Impact of Pauper Settlement 1691–1834', *Past and Present*, 73 (1976), 42–74; K. D. M. Snell, *Parish and Belonging: Community, Identity, and Welfare in England and Wales, 1700–1950* (Cambridge, 2006), 91.

21. Pamela Sharpe, 'Survival Strategies and Stories: Poor Widows and Widowers in Early Industrial England', in Sandra Cavallo and Lyndan Warner (eds), *Widowhood in Medieval and Early Modern Europe* (1999), 229–39.

22. Wales, 'Poverty, Poor Relief and the Life-Cycle', in Smith (ed.), *Land, Kinship, and Life-Cycle*, 358.

23. W. Newman Brown, 'The Receipt of Poor Relief and Family Situation: Aldenham, Hertfordshire 1630–90', in Smith (ed.), *Land, Kinship, and Life-Cycle*, 412–14.

24. John Henderson and Richard Wall (eds), *Poor Women and Children in the European Past* (1994), 18, citing an unpublished paper by Jeremy Boulton.

25. Bothelo, *Old Age and the English Poor Law*, 151–2 and *passim*.

26. Geoffrey L. Hudson, 'Negotiating for Blood Money: War Widows and the Courts in Seventeenth-Century England', in Jenny Kermonde and Garthine Walker (eds), *Women, Crime and the Courts in Early Modern England* (1994), 146–69; Amanda Whiting, ' "Some Women Can Shift it Well Enough": A Legal Context for Understanding the Women Petitioners of the Seventeenth-Century English Revolution', *Australian Feminist Law Journal*, 21 (2004), 97 and *passim*.

27. *Essex Quarter Sessions Order Book, 1652–1661*, ed. D. H. Allen (Chelmsford, 1974), p. xxvii.

28. Thanks to Margaret Hunt for advice.

29. GL, MS 1204/1, St Katherine Cree, Workhouse Committee: minute book, 1738–95, fo. 63v.
30. Wales, 'Poverty, Poor Relief and the Life-Cycle', in Smith (ed.), *Land, Kinship, and Life-Cycle*, 351–404.
31. James Stephen Taylor, *Poverty, Migration, and Settlement in the Industrial Revolution: Sojourners' Narratives* (Palo Alto, CA, 1989), 42.
32. Paul Slack, *Poverty and Policy in Tudor and Stuart England* (1988), 194–5.
33. Michael Watts, *The Dissenters: From the Reformation to the French Revolution* (Oxford, 1978), 336–41.
34. For an excellent account of parish apprenticeship, see Steve Hindle, *On the Parish? The Micro-Politics of Poor Relief in Rural England c. 1550–1750* (Oxford, 2004), 191–226, 295–9; Steve Hindle, 'A Cumbrian Family and the Poor Law Authorities, c. 1690–1730', in Helen Berry and Elizabeth Foyster (eds), *The Family in Early Modern England* (Cambridge, 2007), 153.
35. Hindle, *On the Parish?*, 223–6.
36. Katrina Honeyman, *Child Workers in England, 1780–1820: Parish Apprentices and the Making of the Early Industrial Labour Force* (Aldershot, 2007), 207.
37. For a general discussion, see O. Jocelyn Dunlop, *English Apprenticeship and Child Labour: A History* (1912), 248–60; Ivy Pinchbeck and Margaret Hewitt, *Children in English Society*: vol. 1: *From Tudor Times to the Eighteenth Century* (1969), 235–53; Deborah Simonton, 'Apprenticeship: Training and Gender in Eighteenth-Century England', in Maxine Berg (ed.), *Markets and Manufacture in Early Industrial Europe* (1991), 227–58. Pauper apprenticeship is discussed further in Chapter 5.
38. Pamela Sharpe, 'Poor children as Apprentices in Colyton, 1598–1830', *Continuity and Change*, 6 (1991), 266; Simonton, 'Apprenticeship', in Berg (ed.), *Markets and Manufacture*, 227–58.
39. Joan Lane, *Apprenticeship in England, 1600–1914* (1996), 45–6, 83.
40. Michael Dalton, *The Countrey Justice* (1635 edn), 95–6; see also, Dalton, *The Countrey Justice* (1666 edn), 111; Dalton, *The Countrey Justice* (1705 edn), 153.
41. Hindle, *On the Parish?*, 207–8.
42. *Calendar of State Papers Domestic, 1633–4*, 273 (2 Nov. 1633).
43. *Somerset Assize Orders*, ed. Thomas G. Barnes, Somerset Rec. Soc., vol. 65 (1959), 37.
44. John Houghton, *A Collection*, in *Seventeenth-Century Economic Documents*, ed. Joan Thirsk and J. P. Cooper (Oxford, 1972), 302.
45. *County of Buckingham: Calendar to the Sessions Records*, 4 vols 1678–1724, ed. William Le Hardy and Geoffrey L. Reckitt (Aylesbury, 1933–39), vol. 2, p. 399.
46. For further discussion of objectives of the Poor Law authorities, see Chapter 5.
47. Mendelson and Crawford, *Women in Early Modern England*, 86 and n. 55.
48. *Quarter Sessions Records for the County of Somerset*, 4 vols, 1607–77, ed. E. H. Bates, Somerset Rec. Soc., vols 23, 24, 28, 34 (1907–19), vol. 1, p. 336.
49. *Somerset Assize Orders*, ed. Barnes, 64.
50. *OBP*, t17450424–33, Edmund Gilbert (killing: murder, guilty).
51. *OBP*, t17330112–3, John Bennet (killing: murder, part guilty: manslaughter).
52. Ibid.
53. *OBP*, t17360610–32, James Durant (killing: murder, not guilty).
54. *OBP*, t17840225–63, William Wade (killing: murder, not guilty).

55. Steve Hindle and Ruth Wallis Herndon, 'Recreating Proper Families in England and North America: Pauper Apprenticeship in Transatlantic Context', in Ruth Wallis Herndon and John E. Murray (eds), *Children Bound to Labor* (*Ithaca*); I am grateful to the authors for allowing me to read their chapter before publication.

56. A. L. Beier, 'Poverty and Progress in Early Modern England', in A. L. Beier, David Cannadine, and James M. Rosenheim (eds), *The First Modern Society: Essays in English History in Honour of Lawrence Stone* (Cambridge, 1989), 214; Sharpe, 'Poor Children as Apprentices', 263; Hindle, *On the Parish?*, 213.

57. Lane, *Apprenticeship*, 215–16.

58. Joanna Innes, 'Origins of the Factory Acts: the Health and Morals of Apprentices Act, 1802', in Norma Landau (ed.), *Law, Crime, and English Society, 1660–1830* (Cambridge, 2002), 235.

59. *The Diary of Thomas Turner 1745–1765*, ed. David Vaisey (Oxford, 1984), 39, 57, 121.

60. Hindle, *On the Parish?*, 187.

61. Sir Frederick Morton Eden, *The State of the Poor*, 3 vols (1797), vol. 2, pp. 147, 207, 443.

62. *An Account of Several Work Houses for Employing and Maintaining the Poor* (1725), 98.

63. Ibid. 106.

64. *Some Thoughts concerning the Maintenance of the Poor* (1700), 17.

65. [John Cary], *An Account of the Proceedings of the Corporation of Bristol* (1700), 11.

66. C. A., *Candid Remarks on Mr Hanway's Candid Historical Account of the Foundling Hospital* (1760), 16.

67. Honeyman, *Child Workers in England*, 199–213.

68. Alfred Fessler, 'The Official Attitude towards the Sick Poor in Seventeenth-Century Lancashire and Cheshire', *Transactions of the Historic Soc. of Lancashire and Cheshire*, 102 (1950), 111.

69. *OBP*, t17420428–26, Richard Cooley, Charles Newton (theft: burglary, guilty).

70. Hindle, *On the Parish?*, 405–32.

71. *Quarter Sessions Records . . . Somerset*, ed. Bates, vol. 1, p. 283.

72. Eden, *State of the Poor*, vol. 1, p. 448.

73. Thomas Alcock, *Observations on the Defects of the Poor Laws* (Oxford, 1752), 13–17.

74. *Essex Pauper Letters 1731–1837*, ed. Thomas Sokoll (Oxford, 2001), 44–67.

75. Ibid. 608.

76. Ibid. 69–70.

77. Buchanan Sharp, 'Popular Protest in Seventeenth-Century England', in Barry Reay (ed.), *Popular Culture in Seventeenth-Century England* (1988), 287.

78. Hindle, 'A Cumbrian Family', in Berry and Foyster (eds), *Family*, 146–7.

79. Adam Fox, 'Ballads, Libels and Popular Ridicule in Jacobean England', *Past and Present*, 145 (1994), 73–4, and 47–83 *passim*; see also Adam Fox, *Oral and Literate Culture in England, 1500–1700* (Oxford, 2000), 326–7.

80. Susan Dwyer Amussen, *An Ordered Society: Gender and Class in Early Modern England* (Oxford, 1988), 130–1, 152–3; Martin Ingram, *Church Courts, Sex and Marriage in England 1570–1640* (Cambridge, 1987), 165–6; Laura Gowing, *Domestic Dangers: Women, Words, and Sex in Early Modern London* (Oxford, 1996), 94–6, 192; Bernard Capp, 'The Double Standard Revisited:

Plebeian Women and Male Sexual Reputation in Early Modern England', *Past and Present*, 162 (1999), 70–100.

81. Hindle, *On the Parish?*, 433–45.

82. Alcock, *Observations on the Defects of the Poor Laws*, 16–17.

83. Joseph Townsend, *A Dissertation on the Poor* (1786; reprinted Berkeley, 1971), 53.

84. Catharine Capp, *Observations on Charity Schools, female friendly societies, and other subjects connected with the views of the Ladies Committee* (York, 1805), 2–3n.

85. GL, MS 2676/1, St Botolph Aldgate, Pauper examinations, 1742–50.

86. Ibid.

87. Louise A. Tilly and Joan W. Scott, *Women, Work, and Family* (New York, 1978), 12–24, 104–45.

88. Sharpe, *Population and Society*, 299–302.

89. Alice Clark, *Working Life of Women in the Seventeenth Century* (reprinted 1919; 1968).

90. [Richard Dunning], *Bread for the Poor* (Exeter, 1698), 3; and quoted in Eden, *State of the Poor*, vol. 1, p. 251.

91. John Locke, quoted in Eden, *State of the Poor*, vol. 1, p. 246.

92. OBP, t16861013–25, Anne Philmore (killing: other, guilty); Randall Martin, *Women, Murder, and Equity in Early Modern England* (2008), 195.

93. For discussion of the case, see Toni Bowers, *The Politics of Motherhood: British Writing and Culture, 1680–1760* (Cambridge, 1996), 93–5; Martin, *Women, Murder, and Equity*, 175–6.

94. Eden, *State of the Poor*, vol. 1, pp. 625–30.

95. Quoted in Leonore Davidoff, 'The Family in Britain', in F. M. L. Thompson (ed.), *The Cambridge Social History of Britain 1750–1950*, 3 vols (Cambridge, 1990), vol. 2, p. 96.

96. LMA, A/FH/A/8/1/1/2, Petitions for admission, 1770–1.

97. Philippa Maddern, ' "In myn own house": The Troubled Connections between Servant Marriages, Late-Medieval English Household Communities and Early Modern Historiography', in Stephanie Tarbin and Susan Broomhall (eds), *Women, Identities and Communities in Early Modern Europe* (Aldershot, 2008), 45–59.

98. LMA, A/FH/A/8/1/1/4, Petitions for admission, 1773.

99. Ibid.

100. Susannah R. Ottaway, 'The Old Woman's Home in Eighteenth-century England', in Botelo and Thane (eds), *Women and Ageing*, 115.

101. Margaret Spufford, *The Great Reclothing of Rural England: Petty Chapmen and their Wares in the Seventeenth Century* (1984), 23–4, 43, 52–4.

102. *The Autobiography of Francis Place (1771–1854)*, ed. Mary Thale (Cambridge, 1972), 116.

103. E. A. Wrigley, 'A Simple Model of London's Importance in Changing English Society and Economy, 1650–1750', *Past and Present*, 37 (1965), 49.

104. John Landers, *Death and the Metropolis: Studies in the Demographic History of London 1670–1830* (Cambridge, 1993), 286–7.

105. Margaret Hunt, 'Women and the Fiscal-imperial State in the Late Seventeenth and Early Eighteenth Centuries', in Kathleen Wilson (ed.), *A New Imperial History: Culture, Identity, and Modernity in Britain and Empire, 1660–1840* (Cambridge, 2004), 30–1.

106. Landers, *Death and the Metropolis*, 288.
107. 7 Jac. I c. 4, *Statutes of the Realm*, vol. 4, p. 1161.
108. *Borough Session Papers 1653–1688, Portsmouth Record Series*, ed. Arthur J. Willis and Margaret J. Hoad (Chichester, 1971), 6.
109. *County of Buckingham:* ed. Hardy and Reckitt, vol. 3, p. 195.
110. *Justice in Eighteenth-Century Hackney: The Justicing Notebook of Henry Norris and the Hackney Petty Session Book*, ed. Ruth Paley, London Rec. Soc., vol. 28 (1991), pp. xxiv, 105.
111. Ibid. 12.
112. GL, MS 12818A/4, Christ's Hospital Presentation papers, 1686–7, Gardner.
113. Ibid. William Walker.
114. E. M. Hampson, *The Treatment of Poverty in Cambridgeshire 1597–1834* (Cambridge, 1934), 140–1.
115. K. D. M. Snell, *Annals of the Labouring Poor: Social Change and Agrarian England, 1660–1900* (Cambridge, 1985), 360–3.
116. Joanne Bailey, *Unquiet Lives: Marriage and Marriage Breakdown in England, 1660–1800* (Cambridge, 2003), 170–8.
117. Taylor, *Sojourners' Narratives*, 43–4.
118. *Letters of John Paige, London Merchant 1648–1658*, ed. George F. Steckley, London Rec. Soc., vol. 21 (1984), 77.
119. Hunt, 'Women and the Fiscal-imperial State', in Wilson (ed.), *A New Imperial History*, 29–47.
120. *The Reverend Richard Baxter's Last Treatise: The Poor Husbandman's Advocate* (1691), ed. F. J. Powicke (Manchester, 1926), 27–8.
121. Peter Laslett, 'Parental Deprivation in the Past', in his *Family Life and Illicit Love in Earlier Generations: Essays in Historical Sociology* (Cambridge, 1977), 162–3, 162 n. 4.
122. Ibid. 166.
123. *Chelsea Settlement and Bastardy Examinations 1733–1766*, ed. Tim Hitchcock and John Black, London Rec. Soc., vol. 33 (1999), 150.
124. Taylor, *Sojourners' Narratives*, 17.
125. Ibid. 97.
126. Somerset RO, DD/SE/45/1, Petitions to Bruton Hospital, no. 75.
127. A. L. Beier, 'The Social Problems of an Elizabethan Country Town: Warwick, 1580–90', in Peter Clark (ed.), *County Towns in Pre-industrial England* (Leicester, 1981), 61.
128. Graham Mayhew, 'Life-Cycle Service and the Family Unit in Early Modern Rye', *Continuity and Change*, 6 (1991), 204.
129. K. D. M. Snell and J. Millar, 'Lone-Parent Families and the Welfare State: Past and Present', *Continuity and Change*, 2 (1987), 392–3.
130. See Maxine Berg, *The Age of Manufactures 1700–1820: Industry, Innovation and Work in Britain*, 2nd edn (1994), 136–65; Sharpe, *Adapting to Capitalism*.
131. Jane Humphries, 'Female-Headed Households in Early Industrial Britain: The Vanguard of the Proletariat', *Labour History Review*, 63 (1998), 36, 40.
132. Sara Horrell, Jane Humphries, Hans-Joachim Voth, 'Stature and Relative Deprivation: Fatherless Children in Early Industrial Britain', *Continuity and Change*, 13 (1998), 73–115.
133. Wales, 'Poverty, Poor Relief and the Life-Cycle', in Smith (ed.), *Land, Kinship, and Life-Cycle*.

134. *The Justicing Notebook of Henry Norris*, ed. Paley, 80.
135. GL, MS 1204/1, St Katherine Cree, Workhouse committee, fo. 14.
136. Ibid. fo. 12.
137. *OBP*, t17900424–26, Lucy Acor (killing: murder, not guilty).
138. Hindle, *On the Parish?*, 223–6; Peter Kirby, *Child Labour in Britain, 1750–1870* (Basingstoke, 2003), 1–5.
139. Ibid. 4.
140. John Gillis, *For Better, For Worse: British Marriages, 1600 to the Present* (New York, 1985), 116–18.
141. Sarah Lloyd, ' "Agents in their own Concerns"? Charity and the Economy of Makeshifts in Eighteenth-Century Britain', in King and Tomkins (eds), *The Poor in England*, 111–12.
142. Wales, 'Poverty, Poor Relief and the Life-Cycle', in Smith (ed.), *Land, Kinship, and Life-Cycle*, 375–6, 378.
143. *The Norwich Census of the Poor 1570*, ed. J. F. Pound, Norfolk Rec. Soc., vol. 40 (1971), 85.
144. [Daniel Defoe], *The Just Complaint of the Poor Weavers* (1729), 29.
145. Berg, *The Age of Manufactures*, 144–7.
146. Sara Horrell and Jane Humphries, ' "The Exploitation of Little Children": Child Labour and the Family Economy in the Industrial Revolution', *Explorations in Economic History*, 32 (1995), 490, 485–516.
147. Ibid. 490–3.
148. Hugh Cunningham, 'The Employment and Unemployment of Children in England c. 1680–1851', *Past and Present*, 126 (1990), 115–50.
149. James Lackington, *Memoirs of the First Forty-Five Years of James Lackington* (1794; facs. edn New York, 1974), 30.
150. Richard Wall, 'Leaving Home and the Process of Household Formation in Pre-industrial England', *Continuity and Change*, 2 (1987), 94, refers to 'the parental home'.
151. Greg T. Smith, 'Expanding the Compass of Domestic Violence in the Hanoverian Metropolis', *Journal of Social History*, 41 (2007), 40–1.
152. Margaret Pelling, 'Old Age, Poverty, and Disability in Early Modern Norwich', in Margaret Pelling and Richard M. Smith (eds), *Life, Death, and the Elderly: Historical Perspectives* (1991), 87–90.
153. Peter Laslett, 'Clayworth and Cogenhoe', in Laslett, *Family Life and Illicit Love*, 58.
154. *The Office of Christian Parents* (Cambridge, 1616), 130–2.
155. *Songs, Carols and Other Miscellaneous Poems . . . Richard Hill's Commonplace Book*, ed. Roman Dyboski, *Early English Text Society*, vol. 101 (1907), 120–5, 128.
156. Laslett, 'Parental Deprivation', in Laslett, *Family Life and Illicit Love*, 165–6.
157. Jeremy Boulton, ' "It is Extreme Necessity That Makes Me Do This": Some "Survival Strategies" of Pauper Households in London's West End during the Early Eighteenth Century', *International Review of Social History*, 45 (2000), 60.
158. GL, MS 1204/1, St Katherine Cree, Workhouse committee, fo. 66.
159. Ibid., fos. 66v–67.
160. Richard Burn, *Justice of the Peace, and Parish Officer*, 2 vols (1755 edn), vol. 2, p. 202.

161. James Burrow, *A Series of Decisions of the Court of King's Bench upon Settlement Cases* (1768), vol. 1, p. 3. However, if a widow gained a settlement in her own right, she could give it to her children.

162. *Essex Quarter Sessions*, ed. Allen, 76.

163. Burn, *Justice of the Peace* (1755 edn), vol. 2, p. 261. By 1829, editors of Blackstone declared that a stepfather had no obligations even during his wife's life-time, since the Elizabethan Poor Laws extended 'only to relations by blood'; 18th edn, notes by Thomas Lee (1829) vol. 1, 448. (Thanks to Sue Hart for this 19th-cent. reference.)

164. GL, MS 2985, St Dunstan in the West, Minute book of meetings of the guardians of the parish poor children, 1789–1806.

165. Stephen Collins, 'British Stepfamily Relationships, 1500–1800', *Journal of Family History*, 14 (1991), 331–44.

166. *Churchwardens' Presentments*, ed. Hilda Johnstone, Sussex Rec. Soc., vol. 49 (1948), 92.

167. Amy Louise Erickson, *Women and Property in Early Modern England* (1993), 129–51.

168. Ibid. 93–4; Diana O'Hara, *Courtship and Constraint: Rethinking the Making of Marriage in Tudor England* (Manchester, 2000), 221–3.

169. *OBP*, oa17481028, The Ordinary of Newgate's account, Sarah Kenigem; see also *OBP*, t17481012–20, Sarah Kennigem (theft: theft from a specified place, guilty).

170. See Elenor Adams, in Chapter 2; *OBP*, t16831212–2, Elenor Adams (killing: infanticide, guilty).

171. *OBP*, t17390117–25, John Marsland (sexual offences: rape, guilty).

172. Contemporaries termed a child whose father had died an orphan.

173. Eden, *State of the Poor*, vol. 1, p. 627.

174. *The Assembly Books of Southampton*, ed. J. W. Horrocks, 4 vols, Southampton Rec. Soc., vols. 19, 21, 24, 25 (1917–25), vol. 3, p. 18.

175. Marina Warner, *From the Beast to the Blonde: On Fairy Tales and their Tellers* (1995), 213, and *passim*.

176. Renzo Derosas and Osamu Saito, 'Introduction', in Renzo Derosas and Michel Oris (eds), *When Dad Died: Individuals and Families Coping with Family Stress in Past Societies* (Berne, 2002), 9. Thanks to Margaret Hunt for this reference.

177. *OBP*, t16931012–17, Mary Nace (theft: simple grand larceny, guilty).

178. *OBP*, t16860707–12, Elizabeth Battison (killing: other, guilty).

179. *OBP*, t17960217–37, Thomas Davenport (sexual offences: rape, guilty).

180. *OBP*, t17670909–1, James Brownrigg, Elizabeth his wife, John their son (killing: murder, not guilty, guilty, not guilty).

181. *OBP*, t17590425–15, Elizabeth Ricketts (theft: simple grand larceny, guilty, transported).

182. *Early Essex Town Meetings: Braintree, 1619–1636: Finchingfield, 1626–36*, ed. F. G. Emmison (1970), 34–5.

183. Taylor, *Sojourners' Narratives*, 43.

184. John Broad, *Transforming English Rural Society: The Verneys and the Claydons, 1600–1820* (Cambridge, 2004), 186.

185. *OBP*, t16870512–34, William Webb (sexual offences: rape, not guilty).

186. I have benefited from discussion with Sue Hart who is writing about remarriage in the 19th cent. Australian colonies.

187. *OBP*, t17490113–11, John Osborne (sexual offences: rape, not guilty).

188. *Assembly Books of Southampton*, ed. Horrocks, vol. 1, p. 52.

189. Donna T. Andrew, ' "To the Charitable and Humane": Appeals for Assistance in the Eighteenth Century London Press', in Hugh Cunningham and Joanna Innes (eds), *Charity, Philanthropy, and Reform: From the 1690s to the 1850s* (Basingstoke, 1998), 101.

190. GL, MS 9192/1, St Ann Blackfriars, Peter Joye's Charity School: Trustees' minute book, 1717–44, 326.

191. GL, MS 12806/5, Christ's Hospital Court Minutes, 1649–1661, Aug. 1655, 405.

192. Lloyd, ' "Agents in their own Concerns"?', in King and Tomkins (eds), *The Poor in England*, 100–36.

193. GL, MS 9192/1, St Ann Blackfriars, Peter Joye's Charity School minutes, 132.

194. Ibid. 299.

195. Ibid. 329.

196. Ibid. 59.

197. CUL, SPCK, C 1/6, Abstract Letter book, 1715–1716, 25 Aug. 1715, 19 Sept. 1715.

198. CUL, SPCK, CR1/8, Abstract Letter book, 1717–1718, no. 5272.

199. GL, MS 9192/1, St Ann Blackfriars, Peter Joye's Charity School minutes, 466–7.

200. GL, MS 12828/3, Christ's Hospital Court Letter Book, 1684–1703, 272; E. H. Pearce, *Annals of Christ's Hospital* (1901), 101–4.

201. Pearce, *Annals of Christ's Hospital* 127, 248.

202. GL, MS 12806/9, Christ's Hospital, Court Minutes, 1699–1718, fos. 142–3.

203. Lloyd, ' "Agents in their own Concerns"?', in King and Tomkins (eds), *The Poor in England*, 113.

204. Boulton, ' "Survival Strategies" of Pauper Households', 66.

205. Carol Kazmierczak Manzione, *Christ's Hospital of London, 1552–1598: A Passing Deed of Pity* (Selinsgrove, 1995), 147.

206. *Christ's Hospital Admissions, etc*, ed. G. A. T. Allan (1937), 249.

207. Ibid. 249.

208. Ibid. 100, 166.

209. Pearce, *Annals of Christ's Hospital*, 35.

210. For example, *Christ's Hospital Admissions*, ed. Allan, 118, 166, 167, 208, 218, 241.

211. Ibid. 117.

212. Ibid. 125.

213. GL, MS 12818A, Christ's Hospital Presentation Papers, 1674–5.

214. Ibid. John Catesbee, [alphabetically filed].

215. Ibid. John Draynor.

216. Ibid. Obadiah Marshall.

217. Ibid. William Carter.

218. Ibid. Thomas Butt.

219. Ibid. Ralph Franklin.

220. Alysa Levene, 'The Origins of the Children of the London Foundling Hospital, 1741–1760: A Reconsideration', *Continuity and Change*, 18 (2003), 201–35.

221. Levene, *Childcare, Health and Mortality at the London Foundling Hospital, 1741–1800: 'Left to the Mercy of the World'* (2007), 40–2.

222. LMA, A/FH/A/11/2/4, Petitions for return of children, 1763.

223. LMA, A/FH/A/8/1/1/3, Petitions for admission, 1772.

224. LMA, A/FH/A/8/1/1/6, Petitions for admission, 1775.

225. T. F. Thistleton-Dyer, *Old English Social Life as told by the Parish Register* (1898), 174–5.

226. GL, MS 2676/2, St Botolph Aldgate, Pauper examinations, 1750–1757.

227. *OBP*, t17890225–1, William Patmore (killing: murder, not guilty).

228. *Oxford English Dictionary Online*: http://dictionary.oed.com/.

229. For 18th cent. attitudes to the sale of bodies as commodities, see Ruth Richardson, *Death, Dissection and the Destitute* (1987).

230. *OBP*, t17360721–36, Robert Hussey (sexual offences: bigamy, guilty).

231. J. A. Sharpe, *Crime in Seventeenth-Century England: A County Study* (Cambridge, 1983), 67–8.

232. *OBP*, t17360721–36, Robert Hussey (sexual offences: bigamy, guilty).

233. *OBP*, oa17241207, The Ordinary of Newgate's Account, Lewis Hussar.

234. Michael MacDonald, *Mystical Bedlam: Madness, Anxiety, and Healing in Seventeenth-Century England* (Cambridge, 1981), 20, 51–3, 77–8.

235. Ibid. 125–8.

236. Vanessa McMahon, *Murder in Shakespeare's England* (2004).

237. Mary E. Fissell, *Vernacular Bodies: The Politics of Reproduction in Early Modern England* (Oxford, 2004), 53–89.

238. *Murthur Will Out, or, a True and Faithful Relation of an Horrible Murther committed thirty three years ago, by an Unnatural Mother . . .*, 30 Nov. [1675], 2–3.

239. J. M. Beattie, *Crime and the Courts in England, 1660–1800* (Oxford, 1986), 117–24; Josephine McDonagh, *Child Murder and British Culture, 1720–1900* (Cambridge, 2003).

240. *OBP*, t17340227–32, Judith Defour (killing: murder, guilty).

241. *OBP*, t17680518–39, Mary Hindes (killing: murder, guilty).

242. *OBP*, t17611209–26, Mary Hindes (killing: murder, not guilty).

243. Ibid.

244. *OBP*, t17680518–39, Mary Hindes (killing: murder, guilty).

245. Ibid.

246. MacDonald, *Mystical Bedlam*, 82–4.

247. N. Partridge and J. Sharp, *Blood for Blood* (1670), 14–15, 18.

248. *The Cruel Mother* (1708), 5 and *passim*.

249. *OBP*, t17670115–24, John Williamson (killing: murder, guilty).

250. *The Tyburn Chronicle: Or, Villainy Display'd in all its Branches* (1768), vol. 4, p. 224; *A Full and Authentic Account of John Williamson, Who was executed in Moorfields* (1767).

251. *A Full and Authentic Account of John Williamson*, 2, 4.

252. Akihito Suzuki, 'The Household and the Care of Lunatics in Eighteenth-Century London', in Peregrine Horden and Richard Smith (eds), *The Locus of Care: Families, Communities, Institutions and the Provision of Welfare since Antiquity* (1998), 153–75; see also, Amanda Berry, 'Community Sponsorship and the Hospital Patient in Late Eighteenth-Century England', in Horden and Smith (eds), *The Locus of Care*, 126–50.

253. *A Full and Authentic Account of John Williamson*, 18–19.

254. *OBP*, t17670115–24, John Williamson (killing: murder, guilty).

255. *Autobiography of Francis Place*, ed. Thale, 116–17, 127.

256. Westminster Muniment Room, Coroners' Inquests 1760 to December 1771, 17 Jan. 1765, St Mary Le Strand (compiled by Tim Hitchcock).

5. CIVIC FATHERS OF THE POOR

1. Robert Bromley, *A Sermon preached in the Chapel of the Hospital for the Maintenance and Education of Exposed and Deserted Young Children* (1770), 13.
2. Ibid. 4.
3. Susan Dwyer Amussen, *An Ordered Society: Gender and Class in Early Modern England* (Oxford, 1988); Anthony Fletcher and John Stevenson, 'Introduction', in Fletcher and Stevenson (eds), *Order and Disorder in Early Modern England* (Cambridge, 1985), 31–3. For continuities, see Kathleen M. Davies, 'Continuity and Change in Literary Advice on Marriage', in R. B. Outhwaite (ed.), *Marriage and Society: Studies in the Social History of Marriage* (1981), 58–80.
4. *An Account of Marriage* (1672), [Bodl, Wood 750 (2)], 17.
5. Alexandra Shepard, 'Manhood, Credit and Patriarchy in Early Modern England c. 1580–1640', *Past and Present*, 167 (2000), 75–106.
6. See Gordon J. Schochet, *Patriarchalism in Political Thought: The Authoritarian Family and Political Speculation and Attitudes Especially in Seventeenth-Century England* (Oxford, 1975); Carole Pateman, *The Sexual Contract* (Stanford, CA, 1988).
7. Mary Astell, *Reflections upon Marriage*, 3rd edn (1706), in Bridget Hill (ed.), *The First English Feminist: Reflections upon Marriage and Other Writings by Mary Astell* (1986), 76.
8. BL, MS Additional 72516, fo. 57, Sir Charles Cottrell to Elizabeth Trumbull, Nov. 1687; thanks to Sara Mendelson for her transcription of these letters.
9. *The Office of Christian Parents* (Cambridge, 1616), 1.
10. Amanda Whiting, ' "Some Women Can Shift it Well Enough": A Legal Context for Understanding the Women Petitioners of the Seventeenth-Century English Revolution', *Australian Feminist Law Journal*, 21 (2004), 97 and *passim*.
11. Robert Ram, *The Countrymans Catechisme* (1655), 39.
12. H[ugh] P[eters], *Good Work for a Good Magistrate* (1651), 26.
13. Samuel Hartlib, *London's Charity Inlarged, Stilling the Orphans Cry* (1650), [16].
14. Hugh Cunningham, *The Children of the Poor: Representations of Childhood Since the Seventeenth Century* (Oxford, 1991).
15. John Moore, *The Crying Sin of England of Not Caring for the Poor* (1653), 2–6.
16. Lotte Mulligan and Judith Richards, 'A "Radical" Problem: The Poor and the English Reformers in the Mid-Seventeenth Century', *JBS*, 29 (1990), 118–46.
17. Ian Green, *The Christian's ABC: Catechisms and Catechizing in England c. 1530–1740* (Oxford, 1996), 452–60.
18. Sir Josiah Child, *The New Discourse of Trade* (1693), 68–73; Firman quoted in Sidney and Beatrice Webb, *English Poor Law History. Part 1: The Old Poor Law* (1927), 106.
19. Quoted in Paul Langford, *Public Life and the Propertied Englishman 1698–1798* (Oxford, 1991), 509.
20. Richard Burn, *The History of the Poor Laws* (1764), 168.
21. *Casuistical Morning Exercises: preached 1689; no. 17 by Dan Burgess*, 423v.
22. CUL, SPCK, CS2/3, Draft letter book out of Henry Newman, fo. 14, 8 May 1713.
23. P[eters], *Good Work for a Good Magistrate*, 26.

24. Michael Grossberg, *Governing the Hearth: Law and the Family in Nineteenth-Century America* (Chapel Hill, 1985).

25. Peter W. Bardaglio, *Reconstructing the Household: Families, Sex, and the Law in the Nineteenth-Century South* (Chapel Hill, 1995), p. xvi.

26. James Stephen Taylor, 'The Impact of Pauper Settlement, 1691–1843', *Past and Present*, 73 (1976), 42–3, 58.

27. Thomas Garden Barnes, *Somerset 1625–1640: A County's Government during Personal Rule* (1961), 172–202; Kevin Sharpe, *The Personal Rule of Charles I* (New Haven, 1992), 401–506.

28. Michael J. Braddick, *State Formation in Early Modern England c. 1550–1700* (Cambridge, 2000), 165–71.

29. W. Newman Brown, 'The Receipt of Poor Relief and Family Situation: Aldenham, Hertfordshire 1630–90', in Richard M. Smith (ed.), *Land, Kinship, and Life-Cycle* (Cambridge, 1984), 419–22; Joan Kent, 'The Rural "Middling Sort" in Early Modern England, circa 1640–1740: Some Economic, Political Socio-Cultural Characteristics', *Rural History*, 10 (1999), 19–54; H. R. French, 'Social Status, Localism, and the "Middle Sort of People" in England 1620–1750', *Past and Present*, 166 (2000), 66–99.

30. Paul Slack, *The English Poor Law, 1531–1782* (Basingstoke, 1990), 28–9.

31. Taylor, 'Impact of Pauper Settlement', 58.

32. Lynn Hollen Lees, *The Solidarities of Strangers: The English Poor Laws and the People, 1700–1948* (Cambridge, 1998), 33.

33. *Hints and Cautions...St Giles in the Fields and St George Bloomsbury* (1781; reprinted 1797), 4.

34. E. H. Pearce, *Annals of Christ's Hospital* (1901), 22–3; Frank Freeman Foster, *The Politics of Stability: A Portrait of the Rulers in Elizabethan London* (1977), 59–60, 63; Carol Kazmierczak Manzione, *Christ's Hospital of London, 1552–1598: A Passing Deed of Pity* (Selinsgrove, 1995), 121–37.

35. Foster, *Politics of Stability*, 60, 143.

36. Margaret Pelling, 'Child Health as a Social Value in Early Modern England', in Margaret Pelling, *The Common Lot: Sickness, Medical Occupations and the Urban Poor in Early Modern England* (1998), 112.

37. Susan C. Lawrence, *Charitable Knowledge: Hospital Pupils and Practices in Eighteenth-Century London* (Cambridge, 1996), 46.

38. *Richard Hutton's Complaints Book: The Notebook of the Steward of the Quaker Workhouse at Clerkenwell, 1711–1737*, ed. Timothy V. Hitchcock, London Rec. Soc., vol. 24 (1987), p. vii and n. 1.

39. Shelley Burt, *Virtue Transformed: Political Argument in England, 1668–1740* (Cambridge, 1992), 158.

40. John Broad, 'Housing the Rural Poor in Southern England, 1650–1850', *Agricultural History Review*, 42 (2000), 152.

41. Craig Rose, 'Politics and the London Royal Hospitals, 1683–92', in Lindsay Granshaw and Roy Porter (eds), *The Hospital in History* (1989), 123–48.

42. Braddick, *State Formation*, 177–290.

43. Quoted by Nicholas Rogers, 'Impressment and the Law in Eighteenth-Century Britain', in Norma Landau (ed.), *Law, Crime, and English Society, 1660–1830* (Cambridge, 2002), 74.

44. Langford, *Public Life and the Propertied Englishman*, 437–509; Paul Slack, *From Reformation to Improvement: Public Welfare in Early Modern England* (Oxford, 1999), 165.

45. Anne Borsay, *Medicine and Charity in Georgian Bath: A Social History of the General Infirmary, c. 1739–1830* (Aldershot, 1999), especially 304–37.

46. For excellent accounts of policies towards poverty in early modern England, see Paul Slack, *Poverty and Policy in Tudor and Stuart England* (1988) and Steve Hindle, *On the Parish? The Micro-Politics of Poor Relief in Rural England c. 1550–1750* (Oxford, 2004).

47. For recent discussion of the franchise and independence, see Michael Mendle (ed.), *The Putney Debates of 1647: The Army, the Levellers, and the English State* (Cambridge, 2001).

48. Cynthia B. Herrup, *A House in Gross Disorder: Sex, Law, and the 2nd Earl of Castlehaven* (New York, 1999); David Turner, ' "Nothing is so secret but shall be revealed": The Scandalous Life of Robert Foulkes', in Tim Hitchcock and Michèle Cohen (eds), *English Masculinities 1600–1800* (1999), 169–92.

49. *Letters of John Holles 1587–1637*, ed. P. R. Seddon, Thoroton Soc., vol. 31 (1975), 266.

50. Sara Mendelson and Patricia Crawford, *Women in Early Modern England, 1550–1720* (Oxford, 1998), 52, 57.

51. Izaak Walton, *The Lives of John Donne, Sir Henry Wotton, Richard Hooker, George Herbert and Robert Sanderson* (1940), 292.

52. Patricia Crawford, *Women and Religion in England, 1500–1720* (1993), 165.

53. Phyllis Mack, *Visionary Women: Ecstatic Prophecy in Seventeenth-Century England* (Berkeley, 1992), 289–92.

54. *A Living testimony . . . from our Women's Meeting* (1685), 2–3.

55. Claire S. Schen, *Charity and Lay Piety in Reformation London, 1500–1620* (Aldershot, 2002), 177.

56. Donna T. Andrew, *Philanthropy and Police: London Charity in the Eighteenth Century* (Princeton, 1989), 87.

57. David Owen, *English Philanthropy, 1660–1960* (Cambridge, MA, 1965); Andrew, *Philanthropy and Police*.

58. R. H. Nichols and F. A. Wray, *The History of the Foundling Hospital* (1935), 16; Lisa Zunshine, *Bastards and Foundlings: Illegitimacy in Eighteenth-Century England* (Columbus, OH, 2005), 103.

59. *Correspondence of the Foundling Hospital Inspectors in Berkshire, 1757–1768*, ed. Gillian Clark, Berkshire Rec. Soc., vol. 1 (1994), p. xxvii.

60. M. G. Jones, *The Charity School Movement: A Study of Eighteenth-Century Puritanism* (Cambridge, 1938).

61. Priscilla Wakefield, *Reflections on the Present Condition of the Female Sex* (1798; New York, 1974), 180.

62. Francis Bacon, 'Of Marriage and Single Life', *Essays* (1906), 21.

63. Patricia Crawford, 'The Construction and Experience of Maternity', in Patricia Crawford, *Blood, Bodies and Families in Early Modern England* (2004), 81–8.

64. Quoted in Peter Earle, *A City Full Of People: Men and Women of London 1650–1750* (1994), 28.

65. OBP, 0a17340709, The Ordinary of Newgate's Account, Thomas Taverner.

66. John Gregory, *A Father's Legacy to His Daughter* (1774; New York, 1974), 34.

67. *Quarter Sessions Records for the County of Somerset*, 4 vols 1607–77, ed. E. H. Bates, Somerset Rec. Soc., vols 23, 24, 28, 34 (1907–19), vol. 2, p. xxi.

68. [Isaac Maddox], *The Wisdom and Duty of Preserving Destitute Infants. A Sermon . . .* (1753), 10.

69. *Some Considerations on the Necessity and Usefulness of the Royal Charter establishing a Hospital* (1740), 18.
70. Ibid. 13.
71. 5 Geo. I c. 8, Burn, *History of the Poor Laws*, 101.
72. Anne M. Scott, *Piers Plowman and the Poor* (Dublin, 2004), 37–47.
73. See Carol Lee Bacchi, *Women, Policy and Politics: The Construction of Policy Problems* (1999).
74. Leonard Lee, *A Remonstrance Humbly Presented to ... Parliament touching the insupportable increase of the poore in this Land* (1645), 3–4.
75. Hindle, *On the Parish?*, 453.
76. Slack, *From Reformation to Improvement*.
77. Shepard, 'Manhood, Credit and Patriarchy', 84–7, 89.
78. Steve Hindle, 'Dependency, Shame and Belonging: Badging the Deserving Poor, c. 1550–1750', *Cultural and Social History*, 1 (2004), 6–35; Hindle, *On the Parish?*, 433–45.
79. Keith Wrightson, 'Mutualities and Obligations: Changing Social Relationships in Early Modern England', Raleigh Lecture, 2005.
80. Braddick, *State Formation*, 163–4.
81. *An Ease for Overseers of the Poore* (Cambridge, 1601), 26.
82. Moore, *The Crying Sin of England*, [11].
83. Joseph Lee, *Considerations Concerning the Commone Fields and Inclosures* (1654), 25.
84. George Smalridge, *The Royal Benefactress: Or, the Great Charity of Educating Poor Children [sermon]* (1710), 20, 37.
85. Valerie Fildes, 'Maternal Feelings Re-assessed: Child Abandonment and Neglect in London and Westminster, 1550–1800', in Valerie Fildes (ed.), *Women as Mothers in Pre-Industrial England* (1990), 143.
86. 'The Royal Charter establishing an Hospital for the Maintenance and Education of Exposed and Deserted Young Children', printed in Nichols and Wray, *History of the Foundling Hospital*, 329–36.
87. *Some Considerations ... establishing a Hospital*, 19.
88. Ibid. 2, 6.
89. Cf. Lawrence Stone, *The Family, Sex and Marriage in England, 1500–1800* (1977), 475.
90. [Richard Dunning], *Bread for the Poor* (1698), quoted in Sir Frederick Morton Eden, *The State of the Poor*, 3 vols (1797), vol. 1, p. 249; also p. 496.
91. Eden, *The State of the Poor*, vol. 1, p. 259.
92. *William Lambarde and Local Government*, ed. Conyers Read, (Ithaca, 1962), 179–84, quotation on 183.
93. *Ease for Overseers*, 26.
94. *'This Little Commonwealth': Layston Parish Memorandum Book, 1607– c. 1650 and 1704–c. 1747*, ed. Heather Falvey and Steve Hindle, Hertfordshire Record Publications, vol. 19 (2003), 66.
95. R[ichard] H[aines], *Provision for the Poor: Or, Reasons for the Erecting of a Working-Hospital in every County* (1678), 6.
96. Hugh Cunningham, 'The Employment and Unemployment of Children in England c. 1680–1851', *Past and Present*, 126 (1990), 115–50.
97. R[ichard] H[aines], *Proposals for Building in Every County a Working Almshouse* (1677), 1, 6.
98. John Downame, *The Plea of the Poor* (1616), 238.

99. 'This Little Commonwealth', ed. Falvey and Hindle, 66.
100. Hindle, On the Parish?, 223.
101. Locke quoted in Eden, State of the Poor, vol. 1, p. 246.
102. [Dunning], Bread for the Poor, 6.
103. Toni Bowers, The Politics of Motherhood: British Writing and Culture, 1680–1760 (Cambridge, 1996), 1–4.
104. [Maddox], Wisdom and Duty of Preserving Destitute Infants, 6, 14–15.
105. Michael Dalton, The Countrey Justice (1635 edn), 95.
106. H[aines], Provision for the Poor, 4–5.
107. Nichols and Wray, History of the Foundling Hospital, 16.
108. For details of legislation, see Webb and Webb, The Old Poor Law; Slack, Poverty and Policy, 113–37.
109. Ease for Overseers, 27; Joseph Keble, An Assistance to Justices of the Peace (1683), 479–80, 503, 514, 521.
110. Pelling, 'Child Health as a Social Value', in Pelling, Common Lot, 109.
111. County of Buckingham: Calendar to the Sessions Records, 4 vols 1678–1724, ed. William Le Hardy and Geoffrey L. Reckitt (Aylesbury, 1933–39), vol. 2, p. 177.
112. Steve Hindle, The State and Social Change in Early Modern England, c. 1550–1640 (Basingstoke, 2000), 54.
113. A. L. Beier, Masterless Men: The Vagrancy Problem in England 1560–1640 (1985), 171–5.
114. Steve Hindle and Ruth Wallis Herndon, 'Recreating Proper Families in England and North America: Pauper Apprenticeship in Transatlantic Context', in Ruth Wallis Herndon and John E. Murray (eds), Children Bound to Labor: Pauper Apprenticeship in Early America (Ithaca, 2009), 48. I am grateful for the kindness of the authors in allowing me to read their chapter before publication.
115. Hindle, On the Parish?, 271–82.
116. Whiting, ' "Some Women Can Shift it Well Enough" ', 97 and passim.
117. Geoffrey W. Oxley, Poor Relief in England and Wales, 1601–1834 (1974), 75–6; Hindle, On the Parish?, 65–6.
118. Books of Examinations and Depositions 1570–1594, ed. Gertrude H. Hamilton, Southampton Rec. Soc., vol. 9 (1914), 51.
119. Shannon McSheffrey, 'Men and Masculinity in Late Medieval London Civic Culture: Governance, Patriarchy and Reputation', in Jacqueline Murray (ed.), Conflicted Identities and Multiple Masculinities: Men in the Medieval West (New York, 1999), 254.
120. Pelling, 'Child Health as a Social Value', in Pelling, Common Lot, 109; Pamela Sharpe, 'Poor Children as Apprentices in Colyton, 1598–1830', Continuity and Change, 6 (1991), 1–18.
121. Joan Kent, 'The Centre and the Localities: State Formation and Parish Government in England, Circa 1640–1740', Historical Journal, 38 (1995), 390–1.
122. Valerie Pearl, 'Puritans and Poor Relief: The London Workhouse, 1649–1660', in Donald Pennington and Keith Thomas (eds), Puritans and Revolutionaries: Essays in Seventeenth-Century History presented to Christopher Hill (Oxford, 1978), 206–32; Paul Slack, 'Hospitals, Workhouses and the Relief of the Poor in Early Modern London', in Ole Peter Grell and Andrew Cunningham (eds), Health Care and Poor Relief in Protestant Europe 1500–1700 (1997), 239–42.
123. Timothy V. Hitchcock, 'The English Workhouse: A Study in Institutional Poor Relief in Selected Counties, 1696–1750' (DPhil thesis, Oxford, 1985), 23; Tim Hitchcock, Down and Out in Eighteenth-Century London (2004), 132–3.

124. *Some Thoughts concerning the Maintenance of the Poor* (1700), 12.
125. *An Account of Several Work Houses for Employing and Maintaining the Poor* (1725), 95.
126. *An Account of the General Nursery, or Colledg of Infants* (1686), 12.
127. *Account of Several Work Houses*, 84.
128. 1723 *Act For Amending the Laws Relating to Settlement and Employment and Relief of the Poor*; Slack, *English Poor Law*, 40–4.
129. H[aines], *Proposals for Building…a Working Almshouse*, 11.
130. *An Account of the General Nursery*, 2.
131. *An Account of Several Work Houses*, 37.
132. Ibid. 65.
133. Ibid. 23.
134. Ibid. 93.
135. Ibid. 3–5.
136. William Bailey, *A Treatise on the better Employment…of the Poor in Workhouses* (1758), 18.
137. 14 Eliz. I c. 5; Ann Kussmaul, *Servants in Husbandry in Early Modern England* (Cambridge, 1981), 166–7; Deborah Simonton, 'Apprenticeship: Training and Gender in Eighteenth-Century England', in Maxine Berg (ed.), *Markets and Manufacture in Early Industrial Europe* (1991), 229.
138. Mendelson and Crawford, *Women in Early Modern England*, 86.
139. Sharpe, 'Poor Children as Apprentices', 254; Hindle, *On the Parish?*, 213–14.
140. Richard Burn, *The Justice of the Peace*, 2 vols (1755), vol. 2, pp. 198–9; Joanna Innes, 'Origins of the Factory Acts: the Health and Morals of Apprentices Act, 1802', in Norma Landau (ed.), *Law, Crime, and English Society 1660–1830* (Cambridge, 2002), 234.
141. Burn, *Justice of the Peace* (1755 edn), vol. 2, pp. 199–200.
142. Mendelson and Crawford, *Women in Early Modern England*, 89.
143. Michael Nolan, *A Treatise of the Laws for the Relief and Settlement of the Poor*, 2 vols (1805), vol. 2, p. 219.
144. Ibid. 218–19.
145. Kussmaul, *Servants in Husbandry*, 166–7; Simonton, 'Apprenticeship: Training and Gender', in Berg (ed.), *Markets and Manufacture*, 235.
146. Hindle, *On the Parish?*, 205.
147. Steve Hindle, ' "Waste" Children? Pauper Apprenticeship under the Elizabethan Poor Laws, c. 1598–1697', in Penelope Lane, Neil Raven, and K. D. M. Snell (eds), *Women, Work and Wages in England 1600–1850* (Woodbridge, 2004), 28–9.
148. Sharpe, 'Poor Children as Apprentices', 253–70.
149. Hindle, ' "Waste" Children?', in Lane, Raven, and Snell (eds), *Women, Work and Wages*, 34; Hindle, *On the Parish?*, 213.
150. David Pam, *A History of Enfield*, 2 vols (Enfield, 1990), vol. 1, p. 173.
151. *A Calendar of Southampton Apprenticeship Register, 1609–1740*, ed. Arthur J. Willis and A. L. Merson, Southampton Records Ser., vol. 12 (1968), pp. li–lii.
152. Innes, 'Origins of the Factory Acts', in Landau (ed.), *Law, Crime, and English Society*, 235.
153. Hindle, *On the Parish?*, 191–223; see also, Chapter 4.
154. Hindle, *On the Parish?*, 209, 217.
155. Quoted in Joan Lane, *Apprenticeship in England, 1600–1914* (1996), 190–1.
156. 8 and 9 Will. III c. 30, An act for Supplying Some Defects in the Laws for the Relief of the Poor in this Kingdom; Mary B. Rose, 'Social Policy and Business:

Parish Apprenticeship and the Early Factory System 1750–1834', *Business History*, 31 (1989), 5–29; Hindle, *On the Parish?*, 19–203.

157. Paul Griffiths, *Youth and Authority: Formative Experiences in England 1560–1640* (Oxford, 1996), 318–20.

158. Dalton, *Countrey Justice* (1635 edn), 96.

159. *Ease for Overseers*, 27; Hindle and Herndon, 'Recreating Proper Families', in Herndon and Murray (eds), *Children Bound to Labor*.

160. *Kentish Sources*, ed. Elizabeth Melling, vol. 4, *The Poor* (Maidstone, 1964), 128–9.

161. Ibid. 133.

162. Oxley, *Poor Relief*, 76.

163. *Kentish Sources*, ed. Melling, 135.

164. Lane, *Apprenticeship*, 173–4.

165. Rose, 'Social Policy and Business', 15, 21–4.

166. Katrina Honeyman, *Child Workers in England, 1780–1820: Parish Apprentices and the Making of the Early Industrial Labour Force* (Aldershot, 2007), 199–213.

167. Rose, 'Social Policy and Business', 23.

168. Ilana Krausman Ben-Amos, *Adolescence and Youth in Early Modern England* (New Haven, 1994), 100–8.

169. Simonton, 'Apprenticeship: Training and Gender', in Berg (ed.), *Markets and Manufacture*, 235.

170. *OBP*, t16810117-1, Elizabeth Wigenton (killing: murder, guilty).

171. *OBP*, t17450424-33, Edmund Gilbert (killing: murder, guilty).

172. See Chapter 4.

173. *The Ordinary of Newgate ... Behaviour, Confession and Dying Words ... Mabel Hughes* (1755), 5. Thanks to Alison Wall for transcribing this for me.

174. *OBP*, t17550910-41, Mabell Hughes (killing: murder, guilty).

175. *Some Thoughts Concerning the Maintenance of the Poor*, 13.

176. *An Enquiry into the Causes of the Encrease and Miseries of the Poor of England* (1738), 43.

177. Innes, 'Origins of the Factory Acts', in Landau (ed.), *Law, Crime, and English Society*, 230–55.

178. Joanna Innes, 'The Mixed Economy of Welfare in Early Modern England: Assessments of the Options from Hale to Malthus (c. 1683–1803)', in Martin Daunton (ed.), *Charity, Self Interest and Welfare in the English Past* (1996), 139–80; Hugh Cunningham, 'Introduction', in Hugh Cunningham and Joanna Innes (eds), *Charity, Philanthropy, and Reform: From the 1690s to the 1850s* (Basingstoke, 1998), 2.

179. Broad, 'Housing the Rural Poor', 152.

180. *Certain Sermons or Homilies* (1562), 406–24.

181. Keith Thomas, *Religion and the Decline of Magic: Studies of Popular Beliefs in Sixteenth and Seventeenth Century England* (1971), 560–9.

182. Hindle, *On the Parish?*, 115–16.

183. Andrew, *Philanthropy and Police*, 46.

184. Slack, *Poverty and Policy*, 18–22.

185. Andrew, *Philanthropy and Police*, 4–5.

186. Ibid. 203–24.

187. White Kennett, *The Charity of Schools for Poor Children* (1706), 15.

188. Thomas Wilson, *The True Christian Method of Educating the Children of Both the Poor and Rich* (1724), 33.

189. Eden, *State of the Poor*, vol. 2, 440.

190. Strype, *Survey*, quoted in Caroline M. Barron, *London in the Middle Ages: Government and People 1200–1500* (Oxford, 2004), 273.

191. William Lemprière, *A History of the Girls' School of Christ's Hospital, London, Hoddesdon and Hertford* (Cambridge, 1924), 2.

192. GL, MS 12828/3, Christ's Hospital Court Letter Book, 1684-(1703), 200 (emphasis mine).

193. Ian W. Archer, *The Pursuit of Stability: Social Relations in Elizabethan London* (Cambridge, 1991), 154–63.

194. *Christ's Hospital Admissions, etc*, ed. G. A. T. Allan (1937), 103.

195. Pearce, *Annals of Christ's Hospital*, 41.

196. Fildes, 'Child Abandonment and Neglect', in Fildes (ed.), *Women as Mothers*, 146–7. Foundlings were 10% of admissions 1557–99.

197. Pearce, *Annals of Christ's Hospital*, 169, 190.

198. Archer, *Pursuit of Stability*, 157.

199. Pearce, *Annals of Christ's Hospital*, 275–6.

200. Quoted in Lemprière, *History of the Girls' School*, 3.

201. Pearce, *Annals of Christ's Hospital*, 170.

202. *Christ's Hospital Admissions*, ed. Allan, 151; GL, MS 12806/11, Christ's Hospital Court Minutes, 1745–56, [regulations printed at front of volume].

203. GL, MS 12828/3, Christ's Hospital Court Letter Book, 1684–1703, 268, 15 July 1689.

204. Manzione, *Christ's Hospital*, 151.

205. Lemprière, *A History of the Girls' School*, 9.

206. Manzione, *Christ's Hospital*, 151.

207. GL, MS 12828/3, Christ's Hospital Court Letter Book, 1684–1703, 116, 26 March 1687.

208. Pearce, *Annals of Christ's Hospital*, 42.

209. GL, MS 12806/6, Christ's Hospital Court Minutes 1661–1677, fo. 45v.

210. GL, MS 12806/9, Christ's Hospital Court Minutes 1699–1718, fo. 449.

211. Lemprière, *A History of the Girls' School*, 7.

212. Pearce, *Annals of Christ's Hospital*, 41.

213. GL, MS 12806/6, Christ's Hospital Court Minutes, 1661–1677, fo. 57.

214. Eden, *State of the Poor*, vol. 1, p. 246.

215. Jones, *Charity School Movement*: Owen, *English Philanthropy*, 17–35; Langford, *Public Life and the Propertied Englishman*, 490–500; Craig Rose, 'Evangelical Philanthropy and Anglican Revival: The Charity Schools of Augustan London, 1698–1740', *London Journal*, 16 (1991), 35–65; Sarah Lloyd, '"Agents in their own concerns"? Charity and the Economy of Makeshifts in Eighteenth-Century Britain', in Steven King and Allanah Tomkins (eds), *The Poor in England 1700–1850: An Economy of Makeshifts* (Manchester, 2003), 123.

216. William Sharp, *The Aimiableness and Advantage of making Suitable Provision for the Education and Employment of Poor Children: A Sermon* (Oxford, 1755), 18–19 and *passim*.

217. CUL, SPCK, D2/11, Abstract Letter book, 1715–16, 23 March 1715, Tiverton Devon.

218. Jones, *Charity School Movement*, 351–2; Owen, *English Philanthropy*, 20–32; Paul Langford, *A Polite and Commercial People: England 1727–1783* (Oxford, 1992), 128–33.
219. Alannah Tomkins, 'Charity Schools and the Parish Poor in Oxford, 1740–1770', *Midland History*, 22 (1997), 52, 57.
220. Kennett, *The Charity of Schools*, 24.
221. Owen, *English Philanthropy*, 20.
222. GL, MS 9192/1, St Ann Blackfriars, Peter Joye's Charity School: Trustees' minute book, 1717–44, 8–9.
223. Ibid. 479.
224. S. J. Skedd, 'More, Hannah (1745–1833)', *Oxford Dictionary of National Biography* (Oxford, 2004), [http://www.oxforddnb.com/view/article/19179, accessed 12 Sept. 2008].
225. Langford, *Polite and Commercial People*, 500.
226. Alannah Tomkins, 'The Experience of Urban Poverty: A Comparison of Oxford and Shrewsbury 1740 to 1770', (DPhil thesis, Oxford, 1994), 208; Jones, *Charity School Movement*, 105.
227. Owen, *English Philanthropy*, 28; Langford, *Polite and Commercial People*, 132–3.
228. Jones, *Charity School Movement*, 73–96.
229. Daniel Waterland, *Religious Education of Children: recommended in a sermon preach'd in the parish-church of St. Sepulchre, June the 6th, 1723* (1723), 26.
230. William Dawes, *The Excellency of the Charity-Schools* (1713), 14.
231. [Zinzano], *The Servant's Calling* (1725), 4.
232. Kennett, *The Charity of Schools*, 15.
233. George Smalridge, *The Royal Benefactress: Or, the Great Charity of Educating Poor Children [sermon]* (1710), 37.
234. Jones, *Charity School Movement*, 110–34; Andrew, *Philanthropy and Police*, 49–51.
235. Langford, *Polite and Commercial People*, 128–33.
236. K. D. M. Snell, 'The Sunday-School Movement in England and Wales: Child-Labour, Denominational Control and Working-Class Culture', *Past and Present*, 164 (1999), 122–68.
237. Lloyd, ' "Agents in their own concerns"?', in King and Tomkins (eds), *The Poor in England*, 127.
238. Jones, *Charity Schools*, 72.
239. *An Account of the General Nursery*, [10].
240. CUL, SPCK, CR1/6, Abstract Minute book, 1715–16, 263.
241. James C. Scott, *Domination and the Arts of Resistance: Hidden Transcripts* (New Haven, 1990), 2, 58, 67.
242. Cunningham, *Children of the Poor*, 44.
243. *Some Considerations . . . establishing a Hospital*, 6.
244. Bowers, *The Politics of Motherhood*, 1–14.
245. Tony Henderson, *Disorderly Women in Eighteenth-Century London: Prostitution and Control in the Metropolis, 1730–1830* (1999), 182–5.
246. Nichols and Wray, *History of the Foundling Hospital*, 101–7; see *Correspondence of the Foundling Hospital Inspectors in Berkshire*, ed. Clark.
247. Nichols and Wray, *History of the Foundling Hospital*, 56.
248. Ibid. 89, 185–6; John Brownlow, *The History and Objects of the Foundling Hospital*, 4th edn (1881), 73.
249. Nichols and Wray, *History of the Foundling Hospital*, 106–7.

250. Ibid. 94; Tanya Evans, *'Unfortunate Objects': Lone Mothers in Eighteenth-Century London* (2005), 94–5.
251. Brownlow, *Foundling Hospital*, 75; Nichols and Wray, *History of the Foundling Hospital*, 42.
252. LMA, A/FH/A/8/1/1/17, Petitions for admission to the London Foundling Hospital, 1768–99, Mary Gance, 17 Feb. 1790.
253. Lewis Namier and John Brooke (eds), *The House of Commons, 1754–1790*, 3 vols (1964), vol. 3, pp. 146–7.
254. Carolyn Steedman, 'Lord Mansfield's Women', *Past and Present*, 176 (2002), 105–43, esp. 128.
255. Ruth McClure, *Coram's Children: The London Foundling Hospital in the Eighteenth Century* (1981), 205–18.
256. Cf. Ernest Caulfield, *The Infant Welfare Movement in the Eighteenth Century* (New York, 1931); Stone, *Family, Sex and Marriage*, 475.
257. Nichols and Wray, *History of the Foundling Hospital*, 31, 39.
258. [Zinzano], *Servant's Calling*, 19.
259. [Maddox], *Wisdom and Duty of Preserving Destitute Infants*, 6–7.
260. *Regulations for Managing the Hospital for the Maintenance and Education of Exposed and Deserted Children* (1757), 50.
261. Ibid. 40.
262. LMA, A/FH/A/3/1/3, General Court: rough minutes, 1765–91, 8 May 1765.
263. Nichols and Wray, *History of the Foundling Hospital*, 184.
264. Ibid. 187; Rose, 'Social Policy and Business', 11.
265. LMA, A/FH/A/12/1/19/1, Petitions to take apprentices, 1771.
266. McClure, *Coram's Children*, 131–2.
267. Nichols and Wray, *History of the Foundling Hospital*, 191.
268. [Jonas Hanway], *A Candid Historical Account of the Hospital for the Reception of Exposed and Deserted Young Children* (1759), 59.
269. Ibid. 105–6.
270. Ibid. 21–2.
271. Ibid. 13, 34; [Jonas Hanway], *Serious Considerations on the Salutary Design of the Act of Parliament for a Regular, Uniform Register of the Parish Poor* (1762), 14.
272. [Hanway], *Candid Historical Account*, 39, 52.
273. Sydney Smith quoted in Brownlow, *Foundling Hospital*, 65.
274. Owen, *English Philanthropy*, 119–21.
275. Andrew, *Philanthropy and Police*, 181–6, quotation on 183.
276. David Rollison, 'Exploding England: The Dialectics of Mobility and Settlement in Early Modern England', *Social History*, 24 (1999), 1–16.
277. [Robert Johnson], *The New Life of Virginia* (1612), in *American Colonial Tracts Monthly* (Rochester, NY, 1897), 19.
278. Richard Hakluyt, *Discourse on Western Planting* (1584), ed. David B. Quinn and Alison M. Quinn, Hakluyt Society, Extra Ser., vol. 45 (1993), 120. I am grateful to Ruth Wallis Herndon for this quotation and comments on this section generally.
279. John Smith, *A Description of New England* (1616), in *American Colonial Tracts Monthly* (Rochester, NY, 1898), 25–7.
280. Robert C. Johnson, 'The Transportation of Vagrant Children from London to Virginia, 1618–1622', in Howard S. Reinmuth (ed.), *Early Stuart Studies: Essays in Honor of David Harris Willson* (Minneapolis, 1970), 137–51, quotation on 139.

281. Alexander Brown, *The First Republic in America* (Boston, 1908), 353.
282. *The Records of the Virginia Company*, ed. Susan Myra Kingsbury, 4 vols (Washington, 1906–35), vol. 1, p. 269; see also, David R. Ransome, 'Wives for Virginia, 1621', *William and Mary Quarterly*, 3rd ser., 48 (1991), 3–18.
283. Ransome, 'Wives for Virginia', 6; see also, Kathleen M. Brown, 'Women in Early Jamestown', Virtual Jamestown, http://www.virtualjamestown.org/essays/brown_essay.html, accessed 26 Feb. 07.
284. Johnson, 'Transportation of Vagrant Children', 140–4.
285. *Records of the Virginia Company*, ed. Kingsbury, vol. 1, p. 489.
286. Johnson, 'Transportation of Vagrant Children', 147.
287. Charles Edward Banks, *The Planters of the Commonwealth ... 1620–1640* (Baltimore, 1967), 31.
288. Smith, *Colonists in Bondage*, 150–1.
289. Peter Wilson Coldham, 'The "Spiriting" of London Children to Virginia', *The Virginia Magazine of History and Biography*, Richmond, Virginia Historical Soc., vol. 83, July (1975), 280–7, quotation on 281.
290. *Acts and Ordinances of the Interregnum, 1642–1660*, ed. C. H. Firth and R. S. Rait, (1911), vol. 1, 681–2.
291. LMA, MJ/SP/1162 (56) and (117), Middlesex sessions of the peace, 1657.
292. Coldham, 'London Children to Virginia', 287.
293. *Calendar State Papers Colonial 1661–1668: America and West Indies*, ed. W. N. Sainsbury, (1880), 555; see also 220–1.
294. Arlette Farge and Jacques Revel, *The Vanishing Children of Paris: Rumour and Politics before the French Revolution*, trans. C. Miéville (Cambridge, MA, 1991), esp. 104.
295. Crawford, 'Blood and Paternity', in Crawford, *Blood, Bodies, and Families*, 121–3.
296. *Memoirs of Laetitia Pilkington*, ed. A. C. Ellis, 2 vols, (Athens, GA, 1994–7), vol. 1, p. 175.
297. GL, MS 20484, Clayton and Morris, Papers 1698–1702, Account of the Workhouse 5 Nov. 1702; *Queries and answers relating to the transportation of vagrants to Virginia ...* [1700].
298. Abbot Emerson Smith, *Colonists in Bondage: White Servitude and Convict Labour in America* (Chapel Hill, 1947); see also, Alan Atkinson, 'The Free-born Englishman Transported: Convict Rights as a Measure of Eighteenth-Century Empire', *Past and Present*, 144 (1994), 88–115.
299. John H. Elliott, 'Introduction', in Nicholas Canny and Anthony Pagden (eds), *Colonial Identity in the Atlantic World, 1500–1800* (Princeton, 1987), 4–7.
300. Richard Middleton, *Colonial America: A History, 1607–1760* (Cambridge, MA, 1992), 25.
301. Bernard W. Sheehan, *Savagism and Civility: Indians and Englishmen in Colonial Virginia* (Cambridge, 1980), 126–7.
302. Ibid. 181.
303. Ibid. 117.
304. Quoted in Ibid. 126.
305. [Robert Johnson], *The New Life of Virginia* (1612), in *American Colonial Tracts Monthly* (Rochester, NY, 1897), 28.
306. Middleton, *Colonial America*, 36; James Axtell, *After Columbus: Essays in the Ethnohistory of Colonial North America* (New York, 1988), 210–11.

307. H. C. Porter, *The Inconstant Savage: England and the North American Indian 1500–1660* (1979), 434–40, quotation on 439.

308. Sheehan, *Savagism and Civility*, 181.

309. Eulogy quoted by Bowers, *Politics of Motherhood*, 13.

310. Ann Cotton, *An Account of our Late Troubles in Virginia written in (1676)*, in *American Colonial Tracts Monthly* (Rochester, NY, 1898), 5–6; Sheehan, *Savagism and Civility*, 87.

311. Ibid. 180–2.

312. Carole Shammas, 'Anglo-American Household Government in Comparative Perspective', *William and Mary Quarterly*, 3rd ser., 52 (1995), 109–20.

313. Ibid. 113–14.

314. Ruth Wallis Herndon, 'Racialisation and feminization of poverty in early America: Indian women as "the poor of the town" in eighteenth-century Rhode Island', in Martin Daunton and Rick Halpern (eds), *Empire and Others: British Encounters with Indigenous Peoples 1600–1850* (Philadelphia, 1999), 188; Ruth Wallis Herndon, ' "Who Died an Expence to This Town": Poor Relief in Eighteenth-Century Rhode Island', in Billy G. Smith (ed.), *Down and Out in Early America* (Philadelphia, 2003), 137.

315. Herndon, 'Poor Relief', 146–7; Ruth Wallis Herndon and Ella Wilcox Sekatua, 'Colonizing the Children: Indian Youngsters in Servitude in Early Rhode Island', in Colin G. Calloway and Neil Salisbury (eds), *Reinterpreting New England Indian History and the Colonial Experience* (Boston, 2003), 56–70.

316. Linda Colley, *Britons: Forging the Nation 1707–1837* (1992), 371–2.

317. Shammas, 'Anglo-American Household Government', 122.

318. John Murray and Ruth Wallis Herndon, 'Markets for Children in Early America: A Political Economy of Pauper Apprenticeship', *Journal of Economic History*, 62 (2002), 356–82; Ruth Wallis Herndon and John E. Murray, ' "A Proper and Instructive Education": Raising Children in Pauper Apprenticeship', in Herndon and Murray (eds), *Children Bound to Labour*.

319. *The Countryman's Lamentation* (1762), quoted in Herndon and Murray, 'Raising Children in Pauper Apprenticeship'.

320. Edward Terry, *A Voyage to East-India*, 2nd edn (1655), 20–1. Thanks to Joan Thirsk for this reference.

321. *Seventeenth-Century Economic Documents*, ed. Joan Thirsk and J. P. Cooper (Oxford, 1972), 511–12.

322. *Australian Dictionary of Biography*, vol. 1, *1788–1850* (Melbourne, 1966).

323. Patricia Crawford, ' "Civic Fathers" and Children: Continuities from Elizabethan England to the Australian Colonies', *History Australia*, 5 (2008), 04.9.

324. Ruth Frankenberg, *White Women, Race Matters: The Social Construction of Whiteness* (1993).

325. Quoted in Folarin Shyllon, *Black People in Britain, 1555–1833* (Oxford, 1977), 94.

326. Philip D. Morgan, 'Encounters between British and "Indigenous" Peoples, c. 1500–1800', in Daunton and Halpern (eds), *Empire and Others*, 44–5.

327. [Edward Littleton], *Groans of the Plantations . . . Island of Barbados* (1689), sigs. [B4], [C2v].

328. John White, *The Planters Plea . . . 1630*, in *American Colonial Tracts Monthly* (Rochester, NY, 1898), 1–2.

329. Langford, *Polite and Commercial People*, 255; Colley, *Britons*, 255.

330. Slack, *Poverty and Policy*, 205.

331. Hindle, *On the Parish?*, 447, 453.

6. CONCLUDING REFLECTIONS

1. Carole Shammas, 'Response', *William and Mary Quarterly*, 3rd ser., 52 (1995), 164–5.
2. University of Nottingham, Department of Manuscripts and Special Collections, Wentworth papers, CI C 721, Thomas, Viscount Wentworth to Sir Gervase Clifton, 8 Sept. 1638.
3. Sara Mendelson and Patricia Crawford, *Women in Early Modern England, 1550–1720* (Oxford, 1998), 367–8.
4. Helen Berry and Elizabeth Foyster, 'Childless Men in Early Modern England', in Helen Berry and Elizabeth Foyster (eds), *The Family in Early Modern England* (Cambridge, 2007), 158–83.
5. Keith Thomas, 'Puritans and Adultery: The Act of 1650 Reconsidered', in Donald Pennington and Keith Thomas (eds), *Puritans and Revolutionaries: Essays in Seventeenth-Century History Presented to Christopher Hill* (Oxford, 1978), 262; David M. Turner, *Fashioning Adultery: Gender, Sex and Civility in England, 1660–1740* (Cambridge, 2002), 83–115.
6. Turner, *Fashioning Adultery*, 83.
7. *The Genuine Trial of Charles Drew, for the Murder of his own Father* (1740), 36–7.
8. Patricia Crawford, 'Introduction', in Patricia Crawford, *Blood, Bodies and Families in Early Modern England* (2004), 2.
9. Richard Wall, 'Inferring Differential Neglect of Females from Mortality Data', *Annales de Démographie Historique* (1981), 119–40.
10. Mendelson and Crawford, *Women in Early Modern England*, 380–429.
11. John Walter, 'Faces in the Crowd: Gender and Age in the Early Modern English Crowd', in Berry and Foyster (eds), *Family*, 112.
12. E. P. Thompson, 'The Moral Economy of the English Crowd in the Eighteenth Century', *Past and Present*, 50 (1971), 115–18.
13. Walter, 'Faces in the Crowd', in Berry and Foyster (eds), *Family*, 112–3.
14. Anna Clark, *Women's Silence: Men's Violence: Sexual Assault in England, 1770–1845* (1987), 48.
15. *OBP*, t17220907–8, Matthias Brinsden (killing: murder, guilty).
16. Felicity Heal and Clive Holmes, *The Gentry in England and Wales 1500–1700* (1994), 48.
17. Walter, 'Faces in the Crowd', in Berry and Foyster (eds), *Family*, 99–100.
18. For the middling sort, see Christopher Brooks, 'Apprenticeship, Social Mobility and the Middling Sort, 1550–1800', in Jonathan Barry and Christopher Brooks (eds), *The Middling Sort of People: Culture, Society and Politics in England, 1550–1800* (Basingstoke, 1994), 52–83.
19. Steve Hindle, *On the Parish? The Micro-Politics of Poor Relief in Rural England c. 1550–1750* (Oxford, 2004), 281–2.
20. James Knight, *A Sermon...At the Anniversary Meeting of the Children Educated in the Charity School* (1720), 23–4.
21. John R. Gillis, *For Better, For Worse: British Marriages, 1600 to the Present* (Oxford, 1985), 114.
22. Diana O'Hara, *Courtship and Constraint: Rethinking the Making of Marriage in Tudor England* (Manchester, 2000), 225–6.
23. Margaret Spufford, 'Who Made a Will in Village Society?', in Margaret Spufford, *Figures in the Landscape: Rural Society in England, 1500–1700* (Aldershot, 2001), 155–9.

24. Cf. Rosemary O'Day, *Women's Agency in Early Modern Britain and the American Colonies* (Harlow, 2007), 179.

25. Old Bailey case, 1736, quoted by Joanne McEwan, 'Negotiating Support: Crime and Women's Networks in London and Middlesex, c. 1730–1820' (PhD thesis, University of Western Australia, 2009), 212.

26. Heal and Holmes, *The Gentry in England*, 38–47.

27. Lawrence Stone, *Road to Divorce: England 1530–1987* (Oxford, 1990), 122–4; R. B. Outhwaite, *Clandestine Marriage in England, 1500–1850* (1995), 75–97.

28. *Parliamentary History of England*, vol. 15 (1813), 82.

29. Amy Louise Erickson, *Women and Property in Early Modern England* (1993), 85; Peter Rushton, 'Property, Power and Family Networks: The Problem of Disputed Marriage in Early Modern England', *Journal of Family History*, 11 (1986), 210.

30. Margaret Spufford, *Contrasting Communities: English Villagers in the Sixteenth and Seventeenth Centuries* (Cambridge, 1974), 142.

31. Alan Macfarlane, *Marriage and Love in England: Modes of Reproduction 1300–1840* (Oxford, 1986), 264; Erickson, *Women and Property*, 88.

32. Erickson, *Women and Property*, 86.

33. Martin Ingram, 'Spousals Litigation in the English Ecclesiastical Courts c. 1350–c. 1640', in R. B. Outhwaite (ed.), *Marriage and Society: Studies in the Social History of Marriage* (1981), 35–7, 44–5; Rushton, 'Property, Power and Family Networks', 205–19; O'Hara, *Courtship and Constraint*, 237–8.

34. Erickson, *Women and Property*, 93.

35. Benjamin Coole, *Miscellanies: ... Being the Advice of a Father to his Children* (1712), sig. [a3v].

36. Louis B. Wright (ed.), *Advice to A Son*, (Ithaca 1962), p. xv.

37. John Locke, *Two Treatises*, Bk. II. §65 (1924 edn), 147–9.

38. For an excellent brief discussion of the dynamics of gentry families, see Heal and Holmes, *The Gentry in England*, 48–96.

39. Rachel Weil, *Political Passions: Gender, the Family and Political Argument in England 1680–1714* (Manchester, 1999), 25; Linda Pollock, 'Rethinking Patriarchy and the Family in Seventeenth-Century England', *Journal of Family History*, 23 (1998), 3–27.

40. Jonathan Dewald, 'Deadly Parents: Family and Aristocratic Culture in Early Modern France', in Barbara B. Diefendorf and Carla Hesse (eds), *Culture and Identity in Early Modern Europe 1500–1800: Essays in Honor of Natalie Zemon Davis* (Ann Arbor, 1993), 223–36, esp. 233–4.

41. Cf. Sara Ruddick, *Maternal Thinking: Towards a Politics of Peace* (Boston, 1995), 28–57.

42. James L. Axtell (ed.), *The Educational Writings of John Locke: A Critical Edition* (Cambridge, 1968), 201–3; H. R. F. Bourne, *The Life of John Locke*, 2 vols (1876), vol. 1, p. 80.

43. Thomas Thompson, *An Encouragement Early to Seek the Lord ...* (1708), 4.

44. Lawrence Stone, *The Family, Sex, and Marriage in England, 1500–1800* (1977); Ralph Houlbrooke, *The English Family 1450–1700* (1984), 253–4 and *passim*.

45. John R. Gillis, *A World of their Own Making: Myth, Ritual, and the Quest for Family Values* (Cambridge, MA, 1997), 182.

46. William Blackstone, *Commentaries on the Laws of England*, 4 vols, 1st edn (Oxford, 1765–9), vol. 1, pp. 434–5.

47. Somerset RO, DD/SE/45/1, Petitions to Bruton Hospital, no. 51. For a full analysis of this archive, see Hindle, *On the Parish?*, 155–64.

48. Somerset RO, DD/SE/45/1, Petitions to Bruton Hospital, no. 37.

49. Somerset RO, DD/SE/45/1, Petitions to Bruton Hospital, no. 73.

50. GL, MS 11280/6, St Dionis Backchurch, Churchwardens' vouchers and miscellaneous papers, 1766–72.

51. Bodl, MS Rawlinson B431, A Justice's Notebook, fo. 34.

52. Somerset RO, DD/SE/45/1, Petitions to Bruton Hospital, no. 59.

53. Somerset RO, DD/SE/45/1, Petitions to Bruton Hospital, no. 1.

54. GL, MS 1204/1, St Katherine Cree, Workhouse Committee: minute book, 1738–95, 4.

55. *The Autobiography of Francis Place 1771–1854*, ed. Mary Thale (Cambridge, 1972), 127–8.

56. Ibid. 73.

57. Catharine Capp, *Observations on Charity Schools, female friendly societies, and other subjects connected with the views of the Ladies Committee* (York, 1805), 2–3.

58. *OBP*, t17661217–54, James Field (killing: infanticide, not guilty).

59. John Newson and Elizabeth Newson, *Seven Years Old in the Home Environment* (1976), 398–407.

60. Laura Gowing, *Common Bodies: Women, Touch and Power in Seventeenth-Century England* (2003), 195.

61. *OBP*, t17900424–14, Thomas Hewett Masters (killing: murder, guilty).

62. Barbara H. Rosenwein, 'Worrying about Emotions in History', *American Historical Review*, 107 (2002), 821–45.

63. GL, MS 6888, St Helen Bishopsgate, Petitions for poor relief and sundry papers relating to the workhouse, 1741–5, admitted 1744.

64. GL, MS 4655/2, Worshipful Company of Weavers, Court Minute Book, 20 June 1653, fo. 21.

65. Knibb was acquitted because the midwives were not convinced there had been penetration; *OBP*, t17501205–40, Richard Knibb (sexual offences: rape, not guilty).

66. K. D. M. Snell, *Annals of the Labouring Poor: Social Change and Agrarian England 1660–1900* (Cambridge, 1985), 368.

67. Richard M. Smith, 'Ageing and Well-being in Early Modern England: Pension Trends and Gender Preferences under the English Old Poor Law c. 1650–1800', in Paul Johnson and Pat Thane (eds), *Old Age from Antiquity to Post-Modernity* (1998), 65–6, 70, 91.

68. Susannah Ottaway, 'Providing for the Elderly in Eighteenth-Century England', *Continuity and Change*, 13 (1998), 393.

69. Margaret Pelling, 'Old Age, Poverty, and Disability in Early Modern Norwich', in Margaret Pelling and Richard M. Smith (eds), *Life, Death, and the Elderly: Historical Perspectives* (1991), 88.

70. Spufford, *Contrasting Communities*, 112, 105.

71. Smith, 'Ageing and Well-being', in Johnson and Thane (eds), *Old Age from Antiquity to Post-Modernity*, 65.

72. Susannah R. Ottaway, *The Decline of Life: Old Age in Eighteenth-Century England* (Cambridge, 2004), 2–4.

73. Pat Thane, 'The family lives of old people', in Johnson and Thane (eds), *Old Age from Antiquity to Post-Modernity*, 180–210.

74. Somerset RO, Q/SR/114, fo. 49.
75. LMA, A/FH/A/8/1/1/3, Petitions for admission to the London Foundling Hospital, 1772, Elizabeth Brooks, 30 Dec. 1772.
76. *OBP*, t17850914-185, Mary Graham (deception: perjury, guilty).
77. *The Book of Examinations and Depositions Before the Mayor and Justices of Southampton 1648–1663*, ed. Sheila D. Thomson, Southampton Rec. Soc., vol. 37 (1994), 28.
78. LMA, A/FH/A/8/1/1/2, Petitions for admission, 1770–1.
79. LMA, A/FH/A/8/1/1/3, Petitions for admission, 1772, Elizabeth Brooks, 30 Dec. 1772.
80. George Armstrong, *An Account of the Diseases Most Incident to Children* (1777), 197–8.
81. Sarah Trimmer, *The Oeconomy of Charity: Or, an Address to Ladies concerning Sunday Schools* (1787), 95.
82. 'Tis not otherwise' [1630], in *A Pepysian Garland: Black-letter Broadside Ballads of the years 1595–1639* (1939), ed. Hyder E. Rollins (Cambridge, MA, 1971), 356.
83. David Levine and Keith Wrightson, *The Making of an Industrial Society: Whickham 1560–1765* (Oxford, 1991), 321.
84. Westminster Muniment Room, Coroners' Inquests, 1760 to December 1771, 15 May 1770, St John the Evangelist (compiled by Tim Hitchcock).
85. *John Clare's Autobiographical Writings*, ed. Eric Robinson (Oxford, 1983), 7.
86. *Autobiography of Francis Place*, ed. Thale, 59.
87. Garthine Walker, 'Just Stories: Telling Tales of Infant Death in Early Modern England', in Margaret Mikesell and Adele Seeff (eds), *Culture and Change: Attending to Early Modern Women* (Newark, NJ, 2003), 98–115.
88. Ibid. 105–11.
89. *Women's Worlds in Seventeenth-Century England: A Sourcebook*, ed. Patricia Crawford and Laura Gowing (2000), 281–4; Laura Gowing, 'The Haunting of Susan Lay: Servants and Mistresses in Seventeenth-Century England', *Gender and History*, 14 (2002), 183–201.
90. Stuart Clark, 'French Historians and Early Modern Popular Culture', *Past and Present*, 100 (1983), 69–70.
91. Levine and Wrightson, *Making of an Industrial Society*, 322.
92. *OBP*, t17670115-24, John Williamson (killing: murder, guilty).
93. *OBP*, t17431012-20, Elizabeth Shudrick (killing: infanticide, not guilty).
94. *OBP*, oa17520113, The Ordinary of Newgate's Account, Rachel Beacham.

SELECT BIBLIOGRAPHY

Place of publication London, unless otherwise stated.

PRIMARY SOURCES

MANUSCRIPTS

Bodleian Library, Oxford

MS Rawlinson B431, *A Justice's Notebook.*

Borthwick Institute

PR S. H. 9., Maintenance Orders and Bonds, 1716–1800.

Cambridge University Library

SPCK, CR1/6, Abstract Letter book, 1715–16.
SPCK, CR1/8, Abstract Letter book, 1717–18.
SPCK, CS2/3, Henry Newman's draft letter book out.
SPCK, D2/11, Abstract letter book, 1715–16.

Devon Record Office

Chanter 878, 1679.

Essex Record Office

Calendar of Records, 17.
Q/SR, Sessions rolls, 1589–1624.

Guildhall Library, Manuscripts, London

MS 613/1, St Augustine Watling Street, Vestry and precinct minute books (including some minutes of the joint vestry meetings of the united parishes of St Augustine Watling Street and St Faith under St Paul), 1744–81.

MS 1204/1, St Katherine Cree, Workhouse Committee: minute book, 1738–95.

MSS 2676/1–18, St Botolph Aldgate, Pauper examinations, 1742–90.

MS 2985, St Dunstan in the West, Minute book of meetings of the guardians of the parish poor children, 1789–1806.

MS 3242/1, St Sepulchre Holborn, Minutes of the Guardians of the Poor, 1767–1806.

MS 4655/2, Worshipful Company of Weavers, Court Minute Book, 1653–4.

MS 5841, Worshipful Company of Brewers, James Hickson's Charity (Ordinances for the Free School 1687), 1689–1751.

MS 6888, St Helen Bishopsgate, Petitions for poor relief and sundry papers relating to the workhouse, 1741–5.

MS 7674, St Alban Wood Street, Churchwardens and overseers' accounts, 1627–75.

MS 9083, St Sepulchre Holborn, Middlesex Division: Workhouse Committee Minutes and Orders, 1728–48.

MS 9192/1, St Ann Blackfriars, Peter Joye's Charity School: Trustees' minute book, 1717–44.

MS 10026/1, St Botolph Aldgate, Bonds of indemnity concerning parish poor children, 1587–1741.

MS 10852, St Benet Paul's Wharf, Churchwardens' papers, 1672–1720.

MS 11280/6, St Dionis Backchurch, Churchwardens' vouchers and miscellaneous papers, 1766–72.

MS 12806/2–11, Christ's Hospital Court Minutes, 1567–1756.

MS 12818A, Christ's Hospital Presentation Papers, 1674–1687.

MS 12828/3, Christ's Hospital Court Letter Book, 1684–1703.

MS 18977, All Hallows Lombard Street, Bonds of indemnity for the maintenance of parish poor children bound as apprentices, 1668–1701.

MS 20484, Clayton and Morris, Papers concerning poor relief in the City of London, and the Corporation for the Poor of the City of London and its workhouse in Bishopsgate Street, 1698–1702.

Lambeth Palace Library

Vicar General archive, visitation returns for the diocese of Canterbury, 1786–1935.

London Metropolitan Archives

A/FH/A/3/1/3, General Court: rough minutes, 1765–91.

A/FH/A/6/1/11, Foundling Hospital Correspondence, 1758.

A/FH/A/8/1/1–24, Petitions for admission to the London Foundling Hospital, 1768–99.

A/FH/A/9/1/1, [Foundling Hospital] Billet book, 1741.

A/FH/A/11/2/1–15, Petitions for return of children, 1759–89.

A/FH/A/12/1/2–19/1, Petitions to take apprentices, 1761–71.

A/FH/M/01/005, Documents and books collected by J. Brownlow, 1759.

MJ/SP/1162–1165, Middlesex Sessions of the Peace, 1657.

P91/LEN/1200, St Leonard Shoreditch, Settlement and Bastardy examinations, 1758–64.

Norfolk Record Office

Mayor's court book, 1624–34.

Coroners' inquests, 1691–99.

North Yorkshire Record Office

North Allerton, typed list QSB 1696.

Oxfordshire Record Office

MS Archidiaconal papers, Oxon c. 118 c. 1616–20.

Quarter sessions, Minutes Books, QSM/l/1, 1687–1714.

Shropshire Record Office

QS/2/8, Salop sessions, 1700.

P246/L/1, 1680.

Somerset Record Office

DD/SE/45/1, Petitions to Bruton Hospital.

Q/SR/114, Sessions roll, 1670.

University of Nottingham

Department of Manuscripts and Special Collections.

Clifton Collection.
Wentworth Papers.

Westminster Archives Centre

MS B1168-B1193, St Clement Danes, examinations.
Parish records: St Paul Covent Garden, Guardians and Overseers of Infant Poor Minutes, 1783–95.

Westminster Muniment Room

Coroner's Inquests, 1760–71 (compiled by Tim Hitchcock).

ON-LINE RESOURCES

Seax – Essex Archives Online, from the Essex Record Office, http://seax.essexcc.gov.uk
Proceedings of the Old Bailey, 1674–1913, http://www.oldbaileyonline.org
Oxford English Dictionary Online, http://dictionary.oed.com
Early English Books Online, http://eebo.chadwyck.com/home
Eighteenth Century Collections Online, http://galenet.galegroup.com/
Virtual Jamestown, http://www.virtualjamestown.org/essays/introduction.html

PRINTED PRIMARY SOURCES

A., C., *Candid Remarks on Mr Hanway's Candid Historical Account of the Foundling Hospital* (1760).
Abstract of the orders made by the Court of Quarter Sessions for Shropshire, 1638–1708, ed. R. Lloyd Kenyon (Shrewsbury, 1901).
The Accomplish'd Housewife; or the Gentlewoman's Companion (1745).
Accounts of the Churchwardens of the Paryshe of St Christophers' in London 1572 to 1662, ed. Edwin Freshfield (1885).
Alcock, Thomas, *Observations on the Defects of the Poor Laws* (Oxford, 1752).
An Account of the General Nursery, or Colledg of Infants (1686).
An Account of Marriage (1672) [Bodl, MS Wood 750 (2)].
An Account of Several Work Houses for Employing and Maintaining the Poor (1725).
Armstrong, George, *An Account of the Diseases Most Incident to Children* (1777).
—— *An Essay on the Diseases Most Fatal to Infants*, 2nd edn (1771).
The Assembly Books of Southampton, ed. J. W. Horrocks, 4 vols, Southampton Rec. Soc., vols. 19, 21, 24, 25 (1917–25).
Bacon, *The Papers of Nathaniel Bacon of Stiffkey*, ed. V. Morgan, J. Key, and B. Taylor, Norfolk Rec. Soc., vol. 64 (2000).
Bailey, William, *A Treatise on the better Employment ... of the Poor in Workhouses* (1758).
The 'Bawdy Court' of Banbury: The Act Book of the Peculiar Court of Banbury, Oxfordshire and Northamptonshire 1625–1638, ed. R. K. Gilkes, Banbury Historical Soc., vol. 26 (1997).
Baxter, Richard, *The Poor Man's Family Book* (1674).
—— *Reliquæ Baxterianæ* (1696).
The Reverend Richard Baxter's Last Treatise: The Poor Husbandman's Advocate (1691), ed. F. J. Powicke (Manchester, 1926).
Bettey, J.H., (ed.), *The Casebook of Sir Francis Ashley JP, Recorder of Dorchester 1614–1635*, Dorset Rec. Soc, Vol. 7 (1981).
B[everley], R[obert], *The History and Present State of Virginia*, 4 vols (1705).

Blackstone, William, *Commentaries on the Laws of England*, 4 vols, 1st edn (Oxford, 1765–9); 4th edn (Dublin, 1771); 5th edn (Oxford, 1773).

Books of Examinations and Depositions 1570–1594, ed. Gertrude H. Hamilton, Southampton Rec. Soc., vol. 9 (1914).

The Book of Examinations and Depositions Before the Mayor and Justices of Southampton 1648–1663, ed. Sheila D. Thomson, Southampton Rec. Soc., vol. 37 (1994).

Borough Session Papers 1653–1688, Portsmouth Record Series, ed. Arthur J. Willis and Margaret J. Hoad (Chichester, 1971).

Bott, E[dmund], *A Collection of the Decisions of the Court of King's Bench upon the Poor's Laws*, [1771].

Bourne, H. R. Fox, *The life of John Locke* (1876).

Bromley, Robert, *A Sermon preached in the Chapel of the Hospital for the Maintenance and Education of Exposed and Deserted Children* (1770).

Buchan, William, *Domestic Medicine; Or, the Family Physician* (Edinburgh, 1769).

Bunyan, John, *Grace Abounding to the Chief of Sinners* (1928 edn).

Burgh, James, *Political Disquisitions*, 3 vols (1774–5).

Burn, Richard, *The Justice of the Peace, and Parish Officer*, 2 vols (1755); 14th edn (1780).

—— *The History of the Poor Laws* (1764).

Burrow, James, *A Series of Decisions of the Court of King's Bench upon Settlement Cases*, 2 vols (1768).

A Calendar of Southampton Apprenticeship Register, 1609–1740, ed. Arthur J. Willis and A. L. Merson, Southampton Records Ser., vol. 12 (1968).

Calendar of Bradford-on-Avon Settlement Examinations and Removal Orders, 1725–98, ed. Phyllis Hembry, Wiltshire Rec. Soc., vol. 46 (1990).

Cappe, Catharine, *An Account of Two Charity Schools for the Education of Girls* (York, 1800).

—— *Observations on Charity Schools, female friendly societies, and other subjects connected with the views of the Ladies Committee* (York, 1805).

[Cary, John], *An Account of the Proceedings of the Corporation of Bristol* (1700).

Cellier, Elizabeth, *A Scheme for the Foundation of a Royal Hospital, Harleian Miscellany*, vol. 4 (1744).

Chelsea Settlement and Bastardy Examinations 1733–1766, ed. Tim Hitchcock and John Black, London Rec. Soc., vol. 33 (1999).

Christ's Hospital Admissions, etc, ed. G. A. T. Allan (1937).

Churchwardens' Presentments, ed. Hilda Johnstone, Sussex Rec. Soc., vol. 49 (1948).

Cobbet, Thomas, *A Fruitfull and Useful Discourse touching the honour due from children to parents, and the duty of parents towards their children* (1656).

Clare, *John Clare's Autobiographical Writings*, ed. Eric Robinson (Oxford, 1983).

Cooke, Richard, *A White Sheete, or A Warning for Whoremongers. A Sermon* (1629).

Correspondence of the Foundling Hospital Inspectors in Berkshire, 1757–1768, ed. Gillian Clark, Berkshire Rec. Soc., vol. 1 (1994).

County of Buckingham: Calendar to the Sessions Records, 4 vols, 1678–1724, ed. William Le Hardy and Geoffrey L. Reckitt (Aylesbury, 1933–39).

Dalton, Michael, *The Countrey Justice* (1618); rev. edn (1635); rev. edn (1666); rev. edn (1705); facs. 1618 edn (Amsterdam, 1975).

Dawes, William, *The Excellency of the Charity-Schools* (1713).

[Defoe, Daniel], *The Just Complaint of the Poor Weavers* (1729).

—— *A Tour through the Whole Island of Great Britain* (1724–7), ed. Pat Rogers, 3 vols (1983).

[Dunning, Richard], *Bread for the Poor* (Exeter, 1698).

Early Essex Town Meetings: Braintree, 1619–1636: Finchingfield, 1626–36, ed. F. G. Emmison (1970).

An Ease for Overseers of the Poore (Cambridge, 1601).

Eden, Sir Frederick Morton, *The State of the Poor*, 3 vols (1797).

English Family Life, 1576–1716: An Anthology from Diaries, ed. Ralph Houlbrooke (Oxford, 1988).

Essex Pauper Letters 1731–1837, ed. Thomas Sokoll (Oxford, 2001).

Essex Quarter Sessions Order Book 1652–1661, ed. D. H. Allen (Chelmsford, 1974).

F[irman], T[homas], *Some Proposals for the Imploying of the Poor*, (1678; reprinted 1681).

Firth, C. S. and Rait, R. S. (eds), *Acts and Ordinances of the Interregnum, 1642–1660*, 2 vols (1911).

A Full and Authentic Account of John Williamson, Who was executed in Moorfields (1767).

Gouge, William, *Of Domesticall Duties* (1622).

Gregory, John, *A Father's Legacy to His Daughter* (1774; fasc. edn New York, 1974).

Grey, A., *Debates of the House of Commons 1667–1694*, 10 vols (1769).

H[aines], R[ichard], *Proposals for Building in Every County a Working Almshouse* (1677).

—— *Provision for the Poor: Or, Reasons for the Erecting of a Working-Hospital in every County* (1678).

[Hanway, Jonas], *A Candid Historical Account of the Hospital for the Reception of Exposed and Deserted Young Children* (1759).

—— *An Earnest Appeal for Mercy to the Children of the Poor* (1766).

—— *Letters on the importance of the rising generation of the laboring part of our fellow-subjects*, 2 vols (1767), vol. 1.

—— *Serious Considerations on the Salutary Design of the Act of Parliament for a Regular, Uniform Register of the Parish Poor* (1762).

H[artlib], S[amuel], *London's Charity Inlarged, Stilling the Poor Orphans Cry* (1650).

Heywood, *Oliver Heywood's Life of John Angier of Denton*, ed. Ernest Acton, Chetham Soc., n.s., vol. 97 (1937).

Holles, Gervase, *Memorials of the Holles Family*, ed. A. Wood, Camden Soc., 3rd ser., vol. 55 (1937).

Holles, John, *Letters of John Holles 1587–1637*, ed. P. R. Seddon, 3 vols, Thoroton Soc., vols. 31, 35, 36 (1975–86).

Hoole, Charles, *A New Discovery of the Old Art of Teachinge School* (1661).

Howard-Drake, Jack (ed.), *Oxford Church Courts: Depositions 1581–1586* (Oxford, 1994).

Hutton, *Richard Hutton's Complaints Book: The Notebook of the Steward of the Quaker Workhouse at Clerkenwell, 1711–1737*, ed. Timothy V. Hitchcock, London Rec. Soc., vol. 24 (1987).

Jackson, *James Jackson's Diary, 1650 to 1683*, ed. Francis Grainger, *Transactions of the Cumberland & Westmoreland Antiquarian and Archaeological Soc.*, n.s., vol. 21 (1921).

Janeway, James, *A Token for Children* (1676).

[Johnson, Robert], *The New Life of Virginia*, printed in *American Colonial Tracts Monthly* (Rochester, NY, 1897).

Josselin, *The Diary of Ralph Josselin 1616–1683*, ed. Alan Macfarlane (1976).

Justice in Eighteenth-Century Hackney: The Justicing Notebook of Henry Norris and the Hackney Petty Session Book, ed. Ruth Paley, London Rec. Soc., vol. 28 (1991).

Keble, Joseph, *An Assistance to Justices of the Peace* (1683).

Kennett, White, *The Charity of Schools for Poor Children* (1706).

A Kentish Parson: Selections from the Private Papers of the Revd Joseph Price, Vicar of Brabourne, 1767–1786, ed. G. M. Price Ditchfield and Bryan Keith Lucas (Stroud, 1991).

Kentish Sources, vol. 4, *The Poor*, ed. Elizabeth Melling (Maidstone, 1964).

Lackington, *Memoirs of the Forty-Five First Years of the Life of James Lackington* (1794; fasc. edn New York, 1974).

Lee, Leonard, *A Remonstrance Humbly Presented to...Parliament touching the insupportable increase of the poore in this Land* (1645).

Ligon, Richard, *A True and Exact History of the Island of Barbados* (1657).

Liverpool Town Books 1649–1671, ed. Michael Power, Rec. Soc. of Lancashire and Cheshire, vol. 136 (1999).

Locke, *The Educational Writings of John Locke*, ed. James L. Axtell (Cambridge, 1968).

Maddox, Isaac, *Expediency of Preventative Wisdom: A Sermon Preached before... Lord-Mayor, the Aldermen, and Governors of the Several Hospitals* (1750).

—— *The Wisdom and Duty of Preserving Destitute Infants. A sermon preached at the chapel of the Hospital for Exposed and Deserted Young Children* (1753).

Marsh, Christopher et al., *Songs of the Seventeenth Century: The Ballads* (Belfast, 1994).

Maurice, 'The Revd Henry Maurice's Shropshire diary', ed. Janice V. Cox, *Shropshire Historical Documents: A Miscellany*, Shropshire Rec. Series, vol. 4 (2000), 31–64.

Mayett, *The Autobiography of Joseph Mayett of Quainton, 1783–1839*, ed. Ann Kussmaul, Buckinghamshire Rec. Soc., vol. 23 (1986).

Memoirs of Laetitia Pilkington, ed. A. C. Ellis, 2 vols (Athens, GA, 1994–7).

Mitcham Settlement Examinations, 1784–1814, ed. Blanche Berryman, Surrey Rec. Soc., vol. 27 (1973).

Moore, John, *The Crying Sin of England of Not Caring for the Poor* (1653).

Moss, Robert, *The Providential Division of Men into Rich and Poor and the respective duties thence arising* (1708).

Murthur Will Out, or, a True and Faithful Relation of an Horrible Murther committed thirty three years ago, by an Unnatural Mother..., 30 Nov. [1675].

Narratives of the Poor in Eighteenth-Century Britain, ed. Alysa Levene, 5 vols (2006).

Nolan, Michael, *A Treatise of the Laws for the Relief and Settlement of the Poor*, 2 vols (1805).

Norfolk Quarter Sessions Order Book 1650–1657, ed. D. E. Howell James, Norfolk Rec. Soc., vol. 26 (1955).

The Norwich Census of the Poor 1570, ed. J. F. Pound, Norfolk Rec. Soc., vol. 40 (1971).

Nottinghamshire County Records: notes and extracts from the Nottinghamshire county records of the 17th century, ed. H. Hampton Copnall (Nottingham, 1915).

The Office of Christian Parents (Cambridge, 1616).

A Pepysian Garland: Black-letter Broadside Ballads of the years 1595–1639 (1939), ed. Hyder E. Rollins (Cambridge, MA, 1971).

P[eters], H[ugh], *Good Work for a Good Magistrate* (1651).

Place, *The Autobiography of Francis Place (1771–1854)*, ed. Mary Thale (Cambridge, 1972).

Poor Law Records of Mid Sussex 1601–1835, ed. Norma Pilbeam and Ian Nelson, Sussex Rec. Soc., vol. 83 (1999).

Poverty in Early-Stuart Salisbury, ed. Paul Slack, Wiltshire Rec. Soc., vol. 31 (1975).

Precepts, or Directions for the well ordering and carriage of a mans life, 1636.

Prescott, *The Diary of Henry Prescott LLB, Deputy Registrar of Chester Diocese*, 3 vols, ed. John Addy, Rec. Soc. of Lancashire and Cheshire, vols 127, 132, 133 (1987–97).

Purvis, J. S. (ed.), *Tudor Parish Documents of the Diocese of York*, Cambridge, (1948).

Quarter Sessions Records for the County of Somerset, 4 vols, 1607–77, ed. E. H. Bates, Somerset Rec. Soc., vols 23, 24, 28, 34 (1907–19).

Ram, Robert, *The Countrymans Catechisme* (1655).

Records of the Borough of Nottingham, vol. 4, 1547–1625, ed. W. H. Stevenson, (1882).

Records of the Borough of Nottingham, vol. 5, 1625–1702, ed. W. T. Baker (1882).

The Records of the Virginia Company, ed. Susan Myra Kingsbury, 4 vols (Washington, DC, 1906–35).

Regulations for Managing the Hospital for the Maintenance and Education of Exposed and Deserted Children (1757).

Rogers, John, *A Treatise of Love* (1629).

The Roxburghe Ballads, ed. W. Chappell (vols 1–3) and J. Woodfall Ebsworth (vols 4–9), 9 vols (Hertford, 1872–99); fasc. edn (New York, 1966).

[Saxby, Mary], *Memoirs of a Female Vagrant written by herself*, Samuel Greatheed (preface) (1806).

Seventeenth-Century Economic Documents, ed. Joan Thirsk and J. P. Cooper (Oxford, 1972).

Sharp, Jane, *The Midwives Book* (1671).

Shaw, *The Family Records of Benjamin Shaw Mechanic of Dent, Dolphinholme and Preston, 1772–1841*, ed. Alan G. Crosby, Rec. Soc. of Lancashire and Cheshire, vol. 130 (1991).

Sheppard, William, *An Epitome of all the Common and Statute Laws of the Nation* (1656).

——— *A Sure Guide for his Majesties Justices of Peace* (1663).

Smalridge, George, *The Royal Benefactress: Or, the Great Charity of Educating Poor Children [sermon]* (1710).

Some Considerations on the Necessity and Usefulness of the Royal Charter establishing a Hospital (1740).

Some Thoughts concerning the Maintenance of the Poor (1700).

Somerset Assize Orders, ed. Thomas G. Barnes, Somerset Rec. Soc., vol. 65 (1959).

Stout, *The Autobiography of William Stout of Lancaster 1665–1752*, ed. J. D. Marshall (Manchester, 1967).

Sussex Coroners' Inquests 1603–1688, ed. R. F. Hunniset (Kew, 1998).

'This Little Commonwealth': Layston Parish Memorandum Book, 1607–c. 1650 & 1704–c. 1747, ed. Heather Falvey and Steve Hindle, Hertfordshire Rec. Publications, vol. 19 (2003).

Tilley, Morris Palmer, A Dictionary of the Proverbs in England in the Sixteenth and Seventeenth Centuries (Ann Arbor, 1950).

Townsend, Joseph, A Dissertation on the Poor (1786; reprinted Berkeley, 1971).

Trimmer, Sarah, The Oeconomy of Charity: Or, an Address to Ladies concerning Sunday Schools (1787).

Turner, The Diary of Thomas Turner 1745–1765, ed. David Vaisey (Oxford, 1984).

Tusser, Thomas, Five Hundred Points of Good Husbandrie, ed. Geoffrey Grigson (Oxford, 1984).

[Underwood, M.], A Treatise of the Disorders of Children; Adapted to Domestic Use, 3 vols (1797), vol. 3.

Varley (als Varlo), Charles, The unfortunate husbandman; an account of the life and travels of a real farmer in Ireland, Scotland, England and America (1768), Desmond Clarke (preface) (1964).

Wadsworth, Thomas, Last Warning to Secure Sinners, 1677.

Wakefield, Priscilla, Reflections on the Present Condition of the Female Sex (1798; facs. edn New York, 1974).

[Warwickshire] Quarter sessions order book, 8 vols, 1625–1696, ed. S. C. Ratcliffe and H. C. Johnson (Warwick, 1935–).

The Westminster City Fathers (The Burgess Court of Westminster) 1585–1901, ed. W. H. Manchee (1924).

Waterland, Daniel, Religious Education of Children: recommended in a sermon preach'd in the parish-church of St. Sepulchre, June the 6th, 1723 (1723).

Wilson, Thomas, The True Christian Method of Educating the Children of Both the Poor and Rich (1724).

Women's Worlds in Seventeenth-Century England: A Sourcebook, ed. Patricia Crawford and Laura Gowing (2000).

Woodforde, The Diary of a Country Parson: The Reverend James Woodforde, vol. 2, 1782–1787, ed. John Beresford (Oxford, 1926).

SECONDARY SOURCES

PUBLISHED WORKS

Adair, Richard, Courtship, Illegitimacy and Marriage in Early Modern England (Manchester, 1996).

Agren, Maria and Erickson, Amy Louise (eds), The Marital Economy in Scandinavia and Britain 1400–1900 (Aldershot, 2005).

Allison, K. J., 'An Elizabethan Village Census', Bulletin of the Institute of Historical Research, 36 (1963), 91–103.

Amussen, Susan Dwyer, '"Being Stirred to Much Unquietness": Violence and Domestic Violence in Early Modern England', Journal of Women's History, 6 (1994), 70–89.

—— 'Elizabeth I and Alice Balstone: Gender, Class, and the Exceptional Woman in Early Modern England', in Betty S. Travitsky and Adele F. Seeff (eds), Attending to Women in Early Modern England (Newark, NJ, 1994).

—— An Ordered Society: Gender and Class in Early Modern England (Oxford, 1988).

—— 'Punishment, Discipline, and Power: The Social Meanings of Violence in Early Modern England', *JBS*, 34 (1995), 1–34.

Andrew, Donna T., *Philanthropy and Police: London Charity in the Eighteenth Century* (Princeton, 1989).

—— '"To the Charitable and Humane": Appeals for Assistance in the Eighteenth Century London Press', in Cunningham and Innes (eds), *Charity, Philanthropy, and Reform*.

Archer, Ian W., *The Pursuit of Stability: Social Relations in Elizabethan London* (Cambridge, 1991).

Bailey, Joanne, *Unquiet Lives: Marriage and Marriage Breakdown in England, 1660–1800* (Cambridge, 2003).

Barker-Benfield, G. J., *The Culture of Sensibility: Sex and Society in Eighteenth-Century Britain* (Chicago, 1992).

Barron, Caroline M., *London in the Middle Ages: Government and People 1200–1500* (Oxford, 2004).

Barry, Jonathan and Brooks, Christopher (eds), *The Middling Sort of People: Culture, Society and Politics in England, 1550–1800* (Basingstoke, 1994).

Beattie, J. M., *Crime and the Courts in England 1660–1800* (Oxford, 1986).

Beier, A. L., *Masterless Men: The Vagrancy Problem in England 1560–1640* (1985).

—— 'Poverty and Progress in Early Modern England', in A. L. Beier, David Cannadine, and James M. Rosenheim (eds), *The First Modern Society: Essays in English History in Honour of Lawrence Stone* (Cambridge, 1989).

—— 'The Social Problems of an Elizabethan Country Town: Warwick, 1580–90', in Peter Clark (ed.), *Country Towns in Pre-industrial England* (Leicester, 1981).

Beier, A. L. and Finlay, Roger (eds), *The Making of the Metropolis: London 1500–1700* (1986).

Ben-Amos, Ilana Krausman, *Adolescence and Youth in Early Modern England* (New Haven, 1994).

—— 'Reciprocal Bonding: Parents and their Offspring in Early Modern England', *Journal of Family History*, 25 (2000), 291–312.

Bennett, Judith M., *History Matters: Patriarchy and the Challenge of Feminism* (Philadelphia, 2006).

Berg, Maxine, *The Age of Manufactures 1700–1820: Industry, Innovation and Work in Britain*, 2nd edn (1994).

—— (ed.), *Markets and Manufacture in Early Industrial Europe* (1991).

Berry, Helen, 'Community Sponsorship and the Hospital Patient in Late Eighteenth-Century England', in Horden and Smith (eds), *The Locus of Care*.

Berry, Helen and Foyster, Elizabeth (eds), *The Family in Early Modern England* (Cambridge, 2007).

Black, John, 'Illegitimacy, Sexual Relations and Location in Metropolitan London, 1735–85', in Hitchcock and Shore (eds), *The Streets of London*.

—— 'Who were the Putative Fathers of Illegitimate Children in London, 1740–1810?', in Levene, Nutt, and Williams (eds), *Illegitimacy in Britain*.

Blaikie, Andrew, *Illegitimacy, Sex, and Society: Northeast Scotland, 1750–1900* (Oxford, 1993).

Bonfield, Lloyd, Smith, Richard M., and Wrightson, Keith (eds), *The World We Have Gained: Histories of Population and Social Structure: Essays presented to Peter Laslett on his Seventieth Birthday* (Oxford, 1986).

Borsay, Anne, *Medicine and Charity in Georgian Bath: A Social History of the General Infirmary, c. 1739–1830* (Aldershot, 1999).

Boswell, John, *The Kindness of Strangers: The Abandonment of Children in Western Europe from Late Antiquity to the Renaissance* (New York, 1988).

Bothelo, L. A., *Old Age and the English Poor Law, 1500–1700* (Woodbridge, 2004).

Bothelo, Lynn and Thane, Pat (eds), *Women and Ageing in British Society since 1500* (2001).

Boulton, Jeremy, '"It is Extreme Necessity That Makes Me Do This": Some "Survival Strategies" of Pauper Households in London's West End during the Early Eighteenth Century', *International Review of Social History*, 45 (2000), 47–69.

—— 'Food Prices and the Standard of Living in London in the "Century of Revolution", 1580–1700', *Economic History Review*, n.s., 53 (2000), 445–92.

—— 'London Widowhood Revisited: The Decline of Female Remarriage in the Seventeenth and Early Eighteenth Centuries', *Continuity and Change*, 5 (1990), 323–55.

—— *Neighbourhood and Society: A London Suburb in the Seventeenth Century* (Cambridge, 1987).

—— 'The Poor among the Rich: Paupers and the Parish in the West End, 1600–1724', in Griffiths and Jenner (eds), *Londoninopolis*.

—— 'Welfare Systems and the Parish Nurse in Early Modern London, 1650–1725', *Family & Community History*, 10 (2007), 127–51.

Bowers, Toni, *The Politics of Motherhood: British Writing and Culture, 1680–1760* (Cambridge, 1996).

Braddick, Michael J., *State Formation in Early Modern England c. 1550–1700* (Cambridge, 2000).

Braddick, Michael J. and Walter, John (eds), *Negotiating Power in Early Modern Society: Order, Hierarchy and Subordination in Britain and Ireland* (Cambridge, 2001).

Broad, John, 'Housing the Rural Poor in Southern England, 1650–1850', *Agricultural History Review*, 42 (2000), 151–70.

—— *Transforming English Rural Society: The Verneys and the Claydons, 1600–1820* (Cambridge, 2004).

Brodsky, Vivien, 'Widows in Late Elizabethan London: Remarriage, Economic Opportunity and Family Orientations', in Bonfield, Smith, and Wrightson (eds), *The World We Have Gained*.

Brooks, Christopher, 'Apprenticeship, Social Mobility and the Middling Sort, 1550–1800', in Barry and Brooks (eds), *The Middling Sort of People*.

Brown, W. Newman, 'The Receipt of Poor Relief and Family Situation: Aldenham, Hertfordshire 1630–90', in Smith (ed.), *Land, Kinship, and Life-Cycle*.

Brownlow, John, *The History and Objects of the Foundling Hospital, with a Memoir of the Founder*, 4th edn (1881).

Buck, Anne, 'Buying Clothes in Bedfordshire: Customers and Tradesmen, 1700–1800', in N. B. Harte (ed.), *Fabrics and Fashions*.

Burghuiere, André, Klapish-Zuber, Christiane, Segalen, Martine, and Zonabend, Françoise, *A History of the Family*, vol. 2, *The Impact of Modernity* (1986), trans. Sarah Hanbury Tenison (Cambridge, 1996).

Burt, Shelley, *Virtue Transformed: Political Argument in England, 1668–1740* (Cambridge, 1992).

Canny, Nicholas and Pagden, Anthony (eds), *Colonial Identity in the Atlantic World, 1500–1800* (Princeton, 1987).

Capp, Bernard, 'The Double Standard Revisited: Plebeian Women and Male Sexual Reputation in Early Modern England', *Past and Present*, 162 (1999), 70–100.

—— *When Gossips Meet: Women, Family, and Neighbourhood in Early Modern England* (Oxford, 2003).

Casey, James, *The History of the Family* (Oxford, 1989).

Caulfield, Ernest, *The Infant Welfare Movement in the Eighteenth Century* (New York, 1931).

Cavallo, Sandra and Warner, Lyndan (eds), *Widowhood in Medieval and Early Modern Europe* (1999).

Chaytor, Miranda, 'Household and Kinship: Ryton in the late 16th and early 17th centuries', *HWJ*, 10 (1980), 25–60.

Clark, Alice, *Working Life of Women in the Seventeenth Century* (1919; reprinted 1968).

Clark, Anna, *Women's Silence, Men's Violence: Sexual Assault in England, 1770–1845* (1987).

Clark, Elaine, 'Mothers at Risk of Poverty in the Medieval English Countryside', in Henderson and Wall (eds), *Poor Women and Children*.

Clark, Peter (ed.), *The Cambridge Urban History of Britain*, vol. 2, 1540–1840 (Cambridge, 2000).

Cockburn, J. S. (ed.), *Crime in England, 1500–1800* (1977).

Coldham, Peter Wilson, 'The "Spiriting" of London Children to Virginia', *The Virginia Magazine of History and Biography*, Richmond, Virginia Historical Soc., vol. 83, July (1975), 280–7.

Coleman, Patrick, Lewis, Jayne, and Kowalik, Jill (eds), *Representations of the Self from the Renaissance to Romanticism* (Cambridge, 2000).

Colley, Linda, *Britons: Forging the Nation 1707–1837* (1992).

Collins, Stephen, 'British Stepfamily Relationships, 1500–1800', *Journal of Family History*, 14 (1991), 331–44.

—— *Step-Parents and Their Children* (1988).

Connell, R. W., *Masculinities* (Sydney, 1995).

Connors, Richard, 'Poor Women, the Parish and the Politics of Poverty', in Hannah Barker and Elaine Chalus (eds), *Gender in Eighteenth-Century England: Roles, Representations and Responsibilities* (1997).

Coster, Will, *Baptism and Spiritual Kinship in Early Modern England* (Aldershot, 2002).

Crawford, Patricia, *Blood, Bodies and Families in Early Modern England* (2004).

—— '"Civic Fathers" and Children: Continuities from Elizabethan England to the Australian Colonies', *History Australia*, 5 (2008), 04.1–16.

—— *Women and Religion in England 1500–1720* (1993).

Cressy, David, *Birth, Marriage, and Death: Ritual, Religion and the Life-Cycle in Tudor and Stuart England* (Oxford, 1997).

—— 'Kinship and Kin Interaction in Early Modern England', *Past and Present*, 113 (1986), 38–69.

Cunningham, Hugh, *Children and Childhood in Western Society since 1500* (1995).

—— *The Children of the Poor: Representations of Childhood since the Seventeenth Century* (Oxford, 1991).

—— 'The Employment and Unemployment of Children in England c. 1680–1851', *Past and Present*, 126 (1990), 115–50.

Cunningham, Hugh and Innes, Joanna (eds), *Charity, Philanthropy, and Reform: From the 1690s to the 1850s* (Basingstoke, 1998).

Daunton, Martin (ed.), *Charity, Self Interest and Welfare in the English Past* (1996).

Daunton, Martin and Halpern, Rick (eds), *Empire and Others: British Encounters with Indigenous Peoples 1600–1850* (1999).

Davidoff, Leonore, 'The Family in Britain', in Thompson (ed.), *Cambridge Social History of Britain*.

—— Doolittle, Megan, Fink, Janet, and Holden, Katherine, *The Family Story: Blood, Contract, and Intimacy, 1630–1960* (1999).

—— McClelland, Keith, and Varikas, Eleni (eds), *Gender and History: Retrospect and Prospect* (Oxford, 2000).

—— and Hall, Catherine, *Family Fortunes: Men and Women of the English Middle Class 1780–1850* (1987).

de Mause, Lloyd (ed.), *The History of Childhood* (New York, 1975).

Derosas, Renzo and Saito, Osamu, 'Introduction', in Renzo Derosas and Michel Oris (eds), *When Dad Died: Individuals and Families Coping with Family Stress in Past Societies* (Berne, 2002).

Dickinson, R. R. and Sharpe, J. A., 'Infanticide in Early Modern England: The Court of Great Sessions at Chester, 1650–1800', in Jackson (ed.), *Infanticide*.

Dolan, Frances E., *Dangerous Familiars: Representations of Domestic Crime in England, 1550–1700* (Ithaca, 1994).

—— 'Household Chastisements: Gender, Authority and "Domestic Violence"', in Patricia Fumerton and Simon Hunt (eds), *Renaissance Culture and the Everyday* (Philadelphia, 1999), 204–25.

Duffy, Eamon, 'The Godly and the Multitude in Stuart England', *Seventeenth Century*, 1 (1986), 31–55.

Dunlop, O. Jocelyn, *English Apprenticeship and Child Labour: A History* (1912).

Earle, Peter, *A City Full Of People: Men and Women of London 1650–1750* (1994).

—— *The Making of the English Middle Class: Business, Society and Family Life in London, 1660–1730* (1989).

Erickson, Amy Louise, 'The Marital Economy in Perspective', in Agren and Erickson (eds), *Marital Economy in Scandinavia and Britain*.

—— *Women and Property in Early Modern England* (1993).

Evans, Tanya, *'Unfortunate Objects': Lone Mothers in Eighteenth-Century London* (2005).

Fessler, Alfred, 'The Official Attitude towards the Sick Poor in Seventeenth-Century Lancashire', *Transactions of the Historic Soc. of Lancashire and Cheshire*, 102 (1950), 85–113.

Fildes, Valerie (ed.), *Women as Mothers in Pre-Industrial England* (1990).

Fildes, Valerie, 'Maternal Feelings Re-assessed: Child Abandonment and Neglect in London and Westminster, 1550–1800', in Fildes (ed.), *Women as Mothers in Pre-Industrial England*.

Fissell, Mary E., *Patients, Power, and the Poor in Eighteenth-Century Bristol* (Cambridge, 1991).

—— *Vernacular Bodies: The Politics of Reproduction in Early Modern England* (Oxford, 2004).

Fletcher, Anthony, *Gender, Sex, and Subordination in England, 1500–1800* (New Haven, 1995).

Fletcher, Anthony and Hussey, Stephen (eds), *Childhood in Question: Children, Parents and the State* (Manchester, 1999).

Fletcher, Anthony and Stevenson, John, 'Introduction', in Fletcher and Stevenson (eds.), *Order and Disorder in Early Modern England* (Cambridge, 1985).

Fontaine, Laurence and Schumbohm, Jurgen (eds), 'Household Strategies for Survival: An Introduction', *International Review of Social History*, Supplement 8, *Household Strategies for Survival 1600–2000: Fission, Faction and Cooperation* (Cambridge, 2000) 1–17.

Fox, Adam, 'Ballads, Libels and Popular Ridicule in Jacobean England', *Past and Present*, 145 (1994), 47–83.

—— *Oral and Literate Culture in England, 1500–1700* (Oxford, 2000).

Foyster, Elizabeth A., *Manhood in Early Modern England: Honour, Sex, and Marriage* (New York, 1999).

—— *Marital Violence: An English Family History, 1660–1857* (Cambridge, 2005).

—— 'Parenting was for Life, not just Childhood: The Role of Parents in the Married Lives of their Children in Early Modern England', *History*, 86 (2001), 313–27.

—— 'Silent Witnesses? Children and the Breakdown of Domestic and Social Order in Early Modern England', in Fletcher and Hussey (eds), *Childhood in Question*.

Froide, Amy M., *Never Married: Singlewomen in Early Modern England* (Oxford, 2005).

Fumerton, Patricia, *Unsettled: The Culture of Mobility and the Working Poor in Early Modern England* (Chicago, 2006).

Gadd, Ian Anders and Wallis, Patrick (eds), *Guilds, Society and Economy in London 1450–1800* (2002).

Gammon, Julie, '"A Denial of Innocence": Female Juvenile Victims of Rape and the English Legal System in the Eighteenth Century', in Fletcher and Hussey (eds), *Childhood in Question*.

Gilboy, Elizabeth W., *Wages in Eighteenth Century England* (Cambridge, MA, 1934).

Gillis, John R., 'Conjugal Settlements: Resort to Clandestine and Common Law Marriage in England and Wales, 1650–1850', in John Bossy (ed.), *Disputes and Settlements: Law and Human Relations in the West* (Cambridge, 1983).

—— *For Better, For Worse: British Marriages, 1600 to the Present* (New York, 1985).

—— *A World of Their Own Making: Myth Ritual, and the Quest for Family Values* (Cambridge, MA, 1997).

Gowing, Laura, *Common Bodies: Women, Touch and Power in Seventeenth-Century England* (2003).

—— *Domestic Dangers: Women, Words, and Sex in Early Modern London* (Oxford, 1996).

—— 'The Haunting of Susan Lay: Servants and Mistresses in Seventeenth-Century England', *Gender and History*, 14 (2002), 183–201.

—— 'Giving Birth at the Magistrate's Gate: Single Mothers in the Early Modern City', in Tarbin and Broomhall (eds), *Women, Identities and Communities*.

——'Ordering the Body: Illegitimacy and Female Authority in Seventeenth-Century England', in Braddick and Walter (eds), *Negotiating Power*.

——'Secret Births and Infanticide in Seventeenth-Century England', *Past and Present*, 156 (1997), 87–115.

Grassby, Richard, *Kinship and Capitalism: Marriage, Family, and Business in the English-Speaking World, 1580–1740* (Cambridge, 2001).

Green, Ian, *The Christian's ABC: Catechisms and Catechizing in England c. 1530–1740* (Oxford, 1996).

Griffiths, Paul, *Youth and Authority: Formative Experiences in England 1560–1640* (Oxford, 1996).

Griffiths, Paul and Jenner, Mark S. R. (eds), *Londoninopolis: Essays in the Cultural and Social History of Early Modern London* (Manchester, 2000).

Hair, P. E. H., 'Bridal Pregnancy in Rural England in Earlier Centuries', *Population Studies*, 20 (1966), 233–43.

—— 'Bridal Pregnancy in Earlier Rural England Further Examined', *Population Studies*, 24 (1970), 59–70.

Hajnal, H. J., 'Age at Marriage and Proportions Marrying', *Population Studies*, 7 (1953), 111–36.

Hampson, E. N., *The Treatment of Poverty in Cambridgeshire 1597–1834* (Cambridge, 1934).

Harding, Vanessa, 'Families and Housing in Seventeenth-Century London', *Parergon*, 24 (2007), 114–38.

Harley, David, 'Provincial Midwives in England: Lancashire and Cheshire, 1660–1760', in Hilary Marland (ed.), *The Art of Midwifery: Early Modern Midwives in Europe* (1993).

Harte, N. B. (ed.), *Fabrics and Fashions: Studies in the Economic and Social History of Dress* (1991).

Harvey, Karen and Shepard, Alexandra, 'What have Historians done with Masculinities? Reflections on Five Centuries of British History circa 1500–1950', *JBS*, 44 (2005), 274–80.

Hay, Douglas and Rogers, Nicholas, *Eighteenth-Century English Society: Shuttles and Swords* (Oxford, 1997).

Heal, Felicity and Holmes, Clive, *The Gentry in England and Wales 1500–1700* (1994).

Helmholz, R. H., 'Harboring Sexual Offenders: Ecclesiastical Courts and Controlling Misbehavior', *JBS*, 37 (1998), 258–86.

—— 'Support Orders, Church Courts, and the Rule of *Filius Nullius*: A Reassessment of the Common Law' (1977), in his *Canon Law and the Law of England* (1987).

Henderson, John and Wall, Richard (eds), *Poor Women and Children in the European Past* (1994).

Henderson, Tony, *Disorderly Women in Eighteenth-Century London: Prostitution and Control in the Metropolis, 1730–1830* (1999).

Herndon, Ruth Wallis, '"Who Died an Expence to This Town": Poor Relief in Eighteenth-Century Rhode Island', in Billy G. Smith (ed.), *Down and Out in Early America* (Philadelphia, 2003).

Herndon, Ruth and Sekatua, Ella Wilcox, 'Colonizing the Children: Indian Youngsters in Servitude in Early Rhode Island', in Colin G. Calloway and Neil Salisbury (eds), *Reinterpreting New England Indian History and the Colonial Experience* (Boston, 2003).

Herndon, Ruth Wallis and Murray, John E. (eds), *Children Bound to Labor: Pauper Apprenticeship in Early America* (Ithaca, 2009).

Herndon, Ruth Wallis and Murray, John E., '"A Proper and Instructive Education": Raising Children in Pauper Apprenticeship', in Herndon and Murray (eds), *Children Bound to Labor*.

Herrup, Cynthia B., *A House in Gross Disorder: Sex, Law, and the 2nd Earl of Castlehaven* (New York, 1999).

—— '"To Pluck Bright Honour from the Pale-Faced Moon": Gender and Honour in the Castlehaven Story', *TRHS*, 6th ser., 6 (1996), 137–59.

Hill, Bridget, 'The Marriage Age of Women and the Demographers', *HWJ*, 28 (1989), 129–47.

Hindle, Steve, 'A Cumbrian Family and the Poor Law Authorities, c. 1690–1730', in Berry and Foyster (eds), *Family*.

—— 'Dearth, Fasting and Alms: The Campaign for General Hospitality in Late Elizabethan England', *Past and Present*, 172 (2001), 44–86.

—— 'Dependency, Shame and Belonging: Badging the Deserving Poor, c. 1550–1750', *Cultural and Social History*, 1 (2004), 6–35.

—— 'Hierarchy and Community in the Elizabethan Parish: The Swallowfield Articles of 1596', *Historical Journal*, 42 (1999), 835–51.

—— *On the Parish? The Micro-Politics of Poor Relief in Rural England c. 1550–1750* (Oxford, 2004).

—— 'The Problem of Pauper Marriage in Seventeenth-Century England', *TRHS*, 6th ser., 8 (1998), 71–89.

—— 'A Sense of Place? Becoming and Belonging in the Rural Parish, 1550–1650', in Shepard and Withington (eds), *Communities in Early Modern England*.

—— 'The Shaming of Margaret Knowsley: Gossip, Gender and the Experience of Authority in Early Modern England', *Continuity and Change*, 9 (1994), 391–419.

—— *The State and Social Change in Early Modern England, c. 1550–1640* (2000).

—— '"Waste" Children? Pauper Apprenticeship under the Elizabethan Poor Laws, c. 1598–1697', in Lane, Raven, and Snell (eds), *Women, Work and Wages in England*.

—— and Herndon, Ruth Wallis, 'Recreating Proper Families in England and North America: Pauper Apprenticeship in Transatlantic Context', in Herndon and Murray (eds), *Children Bound to Labor*.

Hirsch, Marianne and Keller, Evelyn Fox (eds), *Conflicts in Feminism* (New York, 1990).

Hitchcock, Tim, 'Begging on the Streets of Eighteenth-Century London', *JBS*, 44 (2005), 478–98.

—— *Down and Out in Eighteenth-Century London* (2004).

—— '"Unlawfully begotten on her body": Illegitimacy and the Parish Poor in St Luke's Chelsea', in Hitchcock, King, and Sharpe (eds), *Chronicling Poverty*.

—— and Cohen, Michèle (eds), *English Masculinities 1600–1800* (1999).

—— King, Peter, and Sharpe, Pamela (eds), *Chronicling Poverty: The Voices and Strategies of the English Poor, 1640–1840* (Basingstoke, 1997).

—— and Shore, Heather (eds), *The Streets of London: From the Great Fire to the Great Stink* (2003).

Hoffer, Peter C. and Hull, N. E. H., *Murdering Mothers: Infanticide in England and New England 1558–1803* (New York, 1981).

Honeyman, Katrina, *Child Workers in England, 1780–1820: Parish Apprentices and the Making of the Early Industrial Labour Force* (Aldershot, 2007).

Hoppit, Julian, *A Land of Liberty? England 1689–1727* (Oxford, 2000).

Horden, Peregrine and Smith, Richard (eds), *The Locus of Care: Families, Communities, Institutions and the Provision of Welfare since Antiquity* (1998).

Horrell, Sara and Humphries, Jane, '"The Exploitation of Little Children": Child Labour and the Family Economy in the Industrial Revolution', *Explorations in Economic History*, 32 (1995), 485–516.

Horrell, Sara, Humphries, Jane, and Voth, Hans-Joachim, 'Stature and Relative Deprivation: Fatherless Children in Early Industrial Britain', *Continuity and Change*, 13 (1998), 73–115.

Horwitz, Henry, '"The mess of the middle class" revisited: the case of the "big bourgeoisie" of Augustan London', *Continuity and Change*, 2 (1987), 263–96.

Houlbrooke, Ralph, *Church Courts and the People during the English Reformation 1520–1570* (Oxford, 1979).

—— *The English Family 1450–1700* (1984).

—— *Religion and the Family in England 1480–1750* (Oxford, 1998).

Humphries, Jane, 'Female-Headed Households in Early Industrial Britain: The Vanguard of the Proletariat', *Labour History Review*, 63 (1998), 31–65.

Hunt, Margaret R., *The Middling Sort: Commerce, Gender, and the Family in England 1680–1780* (Berkeley, CA, 1996).

—— 'Wife beating, Domesticity and Women's Independence in Eighteenth-Century London', *Gender and History*, 4 (1992), 10–33.

—— 'Women and the Fiscal-Imperial State in the Late Seventeenth and Early Eighteenth Centuries', in Kathleen Wilson (ed.), *A New Imperial History: Culture, Identity, and Modernity in Britain and Empire, 1660–1840* (Cambridge, 2004).

Hurl, Jennine, '"She being bigg with child is likely to miscarry": Pregnant Victims Prosecuting Assault in Westminster, 1685–1720', *London Journal*, 24 (1999), 18–33.

Hurl-Eamon, J., *Gender and Petty Violence in London, 1680–1720* (Columbus, OH, 2005).

Ingram, Martin, *Church Courts, Sex and Marriage in England 1570–1640* (Cambridge, 1987).

—— 'Spousals Litigation in the English Ecclesiastical Courts c. 1350–c. 1640', in Outhwaite (ed.), *Marriage and Society*.

—— 'The Reform of Popular Culture? Sex and Marriage in Early Modern England', in Reay (ed.), *Popular Culture*.

—— 'Child Sexual Abuse in Early Modern England', in Braddick and Walter (eds), *Negotiating Power*.

Innes, Joanna, 'The Mixed Economy of Welfare in Early Modern England: Assessments of the Options from Hale to Malthus (c. 1683–1803)', in Daunton (ed.), *Charity, Self Interest and Welfare*.

—— 'Origins of the Factory Acts: The Health and Morals of Apprentices Act, 1802', in Landau (ed.), *Law, Crime, and English Society*.

Jackson, Mark, *New-Born Child Murder: Women, Illegitimacy and the Courts in Eighteenth-century England* (Manchester, 1996).

—— 'Suspicious Infant Deaths: The Statute of 1624 and Medical Evidence at Coroners' Inquests', in Michael Clark and Catherine Crawford (eds), *Legal Medicine in History* (Cambridge, 1994).

—— (ed.), *Infanticide: Historical Perspectives on Child Murder and Concealment, 1550–2000* (Aldershot, 2002).

Johnson, Paul and Thane, Pat (eds), *Old Age from Antiquity to Post-Modernity* (1998).

Johnson, Robert C., 'The Transportation of Vagrant Children from London to Virginia, 1618–1622', in Howard S. Reinmuth (ed.), *Early Stuart Studies: Essays in Honor of David Harris Willson* (Minneapolis, 1970).

Jones, M. G., *The Charity School Movement: A Study of Eighteenth Century Puritanism in Action* (Cambridge, 1938).

Kent, D. A., 'Ubiquitous but Invisible: Female Domestic Servants in Mid-Eighteenth Century London', *HWJ*, 28 (1989), 111–28.

Kent, Joan, 'The Centre and the Localities: State Formation and Parish Government in England, Circa 1640–1740', *Historical Journal*, 38 (1995), 363–404.

—— 'The Rural "Middling Sort" in Early Modern England, circa 1640–1740: Some Economic, Political Socio-Cultural Characteristics', *Rural History*, 10 (1999), 19–54.

Kermonde, Jenny and Walker, Garthine (eds), *Women, Crime and the Courts in Early Modern England* (1994).

Kilday, Anne-Marie and Watson, Katherine, 'Child Murder in Georgian England', *History Today*, 55 (2005), 40–6.

King, Peter, *Crime, Justice and Discretion in England 1740–1820* (Oxford, 2000).

King, Steven, 'The Bastardy Prone Sub-society Again: Bastards and Their Fathers and Mothers in Lancashire, Wiltshire, and Somerset, 1800–1840', in Levene, Nutt, and Williams (eds), *Illegitimacy in Britain*.

—— 'Poor Relief and English Economic Development Reappraised', *Economic History Review*, n.s., 50 (1997), 360–8.

—— *Poverty and Welfare in England 1700–1850: A Regional Perspective* (Manchester, 2000).

King, Steven and Tomkins, Alannah (eds), *The Poor in England 1700–1850: An Economy of Makeshifts* (Manchester, 2003).

King, Walter J., 'Punishment for Bastardy in Early Seventeenth-Century England', *Albion*, 10 (1978), 130–51.

Kirby, Peter, *Child Labour in Britain, 1750–1870* (Basingstoke, 2003).

Kussmaul, Ann, *A General View of the Rural Economy in England, 1538–1840* (Cambridge, 1990).

—— *Servants in Husbandry in Early Modern England* (Cambridge, 1981).

Lancaster, Jane B., Altmann, Jeanne, Rossi, Alice C., and Sherrod, Lonnie R. (eds), *Parenting Across the Lifespan: Biosocial Dimensions* (New York, 1987).

Landau, Norma (ed.), *Law, Crime, and English Society, 1660–1830* (Cambridge, 2002).

—— 'The Laws of Settlement and the Surveillance of Immigration in Eighteenth-Century Kent', *Continuity and Change*, 3 (1988), 391–420.

Landers, John, *Death and the Metropolis: Studies in the Demographic History of London 1670–1830* (Cambridge, 1993).

Lane, Joan, *Apprenticeship in England, 1600–1914* (1996).

Lane, Penelope, 'Work on the Margins: Poor Women and the Informal Economy of the Eighteenth and Early Nineteenth-Century Leicestershire', *Midland History*, 22 (1997), 85–99.

Lane, Penelope, Raven, Neil, and Snell, K. D. M. (eds), *Women, Work and Wages in England, 1600–1850* (Woodbridge, 2004).

Langbein, John H., *The Origins of the Adversary Criminal Trial* (Oxford, 2003).

Langelüddecke, Henrik, '"Patchy and Spasmodic": The Response of Justices of the Peace to Charles I's Book of Orders', *English Historical Review*, 113 (1998), 1231–48.

Langford, Paul, *A Polite and Commercial People: England 1727–1783* (Oxford, 1989).

—— *Public Life and the Propertied Englishman 1689–1798* (Oxford, 1991).

Laslett, Peter, *Family Life and Illicit Love in Earlier Generations: Essays in Historical Sociology* (Cambridge, 1977).

Laslett, Peter, and Wall, Richard (eds), *Household and Family in Past Time* (Cambridge, 1974).

Laslett, Peter, Oosterveen, Karla, and Smith, Richard M. (eds), *Bastardy and its Comparative History: Studies in the History of Illegitimacy and Marital Nonconformism in Britain, France, Germany, Sweden, the United States, Jamaica, and Japan* (1980).

Laurence, Anne, '"Begging pardon for all mistakes or errors in this writeing I being a woman and doing itt myself": Family Narratives in some Early Eighteenth-Century Letters', in James Daybell (ed.), *Early Modern Women's Letter Writing, 1450–1700* (Basingstoke, 2001).

Lees, Lynn Hollen, *The Solidarities of Strangers: The English Poor Laws and the People, 1700–1948* (Cambridge, 1998).

Lemprière, William, *A History of the Girls' School of Christ's Hospital, London, Hoddesdon and Hertford* (Cambridge, 1924).

Leonard, E. M., *The Early History of English Poor Relief* (Cambridge, 1900).

Levene, Alysa, *Childcare, Health and Mortality at the London Foundling Hospital, 1741–1800: 'Left to the mercy of the world'* (2007).

—— 'The Mortality Penalty of Illegitimate Children: Foundlings and Poor Children in Eighteenth-Century England', in Levene, Nutt, and Williams (eds), *Illegitimacy in Britain*.

—— 'The Origins of the Children of the London Foundling Hospital, 1741–1760: A Reconsideration', *Continuity and Change*, 18 (2003), 201–35.

Levene, Alysa, Nutt, Thomas, and Williams, Samantha (eds), *Illegitimacy in Britain, 1700–1920* (Basingstoke, 2005).

Levine, David, *Family Formation in an Age of Nascent Capitalism* (New York, 1977).

Levine, David and Wrightson, Keith, *The Making of an Industrial Society: Whickham 1560–1765* (Oxford, 1991).

Linebaugh, Peter and Rediker, Marcus, *The Many-Headed Hydra: Sailors, Slaves, Commoners, and the Hidden History of the Revolutionary Atlantic* (Boston, 2000).

Lloyd, Sarah, '"Agents in their own concerns"? Charity and the Economy of Makeshifts in Eighteenth-Century Britain', in King and Tomkins (eds), *The Poor in England 1700–1850*.

McClure, Ruth, *Coram's Children: The London Foundling Hospital in the Eighteenth Century* (1981).

McDonagh, Josephine, *Child Murder and British Culture, 1720–1900* (Cambridge, 2003).

MacDonald, Michael, *Mystical Bedlam: Madness, Anxiety, and Healing in Seventeenth-Century England* (Cambridge, 1981).

Macfarlane, Alan, *The Family Life of Ralph Josselin, a Seventeenth-Century Clergyman: An Essay in Historical Anthropology* (Cambridge, 1970).

—— *Marriage and Love in England: Modes of Reproduction 1300–1840* (Oxford, 1986).

Macfarlane, Stephen, 'Social Policy and Poor in the Later Seventeenth Century', in Beier and Finlay (eds), *The Making of the Metropolis*.

McIntosh, Marjorie Keniston, *Controlling Misbehavior in England, 1370–1600* (Cambridge, 1998).

MacKinnon, A. D., '"Charity is worth it when it looks that good": Rural Women and Bequests of Clothing in Early Modern England', in Tarbin and Broomhall (eds), *Women, Identities and Communities*.

—— 'The Godly Family of the Seventeenth Century and John Howard's Australia', in Delys Bird, Wendy Were, and Terri-ann White (eds), *Future Imaginings: Sexualities and Genders in the New Millennium* (Nedlands, 2003).

McMahon, Vanessa, *Murder in Shakespeare's England* (2004).

Maddern, Philippa, '"In myn own house": The Troubled Connections between Servant Marriages, Late-Medieval English Household Communities and Early Modern Historiography', in Tarbin and Broomhall (eds), *Women, Identities and Communities*.

Malcolmson, R. W., 'Infanticide in the Eighteenth Century', in Cockburn (ed.), *Crime in England*.

Manzione, Carol Kazmierczak, *Christ's Hospital of London, 1552–1598: A Passing Deed of Pity* (Selinsgrove, 1995).

Marshall, Dorothy, *The English Poor in the Eighteenth Century: A Study in Social and Administrative History* (1926; reprinted 1969).

Martin, Randall, *Women, Murder, and Equity in Early Modern England* (2008).

Mayhew, Graham, 'Life-Cycle Service and the Family Unit in Early Modern Rye', *Continuity and Change*, 6 (1991), 201–26.

Meldrum, Tim, *Domestic Service and Gender 1660–1750: Life and Work in the London Household* (2000).

—— 'London Domestic Servants from Depositional Evidence, 1660–1750: Servant–Employer Sexuality in the Patriarchal Household', in Hitchcock, King, and Sharpe (eds), *Chronicling Poverty*.

Mendelson, Sara and Crawford, Patricia, *Women in Early Modern England, 1550–1720* (Oxford, 1998).

Mikalachki, Jodi, 'Women's Networks and the Female Vagrant: A Hard Case', in Susan Frye and Karen Robertson (eds), *Maids and Mistresses, Cousins and Queens: Women's Alliances in Early Modern England* (Oxford, 1999).

Muldrew, Craig, *The Economy of Obligation: The Culture of Credit and Social Relations in Early Modern England* (New York, 1998).

Mulligan, Lotte and Richards, Judith, 'A "Radical" Problem: The Poor and the English Reformers in the Mid-Seventeenth Century', *JBS*, 29 (1990), 118–46.

Murphy, Terence R., '"Woful Childe of Parents Rage": Suicide of Children and Adolescents in Early Modern England, 1507–1710', *Sixteenth Century Journal*, 17 (1986), 259–70.

Murray, John and Herndon, Ruth Wallis, 'Markets for Children in Early America: A Political Economy of Pauper Apprenticeship', *Journal of Economic History*, 62 (2002), 356–82.

Nichols, R. H. and Wray, F. A., *The History of the Foundling Hospital* (1935).

Nutt, Thomas, 'The Paradox and Problems of Illegitimate Paternity in Old Poor Law Essex', in Levene, Nutt, and Williams (eds), *Illegitimacy in Britain*.

O'Day, Rosemary, *The Family and Family Relationships 1500–1900: England, France, and the United States of America* (1994).

O'Hara, Diana, *Courtship and Constraint: Rethinking the Making of Marriage in Tudor England* (Manchester, 2000).

Ottaway, Susannah R., *The Decline of Life: Old Age in Eighteenth-Century England* (Cambridge, 2004).

—— 'The Old Woman's Home in Eighteenth-Century England', in Bothelo and Thane (eds), *Women and Ageing*.

—— 'Providing for the Elderly in Eighteenth-Century England', *Continuity and Change*, 13 (1998), 391–418.

Outhwaite, R. B., *Clandestine Marriage in England, 1500–1850* (1995).

—— ' "Objects of Charity": Petitions to the London Foundling Hospital, 1768–72', *Eighteenth-Century Studies*, 32 (1999), 497–510.

—— (ed.), *Marriage and Society: Studies in the Social History of Marriage* (1981).

Overton, Mark, *Agricultural Revolution in England: The Transformation of the Agrarian Economy 1500–1850* (Cambridge, 1996).

Owen, David, *English Philanthropy 1660–1960* (Cambridge, MA, 1965).

Oxley, Geoffrey W., *Poor Relief in England and Wales, 1601–1834* (1974).

Panter-Brick, Catherine and Smith, Malcolm T. (eds), *Abandoned Children* (Cambridge, 2000).

Payne, Dianne, 'Rhetoric, Reality and the Marine Society', *London Journal*, 30 (2005), 66–84.

Pearce, E. H., *Annals of Christ's Hospital*, 1901.

Pearl, Valerie, 'Puritans and Poor Relief: The London Workhouse, 1649–1660', in Pennington and Thomas (eds), *Puritans and Revolutionaries*.

—— 'Social Policy in Early Modern London', in Hugh Lloyd-Jones, Valerie Pearl, and Blair Worden (eds), *History and Imagination* (1981).

Pelling, Margaret, *The Common Lot: Sickness, Medical Occupations and the Urban Poor in Early Modern England* (1998).

—— 'The Women of the Family? Speculations around Early Modern British Physicians', *Social History of Medicine*, 8 (1995), 383–401.

—— (with Frances White), *Medical Conflicts in Early Modern London: Patronage, Physicians, and Irregular Practitioners 1550–1640* (Oxford, 2003).

Pelling, Margaret, and Smith, Richard M. (eds), *Life, Death, and the Elderly: Historical Perspectives* (1991).

Pennington, Donald and Thomas, Keith (eds), *Puritans and Revolutionaries: Essays in Seventeenth-Century History Presented to Christopher Hill* (Oxford, 1978).

Perrier, Sylvie, 'The Blended Family in *Ancien Régime* France: A Dynamic Family Form', *History of the Family*, 3 (1998), 459–71.

Perry, Ruth, 'Colonising the Breast: Sexuality and Maternity in Eighteenth-Century England', *Journal of the History of Sexuality*, 2 (1991), 204–34.

Pinchbeck, Ivy and Hewitt, Margaret, *Children in English Society*, 2 vols (1969).

Plumb, J. H., 'The New World of Children in Eighteenth-Century England', *Past and Present*, 67 (1975), 64–95.

Pollock, Linda A., 'Childbearing and Female Bonding in Early Modern England', *Social History*, 22 (1997), 286–306.

—— *Forgotten Children: Parent-Child Relations from 1500–1900* (1983).

—— 'Living on the Stage of the World: The Concept of Privacy among the Elite of Early Modern England', in Adrian Wilson (ed.), *Rethinking Social History: English Society 1570–1920 and its Interpretation* (Manchester, 1993).

—— 'Rethinking Patriarchy and the Family in Seventeenth-Century England', *Journal of Family History*, 23 (1998), 3–27.

—— 'Training a Child in the Way He/She Should Go. Cultural Transmission and Child-Rearing within the Home in England, circa 1550–1800', in Johan Sturm, Jeroen Dekker, Richard Aldrich, and Frank Simon (eds.), *Education and Cultural Transmission, Paedagogica Historica: International Journal of the History of Education*, supplementary series, 11 (1996), 79–103.

Postles, Dave, 'Surviving Lone Motherhood in Early-Modern England', *Seventeenth Century*, 21 (2006), 160–83.

Pound, John, *Poverty and Vagrancy in Tudor England*, 2nd edn (1986).

Pullan, Brian, *Orphans and Foundlings in Early Modern Europe* (Reading, 1989).

Quaife, G. R., *Wanton Wenches and Wayward Wives: Peasants and Illicit Sex in Early Seventeenth Century England* (1979).

Rabin, Dana Y., 'Searching for the Self in Eighteenth-Century English Criminal Trials, 1730–1800', *Eighteenth-Century Life*, 27 (2003), 85–106.

——— 'Beyond "Lewd Women" and "Wanton Wenches": Infanticide and Child-Murder in the Long Eighteenth Century', in Thorn (ed.), *Writing British Infanticide*.

Ransome, David R., 'Wives for Virginia, 1621', *William and Mary Quarterly*, 3rd ser., 48 (1991), 3–18.

Reay, Barry (ed.), *Popular Culture in Seventeenth-Century England* (1988).

Rogers, Nicholas, 'Carnal Knowledge: Illegitimacy in Eighteenth-Century Westminster', *Journal of Social History*, 23 (1989), 355–75.

Roper, Lyndal, *The Holy Household: Women and Morals in Reformation Augsburg* (Oxford, 1989).

——— *Oedipus and the Devil: Witchcraft, Sexuality and Religion in Early Modern Europe* (1994).

——— *Witch Craze: Terror and Fantasy in Baroque Germany* (New Haven, 2004).

Roper, Michael and Tosh, John (eds), *Manful Assertions: Masculinities in Britain since 1800* (1991).

Rose, Craig, 'Evangelical Philanthropy and Anglican Revival: the Charity Schools of Augustan London, 1698–1740', *London Journal*, 16 (1991), 35–65.

——— 'Politics and the London Royal Hospitals, 1683–92', in Lindsay Granshaw and Roy Porter (eds), *The Hospital in History* (1989).

Rose, Mary B., 'Social Policy and Business; Parish Apprenticeship and the Early Factory System 1750–1834', *Business History*, 31 (1989), 5–29.

Rowlands, Alison, ' "In Great Secrecy": The Crime of Infanticide in Rothenburg ob der Tauber, 1501–1618', *German History*, 15 (1997), 179–99.

Ruddick, Sara, *Maternal Thinking: Towards a Politics of Peace* (Boston, 1995).

Rule, John, 'The Manifold Causes of Rural Crime: Sheep-Stealing in England, c. 1740–1840', in John G. Rule (ed.), *Outside the Law: Studies in Crime and Order, 1650–1850* (Exeter, 1982).

Rushton, Peter, 'The Matter in Variance: Adolescents and Domestic Conflict in the Pre-Industrial Economy of Northeast England, 1600–1800', *Journal of Social History*, 25 (1991–2), 89–107.

——— 'Property, Power and Family Networks: The Problem of Disputed Marriage in Early Modern England', *Journal of Family History*, 11 (1986), 205–19.

Schen, Claire S., *Charity and Lay Piety in Reformation London, 1500–1620* (Aldershot, 2002).

——— 'Women and the London Parishes, 1500–1620', in Katherine L. French, Gary G. Gibbs, and Beat A. Kümin (eds), *The Parish in English Life 1400–1600* (Manchester, 1997).

Schochet, Gordon J., *Patriarchalism in Political Thought: The Authoritarian Family and Political Speculation and Attitudes Especially in Seventeenth-Century England* (Oxford, 1975).

Schwartz, L. D., 'The Standard of Living in the Long Run: London 1700–1800', *Economic History Review*, n.s., 38 (1985), 24–41.

Shammas, Carole, 'Anglo-American Household Government in Comparative Perspective', *William and Mary Quarterly*, 3rd ser., 52 (1995), 104–44; 'Response', ibid. 163–6.

Sharp, Buchanan Sharp, 'Popular Protest in Seventeenth-Century England', in Reay (ed.), *Popular Culture*.

Sharpe, J. A., *Crime in Seventeenth-Century England: A County Study* (Cambridge, 1983).

Sharpe, Pamela, *Adapting to Capitalism: Working Women in the English Economy, 1700–1850* (Basingstoke, 1996; reprinted Basingstoke, 2000).

—— 'Poor Children as Apprentices in Colyton, 1598–1830', *Continuity and Change*, 6 (1991), 253–70.

—— *Population and Society in an East Devon Parish: Reproducing Colyton 1540–1840* (Exeter, 2002).

—— 'Population and Society', in Clark (ed.), *Cambridge Urban History of Britain*.

—— 'Survival Strategies and Stories: Poor Widows and Widowers in Early Industrial England', in Cavallo and Warner (eds), *Widowhood in Medieval and Early Modern Europe*.

Sheehan, Bernard W., *Savagism and Civility: Indians and Englishmen in Colonial Virginia* (Cambridge, 1980).

Shepard, Alexandra, 'Manhood, Credit and Patriarchy in Early Modern England c. 1580–1640', *Past and Present*, 167 (2000), 75–106.

—— *Meanings of Manhood in Early Modern England* (Oxford, 2003).

—— and Withington, Phil (eds), *Communities in Early Modern England: Networks, Place, Rhetoric* (Manchester, 2000).

Simonton, Deborah, 'Apprenticeship: Training and Gender in Eighteenth-Century England', in Berg (ed.), *Markets and Manufacture*.

Slack, Paul, *The English Poor Law, 1531–1782* (Basingstoke, 1990).

—— *From Reformation to Improvement: Public Welfare in Early Modern England* (Oxford, 1999).

—— 'Great and Good Towns 1540–1700', in Clark (ed.), *The Cambridge Urban History of Britain*, vol. 2, *1540–1740*.

—— *Poverty and Policy in Tudor and Stuart England* (1988).

—— 'Vagrants and Vagrancy in England, 1598–1664', *Economic History Review*, n.s., 27 (1974), 360–79.

Smith, Greg T., 'Expanding the Compass of Domestic Violence in the Hanoverian Metropolis', *Journal of Social History*, 41 (2007), 31–54.

Smith, Lisa, 'The Relative Duties of a Man: Domestic Medicine in England and France, ca. 1685–1740', *Journal of Family History*, 31 (2006), 237–58.

Smith, Richard M., 'Ageing and Well-being in Early Modern England: Pension Trends and Gender Preferences under the English Old Poor Law c. 1650–1800', in Johnson and Thane (eds), *Old Age from Antiquity to Post-Modernity*.

—— (ed.), *Land, Kinship, and Life-Cycle* (Cambridge, 1984).

Smith, Steven R., 'The London Apprentices as Seventeenth-Century Adolescents', *Past and Present*, 61 (1973), 149–61.

Snell, K. D. M., *Annals of the Labouring Poor: Social Change and Agrarian England 1660–1900* (Cambridge, 1985).

—— *Parish and Belonging: Community, Identity, and Welfare in England and Wales, 1700–1950* (Cambridge, 2006).

—— 'The Sunday-School Movement in England and Wales: Child-Labour, Denominational Control and Working-Class Culture', *Past and Present*, 164 (1999), 122–68.

Snell, K. D. M. and Millar, J., 'Lone-parent Families and the Welfare State: Past and Present', *Continuity and Change*, 2 (1987), 387–422.

Spufford, Margaret, *Contrasting Communities: English Villagers in the Sixteenth and Seventeenth Centuries* (Cambridge, 1974).

—— 'The Cost of Apparel in Seventeenth-Century England, and the Accuracy of Gregory King', *Economic History Review*, n.s., 53 (2000), 677–705.

—— *Figures in the Landscape: Rural Society in England, 1500–1700* (Aldershot, 2001).

—— 'First Steps in Literacy: The Reading and Writing Experience of the Humblest Seventeenth-Century Spiritual Autobiographers', *Social History*, 4 (1979), 407–53.

—— *The Great Reclothing of Rural England: Petty Chapmen and their Wares in the Seventeenth Century* (1984).

—— *Small Books and Pleasant Histories: Popular Fiction and its Readership in Seventeenth-Century England* (1981).

—— (ed.), *The World of Rural Dissenters, 1520–1725* (Cambridge, 1995).

Stapleton, Barry, 'Inherited Poverty and Life-Cycle Poverty: Odiham, Hampshire, 1650–1850', *Social History*, 18 (1993), 339–55.

Steedman, Carolyn, 'Lord Mansfield's Women', *Past and Present*, 176 (2002), 105–43.

Stone, Lawrence, *The Family, Sex and Marriage in England, 1500–1800* (1977).

—— *Uncertain Unions: Marriage in England 1660–1753* (Oxford, 1992).

Suzuki, Akihito, 'The Household and the Care of Lunatics in Eighteenth-Century London', in Horden and Smith (eds), *The Locus of Care*.

Sweet, Rosemary and Lane, Penelope (eds), *Women and Urban Life in Eighteenth-Century England: 'On the Town'* (Aldershot, 2003).

Tadmor, Naomi, 'The Concept of the Household-Family in Eighteenth-Century England', *Past and Present*, 151 (1996), 581–601.

—— *Family and Friends in Eighteenth Century England: Household, Kinship and Patronage* (Cambridge, 2001).

—— 'Women and Wives: The Language of Marriage in Early Modern English Biblical Translations', *HWJ*, 62 (2006), 1–27.

Tarbin, Stephanie and Broomhall, Susan (eds), *Women, Identities and Communities in Early Modern Europe* (Aldershot, 2008).

Taylor, James Stephen, 'The Impact of Pauper Settlement, 1691–1834', *Past and Present*, 73 (1976), 42–74.

—— 'Philanthropy and Empire: Jonas Hanway and the Infant Poor of London', *Eighteenth-Century Studies*, 12 (1979), 285–305.

—— *Poverty, Migration, and Settlement in the Industrial Revolution: Sojourners' Narratives* (Palo Alto, CA, 1989).

Thane, Pat, 'The Family Lives of Old People', in Johnson and Thane (eds), *Old Age from Antiquity to Post-Modernity*.

Thirsk, Joan, *Food in Early Modern England: Phases, Fads, Fashions 1500–1760* (2007).

—— *The Rural Economy of England: Collected Essays* (1984).

—— (ed.), *The Agrarian History of England and Wales*, vol. 4, 1500–1640 (Cambridge, 1967).

Thistleton-Dyer, T. F., *Old English Social Life as told by the Parish Register* (1898).

Thomas, Keith, 'Puritans and Adultery: The Act of 1650 Reconsidered', in Pennington and Thomas (eds), *Puritans and Revolutionaries*.

Thompson, E. P., 'Happy Families', in his *Persons and Polemics* (1994).

Thomas, Keith, *Religion and the Decline of Magic: Studies of Popular Beliefs in Sixteenth and Seventeenth Century England* (1971).

Thompson, F. M. L. (ed.), *The Cambridge Social History of Britain 1750–1950*, 3 vols (Cambridge, 1990).

Thorn, Jennifer (ed.), *Writing British Infanticide: Child-Murder, Gender, and Print, 1722–1859* (Newark, NJ, 2003).

Tilly, Louise A. and Scott, Joan W., *Women, Work, and Family* (New York, 1978).

Tomkins, Alannah, 'Charity Schools and the Parish Poor in Oxford, 1740–1770', *Midland History*, 22 (1997), 51–70.

Tosh, John, 'Authority and Nurture in Middle-Class Fatherhood: The Case of Early and Mid-Victorian England', *Gender and History*, 8 (1996), 48–64.

Trumbach, Randolph, *Sex and the Gender Revolution* (Chicago, 1998).

Turner, David M., *Fashioning Adultery: Gender, Sex and Civility in England, 1660–1740* (Cambridge, 2002).

Walby, Sylvia, *Theorizing Patriarchy* (Oxford, 1990).

Wales, Tim, 'Poverty, Poor Relief and the Life-Cycle: Some Evidence from Seventeenth-Century Norfolk', in Smith (ed.), *Land, Kinship, and Life-Cycle*.

Walker, Garthine, *Crime, Gender and the Social Order in Early Modern England* (Cambridge, 2003).

—— 'Expanding the Boundaries of Female Honour in Early Modern England', *TRHS*, 6th ser., 6 (1996), 235–45.

—— 'Just Stories: Telling Tales of Infant Death in Early Modern England', in Margaret Mikesell and Adele Seeff (eds), *Culture and Change: Attending to Early Modern Women* (Newark, NJ, 2003).

—— 'Rereading Rape and Sexual Violence in Early Modern England', *Gender and History*, 10 (1998), 1–25.

Wall, Richard, 'The Age at Leaving Home', *Journal of Family History*, 3 (1978), 181–202.

—— 'Inferring Differential Neglect of Females from Mortality Data', *Annales de Démographie Historique* (1981), 119–40.

—— 'Leaving Home and the Process of Household Formation in Pre-industrial England', *Continuity and Change*, 2 (1987), 77–101.

Walter, John, 'Faces in the Crowd: Gender and Age in the Early Modern English Crowd', in Berry and Foyster (eds), *Family*.

Warner, Jessica and Griller, Robin, ' "My Pappa Is out, and My Mamma Is Asleep": Minors, their Routine Activities, and Interpersonal Violence in an Early Modern Town, 1653–1781', *Journal of Social History*, 36 (2003), 561–84.

Warner, Marina, *From the Beast to the Blonde: On Fairy Tales and their Tellers* (1995).

Webb, Sidney and Webb, Beatrice, *English Poor Law History: Part 1: The Old Poor Law* (1927).

Whiting, Amanda, ' "Some Women Can Shift it Well Enough": A Legal Context for Understanding the Women Petitioners of the Seventeenth-Century English Revolution', *Australian Feminist Law Journal*, 21 (2004), 77–100.

Williams, Samantha, 'Poor Relief, Labourers' Households and Living Standards in Rural England c. 1770–1835: A Bedfordshire Case Study', *Economic History Review*, n.s., 58 (2005), 485–519.

Wilson, Adrian, 'Illegitimacy and its Implications in Mid-Eighteenth-Century London: The Evidence of the Foundling Hospital', *Continuity and Change*, 4 (1989), 103–64.

Wood, Andy, *The Politics of Social Conflict: The Peak Country 1520–1770* (Cambridge, 1999).

Woodward, Donald, *Men at Work: Labourers and Building Craftsmen in the Towns of Northern England, 1450–1750* (Cambridge, 1995).

—— *Survival in a Harsh Environment: Life in Tudor and Stuart England* (Hull, 1996).

Wrightson, Keith, *Earthly Necessities: Economic Lives in Early Modern Britain* (New Haven, 2000).

—— *English Society 1580–1680* (1982).

—— 'The Family in Early Modern England: Continuity and Change', in S. Taylor, R. Connors, and C. Jones (eds), *Hanoverian Britain and Empire: Essays in Memory of Philip Lawson* (Woodbridge, 1998), 1–22.

—— 'Infanticide in Earlier Seventeenth-Century England', *Local Population Studies*, 15 (1975), 10–22.

—— 'The Nadir of English Illegitimacy in the Seventeenth Century', in Laslett, Oosterveen, and Smith (eds), *Bastardy.*

Wrightson, Keith and Levine, David, *Poverty and Piety in an English Village: Terling, 1525–1700* (New York, 1979).

Wrigley, E. A., 'Marriage, Fertility and Population Growth in Eighteenth-Century England', in Outhwaite (ed.), *Marriage and Society.*

—— 'A Simple Model of London's Importance in Changing English Society and Economy, 1650–1750, *Past and Present*, 37 (1965), 44–70.

—— and Schofield, R. S., *The Population History of England 1541–1871: A Reconstruction* (Cambridge, 1989).

Wrigley, E. A., Davies, R. S., Oeppen, J. E., and Schofield, R. S., *English Population History from Family Reconstitution* (Cambridge, 1997).

Zunshine, Lisa, *Bastards and Foundlings: Illegitimacy in Eighteenth-Century England* (Columbus, OH, 2005).

THESES

Black, John, 'Illegitimacy and the Urban Poor in London, 1740–1830' (PhD thesis, London University, 2000).

Hitchcock, Timothy V., 'The English Workhouse: A Study in Institutional Poor Relief in Selected Counties, 1696–1750' (DPhil thesis, Oxford University, 1985).

McEwan, Joanne, 'Negotiating Support: Crime and Women's Networks in London and Middlesex, c. 1730–1820' (PhD thesis, University of Western Australia, 2009).

Nutt, Thomas, 'Illegitimacy and the Poor Law in Late-Eighteenth and Early-Nineteenth Century England' (PhD thesis, Cambridge University, 2006).

Payne, Dianne, 'Children of the Poor in London 1700–1780' (PhD thesis, University of Hertfordshire, 2008).

Riley, Kate, 'The Good Old Way Revisited: The Ferrar Family of Little Gidding, c. 1625–1637' (PhD thesis, University of Western Australia, 2007).

Tomkins, Alannah, 'The Experience of Urban Poverty: A Comparison of Oxford and Shrewsbury 1740 to 1770' (DPhil thesis, Oxford University, 1994).

UNPUBLISHED PAPERS

Levene, Alysa, 'Children and Hospitals before Children's Hospitals', NEER conference paper, UWA, Perth, July 2007.

Nutt, Thomas, ' "There may be supposed something of natural affection": father-hood, affiliation and the maintenance of illegitimate children in eighteenth, and early-nineteenth century England', NEER conference paper, UWA, Perth, July 2007.

Sharpe, Pamela, ' "The Tender Lungs of Children": Infant and Child Morbidity and Short Stature in Nineteenth-Century England', NEER conference paper, UWA, Perth, July 2007.

Wales, Tim, 'Work, Learning and the Fear of God: The English Poor Laws and the Young, c. 1570–c. 1700', conference paper (expanded), 1986.

INDEX

abandoned children, *see* children
abortion 41
abuse 145, 159, 216, 234;
  at hands of nurses 65–6, 169,
    183, 217;
  neglect 166, 176, 206, 242;
  of schoolteachers 146, 181;
  sexual 142–3, 146–7, 250;
  see also incest; violence
accidents 4, 140, 139
Acor, Lucy 169
Acts of Parliament, *see* statutes
Adair, Richard 96
Adams, Elenor 82
adolescence
  age at which poor children deemed
    to have reached 136–7, 214;
  as age for economic
    semi-independence 24, 113–14;
  later for children of the 'middling
    sort' 137, 244
adoptions
  formal 106;
  informal 21, 47, 107, 184, 228;
  secret 107
adultery 33, 35, 105, 162, 140
affection 148, 160–1, 230, 254;
  historians' views of 17;
  lack/denial of 147, 222, 239;
  maternal 18, 30, 70–1, 203, 250;
  natural 30, 74;
  paternal 108–10, 228, 246
affiliation, filiation 67, 77–8, 96,
    103, 108
age at leaving home 137, 172
Alban, Ann 106
Alcock, Thomas 161
Aldridge, Anne 91
Aldworth, William 79
alehouse, innkeepers 88, 89, 147
Allen, Franch 97
Allhallowes, Humphery 103

Anderson, Richard 179
Andrew, Donna 219, 231
Anguish, Thomas 198
apprentices 92, 244; *see also* parish
    apprentices
Armstrong, George, physician 120,
    123, 129, 252
army 92, 192, 198
Arnold, Mary 104
Arrowsmith, Stephen 146
Ashley, Sir Francis, justice 97
Astell, Mary 195
Aviary, Sarah 57
Axholl, Sollesy 123
Aylmer, Mary 106

baby substitution plot 1–2
Bacon, Francis 201
Baker, Leah 101
ballads, popular, as social commen-
    tary 25, 89, 92, 106, 136, 150,
    162, 173
Banes: Agnes 69; James 69
Banks, Elizabeth 85
baptism
  as data for historical demography
    10, 31;
  child given name of father or
    parish 51, 84, 85, 93, 106;
  of illegitimate children 31, 109;
  records of 32, 62
Barber, Sarah 71
Barnard, John 81, 107
Barnes, Mary 63
Bartlet, Jonathan 95
'bastard-bearers' 30–1, 34, 37,
    39, 93, 202–3
bastardy
  attitudes towards 32, 35;
  consequences of allegations 81,
    85, 96;
  depositions 49, 64, 80, 96, 108;

345